More praise for

OUR LINCOLN

"[An] absorbing anthology of essays. . . . By assembling a stellar cast of historians with the specific task of assessing Lincoln's life within the context of his times, Foner does a fine job of demonstrating why this man still exerts such a powerful hold on the American imagination."

—*Sunday Business Post*

"This collection . . . by some of the most prominent authorities . . . is especially commendable." —*Philadelphia Inquirer*

"As the bicentennial of our 16th president's birth approaches, these provocative essays constitute a perfect sneak-preview of a good portion of the likely scholarly agenda." —*Kirkus Reviews*

"This is a must-read in the bicentennial year of Abraham Lincoln's birth. Eric Foner has assembled the crème de la crème of Abraham Lincoln scholars to give a contemporary analysis of the 16th president."

—Frank J. Williams, founding Chair of the Lincoln Forum and Chief Justice of the Rhode Island Supreme Court

"The writers look well past the obvious to flesh out intriguing relations in the forces that shaped Lincoln's leadership." —Seth Sandronsky, *Words*

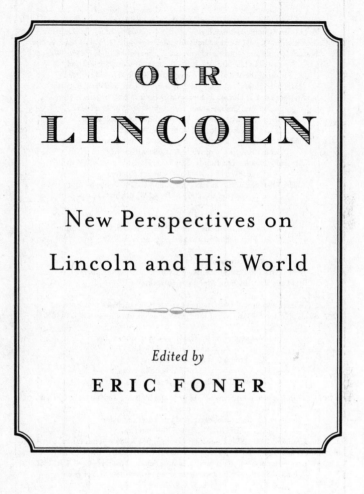

OUR
LINCOLN

New Perspectives on
Lincoln and His World

Edited by

ERIC FONER

W. W. NORTON & COMPANY

New York   London

Copyright © 2008 by W. W. Norton & Company, Inc.
Preface copyright © 2008 by Eric Foner
"A. Lincoln, Commander in Chief" copyright © 2008 by James M. McPherson
"The Constitution and Civil Liberties Under Lincoln" copyright © 2008 by Mark E. Neely, Jr.
"Abraham Lincoln and Jacksonian Democracy" copyright © 2008 by Sean Wilentz
"Visualizing Lincoln: Abraham Lincoln as Student, Subject, and
Patron of the Visual Arts" copyright © 2008 by Harold Holzer
"Natural Rights, Citizenship Rights, States' Rights, and Black Rights:
Another Look at Lincoln and Race" copyright © 2008 by James Oakes
"Lincoln and Colonization" copyright © 2008 by Eric Foner
"Allies for Emancipation?: Lincoln and Black Abolitionists"
copyright © 2008 by Manisha Sinha
"Lincoln's Sacramental Language" copyright © 2008 by Andrew Delbanco
"Lincoln's Religion" copyright © 2008 by Richard Carwardine
"Abraham Lincoln: The Family That Made Him, the Family He Made"
copyright © 2008 by Catherine Clinton
"The Theft of Lincoln in Scholarship, Politics, and Public Memory"
copyright © 2008 by David W. Blight

All rights reserved
Printed in the United States of America
First published as a Norton paperback 2009

For information about permission to reproduce selections from this book,
write to Permissions, W. W. Norton & Company, Inc.,
500 Fifth Avenue, New York, NY 10110

For information about special discounts for bulk purchases, please contact
W. W. Norton Special Sales at specialsales@wwnorton.com or 800-233-4830

Manufacturing by The Courier Companies, Inc.
Book design by JAM Design
Production manager: Andrew Marasia

Library of Congress Cataloging-in-Publication Data

Our Lincoln : new perspectives on Lincoln and his world / edited by Eric Foner.
p. cm.
Includes bibliographical references and index.
ISBN 978-0-393-06756-9 (hardcover)
1. Lincoln, Abraham, 1809–1865. 2. Lincoln, Abraham, 1809–1865—Political and social views.
3. Lincoln, Abraham, 1809–1865—Military leadership. 4. Presidents—United States—Biography.
5. United States—History—19th century. 6. United States—History—Civil War, 1861–1865.
7. United States—Politics and government—1861–1865. I. Foner, Eric.
E457.O97 2008
973.7092—dc22
[B]

2008017096

ISBN 978-0-393-33705-1 pbk.

W. W. Norton & Company, Inc.
500 Fifth Avenue, New York, N.Y. 10110
www.wwnorton.com

W. W. Norton & Company Ltd.
Castle House, 75/76 Wells Street, London W1T 3QT

1 2 3 4 5 6 7 8 9 0

To the Memory of

James P. Shenton

(1925–2003)

Contents

PART III: THE MAN

PART IV: POLITICS AND MEMORY

List of Illustrations

Preface

In April 1876, Frederick Douglass delivered a celebrated oration at the unveiling in Washington, D.C. of the Freedmen's Monument, a statue that depicts Abraham Lincoln conferring freedom on a kneeling slave. "No man," the former abolitionist remarked, "can say anything that is new of Abraham Lincoln." This did not, however, prevent Douglass from offering some strikingly original reflections on Lincoln's attitudes and policies regarding slavery and race. Nor, in the ensuing 130 years, has Douglass's admonition deterred innumerable historians, biographers, journalists, lawyers, literary critics, and psychologists from trying to say something new about Lincoln. More words have been written about Lincoln than any historical personage except Jesus Christ. There are scores of biographies of every size, shape, and description, as well as books on Lincoln's views about everything from cigarette smoking to Judaism. Is it possible in the early twenty-first century to say something new about Lincoln? The contributors to *Our Lincoln* believe it is, if one takes as a starting point the complex interrelationship between the man and the times in which he lived.

In some ways, the past two decades have been a golden age of Lincoln scholarship. An unprecedented number of important works have appeared; many of them are cited in the notes for the essays that follow. They include biographies and studies of one or another aspect of Lincoln's career, such as his law practice, speeches, racial attitudes, and psychology. Undoubtedly, more will be forthcoming as the bicentennial of his birth in 1809 approaches. In addition, thanks to the work of indefatigable scholars like Michael Burlingame, Douglas L. Wilson, Rodney O. Davis, and the staff of the Lincoln Legal Papers project, thousands of primary sources directly relevant to Lincoln's life have for the first time become widely available to scholars in printed documentary collections and on compact discs. Simultaneously, the basic raw materials for the study of Lincoln—his collected works, the Lincoln Papers at the Library of Congress, the *Official Records* of the Civil War, the *Congressional Globe*—have been made available in digital form online. Documents previously hidden in obscure repositories and collections are now easily accessible to scholars.

Many recent books offer striking new insights into Lincoln's career. Too often, however, as James Oakes points out in a recent review essay in the journal *Civil War History*, the dramatic expansion of available material somehow seems to have gone hand in hand with a narrowing of focus. Previous generations of scholars strove to place Lincoln in a broad political and social context. They published works with titles like *Lincoln and the Radicals, Lincoln and the Negro, Lincoln and the War Governors*. In too many recent studies, however, the wider world slips from view. To understand Lincoln, it seems, one has to study only the man himself.

This development is puzzling, since the new writing on Lincoln has coincided with an even larger body of scholarship that has reshaped our understanding of the nineteenth-century world in which Lincoln lived. Historians have offered innovative insights on subjects central to an understanding of Lincoln: the market revolution, the nineteenth-century family, the politics of slavery and antislavery, the transformation of American religion, the rise of nationalism, and emancipation as a transnational experience. With some exceptions, however, these two scholarly trends—a renewed interest in Lincoln and a rethinking of his world—have remained disconnected from each other. If some Lincoln scholars have slighted his historical context, historians of nineteenth-century America more generally have failed to spell out the implications of their new work for understanding Lincoln.

Our Lincoln aims to bring to bear on the study of Lincoln some of the new interpretations of Lincoln's era, in the hope of producing a more nuanced understanding of both the man and his world. In assembling the contributors, I have tried to balance scholars who have already produced important works on Lincoln with others who have never written directly about him, but whose work has shed new light on nineteenth-century America. Taken together, these essays offer new perspectives on long-debated issues and exemplify how recent scholarship on Lincoln's world helps illuminate in new ways his own life and career.

The book's first section examines crucial aspects of Lincoln's political career and years in the White House. James M. McPherson reflects the most up-to-date approach to writing the history of war by insisting on the interdependency of politics, strategy, and tactics, all key aspects of presidential leadership. Mark Neely adds a new dimension to the long-debated issue of civil liberties in wartime through a careful analysis of some of Lincoln's previously neglected pronouncements on the subject. Drawing on recent work on the history of American democracy, including his own, Sean Wilentz reinterprets Lincoln's relationship to the nineteenth-century political system and the sources of his antislavery and nationalist ideas and practices. And Harold Holzer shows how Lincoln, living in an era in which mass-produced lithographs and photographs contributed to the rapid expansion of the public sphere, consciously strove to shape his own pictorial representation.

Lincoln's ideas and policies regarding slavery and race, the focus of the second section, have long preoccupied historians. The essays in this section move beyond recent either/or debates over whether Lincoln was or was not a racist and whether he or the slaves themselves should be given credit for emancipation. James Oakes reinterprets Lincoln's racial views in light of what we now know about nineteenth-century concepts of citizenship and the complex gradations of rights that accompanied it. My own essay, on Lincoln's long embrace of the idea of "colonizing" emancipated slaves outside the United States (a subject slighted by most of his biographers), draws on recent literature on the colonization movement and on abolitionism to situate Lincoln within the broad spectrum of beliefs and tactics that made up the crusade against slavery. And Manisha Sinha looks at the era's black abolitionists, a group whose centrality to the antislavery struggle recent scholarship has emphasized, to assess their changing views of Lincoln and possible influence upon him.

The third section situates other aspects of Lincoln's life within changes in nineteenth-century American society. Andrew Delbanco examines Lincoln's distinctive literary style, relating it both to the moral power of his convictions and to the ongoing democratization of public language. Richard Carwardine shows how Lincoln, although hardly an evangelical Christian, responded to his era's religious revolution, frequently echoing the language of revivalist Protestantism and shrewdly mobilizing the churches in support of the war effort. And Catherine Clinton shows how the contrast between the patriarchal family in which Lincoln grew up and the companionate marriage he forged with his wife, Mary, reflected the far-reaching transformation of nineteenth-century family life.

Lincoln occupies a unique place not only in our country's actual history but in American ideology, mythology, and memory. In the volume's final essay, David W. Blight, whose own work has helped spark historians' current concern with historical memory, dissects how today's Republican Party, with a center of gravity located in the white South, has tried to use its history as the "party of Lincoln" to appeal to African Americans while subtly redefining the legacy of emancipation as "color blindness" to avoid offending conservative voters.

No single theme unites these essays, nor have I made any effort to impose a uniformity of interpretation upon them. Overall, however, Lincoln emerges as a man powerfully shaped by the currents of social and political transformation in nineteenth-century America. He changed as his society changed, but his own actions helped remake his world. He was a man of his time yet able to transcend it, probably as good a definition of greatness as any.

The title of this volume, *Our Lincoln*, alludes, in the first place, to the collective task of rethinking Lincoln undertaken by eleven individual scholars. But it is also meant to suggest that two centuries after his birth Lincoln remains in many ways our contemporary. Issues central to these essays—presidential leadership, constitutional liberty in wartime, the relationship between religion and politics, the definition of American citizenship, the legacy of slavery—are as current as today's newspapers. So long as these remain unresolved challenges in American life, Lincoln will remain central to an understanding of ourselves as a nation and a people.

—Eric Foner
November 2007

Note: The dedication of this volume offers a small tribute to an extra-ordinary teacher with a passion for history and an unrivaled commitment to his students. It was in the classes of James P. Shenton that I first encountered Lincoln and the Civil War era, and three other contributors, Professors Delbanco, Sinha, and Wilentz, also knew him as mentor or colleague.

PART I

THE

PRESIDENT

1

A. Lincoln,
Commander in Chief

James M. McPherson

When the American Civil War began with the Confederate attack on Fort Sumter, United States President Abraham Lincoln was far less prepared for the task of commander in chief than his southern adversary. Jefferson Davis had graduated from West Point (in the lowest third of his class, to be sure), commanded a regiment that fought intrepidly at Buena Vista in the Mexican War, and served as an outstanding secretary of war in the Franklin Pierce administration from 1853 to 1857. Lincoln's only military experience had come twenty-nine years earlier, when he was captain of a militia unit that saw no action in the Black Hawk War. During Lincoln's one term in Congress, he made a speech in 1848 mocking his military career. "Did you know I am a military hero?" he said. "I fought, bled, and came away" after "charges upon the wild onions" and "a good many bloody struggles with the Musquetoes."[1]

When he called state militia into federal service on April 15, 1861, to put down "combinations too powerful to be suppressed by the ordinary course of judicial proceedings," Lincoln therefore faced a steep learning curve as commander in chief. He was a quick study, however; his experience as a largely self-taught lawyer with a keen analytical mind who had mastered Euclidean geometry for mental exercise enabled him to learn quickly on the job. He read and absorbed works on military history and strategy; he observed the successes and failures of his own and the enemy's military commanders and drew apt conclusions; he made mistakes and learned from them; he applied his large quotient of common sense to slice through the obfuscations and excuses of military subordinates. By 1862 his grasp of strategy and operations was firm enough almost to justify the overstated but not entirely wrong conclusion of historian T. Harry Williams: "Lincoln stands out as a great war president, probably the greatest in our history, and a great natural strategist, a better one than any of his generals."[2]

Williams belonged to a generation of historians who recognized that Lincoln's role as commander in chief was central to his place in history. The sixteenth president has been (so far) the only one whose presidency was wholly bounded by war. On the day Lincoln took office, the first document placed on his desk was a letter from Major Robert Anderson at Fort Sumter informing him that the garrison there must be withdrawn or resupplied at the risk of war. Lincoln chose to take that risk. Four years later he was assassinated five days after General Robert E. Lee surrendered at Appomattox but while several Confederate armies were still in the field.

During those four years Lincoln spent more time in the War Department telegraph office than anywhere else except the White House or his summer residence at the Soldiers' Home. Military matters required more of his time and energy than anything else. He rarely left Washington except to visit the Army of the Potomac at the front, as he did eleven times for a total of forty-two days with the army. As T. Harry Williams and other historians who were writing during the era from the 1920s to the 1960s understood, not only Lincoln's success or failure as president but also the very survival of the *United* States depended on how he performed his duties as a military leader.[3]

Since the 1960s, however, military history has fallen out of fashion among professional academic historians. Social history in its various forms that focus on themes of race, class, ethnicity, and gender has replaced political, diplomatic, and especially military history as a leading historiographical category. This change affected scholarship about Lincoln. One of the best reference works on Lincoln, Mark E. Neely's *The Abraham Lincoln Encyclopedia* (1982), devoted less than 5 percent of its space to military matters. Of the seventeen collected essays on Lincoln published in 1987 by the late Don E. Fehrenbacher, one of the foremost Lincoln scholars of his time, not one dealt with the president as a military leader. On the 175th anniversary of Lincoln's birth in 1984, Gettysburg College hosted a conference on recent Lincoln scholarship. There were three sessions on psychobiography, two on the assassination, two on Lincoln's image in photographs and popular prints, one each on his economic ideas, religion, humor, Indian policy, and slavery. But there were no sessions on Lincoln as commander in chief—a remarkable irony, given the site of the conference. In 1994 the historian Merrill Peterson published his splendid study *Lincoln in American Memory*, highlighting 130 years of the sixteenth president's image in American historiography and popular culture. There are chapters on Lincoln and the South, religion, politics, Reconstruction, civil rights, and several other themes, but no chapter on Lincoln and the army.[4]

Perhaps it is time to recognize the truth expressed by Lincoln himself in his second inaugural address when the Civil War had been raging for almost four years: On "the progress of our arms . . . all else chiefly depends."[5] "All else" included many of the questions and developments that social historians consider important: the fate of slavery; the definition of freedom; the destruction of the Old South's socioeconomic system and the triumph of entrepreneurial free labor capitalism as the national norm; a new definition of American nationalism; the origins of a new system of race relations; the very survival of the United States in a manner that laid the foundations for the nation's emergence as a world power.

The issue of slavery and its abolition offers a striking illustration of this point. Much recent writing about the wartime emancipation of hundreds of thousands of slaves has viewed this process mainly through the lens of social history, "history from the bottom up." Of their own volition many slaves escaped from their masters and won freedom by coming into Union lines. But this process could not have occurred if there had been no Union lines to which they could escape. And in most cases it was the military lines that came to the slaves, not vice versa, as northern armies penetrated deeper into the South. It was the commander in chief of these armies who oversaw these events and who made the crucial decisions to convert a *strategy* of liberating slaves to weaken the Confederacy into a *policy* of abolishing slavery as a war aim second in importance only to preserving the Union. Freedom quite literally came from the barrel of a gun. The story of how this happened cannot be fully understood without at least some attention to military history.

As commander in chief in time of war a president performs or oversees five functions in diminishing order of direct activity: policy, national strategy, military strategy, operations, and tactics. Neither Lincoln nor anyone else defined these functions in a systematic way during the Civil War. If they had, their definitions might have looked something like this: *Policy* refers to war aims, the political goals of the nation in time of war. *National Strategy* refers to mobilization of the political, economic, diplomatic, and psychological as well as military resources of the nation to achieve these war aims. *Military Strategy* refers to plans for the employment of armed forces to win military victories that will further the political goals. *Operations* refers to the actual organization, logistics, and movements of armies in particular campaigns to carry out the purposes of military strategy. *Tactics* refer to the formations and fighting of an army in actual battle.

As president of the nation and leader of his party as well as commander in chief, Lincoln was principally responsible for shaping and defining national policy. From first to last, that policy was preservation of the United States as one nation, indivisible, and as a republic based on majority rule. In May 1861 he explained that "the central idea pervading this struggle is the necessity that is upon us, of proving that popular government is not an absurdity. We must settle this question now, whether in a free government the minority have the right to break up the government whenever they choose."[6] Secession "is the essence of anarchy," said Lincoln on another occasion, for if one state may secede at will, so may any other until there is no government and no nation. In the Gettysburg Address, Lincoln offered his most eloquent statement of policy: The war was a test of whether the nation conceived in 1776 "might live" or would "perish from the earth." This issue of national sovereignty over a union of all the states was nonnegotiable. No compromise between a sovereign *United* States and a separately sovereign *Confederate* States was possible. This issue "is distinct, simple, and inflexible," said Lincoln in 1864. "It is an issue which can only be tried by war, and decided by victory."[7]

Lincoln's frequent statements of policy were indeed distinct and inflexible. The next level of his duty as commander in chief was to mobilize the means to achieve that policy by winning the war. The president, of course, shared with Congress and key cabinet members the tasks of raising, organizing, and sustaining an army and navy, preventing foreign intervention in the conflict, and maintaining public support for the war. But no matter how much this national strategy required maximum effort at all levels of government and society, the ultimate responsibility was the president's in his dual roles as head of government and commander in chief. And this responsibility was as much a political as a military one, especially in a civil war whose origins lay in a political conflict and was precipitated by political decisions. Although Lincoln never read Karl von Clausewitz's famous treatise *On War* (*Vom Kriege*), his actions were a consummate expression of Clausewitz's central argument: "The political objective is the goal, war is the means of reaching it, and means can never be considered in isolation from their purpose. Therefore, it is clear that war should never be thought of as *something autonomous* but always as an instrument of policy."[8]

Some professional military men tended to think of war as "something autonomous" and deplored the intrusion of political considerations into military matters. Take the notable example of "political generals." Lincoln appointed numerous prominent politicians with little or no military training or experience to the rank of brigadier or major general. Some of them received these appointments so early in the war that they subsequently outranked professional, West Point–educated officers. Lincoln also commissioned important ethnic leaders as generals with little regard to their military merits. Some of these political and ethnic generals proved to be incompetent on the battlefield. "It seems but little better than murder to give important commands to such men as [Nathaniel] Banks, [Benjamin] Butler, [John] McClernand, and Lew Wallace," said the thoroughgoing professional Henry W. Halleck in 1864, "but it seems impossible to prevent it."[9]

Historians who likewise deplore the abundance of political generals sometimes cite an anecdote to mock the process. One day in 1862, so the story goes, Lincoln and Secretary of War Edwin M. Stanton were going over a list of colonels for promotion to brigadier general. Coming to the name of Alexander Schimmelfennig, the president said that "there has got to be something done unquestionably in the interest of the Dutch, and to that end I want Schimmelfennig appointed." Stanton protested that there were better qualified German Americans. "No matter about that," said Lincoln, "his name will make up for any difference there may be."[10]

General Schimmelfennig is remembered today mainly for hiding three days in a woodshed next to a pigpen to escape capture at Gettysburg. Other political generals are also remembered more for their military defeats or supposed blunders than for any positive achievements:

Nathaniel Banks for the Red River campaign and other defeats; John C. Frémont for the mess he made of affairs in Missouri and western Virginia; Daniel Sickles for endangering the Army of the Potomac and losing his leg by moving out to the Peach Orchard at Gettysburg; Benjamin Butler for alleged corruption in New Orleans and for botching the first attack on Fort Fisher; and so on.

Often forgotten are the excellent military records of some political generals like John A. Logan and Francis P. Blair (among others). And some West Pointers, notably Ulysses S. Grant and William T. Sherman, might have languished in obscurity if it had not been for the initial sponsorship of Grant by Congressman Elihu B. Washburne and of Sherman by his brother John, a U.S. senator. Even if all political generals, or generals in whose appointments politics played a part, turned out to have mediocre military records, however, the process would have had a positive impact on *national* strategy. The main purpose of commissioning prominent political and ethnic leaders was to mobilize their constituencies for the war effort. The United States Army on the eve of the war consisted of approximately 16,400 men, of whom about 1,100 were commissioned officers. Of these officers, some 25 percent resigned to join the Confederate army. By April 1862, when the war was a year old, the volunteer Union army consisted of 637,000 men. This mass mobilization could not have taken place without an enormous effort by local and state politicians as well as by prominent ethnic leaders. In New York City, for example, the Tammany Democrat Daniel Sickles raised a brigade and earned a commission as brigadier general, the Irish-born Thomas Meagher helped raise the famous Irish Brigade, and the German American leader Carl Schurz helped raise several German regiments and eventually became a major general. Northern state governors, nearly all Republicans, played an essential part in raising and organizing volunteer regiments, and claimed brigadier generalships for their political allies in return. At the same time Lincoln needed the allegiance of prominent Democrats like John McClernand and John Logan in southern Illinois, for example, where support for the war was questionable. These two men "have labored night and day to instruct their fellow citizens in the true nature of the contest," acknowledged the Republican *Chicago Tribune* in September 1861, "and to organize their aroused feelings into effective military strength. They have succeeded nobly."[11] Both eventually became major generals. And of course, prominent Republicans could not be ignored. Lincoln's party supplied most of the energy and manpower for the war effort. John C. Frémont, who had been the first Republican presidential candidate in 1856, and Nathaniel P. Banks, former Speaker of the House and governor of Massachusetts, were made major generals early in the war.

By the war's second year the need for politically motivated commissions to cement allegiances and to reward support had declined. Performance in action became the principal determinant for promotion, though politics could never be completely absent from the process. With Lincoln's approval, the War Department issued General Order No. 111 in August 1862 stipulating that "hereafter no appointments of major generals or brigadier generals will be given except to officers of the regular army for meritorious and distinguished service during the war, or to volunteer officers who, by some successful achievement in the field shall have displayed the military abilities required for the duties of a general officer." This order was sometimes honored in the breach. Schimmelfennig, for example, was promoted to brigadier general in November 1862, while Carl Schurz and Julius Stahel were promoted to major general in January 1863—all in the name of rewarding "our sincere friends" in the German American community, as Lincoln put it.[12]

Nevertheless, General Order No. 111 did herald the advent of a more professional criterion for promotion in the Union army. The national strategy of mobilizing political support for the war through military patronage had served its purpose. "The political generals' reputation for battlefield defeats is certainly accurate for many in this group," writes the most recent historian of the subject, "but this orthodox caricature neglects their vital contribution in rallying support for the war and convincing the people to join the mass citizen army as volunteers." Lincoln would have agreed.[13]

Some of the higher-ranking political generals helped shape military strategy and thus straddled the boundary between national and military strategy. Another important issue that began as a question of national strategy eventually crossed the boundary to become policy as well. That was the issue of slavery and emancipation. During the war's first year, one of Lincoln's top priorities was to keep border state unionists and northern antiabolitionist Democrats in his war coalition. He feared, with good reason, that the balance in three border slave states might tip to the Confederacy if his administration took a premature step toward emancipation. When General Frémont issued a military order freeing the slaves of Confederate supporters in Missouri, Lincoln revoked it in order to quell an outcry from the border states and northern Democrats. To sustain Frémont's order, Lincoln believed, "would alarm our Southern Union friends, and turn them against us—perhaps ruin our rather fair prospect for Kentucky. . . . I think that to lose Kentucky is nearly the same as to lose the whole game. Kentucky gone, we can not hold Missouri, nor as I think, Maryland. These all against us, and the job on our hands is too large for us. We would as well consent to separation at once, including the surrender of this capitol."[14]

During the next nine months, however, the thrust of national strategy shifted away from conciliating the border states and antiemancipation Democrats. The antislavery Republican constituency grew louder and more demanding. The argument that the slave power had brought on the war and that reunion with slavery would only sow the seeds of another war became more insistent. The evidence that slave labor sustained the Confederate economy and the logistics of Confederate armies grew stronger. Counteroffensives by southern armies in the summer of 1862 wiped out many of the Union gains of the winter and spring. Many northerners, including Lincoln, became convinced that bolder steps were necessary. To win the war over an enemy fighting *for* and sustained *by* slavery, the North must strike *at* slavery.

In July 1862 Lincoln decided on a major change in national strategy. Instead of deferring to the border states and northern Democrats, he would activate the dynamism of the northern antislavery majority that had elected him and mobilize the potential of black manpower by issuing a proclamation of freedom for slaves in rebellious states. "Decisive and extreme measures must be adopted," Lincoln told members of his cabinet according to Secretary of the Navy Gideon Welles. Emancipation was "a military necessity, absolutely necessary to the preservation of the Union. We must free the slaves or be ourselves subdued. The slaves [are] undeniably an element of strength to those who have their service, and we must decide whether that element should be with us or against us. . . . We [want] the army to strike more vigorous blows. The administration must set the army an example and strike at the heart of the rebellion."[15]

After a two-month wait for a Union military victory to give an emancipation edict credibility as a positive war measure instead of a desperate appeal for a slave uprising, Lincoln issued a preliminary proclamation five days after the battle of Antietam. It warned that on January 1, 1863, the president would invoke his war powers as commander in chief to seize enemy property (slaves) by proclaiming emancipation in all states or parts of states in rebellion. January 1 came, the rebellion still raged, and Lincoln issued his historic proclamation.

Emancipation thus became a crucial part of the North's national strategy by trying to convert a Confederate resource to Union advantage. But this step opened up a potential inconsistency between national strategy and policy. The Emancipation Proclamation might free many slaves if northern armies could conquer the states to which it applied. But what about slaves in the states to which it did not apply? Could the North fight a war using the strategy of emancipation to restore a Union in which slavery still existed and to uphold a Constitution that still sanctioned bondage? During the last two years of the war the abolition of slavery evolved from a *means* of winning the war to a *war aim*, from national strategy to national policy. Lincoln was reelected in 1864 on a platform calling for "unconditional surrender" of the Confederacy *and* a Thirteenth Amendment to abolish slavery everywhere and forever.[16]

Lincoln's shift from a national strategy of opposing the recruitment of black soldiers to one of vigorous support for that action lagged a few months behind his similar shift on emancipation. The idea of putting arms in the hands of black men provoked even greater hostility among Democrats and border state unionists than emancipation itself. In August 1862 Lincoln told delegates from Indiana who offered to raise two black regiments that "the nation could not afford to lose Kentucky at this crisis" and that "to arm the negroes would turn 50,000 bayonets from the loyal border States against us that were for us."[17]

Three weeks later, however, the president quietly authorized the War Department to begin organizing black regiments on the South Carolina Sea Islands. The Emancipation Proclamation openly endorsed the recruitment of black soldiers and sailors. And by March 1863 Lincoln had told his military governor of occupied Tennessee that "the colored population is the great *available* and yet *unavailed* of, force for restoring the Union. The bare sight of fifty thousand armed, and drilled black soldiers on the banks of the Mississippi, would end the rebellion at once. And who doubts that we can present that sight, if we but take hold in earnest."[18]

This prediction proved overoptimistic, but in August 1863 after black regiments had proved their worth at Fort Wagner and elsewhere, Lincoln told opponents of their employment that in the future "there will be some black men who can remember that, with silent tongue, and clenched teeth, and steady eye, and well-poised bayonet, they have helped mankind on to this great consummation; while, I fear, there will be some white ones, unable to forget that, with malignant heart, and deceitful speech, they have strove to hinder it." A year later, with more than a hundred thousand black men under arms, Lincoln considered their contribution essential to victory. Without those soldiers, he said, "we can not longer maintain the contest . . . & we would be compelled to abandon the war in 3 weeks."[19]

Lincoln's dominant role in determining policy and national strategy is scarcely surprising. But he also took a more active, hands-on part in shaping military strategy than presidents have done in most other wars. This was not necessarily by choice. Lincoln's lack of military training inclined him at first to defer to General-in-Chief Winfield Scott, America's most celebrated soldier since George Washington. But Scott's age, poor health, and lack of energy placed a greater burden on the president. Lincoln was also disillusioned by Scott's advice in March 1861 to yield both Forts Sumter and Pickens and by the seemingly passive strategy of the Anaconda Plan. Scott's successor, General George B. McClellan, proved an even greater disappointment to Lincoln. Nor did Don Carlos Buell, Henry W. Halleck, John Pope, Ambrose Burnside, Joseph Hooker, or William S. Rosecrans measure up to his initial expectations. When Ulysses S. Grant became general-in-chief in March 1864, Lincoln told him (according to Grant's memoirs) that "he had never professed to be a military man or to know how campaigns should be conducted, and never wanted to interfere in them: but that procrastination on the part of commanders" had compelled him to take a more active part.[20]

Grant's account does not ring entirely true. But it is certain that "procrastination," especially by McClellan and Buell, caused Lincoln to become in effect his own general-in-chief as well as commander in chief during key campaigns. Perhaps he should have played an even more assertive role. In early December 1861, after McClellan had been commander of the Army of the Potomac for more than four months and had done little with it except conduct drills and reviews, Lincoln drew on his reading and discussions of military strategy to propose a campaign against Confederate General Joseph E. Johnston's army occupying the Manassas-

Centreville sector twenty-five miles from Washington. Under Lincoln's plan, part of the Army of the Potomac would feign a frontal attack while the rest would use the Occoquan Valley to move up on the flank and rear of the enemy, cut its rail communications, and catch it in a pincers.[21]

It was a good plan; indeed it was precisely what Johnston most feared. McClellan rejected it in favor of his proposal for a deeper flanking movement all the way south to Urbana on the Rappahannock River. Lincoln posed a series of questions to McClellan, asking him why his distant-flanking strategy was better than Lincoln's short-flanking plan. Three sound premises underlay Lincoln's questions: First, the enemy army, not Richmond, should be the objective; second, Lincoln's plan would enable the Army of the Potomac to operate near its own base (Alexandria) while McClellan's plan, even if successful, would draw the enemy back toward *his* base (Richmond) and lengthen the Union supply line; and third, "does not your plan involve a greatly larger expenditure of *time* . . . than mine?"[22]

McClellan brushed off Lincoln's questions and proceeded with his own plan, bolstered by an 8–4 vote of his division commanders in favor of it, which caused Lincoln reluctantly to acquiesce. Johnston then threw a monkey wrench into McClellan's Urbana strategy by withdrawing from Manassas to the south bank of the Rappahannock—in large part to escape from the kind of maneuver Lincoln had proposed. McClellan now shifted his campaign all the way to the Virginia peninsula between the York and James rivers. Instead of attacking the line near Yorktown held by fewer than seventeen thousand Confederates in early April with his own army, then numbering seventy thousand, McClellan settled down for a siege that would give Johnston time to bring his whole army down to the peninsula. An exasperated Lincoln telegraphed McClellan on April 6: "I think you better break the enemies' line from York-town to War-wick River, at once. They will probably use *time*, as advantageously as you can." McClellan's only response was to comment petulantly in a letter to his wife that "I was much tempted to reply that he had better come & do it himself."[23]

Three days later Lincoln wrote McClellan a letter reiterating what was becoming a hallmark of his strategic thinking, the importance of time. "By delay the enemy will relatively gain upon you—that is, he will gain faster, by *fortifications* and *re-inforcements*, than you can by re-inforcements alone."[24] Lincoln's point was exactly right. McClellan's repeated delays yielded the initiative time and again to Johnston and then to Robert E. Lee, and ruined McClellan's Peninsula campaign.

In his April 9 letter to the general, Lincoln enunciated another major theme of his military strategy: The war could be won only by fighting the enemy rather than by endless maneuvers and sieges to occupy *places*. "Once more," wrote Lincoln, "let me tell you, it is indispensable to *you* that you strike a blow. You will do me the justice to remember I always insisted, that going down the Bay in search of a field, instead of fighting at or near Manassas, was only shifting, and not surmounting, a difficulty—that we would find the same, or equal intrenchments, at either place. The country will not fail to note—is now noting—that the present hesitation to move upon an intrenched enemy, is but the story of Manassas repeated." Lincoln assured McClellan that "I have never written you, or spoken to you, in greater kindness of feeling than now, nor with a fuller purpose to sustain you. . . . *But you must act*."[25]

But the general who acquired the nickname of Tardy George never learned that lesson. The same was true of several other generals who did not live up to Lincoln's expectations. They seemed to be paralyzed by responsibility for the lives of their men as well as the fate of their army and nation. This intimidating responsibility made them risk-averse. Afraid of a failure that might lose everything, they chose the safe course of doing as little as possible. This risk-averse behavior especially characterized commanders of the Army of the Potomac, who operated in the glare of media publicity with the government in Washington looking over their shoulders. In contrast, officers like Ulysses S. Grant, George H. Thomas, and Philip H. Sheridan got their start in the western theater hundreds of miles distant, where they worked their way up from command of a regiment step by step to larger responsibilities away from media attention. They were able to grow into these responsibilities and to learn the necessity of taking risks without the fear of failure that paralyzed McClellan.

General William T. Sherman was something of an exception that proved the rule. Thrust into command of the entire Department of the Cumberland in October 1861, he broke down under the pressure and had to be removed. He started over again as the officer in charge of a supply base at Cairo, Illinois, under Grant, and then found himself as a division commander at Shiloh, which became the solid bottom rung for his successful climb up the ladder of command. In 1864 Sherman persuaded

Grant and an initially reluctant Lincoln to let him take the greatest risk of all, to cut loose from his base and march through the enemy heartland 285 miles from Atlanta to the sea. This spectacular feat evoked from Lincoln praise for the risk-taking characteristics he wanted in a general: "When you were about leaving Atlanta for the Atlantic coast, I was *anxious*, if not fearful; but feeling that you were the better judge, and remembering that 'nothing risked, nothing gained' I did not interfere. Now, the undertaking being a success, the honor is all yours; for I believe none of us went farther than to acquiesce."[26]

In October 1862, after the battle of Antietam, Lincoln had prodded McClellan to pursue and attack the retreating Confederates more aggressively by offering the same "nothing risked, nothing gained" advice. "I say 'try,'" the commander in chief told McClellan; "if we never try, we shall never succeed." But the general did not try. Lincoln finally gave up on him and removed McClellan from command. He could no longer "bore with an auger too dull to take hold," he told one of McClellan's supporters.[27]

Meanwhile Lincoln's frustration with the lack of activity in the Kentucky-Tennessee theater had elicited from him an expression of an important strategic concept. Generals Halleck and Buell commanded in the two western theaters separated by the Cumberland River. Lincoln urged them to cooperate in a joint campaign against the Confederate army defending a line from eastern Kentucky to the Mississippi River. Both responded in early January 1862 that they were not yet ready. On the back of a copy of a letter from Halleck explaining why he could not move against the Confederate defenses at Columbus, Kentucky, Lincoln wrote: "It is exceedingly discouraging. As everywhere else, nothing can be done."[28]

Lincoln was provoked by Halleck's pedantic explanation of why he and Buell could not cooperate. "To operate on *exterior* lines against an enemy occupying a central position will fail," wrote Halleck. "It is condemned by every military authority I have ever read." By this time Lincoln had read some of those authorities (including Halleck) and was prepared to challenge the general's reasoning. "I state my general idea of the war," he wrote to both Halleck and Buell, "that we have the *greater* numbers, and the enemy has the *greater* facility of concentrating forces upon points of collision; that we must fail, unless we can find some way to making *our* advantage an over-match for his; and that this can be only done by menacing him with superior forces at *different* points, at the *same* time; so that we can safely attack, one, or both, if he makes no change; and if he *weakens* one to strengthen the other, forbear to attack the strengthened one, but seize and hold the weakened one, gaining so much."[29]

Lincoln clearly expressed here what military theorists define as "concentration in time" to counter the Confederacy's advantage of interior lines that enabled southern forces to concentrate in space. The geography of the war required the North to operate generally on exterior lines while the Confederacy could use interior lines to shift troops to the point of danger. By advancing on two or more fronts simultaneously, Union forces could neutralize this advantage, as Lincoln understood but Halleck and Buell seemed unable to grasp.

Not until Grant became general-in-chief in 1864 did Lincoln have a commander in place who carried out this strategy. In his final report on the 1864–65 campaigns that won the war, Grant noted that prior to these operations, Union armies in different theaters had "acted independently and without concert, like a balky team, no two ever pulling together." Employing concentration in time, Grant ordered five separate Union armies to operate from exterior lines against as many smaller Confederate armies to prevent any of them from reinforcing another. Lincoln was impressed. He told his private secretary John Hay that Grant's plans reminded him of his own "suggestion so constantly made and as constantly neglected, to Buell & Halleck et al to move at once upon the enemy's whole line so as to bring into action to our advantage our great superiority in numbers."[30]

Grant's strategy of attacking the enemy wherever he found them also carried out Lincoln's strategy of trying to cripple the enemy army as far from Richmond (or any other base) as possible rather than maneuver to occupy or capture *places*. From February to June 1862, Union forces had enjoyed remarkable success in capturing Confederate territory and cities along the south Atlantic coast and in Tennessee and the lower Mississippi Valley, including the cities of Nashville, New Orleans, and Memphis. But Confederate counteroffensives in the summer recaptured much of this territory (though not these cities). Clearly, the conquest and occupation of places would not win the war so long as enemy armies remained capable of reconquering them.

Lincoln viewed these Confederate offensives more as an opportunity than a threat. When the Army of Northern Virginia began to move north in the campaign that led to Gettysburg, General Hooker proposed to cut in behind them and attack Richmond. Lincoln rejected the idea. "*Lee's* Army, and not *Richmond*, is your true objective point," he wired Hooker on June 10, 1863. "If he comes toward the Upper Potomac, follow on his flank, and on the inside track, shortening your [supply] lines, whilst he lengthens his. Fight him when opportunity offers." A week later, as the enemy was entering Pennsylvania, Lincoln told Hooker that this invasion "gives you back the chance that I thought McClellan lost last fall" to cripple Lee's army far from its base.[31]

Hooker's complaints and bickering with Halleck finally caused Lincoln to replace Hooker on June 28 with George Gordon Meade, who punished but did not destroy Lee at Gettysburg. When the rising Potomac trapped Lee in Maryland, Lincoln urged Meade to close in for the kill. If Meade could "complete his work, so gloriously prosecuted thus far," said Lincoln, "by the literal or substantial destruction of Lee's army, the rebellion will be over."[32]

Lincoln was distressed by Meade's congratulatory order to his army on July 7, which closed with the words that the country now "looks to the army for greater efforts to drive from our soil every vestige of the presence of the invader." "Great God!" cried Lincoln. "This is a dreadful reminiscence of McClellan," who had proclaimed a great victory when the enemy retreated across the river after Antietam. "Will our Generals never get that idea out of their heads? The whole country is *our* soil." That, after all, was the point of the war.[33]

When word came that Lee had escaped across the Potomac, Lincoln was both angry and depressed. He wrote to Meade: "My dear general, I do not believe you appreciate the magnitude of the misfortune involved in Lee's escape. He was within your easy grasp, and to have closed upon him would, in connection with our other late successes [mainly the capture of Vicksburg and Port Hudson with their thirty-six thousand defenders], have ended the war. As it is, the war will be prolonged indefinitely. . . . Your golden opportunity is gone, and I am distressed immeasurably because of it."[34]

Having gotten these feelings off his chest, Lincoln filed the letter away unsent. But he never changed his mind. And two months later, when the Army of the Potomac was maneuvering and skirmishing again over the devastated land between Washington and Richmond, the president declared that "to attempt to fight the enemy back to his intrenchments in Richmond . . . is an idea I have been trying to repudiate for quite a year. . . . I have constantly desired the Army of the Potomac, to make Lee's army, and not Richmond, it's [sic] objective point. If our army can not fall upon the enemy and hurt him where he is, it is plain to me it can gain nothing by attempting to follow him over a succession of intrenched lines into a fortified city."[35]

Five times in the war Lincoln tried to get his field commanders to trap enemy armies that were raiding or invading northward by cutting in south of them and blocking their routes of retreat: during Stonewall Jackson's drive north through the Shenandoah Valley in May 1862; Lee's invasion of Maryland in September 1862; Braxton Bragg's and Edmund Kirby Smith's invasion of Kentucky in the same month; Lee's invasion of Pennsylvania in the Gettysburg campaign; and Jubal Early's raid to the outskirts of Washington in July 1864. Each time his generals failed him, and in most cases they soon found themselves relieved of command: John C. Frémont and James Shields after failing to intercept Jackson; McClellan after letting Lee get away; Buell after Bragg and Kirby Smith got safely back to Tennessee; and David Hunter after Early's raid. Meade retained his command despite Lincoln's disappointment but played second fiddle to Grant in the war's last year.

In all of these cases the slowness of Union armies trying to intercept or pursue the enemy played a key part in their failures. Lincoln expressed repeated frustration with the inability of his armies to march as light and fast as Confederate armies. Much better supplied than the enemy, Union forces were actually slowed down by the abundance of their logistics. Most Union commanders never learned the lesson pronounced by Confederate General Richard Ewell that "the road to glory cannot be followed with much baggage."[36] Lincoln's efforts to get his commanders to move faster with fewer supplies brought him into active participation at the operational level of his armies. In May 1862 he directed General Irvin McDowell to "put all possible energy and speed into the effort" to trap Jackson in the Shenandoah Valley. "It is, for you, a question of legs. Put in all the speed you can. I have told Frémont as much, and directed him to drive at them as fast as possible."[37] Jackson's troops marched twice as fast as those of Frémont and of McDowell's lead division under Shields, and the Confederates slipped through the trap with hours to spare.

Lincoln was disgusted with the excuses offered by Frémont for not moving faster. The same pattern of excuses from Buell during his pursuit of Bragg after the battle of Perryville and from McClellan after Antietam deepened his disgust. Lincoln told Buell that he could "not understand why we cannot march as the enemy marches, live as he lives, and fight as he fights, unless we admit the inferiority of our troops and our generals."[38] Lincoln probably did not fully appreciate the logistical difficulties of moving large bodies of troops, especially in enemy territory. On the other hand, the president did comprehend the reality expressed by the Army of the Potomac's quartermaster in response to McClellan's incessant requests for more supplies before he could advance after Antietam, that "an army will never move if it waits until all the different commanders report that they are ready and want no more supplies." Lincoln told another general in November 1862 that "this expanding, and piling up of *impedimenta*, has been, so far, almost our ruin, and will be our final ruin if it is not abandoned. . . . You would be better off . . . for not having a thousand wagons, doing nothing but hauling forage to feed the animals that draw them, and taking at least two thousand men to care for the wagons and animals, who otherwise might be two thousand good soliders."[39]

With Grant and Sherman, Lincoln finally had generals in top commands who followed Ewell's dictum about the road to glory and who were willing to demand of their soldiers—and of themselves—the same exertions and sacrifices that Confederate commanders required of their men. After the Vicksburg campaign Lincoln said of General Grant, whose rapid mobility and absence of a cumbersome supply line were a key to its success, that "Grant is my man and I am his the rest of the war!" Perhaps one of the reasons for Lincoln's praise was a tongue-in-cheek report from Elihu Washburne, who traveled with Grant for part of the campaign. "I am afraid Grant will have to be reproved for want of style," Washburne wrote to Lincoln on May 1, 1863. "On this whole march for five days he has had neither a horse nor an orderly or servant, a blanket or overcoat or clean shirt, or even a sword. . . . His entire baggage consists of a toothbrush."[40] To Lincoln, the contrast with the headquarters pomp of a McClellan or Frémont could not have been greater.

Lincoln had opinions about battlefield tactics, but he rarely made suggestions to his field commanders for that level of operations. One exception, however, occurred in the second week of May 1862. Upset by McClellan's monthlong siege of Yorktown without any apparent result, Lincoln and Secretary of War Stanton and Secretary of the Treasury

Salmon P. Chase sailed down to Hampton Roads on May 5 to discover that the Confederates had evacuated Yorktown before McClellan could open with his siege artillery.

Norfolk remained in enemy hands, however, and the feared CSS *Virginia* (former *Merrimack*) was still docked there. On May 7 Lincoln took direct operational control of a drive to capture Norfolk and to push a gunboat fleet up the James River. The president ordered General John Wool, commander at Fort Monroe, to land troops on the south bank of Hampton Roads. Lincoln even personally carried out a reconnaissance to select the best landing place. On May 9 the Confederates evacuated Norfolk before northern soldiers could get there. Two days later the *Virginia*'s crew blew her up to prevent her capture. An officer on the USS *Monitor* wrote that "it is extremely fortunate that the President came down as he did—he seems to have infused new life into everything." Nothing was happening, he said, until Lincoln began "stirring up dry bones." Chase rarely found opportunities to praise Lincoln, but on this occasion he wrote to his daughter: "So has ended a brilliant week's campaign of the President; for I think it quite certain that if he had not come down, Norfolk would still have been in possession of the enemy, and the 'Merrimac' as grim and defiant and as much a terror as ever. . . . The whole coast is now virtually ours."[41]

Chase exaggerated, for the Confederates would have had to abandon Norfolk anyway to avoid being cut off when Johnston's army retreated up the north side of the James River. But Chase's words can perhaps be applied to Lincoln's performance as commander in chief in the war as a whole. He enunciated a clear national policy, and through trial and error evolved national and military strategies to achieve it. The nation did not perish from the earth but experienced a new birth of freedom.

2

The Constitution and Civil Liberties Under Lincoln[1]

MARK E. NEELY, JR.

This essay will focus on three documents that are critical to understanding President Abraham Lincoln's record on civil liberties. The first is *Ex parte Merryman*. In that opinion from the United States Supreme Court, issued in June 1861, Chief Justice Roger B. Taney declared Lincoln's suspension of the writ of habeas corpus unconstitutional. The second is Lincoln's fullest defense of his suspension and its dangerous consequences, the famous letter to Erastus Corning and others, of June 12, 1863. (On June 29, 1863, Lincoln sent a similar letter to a delegation of Ohio Democrats led by Matthew Birchard, and a look at the Birchard letter will supplement the analysis of the more famous Corning letter.) Finally, Lincoln's letter to Governor Thomas Fletcher, of February 20, 1865, an important but neglected policy statement, will shine new light on the restoration of civil liberties in Missouri, the state where they had been the most endangered. The discussion thus will span the years of the Lincoln administration and provide, among other things that history has been lacking up to this time, an appreciation for chronological changes in the policy.

Ex parte Merryman, Roger B. Taney's legal challenge to the suspension of the writ of habeas corpus, stands as one of the most poorly understood of decisions to come from the Supreme Court. Take that very statement itself. Historians still write as though Taney had issued his opinion as a decision of a Baltimore federal circuit court.[2] In the middle of the nineteenth century the justices of the Supreme Court spent only part of their time in Washington, D.C., sitting as members of the Supreme Court. Each justice was also assigned a federal circuit court and rode out from Washington to hear decisions in those lower courts too. Taney sat on the bench in Baltimore, part of his federal circuit, when he first pronounced his decision in the case, but he issued the decision as a justice of the United States Supreme Court.[3]

Here is the sequence of events. Federal soldiers arrested secessionist John Merryman at his home near Cockeysville, Maryland, outside Baltimore, on May 25, 1861, because he was the officer commanding an organized militia armed with United States weapons and training to join the Confederacy. He was arrested at two in the morning and whisked away to Fort McHenry, a federal installation in Baltimore. Merryman's lawyer sought a writ of habeas corpus from Chief Justice Taney himself, in Washington. Taney issued the writ, ordering the soldiers holding Merryman to produce him in court and explain the law for the arrest. Since Lincoln had on April 27 allowed military officers to suspend the writ of habeas corpus along the "military line" reaching from Philadelphia to Washington at any point where "resistance occurs," the soldiers did not comply with the writ and bring Merryman to court.[4]

The chief justice was waiting in Baltimore for the general to produce the prisoner in court (Fort McHenry lay in the city's harbor). So Taney was not really in his chambers at the Supreme Court in Washington when he made his ruling on the case. But the chief justice explained in the decision itself that he had come to the circuit court only as a convenience to the army commander holding the prisoner, so that the general would not be forced to travel a great distance from his command during a war to take care of a legal matter. Taney made it plain that he was issuing the opinion from the Supreme Court "in chambers" and that his jurisdiction to hear the case stemmed from the provision of the Judiciary Act of 1789 giving Supreme Court justices as well as federal judges original jurisdiction in habeas corpus cases for federal prisoners.[5]

After the army refused to produce Merryman because the president had suspended the writ of habeas corpus, Taney went home to write a decision in the case. As the constitutional historian Daniel Farber summarizes it, Taney made three points, and they added up to "a powerful challenge to Lincoln's power":

First, the suspension clause is found in Article I, devoted mostly to the legislative power, not in Article II, devoted to the executive power. This placement seemed unlikely for a constraint on the president. Second, after long struggles on behalf of liberty, the English monarch had been completely deprived of the power to suspend the writ. Would the Framers have given the president more draconian powers than those possessed by George III? Third, eminent judicial authorities and commentators such as Chief Justice Marshall and Justice [Joseph] Story had described the suspension power as congressional. Thus Lincoln's actions contradicted the accepted reading of the clause.[6]

Taney's case was not as powerful as it may seem—but for a reason overlooked in that analysis of his position. The chief justice's considerable power in 1861 derived from the Judiciary Act of 1789 and from John Marshall, his predecessor as chief justice in the early Republic. The fourteenth section of the Judiciary Act gave Taney, as a justice of the United States Supreme Court, original jurisdiction in habeas corpus cases for federal prisoners. John Marshall gave him the power of judicial review. In this instance, Taney, who had famously overturned an act of Congress prohibiting slavery in parts of the territories acquired in the Louisiana Purchase in the *Dred Scott* decision of 1857, did not now have to take on an act of Congress. He was reviewing an order of the president suspending the privilege of the writ of habeas corpus. But Taney was prepared to use the power of judicial review later to undermine the acts of Congress key to mobilizing troops and funding the war.[7] The opportunity simply never arose through appellate jurisdiction.

When John Marshall established or invigorated judicial review in *Marbury v. Madison* in 1803, he too had been concerned with the Judiciary Act of 1789. Marshall had ruled the thirteenth section of that act unconstitutional because it increased the original jurisdiction of the Court. Marshall said that the Constitution itself established the original jurisdiction of the Supreme Court, and Congress could not pass a law that would alter a constitutional mandate. Section 2 of Article III of the Constitution, the article concerned with the powers of the judiciary, stated in part: "In all Cases affecting Ambassadors, other public Ministers and Consuls, and those in which a State shall be Party, the supreme Court shall have original Jurisdiction. In all the other cases before mentioned [in the previous section of the article] the supreme Court shall have appellate Jurisdiction, both as to Law and Fact, with such Exceptions, and under such Regulations as the Congress shall make."[8]

Thus Congress could alter the appellate jurisdiction of the court, but the Constitution itself described the original jurisdiction, and only amendment could alter that. The facts of the case were these. Marbury had asked the court for an order called a writ of mandamus to be served on Secretary of State James Madison. The thirteenth article of the Judiciary Act of 1789 gave the Supreme Court "the power to issue . . . writs of mandamus, in cases warranted by the principles and usages of law, to any Courts appointed, or persons holding office, under the authority of the United States."[9] But such an action constituted original jurisdiction, as Marbury's request for the order went directly to the Supreme Court and did not come to the Court from another court. For that reason Marshall declared Article 13 of the Judiciary Act unconstitutional in 1803.

Roger B. Taney began his opinion in *Ex parte Merryman* by saying:

The application in this case for a writ of habeas corpus is made to me under the 14th section of the judiciary act of 1789, which renders effectual for the citizen the constitutional privilege of the writ of habeas corpus. That act gives to the courts of the United States, as well as to each justice of the supreme court, and to every district judge, power to grant writs of habeas corpus for the purpose of an inquiry into the cause of commitment. The petition was presented to me, at Washington, under the impression that I would order the prisoner to be brought before me there, but as he was confined in Fort McHenry, in the city of Baltimore, which is in my circuit, I resolved to hear it in the latter city, as obedience to the writ, under such circumstances, would not withdraw General Cadwalader, who had him in charge, from the limits of his military command.[10]

The fourteenth section of the Judiciary Act, by which Taney thus claimed power to hear the application, stated in part: "[E]ither of the Justices of the Supreme Court, as well as Judges of the district Courts, shall have power to grant writs of Habeas Corpus for the purpose of an enquiry into the cause of commitment.—Provided that writs of Habeas Corpus shall in no case extend to prisoners in Gaol, unless where they are in custody under or by color of the authority of the United States, or are committed for trial before some Court of the same, or are necessary to be brought into Court to testify."[11]

But we know, for it was the very basis of the establishment of the power of judicial review in *Marbury v. Madison*, that the Constitution established the original jurisdiction of the United States Supreme Court. Congress could not change it, expand it, or shrink it. Was it not just as much an addition to the original jurisdiction of the Supreme Court to give its justices power to issue the writ of habeas corpus as it was to give them the power to issue writs of mandamus? Was this extension of authority to issue writs of habeas corpus in the fourteenth section any more constitutional than the extension of authority to issue writs of mandamus in the thirteenth section?

Roger B. Taney never asked that question. But it is surely worth comment that he did not. Taney grabbed the power. He did not look behind it to see whether jurisdiction was really his, constitutionally. He did not take a clue from John Marshall and check into the constitutionality of the very next section of the Judiciary Act after the one Marshall had famously overturned in *Marbury v. Madison* in 1803. Taney did not question the power of the Supreme Court in this instance. He was too eager to employ it. He did not look behind it to see whether in the desperate circumstances of the United States government in May 1861, he really should as a Supreme Court justice in chambers take jurisdiction of a case that might cause serious constitutional conflict with the commander in chief. When it came to defending the rights of southerners, there was no length to which Taney would not go, as historian Don E. Fehrenbacher pointed out long ago in regard to the *Dred Scott* decision. He continued down that recklessly expansive path in *Ex parte Merryman*. But it may have been simply unconstitutional to do so.

Lincoln's position is not much better understood than Taney's jurisdiction. In the first place, because he was defying a decision of the chief justice of the United States in chambers, the president was more nearly defying the Supreme Court than it might appear if we think of *Ex parte Merryman* as a Baltimore circuit court decision. In the second place, the theory of presidential power from which Lincoln's defiance derived is not well understood either. Constitutional scholar Akhil Reed Amar, for example, defends Lincoln this way: "In his view, the placement of the nonsuspension clause in Congress's Article I rather than the president's

Article II did not impliedly require prior congressional approval. Rather, the Article I location of the clause simply confirmed that ultimately the decision was Congress's. The president could merely act temporarily, as Congress's faithful on-duty servant maintaining the pre-rebellion status quo precisely in order to preserve Congress's options."[12] Such may be a plausible constitutional justification for Lincoln's actions, but it is not the justification the president invoked.

In fact Lincoln invoked more than one justification. He did on occasion discuss the necessity of acting without wasting time when Congress was not in session. But that consideration was of no moment once Congress met, as it did in special session, beginning on July 4, 1861, and in regular session, as it did beginning in December 1861. When Lincoln issued his presidential proclamation of September 24, 1862, suspending the writ of habeas corpus to enforce the recent federal draft, Congress was not in session. Lincoln said not a word about awaiting congressional authorization or acting in lieu of Congress in his proclamation; he said only that "it has become necessary."[13] Perhaps he was preserving Congress's options, but Congress had met and met and met by the autumn of 1862, yet the option had gone unexercised. Finally, on March 3, 1863, Congress authorized the president to suspend the writ of habeas corpus, without passing judgment on the previous suspensions enacted under presidential authority alone. Congress did not thank Lincoln as their "faithful servant" for keeping their options open or taking care of what was "ultimately" their business. It seems very unlikely that members of Congress regarded Lincoln's arrogation of that power as a way of protecting their power.

In June 1863 Lincoln defended his policy on civil liberties in the Corning letter (to be discussed at length later in this article). In the part of it dealing with his conception of presidential power, Lincoln explained: "Ours is a case of Rebellion . . . in fact, a clear, flagrant, and gigantic case of Rebellion; and the provision of the constitution that 'The previlege [sic] of the writ of Habeas Corpus shall not be suspended, unless when in cases of Rebellion or Invasion, the public Safety may require it' is the provision which specially applies to our present case."[14] Again, the president made no mention of Congress even though by that time Congress had acted.

For his part, Lincoln had congressional authorization now, but he did not say so. He still dallied with the "temporary" defense, but it led to confusion in his otherwise clearheaded Corning letter: "[I]f, as has happened," he argued in the summer of 1863, "the executive should suspend the writ, without ruinous waste of time, instances of arresting innocent persons might occur, as are always likely to occur in such cases."[15] The promptness of the suspension had nothing logically to do with the risk of arrest of innocent persons, an unfortunate possibility at any time the writ was suspended (as he said himself).

In another vigorous public letter defending the policy, issued about two weeks after the Corning letter, Lincoln forthrightly stated his view that Article I, section 9 was "improperly called, as I think, a limitation upon the power of congress."[16] And then he made it clear where he thought the power lay:

> This question, divested of the phraseology calculated to represent me as struggling for an arbitrary personal prerogative, is either a question simply who shall decide, or an affirmation that nobody shall decide, what the public safety does require, in cases of Rebellion or Invasion. The constitution contemplates the question as likely to occur for decision, but it does not expressly declare who is to decide it. By necessary implication, when Rebellion or Invasion comes, the decision is to be made, from time to time; and I think the man whom, for the time, the people have, under the constitution, made the commander-in-chief, of their Army and Navy, is the man who holds the power, and bears the responsibility of making it. If he uses the power justly, the same people will probably justify him; if he abuses it, he is in their hands, to be dealt with by all the modes they have reserved to themselves in the constitution.[17]

There was nothing temporary about the president's power in Lincoln's view as expressed in 1863. He now suggested a radical democratic justification with the flavor of a Jacksonian interpretation of the presidency about it. Congress simply did not figure in his view of the question and never had very much. Officially, though, proclamations suspending the writ of habeas corpus after March 3, 1863, began with an invocation of congressional authorization.[18] Or rather, Secretary of State Seward so began the proclamations, for by this time Lincoln was delegating the drafting of the proclamations to others. The proclamation of September 15, 1863, read thus:

> Whereas the Constitution . . . has ordained that the privilege of the Writ
> of Habeas Corpus shall not be suspended unless when in cases of rebellion
> or invasion the public safety may require it, And whereas a rebellion was
> existing on the third day of March, 1863, which rebellion is still existing;
> and whereas by a statute which was approved on that day, it was enacted
> by the Senate and House of Representatives of the United States . . . that,
> during the present insurrection, the President . . . whenever, in his judg-
> ment, the Public safety may require, is authorized to suspend the privi-
> lege of the Writ of Habeas Corpus in any case throughout the United
> States or any part thereof; and whereas in the judgment of the President
> the public safety does require that the privilege . . . shall now be sus-
> pended. . . . Now, therefore, I, Abraham Lincoln, President of the United
> States, do hereby proclaim . . . that the privilege of the Writ of Habeas
> Corpus is suspended.[19]

Such proved to be the language of official proclamations but not the language Lincoln himself used to describe the nature of the power.

In the final analysis, what *Ex parte Merryman* and Lincoln's responses to
criticism of the suspension of the writ of habeas corpus prove is this:
Both the president and the chief justice of the United States were
expanding the power of their branches of government, most likely,
beyond what the Constitution allowed. Lincoln's strong view has long
been recognized as such, but not Taney's. That is what is new in this
interpretation of the *Merryman* decision.

Constitutional scholar Daniel Farber concluded his analysis of the
Lincoln-Taney conflict by asking why Lincoln refused to obey the court
order in the Merryman incident. "[T]he president must enforce the judgments of the federal courts in specific cases, right or wrong," he insisted.
To Farber the only legitimate ground on which Lincoln might have dis-
obeyed the order was jurisdictional: The judge had no power to rule on
the case. Yet Farber ignored the true jurisdictional question in the case as
beneath consideration and did not investigate the Judiciary Act of 1789:
"[T]he question," Farber said, "of whether a case could be brought
directly before the Supreme Court or only by appeal from a lower court,
the issue in *Marbury v. Madison*, clearly does not seem earthshaking
enough to justify non-compliance."[20]

Curiously, Farber did not elaborate any further on what caused such a
question to arise. Once we descend to an analysis of the technicalities of

obedience to a court order, then we have surely descended into the realm of the Judiciary Act and what jurisdiction it gave to the Court. That was the only real jurisdictional question. And that question was substantial indeed. The answer to it reveals definitively, for the first time, the aggressive nature of Roger B. Taney's jurisprudence. Lincoln's ignoring the decision is likewise of great significance, but not because of the outcome for the individual involved in the case (though that must have been earth-shaking enough for John Merryman and his family). There is much to be learned not only from Lincoln's response but from Taney's willing and overeager acceptance of the jurisdictional gift of Section 14 of the Judiciary Act of 1789.

Taken all in all, however, it is possible that in the clash of branches of the United States government embodied in the struggle over habeas corpus and the *Merryman* decision, both the president and the Supreme Court (in chambers) maintained unconstitutional positions aimed at increasing their respective powers. Neither side in the political conflict was going to remain neatly within the lines drawn by the old Constitution of 1787. In the realm of domestic civil liberty, events shaped the Constitution during the Civil War and not the other way around.[21]

Lincoln's defiance of Taney's writ proved hardly inflammatory. He did not reply to Taney immediately, and when he finally did reply (in the president's message to the special session of Congress, which met on July 4, 1861), it was with a general argument and did not refer to the particular decision or to Taney by name or position. Lincoln there presented so labored and cumbersome a style that a careful modern critic of Lincoln's writing suggests the difficulties were deliberate.[22] Whatever the merits and qualities of Lincoln's defense in July 1861, all are agreed that Lincoln wrote a vigorous and memorable defense of the policy later. Lincoln's public letter of June 12, 1863, was a reply to a group of New York Democrats who had protested the recent arrest and trial by military commission of Ohio Democratic politician Clement L. Vallandigham. Because the leader of the protest was a man named Erastus Corning, the letter has come to be called the Corning letter. It was a hair-raising demand for enlisting heart and mind unreservedly in the cause of the nation.

Lincoln began by asserting that secession was a conspiracy, some thirty years in the making; because of all that advanced preparation on the part of the secessionists, the North and South met "on very unequal terms." Lincoln alleged that the southerners "hoped to keep on foot amongst us a most efficient corps of spies, informers, suppliers, and aiders and abettors of their cause." These confederates would operate "under cover of 'Liberty of speech' 'Liberty of the press' and 'Habeas corpus.' " The Confederates "knew" that "their friends would make a question as to who was to suspend" the writ of habeas corpus under the Constitution. All this sedition conducted under the umbrella of liberty of speech and under cover of argument that the president did not have the power to suspend the writ was "part of the enemies' programme."[23] Lincoln thus characterized libertarian critics of the government and defenders of First Amendment freedoms and the privilege of the writ of habeas corpus as Confederate sympathizers and an integral part of Confederate strategy for winning the war.

If such accusations were not enough to silence criticism of the government, Lincoln went on to make very plain that even silence was not good enough as proof of loyalty. "The man who stands by and says nothing, when the peril of this government is discussed, can not be misunderstood. If not hindered, he is sure to help the enemy." Thus the president now demanded a noisy and interventionist patriotism when the war was under debate. "Much more," Lincoln added, "if he talks ambiguously—talks for his country with 'buts' and 'ifs' and 'ands.' "[24] A moment's reflection brings to mind who at the time was speaking for the country with buts and ifs: the loyal opposition. The Democrats affirmed their allegiance to the Union "if" the administration obeyed the Constitution. The Democrats pledged their continuing loyalty "but" not if the goal of the war changed to a fanatical abolition program. The Corning letter pointed to the practical twilight of freedom of speech and the press for the war's loyal opposition. It criminalized silence, and singled out the political opposition as part of the enemies' program in raising a "clamor" of protest against the wrongful arrest of "innocent persons."[25]

To this day the alarming content of this famous letter remains underestimated. In fact the reluctance of most writers on Lincoln to look squarely in the face the stern propositions in the Corning letter speaks volumes about the gentle standards of criticism applied to Lincoln. James G. Randall, for example, the ablest of twentieth-century Lincoln biographers, characterized the Corning letter as "one of those dignified, carefully worded statements addressed to a person or occasion, but intended as a kind of state paper."[26] Surely Lincoln's brawling and pugnacious Corning letter is hardly recognizable in that bloodless image. Randall's student and Lincoln's most able biographer of recent times David Herbert Donald recognized the partisan scrappiness in the Corning letter that Randall had somehow overlooked, but concluded that "it reassured unionists genuinely troubled by an assumption of despotic power on the part of the President."[27] No good Republican was going to say he feared despotic tendencies in the Republican president, but the Corning letter did give some Republican commentators a little pause. Editors at the *New York Tribune*, for example, found Lincoln's constitutional arguments in the letter unanswerable, but they did express doubts about the expediency, as opposed to the right, to arrest Vallandigham. The *Tribune* editors feared that such arrests would give Democrats "pretext for resisting and breaking down the War under the guise of defending Free Speech," and they advised the president to let the opposition "do their worst undisturbed."[28] Editors at the *New York Evening Post*, after commending the president's letter, took note of a significant omission, "the failure to mention the full and satisfactory legislation of the last Congress on the entire subject of arbitrary arrest"—that is, the crucial Habeas Corpus Act of March 3, 1863, authorizing the president to suspend the writ of habeas corpus.[29] In other words, the newspaper quietly chided the president for leaving Congress's authorization out of his justification for the suspension of the writ of habeas corpus. It is difficult to find much reassurance in the propositions laid out in the Corning letter.

Yet another modern Lincoln scholar, a specialist in constitutional matters like Randall, Phillip Shaw Paludan, has remarked this way on the Corning letter and Lincoln's letter on the same subject sent to Ohio Democrats sixteen days later: "The president spent many hours on his letters to New York and Ohio Democrats explaining the stakes and why the constitution justified what he had done, thus bringing a listening audience to his side and justifying the ongoing fight. In a general sense, Lincoln kept the constitutional debate going throughout the war and thus propagandized to persuade the people that their constitutional system was adequate to survive and prosecute a war."[30]

Paludan combined this old-fashioned "constitutional debate" interpretation of the Corning letter with a contradictory emphasis on the letter's immediate war context. "Lincoln held off replying to his critics against his 'attack on civil liberties' until early June 1863," Paludan pointed out, "although they had written him in early May. There was not a pressing need for an immediate answer then. But by early June, Robert E. Lee, fresh from victory at Chancellorsville, was advancing north. One of the reasons he was doing that was because he believed . . . that Northern antiwar protest might signal support for the rebellion. In this environment, Lincoln answered his critics with a sweeping and threatening justification of government suppression of dissent."[31]

Paludan's assertion that Lincoln's attempts to shape public opinion perhaps showed "how the constitutional system should work at its best" denies the letter's most striking feature: It seems to be aimed at silencing debate, not at keeping debate going.[32] As for the context, it is not at all clear that the context was Lee's invasion of the North in June 1863. It is true that Lincoln had for some time previous to June had the elements of the Corning letter sitting around as scraps, fragments, and notes awaiting the proper occasion for defense of his policies on civil liberties. Lincoln had these intimidating arguments at the ready, but the trigger was not Lee's invasion of Maryland. Lee did not cross the Potomac until June 15. Before that, neither Lincoln nor General Joseph Hooker, then commanding the Army of the Potomac, standing in Lee's path, knew exactly what Lee was up to. As late as June 14, Lincoln was suggesting to Hooker that he might attack Lee's army in Virginia somewhere between Fredericksburg and Chancellorsville. Lincoln's reaction to Lee's invasion, when it did come, was just what it should have been: On June 15 he called for the uprising of the militia of the North.[33]

By that time Lincoln had already sent the Corning letter off—to Erastus Corning himself and to the *New York Tribune* for publication to the world—on June 13. He sent it two days before Lee's invasion. In fact, on the day he mailed the letter, the president remained unconcerned enough about developments with Lee's army to plan a boat trip to visit the Army of the Potomac but was turned back by an alarmed General Hooker.[34]

These were trying times for the administration, but Lincoln was as much alarmed by political as military events. The Democratic Party had performed well, under the circumstances, back in the autumn of 1862, making considerable gains in the congressional elections, winning the governorship of New York, and gaining majorities in the legislatures of Indiana and Illinois. It made a fateful miscalculation of the meaning of those election results, however. The Democrats thought they indicated war weariness and apparently decided to turn to agitation for peace and armistice in elections in Connecticut, Pennsylvania, and Ohio in 1863.[35] In fact the American people were not war-weary at all; they were defeat-weary. They did not want the Lincoln administration to quit fighting battles. They wanted the Lincoln administration to quit losing battles.

The Democrats could not have made a more pointed statement of this turn to peace agitation than by nominating Clement Vallandigham for governor of Ohio—on June 11, 1863![36] Surely that sensational political event as much as the military events in northern Virginia triggered Lincoln's release of the Corning letter. Lincoln was responding to the immediate context, all right, but it was as much political context as military. Up to the summer of 1863 the Democrats had generally taken care to preserve their status as a loyal opposition, supporting the war but not necessarily supporting the way the Republicans fought it and certainly not the other policies of the Republican administration. But having misread the election results of the previous autumn, the Democratic Party now seemed to be signaling, not with mere rhetoric but with electoral behavior in nominations for office, a turn to seeking armistice and peace. Vallandigham, while a member of the House of Representatives, had abstained from voting supplies for the troops in the field. He thus violated the unwritten constitution of the United States, a part of which, ever since the demise of the bitterly antiwar Federalist Party after 1815, posited that it was sure death for a party not to vote supplies for the troops in the field. In other words, Lincoln was for the first time beginning to see signs of what he had feared from the start was the only real threat to the American nation (besides the Confederacy itself), the failure of the political parties in the North to agree on supporting the war.

The reason Lincoln had the fragments and notes for what turned out to be the Corning letter at the ready was that he had been mulling the gradual development of Democratic Party policy toward what appeared to be sedition. In retrospect we know that it was making no such turn, but it was hard to tell otherwise from where Lincoln sat. The change in Lincoln's views about the loyalty of the opposition proved temporary, and it was a good thing for the Republic. Lincoln's power with language and argument was great. The Corning letter threatened to unleash the full wrath of American patriotism on northern society itself. The letter proved popular, in no small part because of Lincoln's own careful cultivation of public sentiment. He had the Corning letter printed and franked on his private secretary's account to key leaders in the country. He saw to its publication in the *New York Tribune*, which in turn guaranteed that other newspapers all over the United States would copy the letter from that source. At least seven different pamphlet versions of the Corning letter appeared in 1863, some of them with circulation in the hundreds of thousands.[37]

But the political context changed after the Democrats had suffered defeat in the three important elections of 1863, including a landslide defeat in Ohio. The Democrats would turn back to a war candidate for the presidency in the national election of 1864. Many Republicans at the time were unable or unwilling to take notice of the reversion to the ways of a loyal opposition, especially in light of the notorious "peace plank" in the Democratic presidential platform of 1864 written at its Chicago nominating convention. Presidential candidates in the nineteenth century did not campaign in their own behalf, and the heavy work was left to surrogates. Among Lincoln's was Secretary of State William H. Seward, who delivered what some regarded as the keynote of the Republican campaign in a speech at his hometown, Auburn, New York, on September 3, 1864, as the autumn campaign opened. The speech was titled "Allies of Treason" and questioned the loyalty of the Democrats. By late October, Lincoln felt called upon to repudiate Seward's speech. He did so in response to a "serenade," a more or less spontaneous event in which a band serenaded the president at the White House and the attendant crowd demanded a speech. Lincoln's "response" to the serenaders did not constitute a stump speech, but it contained important information for the electorate nevertheless:

> Something said by the Secretary of State in his recent speech at Auburn, has been construed by some into a threat that, if I shall be beaten at the election, I will, between then and the end of my constitutional term, do what I may be able, to ruin the government.
>
> Others regard the fact that the Chicago Convention adjourned, not sine die, but to meet again, if called to do so by a particular individual, as the intimation of a purpose that if their nominee shall be elected, he will at once seize control of the government. I hope the good people will permit themselves to suffer no uneasiness on either point. . . . [I]f I shall live, I shall remain President until the fourth of next March; and that whoever shall be constitutionally elected therefore in November, shall be duly

installed as President on the fourth of March; and that in the interval I shall do my utmost that whoever is to hold the helm for the next voyage, shall start with the best possible chance to save the ship.[38]

In other words, Lincoln went out of his way, even skirting presidential propriety in the course of it, to reassure the people a month before the election that this was an ordinary American contest between two loyal political parties. He had noted the Democrats' return even if Seward and other Republicans had not.

But if the threat in 1864 was not as great as he had thought it might be in 1863, did the threat of arrest for political opinion remain as grave as it sounded in the Corning letter of 1863? The existing literature on Lincoln and the Constitution leaves us only with knowledge that the president restricted civil liberties during the war. Once circumscribed, were they left restricted, whatever the changing circumstances? Should we think of the blistering tone and scorching content of the Corning letter hanging over public debate for the remainder of the Lincoln administration and up to his very death?[39]

Lincoln began in 1865 to alter policies and practices of internal security to match his understanding that the Democrats constituted a loyal opposition and that threats of sedition in the North were waning. This is nowhere clearer than in the case of the much-neglected letter to Thomas Fletcher of February 20, 1865. This document permits us to see that Lincoln came to realize that he had underestimated the dangers of suspending liberties even temporarily in crisis times. To put it another way, Lincoln not only restricted civil liberties but restored them as well. The Lincoln administration was likely pulling back from vigorous internal security measures after the election of 1864. He had never indulged in the pyrotechnics of the Corning letter sort in the 1864 presidential campaign (though many other Republicans, like Secretary of State Seward, speaking for his cause did so). Though he seems to have had reasonable confidence that the Democrats had more obviously resumed their role as a loyal opposition, Lincoln did breathe an audible sigh of relief when the election was safely over. Two days after the election Lincoln decided to affirm the inevitability of party opposition even in war:

We can not have free government without elections; and if the rebellion could force us to forego or postpone a national election, it might fairly claim to have already conquered and ruined us. The strife of the election is but human-nature practically applied to the facts of the case. What has occurred in this case, must ever recur in similar cases. Human-nature will not change. . . .

But the election, along with its incidental, and undesirable strife, has done good too. It has demonstrated that a people's government can sustain a national election, in the midst of a great civil war. . . . It shows that, even among candidates of the same party, he who is most devoted to the Union, and most opposed to treason, can receive most of the people's votes.[40]

Historians sometimes read those remarks as though Lincoln had said, "We cannot have free government without parties," but that is not quite what he said. Still, what he said was a far cry from his response to the strife of electoral politics in the Corning letter in the previous year.

Early in 1865, in keeping with his more relaxed attitude toward the opposition, Lincoln took positive steps to restore civil liberty—in the state where it had been most restricted, Missouri. Civil liberty was eclipsed in Missouri. Trials by military commission were first instituted there, and almost half of all trials by military commission in the Civil War occurred in Missouri. The state saw more than nine times the number of such trials held in either Kentucky or Maryland, similar border states. Moreover, General Order No. 11, of August 25, 1863, banished some twenty thousand civilians from four counties of Missouri near the Kansas border and thus stood as the most drastic displacement of population of its kind in the whole Civil War, exceeding anything the Union brought about by a single order in the Confederacy itself. President Lincoln specifically approved of "removing the inhabitants of certain counties *en masse*" in a letter written to the general who commanded the department.[41]

The summer of 1863, as we have seen in the case of the Corning letter, was the summer of Lincoln's great political discontent, and marked the period of his most drastic statements on the subject of liberty in the war. He had always been made uneasy by the restrictions of liberty deemed necessary in Missouri; he must have shared the fears that such policies, in the wrong hands and far from the watchful eye of the president, might lead to attempts to eliminate the political opposition. And he knew they inevitably permitted unjust and unnecessary arrests of the innocent.

As early as December 17, 1862, Lincoln sought to restrain Union forces operating in the state. He asked the commander of the Department of the Missouri, "Could the civil authority be reintroduced into Missouri in lieu of the military to any extent, with advantage and safety?"[42] Despite its succinct wording, this must have been a matter of importance to Lincoln because he was at the time distracted by political crisis in Washington. The disastrous Union defeat at Fredericksburg on the thirteenth had led Republican senators to attempt to force Lincoln to reorganize his cabinet and thus submit to their dictation. Nevertheless, the president took time to inquire about the possibility of ending reliance on military authority in distant Missouri. Lincoln had not yet begun to lose his confidence in the loyalty of the opposition, as the results of the fall elections were just in and the Democratic reaction to them not yet fully apparent.

The situation in December 1862 looked different to people stationed in Missouri. Lincoln's proposal went nowhere. The military commander in the state fired back a telegram immediately. "Dispatch received," he reported. "The peace of the State rests on Military power—to relinquish this power would be dangerous."[43] Two days later the provost marshal general for Missouri, the officer who actually exerted military power on civilians directly, sent Lincoln a long letter, the upshot of which was this: "I am convinced of the necessity of maintaining the ascendancy of the Federal Government in Missouri by force."[44]

Lincoln's suggestion caused rumors to run rampant in Missouri and consternation to set in among highly placed Union personnel in the state. Some of these alarms were political. John O'Fallon of St. Louis, one of the wealthiest businessmen in the city, as soon as he got wind of the possibility, wrote Lincoln: "It would result most disastrously to the Union cause; . . . one of its fruits, would be, at the next April election, in this city, the reelection, for the next two years, of the present, secession Mayor, council, &, other city officers."[45]

O'Fallon was old and conservative, a staunch opponent of abolition, but martial law in Missouri could unite left and right in the Republican Party. The leader of the radical antislavery faction, Charles Drake, wrote the president too. "From what I have heard," Drake said, "I am led to believe that the impression has been made on your mind, that Missouri is all quiet and secure." That was untrue, he insisted.[46]

The initial attempt to relax martial law in Missouri failed, and Lincoln may have, more or less, given up on the state as the situation there deteriorated, as factional politics grew bitter and unmanageable there, and as he became increasingly preoccupied with military campaigns farther south. But by 1865 the conditions in the state had changed dramatically. The Confederate invasion of Missouri in the fall of 1864, General Sterling Price's "Raid," had been turned back decisively. It did not seem likely, given the declining fortunes of the Confederacy, that future invasions were possible. That left internal civil strife the only problem in Missouri, which was otherwise at last entirely secured to the Union. Lincoln was now informed that continuing "irregular violence" in northern Missouri was still causing citizens to flee that part of the state. It seemed to the president that there was no longer any good reason for such a situation, and he began to consider not reinforcing the occupying Union forces in Missouri but reaching a long-term political solution to the state's problems of disorder and scaling back Union military force. He telegraphed General Grenville M. Dodge, the recently appointed commander of the Missouri district. "Please gather information," Lincoln wrote, "and consider whether an appeal to the people there to go to their homes, and let one another alone, recognizing as a full right of protection for each, that he lets others alone, and banning only him who refuses to let others alone, may not enable you to withdraw the troops, their presence itself a cause of irritation and constant apprehension, and thus restore peace and quiet & returning prosperity."[47] As in the past, Lincoln got no cooperation from the military authorities in the state. Dodge complained that the "troubles in North Missouri" had only increased since he assumed command because most of the troops previously occupying the area had been pulled away to swell the armies of the Union fighting General John Bell Hood in Tennessee. "Allow me to assure you," Dodge replied, "that the course you propose would be protested against by the State authorities, the legislature, the [constitutional] convention [then meeting to abolish slavery in the state] and by nearly every undoubtedly loyal man in North Missouri, while it would receive the sanction of nearly every disloyal, semi-loyal, and non-committed person there, all such could, under that course live and should want to stay in that country, while every loyal man would have to leave these counties when the disloyal sentiment is in the ascendancy."[48]

Representative William A. Hall had prompted Lincoln's inquiry. The

Missouri congressman was the brother of Willard P. Hall, who had served as lieutenant governor to the conservative Republican governor Hamilton R. Gamble, the man Fletcher replaced.[49] The Halls hailed from St. Joseph, on the Missouri River about halfway between Kansas City and the Iowa line, and Hall thus represented northwestern Missouri.

Obviously, by that late date the bitterly competitive factions in Missouri were split on whether the state was quiet enough to permit the end of martial law, with the conservatives like the Halls wishing to do so and the radicals like Drake opposed. It would be a mistake, however, to think that the Missouri factions divided significantly on questions of constitutionality. The radicals wished to see martial law continued, despite the cooling of Missouri's strife. The conservatives, who opposed martial law in 1865, had not been so constitutionally delicate back in 1861, when they were the beneficiaries of an outright *coup d'état*.[50] Hall and Gamble had always headed an unconstitutional and illegal government. They had been chosen, ironically, by the rump of the old secession convention of 1861, after the secessionists had been driven out of the state and out of the convention by military force. Probably few people would deny that the situation in Missouri at the moment of that government's appointment was dire and that if ever there was a moment to ignore constitutional nicety, that was the moment. But a year later Governor Gamble called the old secession convention into session once again. When the delegates voted to call for gubernatorial elections to be held in the autumn of 1862, Gamble and Hall informed the convention that they regarded that vote as condemnation of their government. After that, many members of the convention changed their minds and voted to retain Gamble's provisional government until the regularly prescribed election date in 1864.[51] Gamble's crisis government had become a self-perpetuating government that shunned the test of election. By the time Lincoln acted to restore constitutional liberties in Missouri, no political faction in the state likely to cooperate with the Republican administration in Washington enjoyed a consistent adherence to constitutionalism. Perhaps for that reason, Lincoln did not choose to pitch his plan for ending martial law in Missouri in terms of constitutional rectitude. He chose a different rhetoric, one of community, which Lincoln was beginning to develop in his letter to Grenville Dodge early in 1865, with its talk of peace and quiet and prosperity.

The appeal had fallen on deaf ears in Dodge's case. William Hall, as a member of the House, was in Washington when Dodge's letter arrived, and Lincoln showed it to him. Hall told Lincoln that Dodge was misinformed and had probably gained his erroneous information from "officers who are themselves in some degree to blame."[52]

Frustrated by resistance from his own military commanders in the state, Lincoln decided to turn to Missouri's civil authorities to end reliance on military force. The time was opportune because Missouri, for the first time in four years, enjoyed a legal and constitutional government as a result of the elections of 1864.

The victor in the election of 1864 in Missouri was a Republican named Thomas C. Fletcher. Soon after his inauguration as governor, Fletcher received a letter from Lincoln. Clearly modeled on the telegram he had sent to General Dodge a couple of weeks earlier, the letter was longer and richly explanatory:

> It seems that there is now no organized force of the enemy in Missouri and yet that destruction of property and life is rampant every where. Is not the cure for this within easy reach of the people themselves? It cannot but be that every man, not naturally a robber or cut-throat, would gladly put an end to this state of things. A large majority in every locality must feel alike upon this subject; and if so they only need to reach an understanding one with another. Each leaving all others alone solves the problem. And surely each would do this but for his apprehension that others will not leave him alone. Can not this mischievous distrust be removed? Let neighborhood meetings be every where called and held, of all entertaining a sincere purpose for mutual security in the future, whatever they may heretofore have thought, said or done about the war or about anything else. Let all such meet and waiving all else pledge each to cease harassing others and to make common cause against whomever persists in making aiding or encouraging further disturbance. The practical means they will best know how to adopt and apply. At such meetings old friendships will cross the memory; and honor and Christian Charity will come in to help.[53]

Though in the past I have treated this letter as a confession of failure of Lincoln's policy in Missouri and did not take it really seriously, I can now see that that was a mistake. Lincoln's suggestions should be regarded not cynically but hopefully as a new policy initiative, and a serious one.

Lincoln did not know he was going to be shot in two months' time. As William C. Harris has shown us, Lincoln had just been reelected and had a mandate for a new administration.[54] He was hopeful. He was optimistic. He was looking forward. Considered in that light, what he suggested to Fletcher can be seen as one of his new policies: He was going to restore civil liberty. Therefore, when a week passed and Lincoln had not received a reply from Governor Fletcher, he sent him a prodding letter: "Have you received my letter of the 20th? I think some such thing as therein suggested, is needed. If you put it before the people, I will direct the Military to cooperate. Please answer."[55] Fletcher was in no mood to take the advice. "It would but madden the true men of this State," he informed the president finally, "to talk to them of reliance on the 'honor' and 'christian charity' of these fiends in human shape."[56]

The reluctance of the Missouri Republicans to do away with martial law in 1865 constituted the real failure of Lincoln's policy on civil liberties and the Constitution. Lincoln had miscalculated. He could not at first believe that liberty could be permanently diminished among the liberty-loving American people. That was the ultimate reassuring premise of the Corning letter. There Lincoln had said, in an unusual scoffing tone, that he was not able "to appreciate the danger . . . that the American people will, by means of military arrests during the rebellion, lose the right of public discussion, the liberty of speech and the press, the law of evidence trial by jury, and Habeas corpus, throughout the indefinite peaceful future. . . any more than I am able to believe that a man could contract so strong an appetite for emetics during temporary illness, as to persist in feeding upon them through the remainder of his healthful life."[57] Missouri proved him wrong. One newspaper correspondent in St. Louis, for example, reported in March 1865, amid rumors of the coming demise of martial law in the state: "So far from being unpopular, it is believed that a large portion of our loyal people are willing to see a provision incorporated in the charter of the city, requiring six months of martial law to be imposed in the city every five years to clean up all the little cases of outraged justice, loose indictments, public corruption and private peculation, which the ordinary courts cannot reach."[58] The St. Louis reporter for the *Chicago Tribune*, quoted here, gave the situation a humorous inflection, but what lay at the bottom of the reluctance to give up martial law in the state was not funny.

In the presidential election of 1864 the number of people who voted in Missouri fell 37 percent from the 1860 level—virtually a whole party's worth of votes. Lincoln received 72,750 votes to McClellan's 31,678 in 1864. Altogether, 104,428 Missourians voted that year. The 1860 presidential contest was a four-way race, and it is not obvious to which party the voters adhered four years later, but then 166,518 Missourians came to the polls, and Lincoln received only 17,028 of their votes. Essentially, the disappearance of more than 62,000 voters in Missouri in 1864 meant that much of the Democratic Party in the electorate in Missouri, likely a majority, had disappeared. Whatever the cause, and military intimidation and fraud at the polls were contributing factors, it made governing more comfortable to have no viable political opposition.[59] Continuing martial law in the state would perpetuate radical Republican rule.

Lincoln steadily maintained in his explanations of internal security policy that he did not want to see the policies used in a partisan manner. Even in the fierce Corning letter, Lincoln retained the careful distinction. Vallandigham, he explained, "was not arrested because he was damaging the political prospects of the administration . . . but because he was damaging the army, upon the existence, and vigor of which, the life of the nation depends."[60] What Lincoln had attempted to guard against in his internal security policy had come to pass in Missouri. Martial law had apparently become the means of eliminating political opposition there. It is no wonder the civil authorities did not respond to Lincoln's appeal to relax martial law in the state.

Lincoln had examined the voter turnout in the election returns of 1864. He likely realized what had happened in Missouri.[61] Recognizing the feared abuse of martial law in Missouri but faced with intransigence from the military authorities and the civil authorities, Lincoln decided to change policy in the state despite the overwhelming opposition of his own political party there. He could not change the civil authorities, but he could, as commander in chief, change the military ones. He could attack the problem without Fletcher's cooperation by appointing a new commander in St. Louis. General Ulysses S. Grant had sent Grenville M. Dodge to Kansas to fight Indians, and though Dodge retained command of the Department of the Missouri, he was no longer in St. Louis, and Lincoln contrived to send General John Pope to St. Louis as commander of the Military Division of Missouri, with orders to wean the state away from martial law. Whether by accident or design, the uncooperative and truculent Dodge was out of the way, and the cooperative Pope was soon on the Missouri scene.

The new general in St. Louis promptly mounted a campaign to win the civil authorities in Missouri over to civilian control of the military. Pope told Fletcher that he "fully believed in the capacity of the American people for self-government," implying that Fletcher seemed not to, to judge from his actions and policies. Pope set about ending martial law in order to relieve the military forces still occupying the state from what he called "the anomalous and anti-American functions which had been forced upon them." He had to point out to the civilian governor that the arguments made by his political faction in Missouri for the policy of martial law "lost their value" when the rebellion was no longer alive. Pope warned of "an alarming and fatal tendency among the people . . . to surrender to the military the execution of the laws, and thus to abandon all safeguards against tyranny and oppression, and to pass unconsciously into a condition of acquiescence in the complete dominion of military authority. Once let the American people abandon themselves to this practice, which indulgence confirms into habit, and their liberties are gone from them forever."[62]

The fact that the military administration was being ordered to restore civil liberties in the North is surely proof positive that Lincoln's second term was aimed at restoring the liberties only temporarily suspended during his first term. Lincoln did not have a relaxed attitude toward the continuance of restrictions when military necessity ceased to justify them. He seemed often on the verge of demanding that martial law cease.

On the other hand, Lincoln had no particular interest in seeing that Congress rather than the president determine when restriction of civil liberties was warranted and when it might be relaxed. And Roger B. Taney's aggressive uses of the Supreme Court left Lincoln with no confidence that he could rely on the judiciary for fair-minded mediation of the difficulties inevitable if a loyal opposition persisted during the war. Even the Corning letter, which revealed Lincoln's deepest doubts about the path the political opposition appeared to be willing to take, found Lincoln hinting, toward the end of it, that he definitely looked forward to better times. Not only would he consider pardoning Vallandigham when the public safety would allow it, but "I further say, that as the war progresses, it appears to me, opinion, and action, which were in great confu-

sion at first, take shape, and fall into more regular channels; so that the
necessity for arbitrary dealing with them gradually decreases. . . . Still, I
must continue to do so much as may seem to be required by the public
safety."[63] The Corning letter itself reveals the susceptibility of Lincoln to
the widespread fears of party opposition in the midst of war, and Lincoln
scholarship has failed up to this point to take full cognizance of that. But
it required a perceptible turn toward new directions by the Democrats in
1863 to provoke those fears.

On the other hand, the Fletcher letter and the previously unknown
policy initiatives taken in its wake by the Lincoln administration in early
1865 are proof of Lincoln's measured response to threats to national security in the North during the Civil War and of the sincerity of his promise
to decrease the pressure on civil liberties as the safety of the public
increased.

The critical tests of internal security policies taken in war are that they
not be used to eliminate the loyal political opposition and that they be
measured, appropriate to the provocation and threat, that they wax and
wane with the extent of the threat. Internal security measures during war
are likely inevitable and always dangerous. Even Lincoln wavered in 1863
when the Democrats took their apparent turn toward peace, and himself
took a scary turn in the direction of silencing criticism of the war. He
came back on track in 1864, however, when the Democrats seemed to settle, early, on nominating a war candidate for president in 1864. His policies were never meant to and never really did threaten the viability of the
Democratic Party. They could, however, be used by others, beyond his
control, to that end, as in Missouri.

Lincoln responded quickly to threats to the national security in the
North, but he also thought constantly about relaxing those measures.[64]
He finally did more than think about it: When Missouri seemed safe from
Confederate invasion but local authorities refused to relax martial law,
Lincoln sent the army in to end martial law in the state.

It is, of course, difficult to say whether Lincoln's response to internal
threats to the nation's security was measured, for there has never been a
threat to the nation as great as the one faced in the Civil War. But a republic in serious danger could hardly ask more of its president than that he
keep an eye on abuses of the policy that might eliminate the loyal opposition and that he take administrative action to relax the policy when the
threats diminished.

On the other hand, this article runs a risk of making villains of the earnest Republicans in Missouri. From another perspective, they had a point. We can see in the rhetoric of "Christian charity" Lincoln began to invoke in dealing with Missouri in 1865, the foreshadowing of the theme of "malice toward none and charity for all" that would appear in March in Lincoln's second inaugural address. Such an optimistic policy may well have been too optimistic for Reconstruction times to come. It is not at all clear that the objectives of Reconstruction, especially protecting the freedmen from the wrath of returning Confederates and unrepentant planters, could be achieved by invocations to forgive and forget and by strict adherence to the old Constitution and the accustomed areas of state authority. But those are questions to be asked about another era and other presidents.

3

Abraham Lincoln
and Jacksonian Democracy

SEAN WILENTZ

I.

Abraham Lincoln was a Whig to begin with. For as long as the Whigs existed, he never supported the candidate of another party. At least until the late 1850s his chief political heroes were Whigs, above all Henry Clay, whom he said he "loved and revered as a teacher and leader." Lincoln became a Republican in 1855, but only after hesitating. He later boasted that he "had stood by the [Whig] party as long as it had a being." As president Lincoln would, according to various recollections, assure moderate southerners and northern conservatives that his instincts were temperate, that he had "always been an old-line Henry Clay Whig," and that "[t]here is still a good deal of old Whig left in me yet."[1]

As recent scholarship has reemphasized the fundamental divisions between Jacksonians and Whigs in the 1830s and 1840s, renewed attention has fallen on Lincoln's Whig loyalties and on the continuities in Lincoln's political outlook. More than ever, Lincoln appears to have been a true-blue Whig not simply in the Illinois legislature and during his two years in Congress but, deep down, for his entire political career, including during his presidency, when he governed, as David Herbert Donald put it more than forty years ago, as "a Whig in the White House."[2] Lincoln's relation to Jacksonian democracy, as construed both as a narrow partisan affiliation and as a broader political movement, seem to have been mainly negative.

We care about Lincoln, though, not because he was a Whig but because he became a Republican. Had he died when his original party did, he would be remembered, if at all, as "Spotty" Lincoln, a one-term congressman, who changed his public position about the Mexican War and ineffectually (and courageously) protested the war policies of President James K. Polk. Once he joined the Republicans, he became the Illinois party's state head, and he never once glanced back in regret at the Whig Party's demise. In telling conservatives that he still had "a good deal of old Whig" left in him, President Lincoln acknowledged that a good deal had also changed.

That Lincoln made his most important political mark as a Republican leader raises questions about the precise character of his Whig loyalties and outlook. Even when he was a devoted Whig partisan, Lincoln, unlike more conservative Whigs, was affected by democratic ideas and practices that shaped the mainstream of both of the major parties of the 1830s and 1840s. Lincoln's conversion to the Republicans also marked him as a certain kind of Whig, an inveterate foe of the Slave Power, at odds with the minority of northern Whigs and the majority of southern Whigs who chose a very different political course in the 1850s.[3]

After 1854, Lincoln certainly upheld ideas of national unity and stability, and of individual social and economic opportunity, which he had championed as a Whig and which became key ideas of his new party. For Lincoln, as for most of the Republican faithful, there was considerable continuity in being a Whig and being a Republican. In speeches during his senatorial campaign against Stephen A. Douglas in 1858, as well as in his famous debates with Douglas, Lincoln cited antislavery passages from "our old leader," Henry Clay, in response to what he called Douglas's efforts to wrap himself in "the giant mantle" of Clay. But Lincoln also looked back to the Declaration of Independence and to Thomas Jefferson—a man widely considered the chief forebear of Jacksonian democracy and whom Lincoln had largely ignored in his public utterances before 1854.[4]

Lincoln was a man of principle but also a shrewd pragmatic politician, who adapted to changing political circumstances. And when he became a Republican, he mingled, as he had not previously, with a substantial minority of dissident former Jacksonian Democrats. These included ex-Democrats who, years before Lincoln's own conversion, had helped hammer out the moderate antislavery constitutionalism that became the core of Republican antislavery ideology and of Lincoln's own politics. In that milieu, where fragments of old party ideologies recombined to form a new Republican whole, Lincoln found himself attracted not simply to Jefferson's egalitarian pronouncements but also to some of the words, ideas, and actions of Andrew Jackson—sometimes as tactical maneuvers but also for more substantive reasons.[5] And by the time he was leading the Union cause as president, some longtime Democrats rallied to him as the embodiment of Jacksonian principles.

II.

On the crucial political questions connected to economic development, Lincoln remained an orthodox Old Northwest, Henry Clay Whig all his life. Regarding the future of the Second Bank of the United States, federal funding of internal improvements, and protective tariffs, he resolutely supported Clay and the American System and denounced the Jacksonians. He thought the hard-money Jacksonians' independent subtreasury system undemocratic as well as financially foolhardy, designed chiefly "for bene-fiting the few at the expense of the many." He condemned the Democrats' alleged abuses of executive power, undertaken by the kinds of ambitious men who, he charged in 1838, "set boldly to the task of pulling down" the nation's established institutions. Although when called upon, he mustered respect for Jackson's "military fame," Lincoln "could never find it in [my] heart to support him as a politician." He held Jackson's handpicked succes-sor, Martin Van Buren, in even lower esteem. Looking forward to Van Buren's defeat in 1840, Lincoln anticipated the nation's purification from Democratic rule, which was "belching forth the lava of political corrup-tion, in a current broad and deep, . . . sweeping with frightful velocity over the whole length and breadth of the land, bidding fair to leave unscathed no green spot or living thing. . . ."[6]

On issues concerning political democracy, though, Lincoln's brand of Whiggery also set him apart from others in his own party, both in Illinois and around the country. Although he was drawn to the fragmented anti-Jackson opposition as early as 1832, Lincoln had strong affinities with those liberal New School Whigs, such as William Seward and Thurlow Weed of New York, who were much more accommodating of democ-racy, including the democratic political tools of the Jacksonians, than Whig conservatives were, and who energized and consolidated the party

during the years immediately before 1840. Unlike the "decided, sanguine" Whig leaders later described by Illinois Democratic leader
Thomas Ford, Lincoln was not "an old federalist" who lacked "confidence in the people for self-government." During his reelection campaign for the state legislature in 1836, he contended that all who bore the
burden of government ought to share in its privileges, meaning all white
men who paid taxes or served in the militia and, he added, "by no means
excluding females." Contrary to conservative Whigs, Lincoln framed his
ideas on political economy not as a defense of the rich and privileged,
whose prosperity would eventually shower down on ordinary citizens,
but as the best means to open economic opportunity directly to humble
individuals. In at least one important clash between Illinois market mod-
ernizers and small yeoman farmers, over a proposed cattle fencing and
breeding law in 1836, Lincoln, a modernizer himself in most respects,
actually sided with the yeomanry.[7]

Having come of age in the 1820s, Lincoln, a paragon of the self-made
man, upheld certain democratic precepts that distinguished his generation
from that of the founders, and that Whigs of his persuasion shared with
the Jacksonians. One historian has described these precepts as a cultural as
well as political fact—a "fraternal democracy," rooted in the male worlds
of government and the law, which emphasized comradeship, equality,
and expressiveness, including expressiveness on the political stump. Riding circuit for weeks at a time, sharing hotel rooms even with his lawyer
opponents, Lincoln certainly fitted the fraternal democratic mold. Hierarchy offended him, including the topsy-turvy hierarchy that some of his
New School Whig colleagues tried to create, vaunting impoverished
beginnings as a sign of superior character. "Lincoln seemed to put himself
at once on an equality with everybody," one of his law partners said. "He
was always easy to approach and thoroughly democratic," said another.
A self-controlled Whig teetotaler, he could not even bring himself to
condemn heavy drinkers, as many Whig temperance reformers did.[8]

Lincoln linked his democratic sensibilities directly to matters of political organization. Antiparty mistrust of professional political organization, which persisted among the Whigs into the 1850s, made little sense
to Lincoln in the face of the changed democratic realities of the 1830s and
1840s. Very early in his political career, he did express a dislike for party
nominating conventions, organized in Illinois by Van Buren's supporters,
as "*subversive of individual freedom and private judgment*." By the early 1840s,

though, Lincoln, bowing to political necessities, was as regular a party man as could be found anywhere, in either party. He endorsed the partisan nominating convention system as a necessity to prevent division of the Whig vote. ("A house divided against itself cannot stand," he declared in defense of the convention system, more than two decades before he turned the same biblical image against slavery's expansion.) He also accepted the idea of rotation of office, both when he sought nomination to Congress ("turn about is fair play," he remarked) and when he stepped aside in 1848 to let another Whig run for his seat in the House of Representatives.[9]

Lincoln repudiated the nativism and anti-Catholicism that gripped the Whig Party far more than it did the Democrats. In 1855, he famously denounced the Know-Nothings, telling Joshua Speed that, should the nation as a whole ever descend to the nativists' level, he "should prefer emigrating to some country where they make no pretense of loving liberty—to Russia, for example, where despotism can be taken pure and without the base alloy of hypocrisy." But Lincoln's antinativism long predated the Know-Nothing American Party. In 1844, when locally based anti-immigrant politics and mob violence broke out in New York, Philadelphia, and other eastern cities, he presented a set of resolutions in Springfield expressing "decided disapprobation" of any attempt to curb naturalization or abridge religious freedom, a statement that won him admiration from Illinois Democrats. To be sure, in the mid-1850s Lincoln the practical politician could adopt a strategic public silence about the Know-Nothings, and even make secret political arrangements with them in Illinois when he thought it suited the Republicans' advantage. But antislavery, not anti-immigration or anti-Catholicism, was to Lincoln the true political cause.[10]

Lincoln recognized the depth of his differences with conservative Whigs—all the more so when the rivalries over slavery between so-called Conscience and Cotton Whigs, which had first emerged in Massachusetts in the late 1840s, persisted even after the party collapsed. Although there were notable exceptions such as the venerable Josiah Quincy, "old federalist" Whigs like Caleb Cushing (who switched to the Democrats in the 1840s), Amos A. Lawrence, Robert Winthrop, Edward Everett, and Rufus Choate were less likely than liberal Whigs like Lincoln to become Republicans. ("Whig principles!" Choate reportedly exclaimed. "I go to the Democrats to find them. They have assumed our principles, one after another, till there is little difference between us.") Lincoln directly and acidulously denounced Choate's description of the Declaration of Independence's opening lines as mere "glittering and sounding generalities" and accused Choate of trying to supplant free government with the principles of "classification, caste, and legitimacy," favored by "crowned heads, plotting against the people."[11]

Indeed Lincoln sensed that a substantial number of ex-Jacksonians were friendlier to his antislavery candidacy against Stephen A. Douglas in 1858 than some of his former fellow Whigs were. "As a general rule," he wrote to his physician and close friend Anson G. Henry, "much of the plain old democracy is with us, while nearly all of the old exclusive silk-stocking whiggery is against us." Lincoln did not mean that most of the old Whigs opposed the Republicans—just "nearly all of the nice exclusive sort." The "exclusive" Whig conservatives' position, Lincoln observed, made perfect sense: "There has been nothing in politics since the Revolution so congenial to their nature, as the present position of the [slaveholder-dominated] great democratic party."[12]

III.

Lincoln's evolving views on antislavery as well as slavery had long departed from those of the traditionalist conservative Whigs and mainstream Democrats, in the North as well as the South. In 1837, when the Illinois General Assembly passed a series of resolutions sternly disapproving "the formation of abolition societies," Lincoln, joined by a Whig colleague, lodged a formal protest, declaring that slavery "is founded on both injustice and bad policy." Although he criticized the abolitionists for their tendency "rather to increase than abate [slavery's] evils," he also resisted his fellow lawmakers' reflexive and fierce antiabolitionism. Less than a year later, and only weeks after the martyrdom of the abolitionist Elijah Lovejoy in Alton, Illinois, Lincoln delivered his famous speech to the Springfield Young Men's Lyceum, with its attacks on "mob law" and its direct reference to events in St. Louis that led directly to Lovejoy's killing. Although devoted to the general topic of "the perpetuation of republican institutions," the speech underscored how Lincoln's views about law and order differed from those of the Whig "gentlemen of property and standing" who approved of and in some instances participated in antiabolitionist violence.[13]

Lincoln also arrived on his own, well before 1840, at certain firm constitutional principles about the slavery issue. Unlike the most ardent abolitionists, Lincoln believed that Congress lacked the constitutional power "to interfere with the institution of slavery in the different States." Unlike mainstream Jacksonians and Whigs, however—and in line with abolitionist petitions subject to tabling in the House of Representatives under the gag rule—he believed that Congress possessed the power to abolish slavery in the District of Columbia without the slave states' approval (although he urged that Congress should exercise that power only at the request of the district's citizens). Together, these views of the limits and potential of congressional power would, when turned to territorial issues in the 1840s and 1850s, become the crucial elements of what one scholar has called the "moderate constitutional antislavery" that propelled the antislavery political parties.[14]

But until 1854 Lincoln was neither inclined nor willing to develop those views into a coherent antislavery ideology or political strategy to take sides on the hustings with those who were. During his one congressional term Lincoln did hammer away at the Polk administration and its war policies; in 1849 he enlarged his earlier support for the abolition of slavery in the District of Columbia by framing and introducing a bill toward that end, which he abandoned when he could not drum up enough allies. Like virtually all northern Whigs and Democrats in the House, he backed the Wilmot Proviso, banning slavery from territories obtained as a result of the war with Mexico. But Lincoln, though an egalitarian liberal, was too much of a partisan Whig, too fearful of schisms that would benefit Democrats, to step far beyond the boundaries of party orthodoxy.

In 1848 he energetically supported his party's nomination of the slaveholder and war hero Zachary Taylor for the presidency, chiefly because he thought Taylor was electable and because the Democratic candidate, the doughface Lewis Cass, would be a disastrous president. Lincoln's fellow antislavery Whig Horace Greeley denounced the convention that chose Taylor as "a slaughterhouse of Whig principles," and for a time he considered supporting the Free-Soil Party, whose platform coincided with his own views. Other antislavery Whigs called Taylor's candidacy "the cup offered by the slaveholders for us to drink," and jumped to the Free-Soilers. Lincoln, however, campaigned hard for the Taylor-Fillmore ticket, and made special appearances in Massachusetts, where he insisted that the Whigs, and not the Free-Soilers headed by the despised Locofoco Martin Van Buren, were the true free-soil alternative.[15]

It was left to the politically oriented abolitionists of the Liberty and Free-Soil parties, aided by Whig and Democratic dissenters, to develop the constitutional and political ideas that eventually informed the antislavery positions adopted by the Republican Party. In 1842, the Liberty Party activist Salmon P. Chase, although a man of Democratic leanings, approached the radical antislavery Whig congressman Joshua R. Giddings with the idea that slavery was purely a creature of state law and could be "confined within the States which admit and sanction it." Giddings endorsed Chase's formulation, and pushed it forward on several fronts, leading to his censure and removal from Congress and his subsequent reelection, a major breakthrough for antislavery politics that, among other things, led to the demise of the gag rule in 1844. In 1845 and 1846, northern Democratic divisions over Texas annexation and Polk administration policies fractured the party, leading first to the Independent Democratic uprising in New Hampshire that elected the antislavery Jacksonian John Parker Hale to the Senate and then to the introduction in the House of the Democratic-sponsored Wilmot Proviso, which opened sectional divisions in Congress over slavery starker than any seen since the Missouri crisis of 1819 to 1821.[16]

In 1848, it was the Free-Soil coalition of antislavery Barnburner Democrats, antislavery Whigs, and Liberty Party veterans that, while diluting the racial egalitarianism of the Liberty Party and hard-core antislavery Whigs, also moved beyond the Wilmot Proviso to demand the complete divorce of slavery and the federal government. "It pledges the new party against the addition of any more Slave States," one political abolitionist wrote of the Free-Soil platform, "and to employ the Federal Government not to limit, localize, and discourage, but to abolish slavery wherever it has the Constitutional power to do so."[17] Here, and in the idea of the Slave Power conspiracy, lay the political origins of what would blossom, after 1854, into the first mass antislavery political party in human history. (Indeed the first Republican Party national platform was actually more circumspect about divorcing slavery and the national government than the Free-Soilers' had been, confining itself to statements about Congress's powers to keep slavery out of the territories.) Yet while the Free-Soilers—including former Jacksonians, descending in their anti-slavery dedication from John P. Hale to Martin Van Buren—expanded the antislavery political cause, Abraham Lincoln retained his loyalties to the Whigs, who in 1848 adopted a national statement of principles that could not have been more evasive on issues connected to slavery.

IV.

Lincoln's decision to support the lesser of the two electable evils in 1848, Taylor over Cass, certainly made cold political sense from a moderate antislavery viewpoint, even if his campaign rhetoric about Taylor as a closet free-soiler was more contrived than it was convincing.* But after the enactment of the Kansas-Nebraska bill and the repeal of the Missouri Compromise in 1854, Whig principles were no longer sufficient to address the burning issues surrounding slavery and slavery's expansion. Lincoln and his fellow antislavery Whigs had to find fresh political bearings. Although, for a time, he may have hoped, like other liberal Whigs, that the northern remnants of the Whig Party could become the vehicle for national antislavery politics, those hopes were dashed amid the political firestorm of 1854. Only the newly emerging fusion of political abolitionists, free-soilers, antislavery Whigs and defecting so-called Independent Democrats—"every true democrat," according to one of their number, "that was too intelligent to be cheated by a name"—contained the numbers as well as the principles required to beat back the southern-dominated Democratic Party and its northern doughface Democratic allies.[18]

A significant but decided minority of the new coalition's supporters, perhaps one in four overall, consisted of former Jacksonian Democrats. Part of the genius of the Republican Party was its ability to unite them with ex-Whigs and Liberty Party men under a single banner. (Lincoln worked with special resolve to foster this harmony, beginning in

---

*As president Taylor did indeed bear out some of Lincoln's contentions, enraging southern Democrats by attempting to admit California and New Mexico directly as free states. He also hoped to court free-soil Whigs back into the Whig Party. But Taylor predicated his action mainly on his desire to suppress sectional discord and his belief that, in any event, slavery would never take root in the newly acquired territories.

1854–55, when he stepped aside in the contest for a U.S. Senate seat from Illinois to allow an ex-Democrat, Lyman Trumbull, to win the election.) The Democrats turned Republicans also added specific themes to the larger body of antislavery thought and rhetoric that proved enormously effective. Claiming that the egalitarian opening portion of the Declaration of Independence was an organic part of American law, stating that the Northwest Ordinance banning bondage revealed the founders' true intentions about slavery, and asserting that any strict construction of the Constitution did not give Congress the power to establish slavery anywhere under its jurisdiction brought a strong Jeffersonian and Democratic aura to the antislavery cause. (The Free-Soil Party's main banner at its Buffalo convention included the lines "'87 and '48/ JEFFERSON AND VAN BUREN/ No Compromise.") The concept of the Slave Power wielded so effectively by the Republicans, including Lincoln, originated in the Jacksonian image of the Money Power, as revised by the hard-money Democratic senator Thomas Morris of Ohio. Antislavery Jacksonians, steeped in antimonopoly politics and defenses of producers' rights, did as much as anyone to create the image of the Democratic Party they had rejected as, in one convert's words, the "tool of the slaveholding oligarchy."[19]

Prior to 1854, Lincoln hardly ever referred, in public or private, to the political wisdom of Thomas Jefferson. Indeed, after Lincoln's death, his old law partner William Herndon wrote that "Mr. Lincoln hated Jefferson as a man" as well "as a politician" (although Herndon's memory is not always to be trusted). Undeniably, though, beginning in 1854, Lincoln, like many other Republicans, continually cited Jefferson on equality and the territorial questions, so much so that for a moment, near the decade's end, Jefferson seemed to have joined Clay as Lincoln's beau ideal of an American statesman. ("All honor to Jefferson," he wrote in 1859, the figure who had pronounced "the definitions and axioms of free society" and whose Declaration of Independence would forever stand as "a rebuke and a stumbling block to . . . re-appearing tyranny and oppression.") Lincoln, also like other Republicans, equated his new party with Jefferson's original Democratic-Republicans, and likened the slaveholder-dominated "so-called democracy of today" with the Federalist Party of John Adams. And by the late 1850s Lincoln was forthright about how his belief in democracy underpinned his antislavery views. "As I would not be a *slave*, so I would not be a *master*," he wrote. "This expresses my idea of democracy. Whatever differs from this, to the extent of the difference, is no democracy."[20]

Lincoln's sudden turn to Jefferson and Jeffersonian democratic rhetoric was striking, and marked off one phase of his political career from another. It did not in itself mark a total rupture with his own political heritage.[21] Henry Clay had, after all, started out his career as a Jeffersonian Democrat; some New England conservatives, including the ex-Federalist Daniel Webster, had begun reconciling themselves to Jefferson, at least rhetorically, in the 1820s; thereafter Whigs as well as Democrats and upholders of virtually every other shade of American political opinion always did their best to get right with the Jefferson image, as, for that matter, did northern doughfaces and some slaveholder Democrats in the 1850s. It is notable, though, that Lincoln turned to Jefferson only after he began becoming a Republican. Even more startling were the Republican Lincoln's approving remarks about some of the ideas and actions of Andrew Jackson. The most familiar of these came in 1861, when Lincoln's initial efforts to suppress secession drew upon certain Jacksonian democratic as well as nationalist themes. But on at least one vital issue during the long crisis that led to secession, the response to the *Dred Scott* decision, what began as a tactical deployment by Lincoln of Jackson's name became a more substantial link to Jacksonian principle.[22]

V.

Although Lincoln could not support Jackson as a politician, he did come to recall with admiration, in specific situations, Jackson's steadfastness and effectiveness as a leader, even before 1854. Several months into Taylor's administration, Lincoln wrote to Secretary of State John Clayton to complain about the effects of the president's weak-kneed appointments and patronage policies, which, he said, were "fixing for the President the unjust and ruinous character of being a mere man of straw" that would "damn us all inevitably." For a better example, Lincoln would have had Taylor look to another White House general: "He must occasionally say, or seem to say, 'by the Eternal,' 'I take the responsibility.' Those phrases were the 'Samson's locks' of Gen. Jackson and we dare not disregard the lessons of experience." In a lighter vein, years later as a Republican, Lincoln fondly retold a familiar anecdote about a boy who asked a companion whether General Jackson could ever get into heaven. "Said the boy, 'He'd get there if he had a mind to.' "[23]

The crises over the Kansas-Nebraska Act and "Bleeding Kansas" shifted Lincoln's perspective on Jackson's presidency. Instead of refighting the old issues about banking, internal improvements, and executive power, Lincoln focused on what he considered Jackson's commendable handling of sectional extremism. Jackson's record made him a more fitting symbol of defiant nationalism, standing up to the southern slaveholders, than Lincoln's Whig hero the Great Conciliator Clay. Lincoln seemed to admire Jackson's steeliness as well as his patriotism. To a cheering rally of Illinois Republicans on July 4, 1856, Lincoln noted how, for many years after the Missouri Compromise, "the people had lived in comparative peace and quiet," with one notable exception: "During Gen. Jackson's administration, the Calhoun Nullifying doctrine sprang up, but Gen. Jackson, with that decision of character that ever characterized him, put an end to it."[24]

Lincoln found Jackson's precedent particularly compelling in the aftermath of the *Dred Scott* decision of 1857—not over slavery or sectionalism *per se* but over the Supreme Court's supposed supremacy in deciding constitutional interpretation. Proslavery southerners hailed Chief Justice Roger B. Taney's ruling in *Dred Scott* as a sacrosanct vindication of slavery and the Constitution, which repudiated the entire basis of what they called Black Republican organization. "Southern opinion upon the subject of southern slavery . . . is now the supreme law of the land," the *Augusta* (Georgia) *Constitutionalist* rejoiced, "and opposition to southern opinion upon this subject is now opposition to the Constitution, and morally treason against the Government."

Northern doughface Democrats, led by Stephen Douglas, reflexively agreed, even though the ruling implicitly barred Douglas's "popular sovereignty" formula on slavery in the territories, just as it did the Republicans' cardinal demand that Congress prohibit slavery in the territories. Unfazed by the contradiction, Douglas and others claimed that even under the *Scott* decision, slavery could not long exist anywhere without majority local support for "appropriate police regulations and local legislation." While trying to square the constitutional circle in the hope of preserving intersectional party unity, the Douglasites charged that the Republicans' protests against the decision amounted to violent resistance—"a deadly blow to our whole Republican system of government," Douglas asserted, "a blow which, if successful would place all our rights and liberties at the mercy of passion, anarchy and violence."[25]

Not all northern Democrats greeted the decision by Jackson's former comrade-in-arms with such equanimity. "I feel quite mortified for the course of this Tawny Lion of Gen. Jackson—it is a great drawback on his fame," one New Yorker wrote. Republicans in general thought the ruling was a farrago of falsehoods and contorted proslavery logic, "entitled to just as much moral weight as would be the judgement of a majority of those congregated in any Washington bar-room," according to Horace Greeley. Lincoln took a slightly—but only slightly—more temperate view. The ruling, he contended, was certainly binding as far as Dred Scott and his family were concerned. Contrary to what Douglas and other Democrats claimed, Lincoln counseled no active resistance to the decision. Normally, he observed, failure to heed, "when fully settled," the Court's decisions as "the general policy of the country" would be "revolution." But Taney's ruling, Lincoln charged, was exceptional, plainly founded on error, at variance with all precedents, and not at all settled. "We know that the court that made it," he declared, in his first public response to the ruling, "has often over-ruled its own decisions, and we shall do what we can to have it to over-rule this." In defense of this peaceful resistance, Lincoln turned to the example of Andrew Jackson and the Bank War.[26]

Lincoln's choice was ironic, perhaps intentionally so, and not simply because he was using Jackson's words to defy a ruling by Jackson's prized ally Roger B. Taney. No Jacksonian policy had perturbed Lincoln more than the destruction of the Second Bank of the United States, an alleged act of executive usurpation that, more than any of Jackson's other actions, brought the Whig Party into being. Yet Lincoln now quoted at length from Jackson's bank veto message, emphasizing those passages where Jackson dismissed objections that the Supreme Court has already proclaimed the bank constitutional. The judicial and legislative precedents concerning a national bank, Jackson said, were divided. Even then, he charged, "[m]ere precedent is a dangerous source of authority, and should not be regarded as deciding questions of constitutional power, except where the acquiescence of the people and the States can be considered well settled." In any event, Lincoln noted, Jackson insisted in his bank veto message "that each public functionary must support the Constitution, '*as he understands it.*' " Lincoln had hardly changed his mind about the Bank of the United States as a wholly constitutional institution. But Jackson's conception of the courts and the Constitution eviscerated the doughfaces' charge that the Republicans, by opposing *Dred Scott*, were fomenting treason.[27]

In part, Lincoln was simply trying to trip up Douglas, who always presented himself as the most loyal of Jacksonians. Turning Old Hickory's words against the Little Giant was the kind of lawyer-politician's debating trick that Lincoln always deployed masterfully. Lincoln never went quite so far as to endorse the democratic view of the courts, which he ascribed to Jefferson, that permitting judges to be the ultimate arbiters of all constitutional questions " 'would place us under the despotism of an oligarchy.' " But the more that Lincoln returned to the issue of judicial supremacy, and to Jackson as a precedent, the bolder he became. "I do not resist it," Lincoln said of *Dred Scott* in an important speech in Chicago in July 1858, but "I am refusing to obey it as a political rule." He declared that were he elected to the Senate, he would defy the ruling and vote to prohibit slavery in a new territory. Douglas's promise to abide by the decision unless and until it was reversed was sheer sophistry, Lincoln claimed. "Somebody has to reverse that decision, since it is made," he argued, "and we mean to reverse it, and we mean to do it peaceably."[28]

Lincoln returned to Jackson and the bank veto during his campaign debates with Douglas in the late summer and autumn of 1858. "[A] decision of the court is to him a '*Thus saith the Lord,*' " he said of Douglas in Ottawa. "It is nothing that I point out to him that his great prototype, Gen Jackson, did not believe in the binding force of decisions." Later, at Galesburg, Douglas replied to Lincoln's gibes by noting that Jackson had acceded to the Court's rulings on the bank until a rechartering was proposed; by contrast, he charged, Lincoln was advocating disobeying the Court. Lincoln's retort, delivered at Quincy, emphasized that as an equal coordinate branch of the government, the executive (like the legislature) had to interpret the Constitution as it saw fit. "I will tell you here that General Jackson once said each man was bound to support the Constitution 'as he understood it.' Now, Judge Douglas understands the Constitution according to the Dred Scott decision, and he is bound to support it as he understands it. [Cheers.] I understand it another way, and therefore I am bound to support it in the way in which I understand it. [Prolonged applause.]"[29] Honest Abe, for once, sounded like Old Hickory.

VI.

Less than three years later, as the secession crisis played itself out in Charleston Harbor, reviving memories of the nullification crisis, Lincoln would have even more reason to turn to Jackson's example. "[P]ut Andrew Jackson's 'union' speech in your inaugural address," the Kentuckian Cassius Clay advised him, even before the 1860 campaign had ended. By December 1860 the veteran Jacksonian turned Republican Francis Blair was reminding Lincoln of Jackson's forceful stance against South Carolina in 1832. (Blair repeated those reminders inside the White House after the inauguration, when it momentarily appeared as if the administration might abandon Fort Sumter without a fight.) "But it may be necessary to put the foot down firmly," Lincoln told the New Jersey General Assembly on his way to Washington, dramatically stamping the stage to enthusiastic cheers. Although in his efforts to appear conciliatory the new president omitted any explicit mention of Jackson in his inaugural address, Jackson's proclamation on nullification was one of the few sources he consulted (along with Webster's famous second reply to Hayne and Henry Clay's speech to the Senate amid the sectional crisis of 1850), and thereafter Jackson's precedent was very much on his mind. After the fall of Sumter, when a committee in Baltimore bade him cease hostilities, Lincoln replied sternly that he would not violate his oath and surrender the government without a blow: "There is no Washington in that—no Jackson in that—no manhood nor honor in that."[30]

The nationalist themes in Lincoln's attacks on secession were of course common to mainstream proto-Whigs as well as to Jackson's proclamation against the nullifiers. In this respect, Lincoln seized on the piece of Jackson's legacy most in line with those of Jackson's opponents (and that many of Jackson's supporters, including Martin Van Buren, opposed). But Jackson also based his attack on the democratic, majoritarian grounds he had expressed in his first message to Congress, ridiculing the effort of a single state—indeed "a bare majority of the voters in any one state"—to repudiate laws approved by the Congress and the president, the people's representatives. Lincoln based the Union effort, in 1861, on fundamentally democratic grounds, proclaiming in his first inaugural that the slavery issue, and with it the divination of God's will, had to be left to "the judgment of this great tribunal, the American people," which had just elected him president.[31]

The vagaries of wartime command also led Lincoln back to Jackson, though as military leader. In mid-1863 a citizens' committee in Albany, led by the industrialist, financier, and mayor Erastus Corning, approved a pair of resolutions censuring the administration over its conduct of the war, including Lincoln's order of military arrests of civilians. The criticisms had been mounting, and Lincoln replied to the New Yorkers directly, defending himself by pointing to General Jackson's declaration of martial law in New Orleans in 1815, for which the general was punished and fined but, thirty years later, vindicated by Congress. Jackson, as earlier, served Lincoln as a convenient figure to deflect attacks on his own conduct, but Lincoln also drew strong parallels between his conduct amid a rebellion and his predecessor's amid an invasion. "[T]he permanent right of the people to public discussion," Lincoln wrote, "the liberty of speech and the press, the trial by jury, the law of evidence, and the Habeas Corpus, suffered no detriment whatever by that conduct of Gen. Jackson, or it's [*sic*] subsequent approval by the American congress." Nor would it suffer because of Lincoln's actions.[32]

VII.

The significance of Lincoln's convergence with certain antislavery elements of Jacksonian democracy, and then with certain of Jackson's political precedents, should not be exaggerated. He certainly found any similarity between himself and Jackson amusing, at least until he became president. (Bidden by Douglas, in 1858, to take the blame for some remarks made by Lyman Trumbull, Lincoln replied, facetiously, "[F]or once in my life I will play General Jackson and to the just extent take the responsibility."[33]) Yet neither should the convergence be ignored. The Republican Lincoln was not a Whig in the White House. As the politics of American democracy altered in the 1840s and 1850s, to confront the long-suppressed crisis over slavery, so the terms of democratic politics broke apart and recombined in ways that defy any neat ideological or political genealogy. Just as the Republican Party of the 1850s absorbed certain elements of Jacksonianism, so Lincoln, whose Whiggery had always been more egalitarian than that of other Whigs, found himself absorbing some of them as well. And some of the Jacksonian spirit resided inside the Lincoln White House.

President Lincoln, Writing the Proclamation of Freedom, January 1, 1863, lithograph based on a painting by David Gilmour Blythe, *Abraham Lincoln Writing the Emancipation Proclamation,* 1863. *(Photo: Library of Congress)*

The pro-Union painter David Gilmour Blythe captured this in a symbolic way, with his fanciful depiction of Lincoln in his office in 1862, writing the Emancipation Proclamation, surrounded by disorder, a bust of James Buchanan hanging at the end of a noose from a bookcase, but another, of Andrew Jackson, sitting upright on a mantelpiece, staring at the president.[34] Although Blythe may not have known it, there was some verisimilitude to his picture. Lincoln's secretaries, Nicolay and Hay, and his son Robert Todd Lincoln left behind memoirs of life inside Lincoln's White House, including scenes inside the large room on the south of the East Wing that served as the president's office. The office's furnishings were simple: a large oak table, covered with cloth, another table for writing, a desk, some chairs, and two hair-covered sofas. The only adornments on the walls were some military maps in wooden frames, a photograph of the English liberal leader John Bright, and, above the fireplace mantel, an old discolored engraving of President Andrew Jackson.[35]

The Republican governor of Oregon Addison C. Gibbs later made the point more prosaically. "I am a supporter of your Administration, but have been a Douglas Democrat," Gibbs told the president, almost exactly a year after Lincoln announced the Emancipation Proclamation, "and see more Jacksonian democracy in the measures of your Administration, than can be found among all your opponants [*sic*]."[36]

4

Visualizing Lincoln:
Abraham Lincoln as Student, Subject,
and Patron of the Visual Arts

HAROLD HOLZER

Of all the American heroes whom Abraham Lincoln idolized—Henry Clay and Thomas Jefferson, to name two[1]—George Washington towered above them all in Lincoln's mind and heart. Once, listening to a group of fellow lawyers enumerating Washington's alleged shortcomings, the customarily jovial Lincoln was said to have brought the conversation to an abrupt end by insisting: "Let us believe, as in the days of our youth, that Washington was spotless. . . ." As Lincoln justified his interruption, "it makes human nature better to believe that one human being was perfect: that human perfection was possible."[2]

The origins of Lincoln's reverence can be traced to his initial exposure to Mason Locke Weems's hagiographical *Life of Washington*, which as late as 1861 he vividly remembered first reading "away back in my childhood." Like other boys, Lincoln never forgot the incidents it recounted. Its gripping stories of heroic soldiers fighting for freedom "fixed themselves upon my imagination," as he later recalled with appreciation.[3] Significantly, Lincoln appreciated the visual contours of the Washington story as well: Along with many of his contemporaries, he was familiar with not only Washington's life story but also his ubiquitous image. It might even be argued that the knowledge of both propelled Lincoln toward a political career that neatly combined words and images. By the time he left Springfield to assume the presidency in 1861, he had left not only a legacy of spoken and published oratory but a visual archive of photographs, paintings, sculpture, and prints.

As early as 1811 Russian diplomat, artist, and author Pavel Svinin was astonished to find that even remote regions of the "Picturesque United States of America" were "glutted with bust portraits of Washington." As Svinin observed in a memoir of his trip, "Every American considers it his sacred duty to have a likeness of Washington in his home, just as we have images of God's saints. Washington's portrait is the finest and sometimes the sole decoration of American homes."[4] Most editions of Parson Weems's book featured a frontispiece engraving of the canonical Gilbert Stuart Athenaeum type of bust portrait of Washington, so it is all but certain that Lincoln saw it for himself at an early age, and likely the image fixed itself on his imagination as vividly as did the narrative.

We know that Lincoln understood the emotional power of these domestic icons if only through one of his funny stories about the response evoked by one crudely displayed Washington likeness. It seemed that an American living in England had grown weary of Englishmen deriding America's greatest hero, so in response he hung a picture of the first president in his host's privy. In Lincoln's view, this seemingly irreverent gesture was in fact "very appropriate . . . for their [*sic*] is Nothing that Will Make an Englishman Shit So quick as the Sight of Genl Washington."[5]

Lincoln seldom lost sight of the general either. Arriving in the federal capital in 1847 to serve his one and only term in Congress, Lincoln surely encountered more of these modest, domestic pictorial tributes to Washington. For the first time he saw monumental public portraits as well, including the formidable John Trumbull paintings of *General George Washington Resigning His Commission to Congress as Commander in Chief of the Army* and the father of his country accepting the *Surrender of Burgoyne at Saratoga*, both imposingly on view in the Capitol Rotunda.[6]

Here in the capital city named in his hero's honor, Lincoln also learned how, wrongly conceived, heroic portraiture might arouse controversy and ridicule. Every day of his term Congressman Lincoln would have encountered Horatio Greenough's much-mocked neoclassical statue of George Washington. The marble anomaly loomed atop its pedestal outside the east steps of the Capitol, past which Lincoln would have strolled daily to work from his boardinghouse, located nearby on the spot where the Library of Congress now stands. Greenough's statue did not lack for ostentation: It was modeled after one of the Seven Wonders of the ancient world, Phidias's legendary sculpture of the Greek god Zeus at

Olympia.[7] Here was Washington as American deity: seated on a throne, half naked, draped in a toga, and holding a scepter. Whether Lincoln thought it ridiculous we do not know, but knowing his sense of humor, we can only imagine what he might have remarked about it.

Of course George Washington himself never posed this way. Greenough modeled his statue's head on Jean-Antoine Houdon's life mask but invented the rest, hiring European models to pose for the bare upper torso. The resulting composite, awkwardly conjoining the artistic traditions of realism and symbolism, was designed not only to resemble its subject but to inspire every citizen who passed in its shadow, certainly to quicken the pulse of any public servant ambitious enough to see himself one day walking in Washington's shoes.

But in an era that was soon to celebrate the rough and ready above the grand and draped, Greenough's statue suffered an ignominious reception. Intended to grace the Capitol Rotunda, it sat there only briefly, while engineers fretted that it was so heavy that it would break through the floor. Ultimately, adverse critical and public reaction, not to mention its gargantuan weight, earned its banishment outdoors. Seeing it even there, a visiting New Yorker wrote home to observe: "It looks like a great . . . Venus of the Bath . . . with a huge napkin lying across his lap and covering his lower extremities, and he preparing to perform his ablutions . . . in the act of consigning his sword to the care of the attendant. . . ."[8]

If Lincoln reacted uncritically to its overt display of the archaic attributes of heroism—unfortunately, he left no specific record of his response—it was probably because he was no stranger himself to the tradition of the meaningfully grand physical gesture as a symbol of authority. Washington's upheld hand in the Greenough statue replicated and reinforced illustrations Lincoln had studied on the prairie from his own childhood copy of William Scott's *Lessons in Elocution*, the primer that introduced him to the art of public speaking and the techniques of gesture. These might well have been the very first professionally engraved portraits the young man ever glimpsed. Scott's book recommended that orators learn not only how to form words but how to accompany them with proper movements of their arms and hands. "The right arm should be held out, with the palm open," advised the book, and then, when lowered, the "left hand raises itself, into exactly the same position as the right was before . . . and so on, from right to left, alternatively, till the speech is ended." Such gestures, the book recommended, could help a speaker "solicit . . . refuse . . . promise . . . threaten . . . dismiss . . . invite . . . entreat . . . express aversion, fear, doubting, denial, asking, affirmation, negation, joy, grief, confusion, penitence. . . ."[9] This was how heroes, and future heroes, declaimed.

All this knowledge and experience help explain why, when the supposedly self-effacing Lincoln finally began to achieve national fame of his own, he made certain that his ascent was, like Washington's, illustrated, and ideally, propelled, by images in several media, whose mutual interdependence has not been fully acknowledged and deserves reexamination. In a sense, Lincoln and image making in America came of age together; the increasing production and proliferation of photographs and print portraits coincided neatly with Lincoln's political rise and not only illustrated but likely influenced his growing prominence.

And while supplying perfect doses of Victorian modesty, he customarily told contemporaries he knew "nothing" about such "matters" as art and was but an "indifferent judge" of his own likenesses, the homely Lincoln seems to have understood from the outset that flattering depictions could be his cosmetic salvation.[10] Thus he often did what he could do to make sure good portraits were produced, even when it was less than convenient, and occasionally distressing, even physically painful to do so. Throughout the relatively brief period of his prominence in national politics, Lincoln was a cooperative subject for artists in all media, posing for more than 120 photographs in the last eighteen years of his life and sitting as well for painters, sketch artists, and sculptors. The pictorial results have been well chronicled in the past, in a number of books on Lincoln photographs, oil portraits, and statues, not to mention the engravings and lithographs that reproduced the original efforts in each of these media and made Lincoln as popular a domestic icon in the late nineteenth century as Washington had been in its first fifty years. But what has seldom been discussed is how mutually interdependent all these branches of art ultimately became and precisely why and how Lincoln facilitated each of the sittings that generated his most familiar images.

If Lincoln would not pose in the classical tradition—that is, he would not hold scepters or other props to help an artist accomplish his ambition—he still made himself generously available to artists who sought to portray him, almost in the time-honored manner of royal sitters and, for a time, no matter how disobliging the process. What made Lincoln, and the artists who depicted him, unique was that they lived during, and made heavy use of, the newest of all artistic media, photography.

As early as 1846, shortly after his election to the House of Representatives, Lincoln posed for his very first photograph, a stiffly formal daguerreotype taken in Springfield by an itinerant camera artist named Nicholas H. Shepherd. Holding immovably still for the lengthy exposure which the newly invented process required, Lincoln could hardly have imagined that he would later become one of the most frequently photographed celebrities of the century or that the new medium would soon be able to supply more than a single-copy souvenir for one's own family to cherish. It remained extremely difficult, as art historians Bates Lowry and Isabel Barrett Lowry have put it, "to turn the sun into an obedient painter."[11]

Through the 1850s, as these pioneering, silverized single images on copper yielded in turn to ambrotypes on glass, ferrotypes on japanned iron, and finally, mass-produced paper prints from glass negatives, Lincoln continued to pose for the occasional photograph, usually at the request of friends and colleagues. These results were not widely reproduced either. Like the first daguerreotype by Shepherd, they remained largely unknown outside the studios where they were made.

As late as 1860, when he quaintly referred to his latest likeness as "my shaddow," Lincoln still understandably regarded photography as little more than a curiosity even if, for the first time, he acknowledged its potential as a means of spreading his image broadly to a wider public. As he noted of the gallery where he had last posed for a photograph that April, "I suppose they . . . can multiply copies indefinitely."[12] But their full potential with large audiences remained untapped and unimagined. Not for another year did the public welcome revolutionary, mass-produced carte de visite photographic prints, along with the tooled leather albums designed to display not only family portraits but likenesses of American heroes.[13]

Not long before the introduction of these visiting card–size photos, Lincoln endured a discomfiting firsthand lesson in the vanishing aesthetic of replicating the human body in heroic art. As he learned that day, posing for public portraits could be time-consuming, painful, even embarrassing. But sculptor Leonard Wells Volk's long-range vision for a Lincoln statue must have seemed irresistible to the presidential aspirant. In March

Photographer unknown, ca. 1865 cabinet photograph of the plaster bust of Lincoln by Leonard Wells Volk, 1860. Volk produced a life mask of Lincoln in March 1860 and then used it as the model for a series of widely reproduced plaster and bronze busts, including this one. The statues became so popular they were in turn photographed and sold as images to decorate parlor walls and family albums. *(Photo courtesy Harold Holzer)*

1860, Lincoln submitted to an "anything but agreeable"[14] wet-plaster life mask meant to facilitate this process and then returned to sit at Volk's Chicago studio in April to pose in the flesh while Volk transformed the mask into a study bust. Once on the premises, while waiting to sit Lincoln even got the opportunity to study Volk's photographs of Greek and Roman statuary, surely among them classical nudes. And then Volk told his subject he "desired to represent his breast and brawny shoulders as nature presented them." Obligingly—and apparently undissuaded by his recollection of the Greenough fiasco in so portraying George Washington—Lincoln, as Volk recalled, promptly "stripped off his coat, waistcoat, shirt, cravat, and collar, threw them on a chair, pulled his undershirt down a short distance, tying his sleeves behind him, and stood up without a murmur for an hour or so" to pose bare-chested.[15]

He might well have been more mortified than he admitted. When the session ended, Lincoln dressed hurriedly and fled the studio. But only a few minutes later he returned, sheepishly explaining to Volk, "I got down on the sidewalk and found I had forgotten to put on my undershirt, and thought it wouldn't do to go through the streets this way." Sure enough, the sculptor glanced behind Lincoln, and saw the sleeves of his undergarment dangling below his frock coat. This time Lincoln let Volk help him get his clothes back on properly.

As it turned out, Volk's original life mask, which sculptor George Grey Barnard later hailed as the best representation ever made of "the most wonderful face left to us,"[16] became the model for several different mass-produced Volk sculptures, including both "nude" and draped neoclassical heroic busts suitable for display in private homes. Eventually the mask also inspired life-size statues for the new State Capitol in Springfield, a copy of which eventually surmounted an obelisk at the Soldiers' and Sailors' Monument in Rochester, New York.[17] These plentiful adaptations, those made for private parlors or public places, justified Lincoln's willingness to help create the kind of heroic art that had immortalized the peerless Washington. And they offered Americans their first opportunities to visualize Abraham Lincoln. But the outlines of that image would soon change. Unlike Washington, the prairie politician was not made for ornate or classically inspired portraiture. But in the Washington tradition, he did become an extremely patient and obliging sitter.

During the presidential campaign of 1860, image makers more often than not visualized the Republican nominee as a plainly dressed, plainspoken, William Henry Harrison–like candidate whose greatest virtue was his rise from frontier obscurity. Lincoln was the subject of an extraordinary outburst of image making that year, typical among them prints that showed the Republican nominee encircled by Lincolnian log rails emblematic of his days as a hardworking frontiersman.[18] Such visual metaphors were key to the development of Lincoln's own enduring, and reputation-enhancing *anti*heroic image, that of a rail-splitter who wore homespun clothes, typically carried a log rail, not a scepter, worked his way up from prairie obscurity through manual labor and devotion to learning, and told the kind of jokes he had privately spun about George Washington's image years before.

It is worth noting that Lincoln hardly chose this image for himself, although he was present at the creation, and his own political handlers introduced the visual metaphors. When his country cousin John Hanks marched down the aisle of the State Republican Convention at Decatur, Illinois, in May 1860, toting log rails purportedly split by Lincoln as a young man thirty years earlier, the banner unfurled beneath the relics proclaimed: "ABRAHAM LINCOLN: The Rail Candidate for President in 1860."[19] Though the stunt had been arranged and financed by local Lincoln supporter Richard J. Oglesby and reportedly left Lincoln "blushing," it created a spontaneous sensation at the convention, which went on to declare Lincoln its favorite son choice for the White House. A spectator sensed immediately that the slogan, and the image it conveyed, were to be "the 'Battle flag,' in the coming contest between 'labor free' and 'labor slave,' between democracy—and aristocracy."[20]

In Lincoln's day, popular prints, even those designed for election campaigns, were conceived of, and distributed by, the publishers themselves, not the political organizations that frequently purchased them in bulk. The mass-produced Lincoln campaign portraits of the 1860 campaign were designed exclusively by the image makers and no doubt accepted gratefully by the candidate and his backers, pleased for the good they could do him by introducing him sympathetically to American voters. As noncommissioned commercial ventures that relied on public patronage to succeed, they reflected the public yearning for a new kind of presidential image, not the imposition of that image on the public. Before the campaign was finished, however, Lincoln became a more active agent in his elevation into the American pantheon of heroes. How and why he did so may help explain how, eventually and uniquely, Lincoln evolved, at least in part through the combined efforts of several portrait genres, into what David Herbert Donald has called an amalgam of "hero" and "demigod."[21] The complex origin of this straightforward image can be traced to the various artistic media that introduced and enshrined it with what amounted to a mutually beneficial conspiracy of creativity.

After 1860 Lincoln began posing for photographers more often, as the fashion grew for cartes de visite and the leather albums that housed them. For several generations, scholars of Lincoln photographs—principally

Frederick Hill Meserve, Stefan Lorant, and Lloyd Ostendorf[22]—have rather too simplistically treated photography as a wholly independent visual genre, as if Lincoln had cooperated with photographers merely to produce a record of his image in that medium alone. In truth, on a surprisingly large and hitherto unrecognized number of occasions, Lincoln sat for photographers not merely to produce new likenesses that could be marketed individually but at the request of artists who often posed them to supplement life sittings in other media. For these artists, Lincoln photographs were not a final visual record but an intermediary visual resource.

For too long historians have underestimated the extent of Lincoln's cooperative participation in such elaborate projects, while overestimating the importance—at least to Lincoln—of the photographs themselves, as appealing as they may have since become to modern observers as authentic records of the man. The truth is, Lincoln posed for photographs—particularly for the very best of his photographs—only when artists suggested that they needed such sittings in order to aid the development of paintings and sculpture, the kind of heroic artistic tributes that had once served George Washington (and appealed to a younger Lincoln).

This tradition of artistic interdependence commenced in 1860. Once nominated for the presidency, Lincoln quickly emerged as a popular subject for painters. So many of the earliest engravings and lithographs had owed undisguised debts to known photographs that more ambitious publishers hired artists to journey to Springfield, Illinois, to produce fresh alternatives that could be reproduced as wholly original campaign print portraiture. But the task proved daunting. "He had a face that defied artistic skill to soften or idealize," remembered Ohio politician Donn Piatt. "When in repose, his face was dull heavy, and repellent. It brightened like a lit lantern when animated. His dull eyes would fairly sparkle with fun, or express as kindly a look as I ever saw, when moved by some matter of human interest."[23] Accurate as they were, photographs did little to disguise Lincoln's sometimes vacant expression, his so-called photographer's face.[24]

Lincoln made it particularly difficult for these first visiting artists by requiring that they draw, paint, or sculpt him while he was "on the jump"[25]—that is, while he greeted visitors or attended to his voluminous correspondence in his campaign headquarters at the Illinois State Capitol. In desperation, the artists turned to the increasingly attractive "crutch" of photographs to supply models that might supplement these unsatisfactory sessions from life. Sculptor Volk may have encouraged Lincoln to pose for his first full-length photographic portrait that year, although no direct evidence of his participation in the project has ever been confirmed. Still, it is clear to the eye that Volk's Lincoln statuettes were based at least in part on the pose.[26] Significantly, what one perceives also is a marked change in the quality of all Lincoln photographs at this time. Suddenly Lincoln was professionally posed, handsomely lighted, and well dressed. There is ample reason to conclude that painters and sculptors had more to do with this change than the camera operators, for the first of these artists not only were in residence in Springfield but accompanied Lincoln to the photography galleries to have his pictures made for their use. There, it is reasonable to assume—and in some cases we have direct evidence of their participation—they personally posed the subject for the cameras in precisely the posture they wanted to capture in oil, crayon, or clay.

The painter Thomas Hicks, who had studied at the Pennsylvania Academy of Fine Arts, the National Academy of Design in New York, and in Paris under Thomas Couture, came to Springfield shortly after the Republican National Convention to execute the very first life portrait of Abraham Lincoln. Hicks was commissioned by the New York print publisher W. H. Schaus, who planned to adapt the result for a campaign lithograph. Hicks arrived in June 1860, won Lincoln's consent for sittings, and began working for an hour each morning at the candidate's well-lit second-floor office inside the State Capitol building.

Hicks later recalled a charmed experience—even when Lincoln's two young sons invaded the office one day, squeezed tubes of the artist's brightest paints onto their palms, and proceeded to smear the walls with bright splotches of red, yellow, and blue. Lincoln even confided to the artist that he had "once read a book which gave an account of some Italian painters and their work in the fifteenth century,"[27] and we can only speculate about whether Lincoln, who had never sat for a painter before, imagined himself repeating the experiences of the sitters of the Renaissance. What Hicks never mentioned is the fact that these one-hour sittings with Lincoln proved insufficient. The artist turned to photography for help.

On June 3, probably acting on his own initiative, photographer Alexander Hesler arrived in Springfield from Chicago to make some campaign pictures of the newly nominated Republican candidate for president. Hesler, who had last photographed Lincoln back in 1857, set up his camera inside the State Capitol and took several fine portraits of candidate Lincoln. Hicks's final work owed an undisguisable debt to what became the most famous of these, a bold profile showing Lincoln with freshly cut hair and a starched white shirt. The photo became an 1860 best seller in its own right.

It also provided crucial aid to Hicks. Whether or not the artist helped Hesler pose Lincoln that day is not definitively known; surely he was present when the pictures were taken. But there can be no doubt that the Hesler photograph became the basis of his painting, which in turn was adapted back in New York as planned for a large W. H. Schaus print by the noted lithographer Leopold Grozelier. Thus three artistic media had together, consciously or not, conspired to spread Lincoln's fame: An artist had used a photograph for a painting, and a lithographer had used a painting for a print. The photographs and prints were mass distributed; the painting went on exhibition to considerable acclaim. It would not be the last time. Importantly, Hicks managed not only to copy the Hesler photograph but, by adding color and illuminating the harsher shadows darkening Lincoln's face, to brighten his appearance considerably. Perhaps it was no accident that when Hicks completed his oil portrait, Lincoln cannily joked that though it gave him "great satisfaction . . . I think the picture has a somewhat pleasanter expression than I usually have, but that, perhaps, is not an objection."[28]

A similar conjoined fate—a dependence on specially commissioned photographic models to supplement life sittings and the artistic inspiration for photographic portraits that has not previously been appreciated—awaited two other painters who followed Hicks to Springfield. Joseph Hill's June 1860 photograph was clearly made in collaboration with painter J. C. Wolfe, who made at least two oil copies before he fled town in advance of his creditors.[29] Painter Thomas M. Johnston, on commission from a Boston print publisher, enjoyed life sittings of his own in Springfield's State House in July, joking that a previous painter, who, notably, had *not* consulted a photograph, had produced a laughable "failure."[30] Not surprisingly, one of the paintings that Johnston created while in town owed an undisguised debt to a photograph made by Springfield's Christopher S. German. Historians have consistently assigned the German pose, for no particular reason, the date of 1858 (although Lincoln consistently looks far more ragged in the pictures indisputably taken during that year of heavy travel and exhausting political debates). There is no reason not to consider seriously the possibility that like the others before and after him, painter Johnston convinced Lincoln that he required a photographic model that he might arrange in the precise pose he desired to capture on canvas and that the German photograph of "1858" was the result and was produced in that same summer of 1860.

In August of that same presidential year came John Henry Brown, a highly respected miniaturist from Philadelphia, dispatched to Springfield by a Pennsylvanian Lincoln supporter with direct instructions to make a handsome likeness of the candidate "whether the original would justify it or not,"[31] according to Lincoln's private secretary, so the result could be adapted into a campaign engraving for that state's all-important voting audience. Although he had been specifically instructed to produce a romanticized portrait, Brown too ended up commissioning a photograph to supplement his life sittings—in this case a now-famous ambrotype that showed Lincoln staring directly into the camera, hair falling carelessly over his forehead, his arms folded almost defiantly. Brown did not use the entire pose in his restricted format (his original miniature on ivory is only four and one-half by five and one-half inches in size), but he did model Lincoln's face after the Preston Butler photograph. The debt of painter to photographer has often been acknowledged, but not the very real possibility that the painter deserves almost all the credit for arranging the compelling camera portrait in the first place, never even imagining its future reputation as a work of art in its own right. As its patron hoped, Samuel Sartain produced a handsome engraved adaptation that was widely circulated in Pennsylvania in October of that year. Lincoln himself pronounced the result "perfect," adding: "To my unpracticed eye, it is without fault."[32]

But Lincoln was getting far more practice than he might have imagined. Leonard Wells Volk was the only sculptor to commission a photograph of Lincoln before he assumed the presidency. In late December 1860, Thomas D. Jones journeyed from Cincinnati on commission by Ohio Republicans to make a marble bust of the president-elect.[33] Although Lincoln agreed to pose for him daily in the artist's makeshift studio in a Springfield hotel, Jones, like others before him, found it too challenging to sketch accurately in pencil or model effectively in clay while Lincoln tended busily to his correspondence. The sculptor admit-

Photograph by Christopher S. German, Springfield, Illinois, January 13, 1861. Sculptor Thomas D. Jones was present for, and probably helped arrange, this pose, the first photographic record of Lincoln to feature his fully grown new whiskers. *(Photo: The Lincoln Museum, Fort Wayne, Indiana, Neg. No. O-42)*

ted that the president-elect was "by far the most difficult subject that I have ever confronted." So on January 13, Jones accompanied Lincoln to the Springfield gallery of C. S. German to see to the creation of a new camera portrait for a "very dear friend," who has never been identified. The friend may well have been Jones himself. Though the resulting photograph has been widely heralded since as the first to show Lincoln with a full beard, the sculptor himself enjoyed the first and most satisfying use

Plaster bust of Abraham Lincoln from life by Thomas D. Jones, Springfield, Illinois, February 1861. Jones enjoyed life sittings with the president-elect but supplemented these opportunities by commissioning, perhaps posing, and certainly adapting the photograph by C. S. German. *(Photo: The Lincoln Museum, Fort Wayne, Indiana, Neg. No. 361)*

of the picture for the successful marble bust that in its early days graced the Red Room in Lincoln's own White House.[34]

An artist cannot be directly credited with inspiring the first photographs taken of Lincoln when he arrived in Washington for his inauguration in late February 1861. Yet it was surely no accident that the resident camera operator at Mathew Brady's newly opened capital gallery, Alexander Gardner, called on a painter to arrange the poses that day. In the end, the artist's wise refusal to fuss with Lincoln helped guarantee the recording of some of his most haunting and eerily vulnerable likenesses. Artist George Henry Story was a tenant in the same building as the Brady studio, and Gardner summoned him to the gallery as soon as Lincoln arrived on February 24, inviting him to pose the picture. In this unique case, the painter attested that he did nothing to wake the sitter from a reverie into which he had drifted while waiting for his sitting. "Mr. Lincoln was seated in a chair wholly absorbed in deep thought, and apparently oblivious to his immediate surroundings," Story remembered. "He did not even raise his eyes, nor did he give any sign of recognition to anything that was taking place about him. I said in an undertone to the operator: 'Bring your instrument here and take the picture.' This was done, and Mr. Lincoln rose and left the room without a word."[35] The result, showing Lincoln all but hidden behind the thickest beard he ever wore and gazing vacantly into the distance, failed to inspire many print reproductions in the United States but apparently looked dignified enough to overseas audiences to inspire a surprising number of European engravers and lithographers through 1865. The soon-outdated pose—Lincoln began paring down his whiskers from the moment he entered the presidency in March—ultimately evolved into a favorite model for French, German, Italian, even Hungarian printmakers.[36]

As far as we know, by contrast, the only artist to center his attention on a little-known 1861 photograph sometimes attributed to C. D. Fredericks[37] was the Philadelphia painter Edward Dalton Marchant. Following the announcement of Lincoln's final Emancipation Proclamation, Marchant was "empowered by a large body of . . . personal and political friends" in his home city to paint the president's portrait for Independence Hall,[38] undoubtedly an attractive proposition for the old admirer of George Washington. Indeed, en route to his inauguration in 1861, Lincoln had paused at the national shrine on Washington's birthday to rousingly, and fatefully, assure a crowd of dignitaries: "I would rather be assassinated on this spot than to surrender it."[39] Surely the prospect of seeing his portrait as an emancipator gracing walls that bore likenesses of Washington and other heroes of the Revolution all but guaranteed his cooperation.

Indeed Lincoln granted Marchant some three months of access to his office at the White House, but the experience, as usual, did not meet the demands of the artist, who admitted, echoing the words of artists who had preceded him into Lincoln's presence, that the president was "the most difficult subject who ever taxed [his] . . . skills as an artist."[40] Marchant ultimately turned for help to the little-known Fredericks photograph, giving it an unexpected twist. Adding a torso and some overt symbolism, he hearkened back to classical iconology, showing the president, dressed in highly formal regalia (a white tie no less), posing before a statue of "Liberty," whose chains break apart symbolically as he takes pen in hand to sign the Emancipation Proclamation. In this instance, one might say, Lincoln had in one sense helped transform classical statuary not by posing self-consciously himself, as he had once done for Leonard Wells Volk, but simply by affixing his name to a document that metaphorically transformed a classical symbol. In the end, Marchant's canvas, and the 1864 campaign engraving it inspired, were quickly forgotten. The original painting, if it was ever exhibited at all inside Independence Hall, remained there only briefly. Ultimately, the portrait was moved to Philadelphia's Union League Club, where it remains to this day. One can only speculate how enduring an image Marchant might have created had he importuned Lincoln to a Washington gallery for an original photograph on which to base his unique vision of the Great Emancipator.

To a sculptor—and a long-forgotten one at that—belongs the seldom recognized honor of inspiring one of the greatest of all Lincoln photographic sessions. Certain that she possessed the talent to produce a bust of the president, Sarah Fisher Ames, wife of the noted portrait painter Joseph Ames, sought sittings from Lincoln in 1863. Though she lacked her husband's artistic reputation, Lincoln granted her request, perhaps in recognition of her service as a nurse in one of Washington's military hospitals.[41] The sculptor is certainly the "Mrs. Ames" to whom Lincoln's assistant private secretary, John M. Hay, referred when he recorded the president's visit to Alexander Gardner's galleries on November 8, 1863: "Went with Mrs Ames to Gardner's gallery & were soon joined by Nico [chief secretary John G. Nicolay] and the Prest. We had a great many pictures taken. Some of the Presdt. the best I have seen."[42] Hay wholly underestimated Mrs. Ames's influence on these results, though without his brief diary entry we would not even know that she was present for their creation.

Gardner's magisterial sitting that Sunday included an iconic close-up portrait, a portrait of Lincoln together with Nicolay and Hay, and two superb likenesses of a self-assured Lincoln seated in a chair, his right arm

Photograph by Alexander Gardner, Washington, November 8, 1863. Long
described as a "Gettysburg" likeness because it was made eleven days before
Lincoln's most famous speech, this and at least one other photo from this
sitting were in fact produced for the use of sculptor Sarah Fisher Ames.
(Photo: The Lincoln Museum, Fort Wayne, Indiana, Neg. No. O-77).

resting leisurely on a table. Ironically, the most famous of these, the full-
face portrait, did not immediately surface publicly, and herein lies a valuable clue to its origins; it first appeared around 1903, when M. T. Rice
acquired Gardner's archive of negatives and published a cropped close-up
that was promptly reproduced and widely copied. The explanation for its
delayed introduction is simple enough, though long ignored: The original uncropped waist-length portrait, together with a mysterious companion shot of Lincoln's rarely viewed left profile, showing the brawny arms
and shoulders that had convinced sculptor Thomas D. Jones that Lincoln

Marble bust of Lincoln by Sarah Fisher Clampitt Ames. Inscribed on back: "Sarah Fisher Ames Sculpt/1868." Armed with the Gardner photographic models made in her presence and possibly posed with her help, Ames produced several successful busts of Lincoln, of which this, the best known, was acquired by the U.S. Senate. *(Courtesy U.S. Capitol Collection, Cat. No. 21.00013)*

was "an athlete of the first order,"[43] both were clearly made specifically for Sarah Fisher Ames for her use as models for her sculpture. Their influence can easily be detected in the otherwise uninspired three-foot-high marble she managed to sell to Congress in 1868.[44] However deficient, the bust, together with the magnificent photographs its creator requested and almost certainly helped pose, recorded Lincoln for posterity at a crucial moment, only days before he reached his rhetorical apogee at Gettysburg. Gardner, however, has traditionally received the credit for these masterpieces; because few have recognized, much less understood, the sculptor's role in sending Lincoln to the gallery and posing the portraits there, Ames has received none of the credit she deserves.

Nor has an artist who, through both paintings and photographs, did more than any other to create the public and private images of Lincoln, Francis B. Carpenter. By the time the New York artist arrived in Washington to paint Abraham Lincoln and his cabinet in 1864, the president was in serious political trouble. The war had raged inconclusively, at great cost in human life and treasure, for two years more, with no end in sight. Lincoln had successfully fought off a challenge to his renomination but now faced General George B. McClellan, whom he had dismissed from army command, as his formidable Democratic opponent for the White House. Lincoln's Emancipation Proclamation may have begun the end of slavery but had sufficiently threatened racist white America to generate huge Republican losses in the off-year elections of 1862 and a serious threat to a second term for the emancipator.

Against this backdrop, it is interesting to note, Lincoln did nothing to encourage the reintroduction of his four-year-old political image as the self-made product of the western frontier. Now, exercising more control than ever over the contours of his public image, he bravely chose to emphasize his authorship of the proclamation, apparently believing that it demanded appropriate heroic tributes in art. "If my name ever goes into history, it will be for this act," he remembered saying as he prepared so sign the final proclamation on January 1, 1863.[45] To artist Carpenter, who proposed painting the entire cabinet on the day it first met to hear the president suggest freedom for the slaves, Lincoln gave unlimited access to the White House, along with six months' time to work out his ideas and the honor of an exhibition in the East Room to display his finished canvas, which the president proclaimed "as good as it can be made."[46]

The press agreed. Even acknowledging its "rawness, lack of finish, and commonplaceness—such as might be expected of a young artist who has grappled with a subject so difficult and yet so interesting now and forever," correspondent Noah Brooks still pronounced the painting "a measurable success." Brooks presciently predicted that its "chief faults which are now noticeable will be remedied in the engraving." As a popular print, he believed, it would be "prized in every liberty-loving household as a work of art, a group of faithful likenesses of the President and cabinet, and as a perpetual remembrance of the noblest event in American history."[47] Such became the case with the publication of Alexander Hay Ritchie's wildly popular engraved adaptation in 1866.

Carpenter's concept was radically different from Marchant's. The New York painter aspired to create a picture that did nothing less than "commemorate this new epoch in the history of Liberty." But while acknowledging that "painters of old had delighted in representations of the birth from the ocean of Venus," meaning the old-fashioned and outdated, America's invigorating new history, he believed, was "no dream of fable, but a substantial fact—the immaculate conception of Constitutional Liberty." It "need borrow no interest from imaginary curtain or column, gorgeous furniture or allegorical statue," Carpenter insisted. It would be free of "the false glitter of tapestry hangings, velvet table-cloths, and marble columns." There would be no "accessories or adjuncts." Art, Carpenter declared, "cannot dwell always among classic forms, nor clothe its concep-

Photograph by Anthony Berger for Mathew B. Brady, Washington, February 9, 1864. One of several photos made on the same day at the Brady Gallery under the supervision of artist Francis B. Carpenter, this pose became the model for Carpenter's portrait of Lincoln in his widely reproduced history painting of the first reading of the Emancipation Proclamation. Today it serves as the model for the current Lincoln portrait on the five-dollar bill. *(Photo: Library of Congress)*

tions in the imagery of an old and worn-out world . . . and its ideals must be wrought out of the strife of a living humanity." As the painter put it, "I had no more right to depart from the facts, than has the historian in his record."[48] With a work free of "accessories or adjuncts," he would elevate the plain man of the people into a national icon.

This proved easier said than done. Life sittings alone did not provide the poses the artist thought best reflected his aspirations. His surviving scrapbook, filled with hasty sketches of both seated and standing Lincolns, testifies to his artistic indecision. For a remedy, Carpenter predictably sought photographic models from which he could paint. As always cooperative, Lincoln agreed to pose before the cameras at Mathew Brady's gallery on February 9, 1864. Brady himself was absent; he was at the front photographing the Civil War. But it turned out to be the day

Lincoln and his son Tad, photographed by Anthony Berger at the Mathew B. Brady Gallery, Washington, February 9, 1864. Taken at the same time as the portrait Carpenter adapted for his emancipation painting—the quintessential public image of Lincoln—this intimate pose inspired the artist to define the president's private image as well. *(Photo: The Lincoln Museum, Fort Wayne, Indiana, Negative No. O-93)*

Oil study of Lincoln by Francis Bicknell Carpenter, Washington, summer 1864. Using the Brady photo as a model and supplementing it with life sittings, the artist produced this painting at the White House. Lincoln supposedly said of it: "I feel that there is more of me in this portrait than in any representation which has ever been made." *(Photo: The Union League Club of New York)*

the Lincoln image—and the primary technology for promulgating it— changed forever. We can safely assume that Carpenter himself arranged the poses, and no one ever did so more brilliantly. The results included the future models for the Lincoln penny, the old five-dollar bill, and the revised five-dollar bill of the twenty-first century, not to mention the quintessential intimate portrait of Abraham Lincoln, the famous photograph with his son Tad. All these poses eventually achieved popularity of their own as photographic keepsakes and further fame as models for engraved and lithographed portraits, coins, stamps, and currency.

But Carpenter was not trying to produce photographic icons that day, even though he did. Nor was he aware that the pictures Brady's photographer took that day would outstrip his painstakingly planned canvas in fame. The artist never even got the credit he deserved for posing them. What he was after at Brady's was merely the perfect pose for his Lincoln canvas. Those on which he lavished special attention were the close-ups of Lincoln's face and a majestic full-figure pose, each a marvelous view of how the president looked just three days shy of his fifty-fifth birthday. But the question of how best to portray Lincoln declaring what the artist believed was a second Declaration of Independence—for a canvas he had every hope would some day hang in the Capitol Rotunda alongside Trumbull's national icon of the first Declaration of Independence—continued to vex Francis B. Carpenter.

Still unsatisfied, the painter ushered Lincoln to Brady's for a second studio session, then, a few weeks later, summoned one of the photographer's camera operators to the White House, where in the president's private office, all but obscured in its weak natural light, Lincoln posed for Brady's cameras under Carpenter's supervision yet again, both sitting and standing, at the very table where he had signed the proclamation on January 1, 1863. Whatever its unavoidable technical flaws, these were breathtaking pictures, the first ever to show a president inside the White House, though the public did not get to see it for generations. And an artist, not a photographer, had arranged them. At last, Carpenter had photographic models worth adapting. He quickly proceeded to work them into both seated and full-figure sketches, as his scrapbook shows.[49] Ultimately, the artist chose to portray Lincoln simply sitting in his chair at the head of the cabinet table, dominating the scene merely by listening, not speaking. The president does not even appear at the center of the canvas. The only major "symbol" visible in the picture is the painting of Andrew Jackson that Lincoln kept in the presidential office.[50]

In appreciation, an influential art journal declared: "The hour has arrived when the necessities of our country not only justify, but inexorably demand, the production of a series of national paintings. . . ." By 1866, undaunted by criticism, Francis B. Carpenter would respond to this call for nation-affirming visual representations by advertising his Emancipation canvas as his own "Great National Picture."[51] The painting, its promoters emphasized, showed an unhesitating Lincoln braving certain political denunciation to issue the order. Lincoln would have been overjoyed to read the New York Tribune's assessment that the picture proved "by all odds, next to Trumbull's Picture of the 'Declaration of Indepen-

A. H. Ritchie after Carpenter, *The First Reading of the Emancipation Proclamation Before the Cabinet*, steel engraving, published by Derby & Miller, New York, 1866. The *New York Evening Post* recommended this enormously popular print as the ideal pictorial tribute with which to "commemorate" emancipation in the American home. *(Photo: The Lincoln Museum, Fort Wayne, Indiana, Negative No. 2825).*

dence'—a picture worth all the rest in the Capitol put together—the best work of this class that has been painted in America."[52]

Lincoln had known those Rotunda paintings intimately in the 1840s. They had helped a young congressman—and, in engraved adaptations, a young nation—visualize national identity and memory. And now a painting of Lincoln himself was declared worthy to be included among them. But it was not to be. Carpenter was no Trumbull.

Yet Americans never entirely lost their taste for heroic art in public places. Francis B. Carpenter did eventually persuade Congress to acquire his realistic Emancipation Proclamation canvas, but only after its engraved adaptation had become a huge best seller. Not until Carpenter found a wealthy patron to buy and donate it did the huge painting earn its place in the Capitol in 1876—not, to the artist's disappointment, in the Rotunda, as the artist always hoped, but on a wall too modest for the canvas outside the Senate chamber, where today only visitors to its galleries can glimpse it. Somehow, a decade after it was painted, Carpenter's immense canvas seemed in a way too small for the hero it celebrated.

The Rotunda instead was to welcome a traditional heroic sculpture carved in Italy by a young American woman named Vinnie Ream, who had also enjoyed life sittings in the White House with Abraham Lincoln to create a portrait bust. But except for the sad, homely face she portrayed realistically, her final statue, commissioned later by Congress, hearkened back to antiquity, portraying Lincoln extending his arm in the classical heroic posture, grasping the Emancipation Proclamation in a gesture meant to suggest the granting of liberty.[53] Public statuary still called for such conventions. Those who held such aspirations for Vinnie Ream's Lincoln statue, also copied in its day by photographers, must have been caught short by some of the violent criticism it aroused, with one newspaper calling it "a frightful abortion."

Were it not for a well-publicized accident, the statue was destined for the same fate as Greenough's banished statue of Washington. But when workers began carting it away, they accidentally smashed the Emancipation Proclamation scroll that the statue clutched in its hand and, in embarrassment, retreated. Vinnie Ream's Lincoln remained where it was first unveiled, its scroll, if not its reputation, quickly restored.[54] (It has since stood in silent witness to countless state funerals, including John F. Kennedy's.) Reversing recent trends in the mutual dependency of artistic media, camera artists now rushed to make copies of Ream's bust and statue and spread its fame exponentially through photography. Even the president's family collected a carte de visite of Ream's original bust for its own family album.[55]

The final artist to wisely seek photographic models to assist him in portraying Lincoln from life, like Sarah Fisher Ames and Francis Bicknell Carpenter before him, also inspired one of the greatest of all the sessions Lincoln enjoyed before the camera. English-born Matthew Henry Wilson, commissioned to paint the president by Secretary of the Navy Gideon Welles, enjoyed at least eight separate life sittings with Lincoln at the White House in February 1865. But these proved insufficient, and Wilson pursued the now time-honored path of accompanying his subject to Gardner's gallery for what proved to be Lincoln's very last visit to a photographer's studio.[56] For generations, the results were believed to have been taken on April 10, 1865,[57] giving added poignancy to the single surviving copy of the final close-up, which showed Lincoln ravaged by his four crisis-filled years in the White House but managing a wan smile at the supposedly imminent prospect of peace. Gardner was able to print but a single copy of the portrait because its glass negative portentously cracked through Lincoln's head. Five days later Lincoln was assassinated.

But the fable proved untrue. It was always dependent on the specious idea that photography always existed as a medium apart, with scant ties to painting and sculpture. As it turned out, Wilson's diaries, first published in 1972, spoiled the story, revealing that the artist accompanied Lincoln to Gardner's not on April 10 but on February 5.[58] Since his painting clearly copied one of the resulting poses, the accuracy of his story is unquestionable, and photo historians ultimately revised their attributions where the Gardner sitting was concerned.

In the now-routine manner of iconographical interdependence, the Wilson painting, based on life sittings and a photograph, in turn inspired a lithograph—in this case a faithful reproduction by Louis Prang[59]—that elevated Lincoln into a new realm beyond politician and emancipator, that of martyr. It was left to Lincoln himself, in his customarily casual manner, to dismiss the final result far less seriously. Glimpsing the work in progress hanging in his White House office, he confided that it reminded him of the story of a westerner whose wife had commissioned his portrait as a birthday present. When she first saw it, she pronounced it "horridly like" the original, "and that"—Lincoln laughed—"seems to me a just criticism of this."[60]

By this time it was not beyond the imagination of one of Lincoln's old friends from Illinois to explain the president's appeal to both classical and more modern artistic tributes by citing not his self-effacement or homeliness but instead the obscure legend of the citizens of ancient Greece who had once staged a competition for a grand new statue of Jupiter. One of the two finalists was "a figure of classical beauty—the perfection of symmetry—a paragon of sculpture—a miracle of art—an image in which glorious life had been arrested at its highest tide—a fit marble ideal of the presiding divinity in the assemblage of the Gods!" The other was "a rough effigy of a human figure—no majesty in its lineaments—no grace in its pose—apparently no art in its execution—no harmony in its relations—no dignity in its bearing." Naturally, the audience made its decision promptly. The first statue was "our Jupiter." The second, "inglorious statue" should be cast into the sea.

But a poet in the crowd begged for a reevaluation. Raise both statues atop their tall pedestals, he urged, and then consider the images anew. A few days later an "eager throng" gathered to rejudge the competitors, to find the "two draped figures . . . poised in mid-air." The draperies were shaken loose, and "the two competitors stood out in bold relief against the pure azure sky." Miraculously, the "favorite had been transformed by the intervening distance. The classical features—the sparkling eye—the luminous countenance, had vanished: but, a greater transformation had been wrought in the other figure, by distance. . . . Life had been impressed upon those hitherto ungainly features—majesty sat enthroned upon those rugged lineaments—the eyes gleamed with the fire of genius . . . and a God stood outlined in classical marble, to the view."

Now, his old friend predicted, the rugged features of Lincoln, seen in the light of history, would one day be "reproduced *ad infinitum* in bronze, granite, and marble, and enshrined in all patriotic hearts, will remain the great central figure of humanity," America's very own Jupiter.[61] He proved correct, but how willingly Lincoln himself had cooperated in this transfiguration, and how closely artists in all media had worked together to forge the result, he never guessed.

Francis B. Carpenter, *The Lincoln Family.* Oil on canvas, ca. 1865. Although commissioned by a New York engraver to create this composite so it could be adapted into a popular print, the artist took so much time to produce it that rival publishers produced Lincoln family images first, and Carpenter lost the credit he deserved for imagining this pose. *(Photo: The New-York Historical Society)*

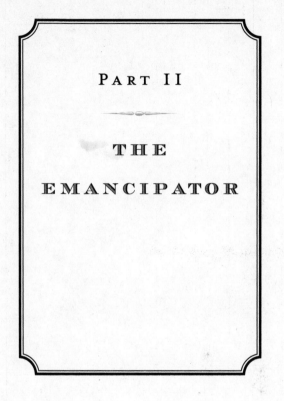

PART II

THE

EMANCIPATOR

5

Natural Rights, Citizenship Rights, States' Rights, and Black Rights: Another Look at Lincoln and Race

JAMES OAKES

Stephen Douglas was the first in a long line of observers frustrated by the inconsistent things Abraham Lincoln had to say about racial equality. In their fifth debate, at Galesburg, Illinois, on October 7, 1858, Douglas complained that when Lincoln went into the northern part of the state "he stood up for negro equality" but that when he went into the southern counties Lincoln "discarded the doctrine and declared that there always must be a superior and inferior race."[1] Lincoln replied by demonstrating that he had said the same things about black inferiority in northern districts, including the district that had elected the abolitionist Owen Lovejoy to Congress, but Douglas was not persuaded. It was true, he said, that Lincoln was willing to endorse racial inequality everywhere in Illinois, but only in the northern parts of the state would Lincoln dare to assert the equality of blacks and whites. A few months earlier in Chicago, for example, Lincoln had asked his audience to "discard all this quibbling about this man and the other man—this race and that race and the other race being inferior, and unite as one people throughout this land, until we shall once more stand up declaring that all men are created equal."[2] Douglas denounced this "Chicago doctrine" as "a monstrous heresy" and condemned Lincoln for refusing to say such things in the southernmost parts of the state.[3]

Pinning Lincoln down on race has proved as difficult for historians as it was for Stephen Douglas. There's a simple reason for this: The evidence for Lincoln's views on the equality of blacks and whites is hopelessly contradictory. String together one set of quotations, and Lincoln comes off as a dyed-in-the-wool white supremacist. Compile a different body of evidence, and Lincoln reads like the purest of racial egalitarians. Compounding the confusion is the fact that so much of what Lincoln had to say about race was so ambiguous that it can be used to support either reading. The only thing Lincoln did make clear was that he disliked talking about race and resented the way Douglas kept forcing the issue.

Stephen Douglas was certain he knew what was going on: Lincoln was tailoring his views "for political effect," playing the race card in the southern counties where audiences expected it and parading his egalitarianism up north where abolitionism and antislavery were more popular. There is something to this, but only something. Like most politicians Lincoln emphasized those convictions most likely to appeal to the particular audience he was addressing. But he was not lying when he told listeners that he had never favored the social and political equality of blacks and whites, just as he was affirming his deepest convictions when he insisted that blacks and whites were equally entitled to the fundamental rights of life, liberty, and the pursuit of happiness. Give all due allowance to Lincoln's political motives and the contradiction is still there. Accordingly most historians have not been satisfied by Douglas's diagnosis. For some the temptation to simplify matters has been irresistible: Lincoln was little more than a mouthpiece for mid-nineteenth-century racism or, alternatively, he didn't have a racist bone in his body. Somewhat more satisfactory have been the efforts to parse Lincoln's various statements and to discern crucial distinctions—between the way he thought about race and the way he thought about slavery, for example, or between his egalitarian view of natural rights and his prejudicial view of social and political rights. This last distinction gets closer to the way Lincoln thought without quite getting there.

Here's a better explanation: Lincoln believed that race relations were regulated at three different levels. At the highest level, the natural rights guaranteed by the Constitution, Lincoln consistently favored the equality of blacks and whites. Below natural rights were the privileges and immunities of citizenship, sometimes called citizenship rights, and at this level Lincoln was cautiously egalitarian during the 1850s and unambiguously so during his presidency. Finally, there were aspects of race relations that fell solely within the purview of states—laws regulating marriage, voting, and jury duty, for example. These matters were determined by state legislatures elected by the people at large. Virtually every concession Lincoln made to racial prejudice concerned this third level.

Lincoln shared many, though by no means all, of the racial prejudices of his fellow Americans. He instinctively thought of the United States as a white man's country, agreed that the founders had imagined their new nation in the same way, believed the western territories existed for the benefit of whites, and said on various occasions that it would be best if blacks and whites were permanently separated. But when he bothered to justify these views Lincoln usually referred not to any notion of innate racial inequality but to the clearly expressed will of a racist white majority. Lincoln's democratic deference to popular opinion explains his perplexing inconsistencies at least as much as his own racial prejudices. He resisted the idea that either natural rights or the privileges and immunities of citizenship were subject to majority rule, and on those matters he was a racial egalitarian. But on issues that were distinctly the prerogative of elected officials in state legislatures Lincoln deferred. As was so often the case in antebellum America, Lincoln's prejudicial views had as much to do with democracy as with racism.

Natural Rights

If Douglas was sure that Lincoln was trimming his racial attitudes to the needs of different audiences, Lincoln complained that Douglas and the Democrats were harping on the issue of racial equality in an effort to avoid the issue of slavery. He responded to one Douglas speech by pointing out that it was made up entirely of "complaints against our tendencies to negro equality" but that it "had ignored the main issue" of slavery.[4] Douglas will "pander to prejudice" by calling us "hard names" such as "Black Republicans."[5] He "pretends to fear" that a Republican victory would result "in the amalgamation of blacks and whites."[6] Because most whites felt a "natural disgust" at the idea of "indiscriminate" racial amalgamation, Lincoln explained, Douglas was "evidently basing his chief hope, upon the chances of being able to appropriate the benefit of that disgust to himself."[7] But these were "flimsy diatribes," Lincoln explained, "perpetrated by the Democracy to divert the public mind from the real issue—the extension or non-extension of slavery."[8] Hoping to "get rid of the fog which obscures the real question," Lincoln dismissed Douglas's claim that the Republicans wanted to make war on southern slavery and introduce "a perfect social and political equality between the white and black races. These are false issues," Lincoln insisted, "upon which Judge Douglas has tried to force a controversy." Lincoln wanted "all extraneous matter thrown out so that men can fairly see the real difference between the parties": The Republicans believe slavery is wrong and ought to be treated as such; the Democrats do not.[9]

Lincoln said it so often, so clearly, and so eloquently that there is no room for doubt: Slavery was wrong because it deprived men and women of the natural rights to which every human being was equally entitled. The Declaration of Independence promised life, liberty, and the pursuit of happiness to all men and women. "If the negro is a man," Lincoln said in his first major antislavery speech, "why then my ancient faith teaches me that 'all men are created equal;' and that there can be no moral right in connection with one man's making a slave of another."[10] This was a life-long conviction on Lincoln's part. He always hated slavery, he said, as much as any abolitionist. He repeatedly described slavery as a moral, social, and political evil; freedom was the natural right of every human being.

For saying such things Stephen Douglas and the Democrats repeatedly denounced Lincoln as an abolitionist, a "Black Republican," and a racial egalitarian. Lincoln in turn condemned Douglas for "debauching" public opinion by speaking of blacks as brutes and animals rather than as men. Douglas would have you believe that those who oppose the enslavement of blacks are somehow "wronging the white man," that there is a "necessary conflict between the white man and the negro." But there is no such conflict, Lincoln declared. "I say that there is room enough for us all to be free."[11] At various points Lincoln questioned the legitimacy of racial categories themselves. Skin color, he warned, cannot possibly justify enslavement because by that rule "you are to be slave to the first man you meet, with fairer skin than your own." Nor would it do to justify slavery on the ground that whites are intellectually superior to blacks, for by that rule "you are to be slave to the first man you meet, with an intellect superior to your own."[12] At one point Lincoln blurted out in frustration against the Democrats' obsession with race: "Negro equality! Fudge! How long, in the government of a God, shall there continue knaves to vend, and fools to gulp, so low a piece of demagogueism as this."[13]

Had Lincoln's chief antagonists been the handful of reactionaries who rejected Jefferson's philosophy root and branch the issue of racial equality would scarcely have arisen. But because Democrats like Douglas professed their commitment to the principles of the Declaration, because they invoked racial arguments to specifically exempt blacks from it, Lincoln had no choice but to confront the racial premises of his opponents. His argument against slavery therefore had to be, at some level, an antiracist argument as well. The Democrats insisted that Jefferson's ideal was never meant to apply to blacks, that "the inferior race" should be granted only those rights and privileges "they are capable of enjoying." Lincoln dismissed such reasoning. "What are these arguments?" he asked. Turn it "whatever way you will," he said, "whether it come from the mouth of a King, an excuse for enslaving the people of his country, or from the mouth of men of one race as a reason for enslaving the men of another race, it is the same old serpent." This was the speech that so enraged Stephen Douglas, the one that ended with Lincoln's plaintive cry for an end to all "this quibbling" over whether this or that race was inferior to the other.[14]

It is not enough, then, to say that Lincoln simply distinguished slavery, which he admittedly hated, from racism, which he openly endorsed. His antislavery argument was in large measure an antiracist argument; the one made no sense without the other. Short of openly repudiating the principles of the Declaration, Lincoln thought, the only way to evade the moral injunction handed down from the founders was to deny what he knew was undeniable: that blacks were human beings. Conversely, the only way Lincoln could claim that blacks and whites were equally entitled to their liberty was to assert their equal humanity. To make his case that blacks were as entitled to their freedom as were whites Lincoln went a long way toward repudiating both racism and the racist demagoguery that went with it.

Freedom—liberty—was not the only natural right with which everyone was endowed. All humans were similarly entitled to the pursuit of happiness, blacks no less than whites. This was one of the most important moral precepts developed by Enlightenment thinkers in the eighteenth century. Throughout history, they argued, most forms of social organization had deprived human beings of the fruits of their labor and thus left in their wake a protracted legacy of indescribable misery. Societies that robbed humans of what they had rightfully earned by the sweat of their brows paid a steep price for this act of theft: They destroyed the individual's incentive to work, undermined the general prosperity, and were thereby doomed to poverty and famine. This was not right. Every living man and woman was entitled to a decent life, a modicum of happiness, free from the debilitating effects of poverty and the haunting fear of starvation. Gratuitous starvation—for society is a human, not a divine, creation. It was therefore immoral to organize a society, any society, in a way that made it impossible for the mass of men and women to rise beyond the destitution that had been humanity's lot for millennia. Here was the moral imperative buried within classical economics. Lincoln translated it into simple proposition: All human beings—blacks and whites, men and women—were equally entitled to the fruits of their labor.[15]

Lincoln probably always believed this, but he said nothing about it in his first major antislavery speech at Peoria in 1854. Not until 1858, in the wake of the *Dred Scott* decision and Douglas's renewed campaign of racial demagoguery, did Lincoln begin to speak more extensively, and emphatically, of every human's right to the fruits of his or her labor. The claim that blacks were inferior to whites, Lincoln said, was nothing more than an updated version of the ancient argument "that says you work and I eat, you toil and I will enjoy the fruits of it." He protested against what he called "the counterfeit logic which concludes that, because I do not want a black woman for a slave I must necessarily have her for a wife." He could just "leave her alone," Lincoln explained, adding that although she was "not my equal" in some respects, "in the right to eat the bread she earns with her own hands without asking leave of any one else, she is my equal and the equal of all others."[16] But although Lincoln repeated this statement a couple of times during his debates with Stephen Douglas in 1858, it was not until 1859 that he began to flesh out his argument into a full-throttle defense of the rights of free labor.

The timing of Lincoln's shift suggests the reason for it. Throughout the 1850s Lincoln's chief antagonist was a northern Democrat, Stephen Douglas, with whom there was no point in arguing the merits of free labor. Only when Lincoln began addressing himself to a wider audience that included proslavery southerners—perhaps with an eye to the upcoming presidential election—did he begin to defend free labor at some length. That happened in the latter half of 1859.

Lincoln had been reading too many eccentric proslavery intellectuals, and like most Republicans he did not appreciate that the vast majority of the slaveholders accepted the basic principle of classical economics, that slaves worked less efficiently than free laborers. Edmund Ruffin was but one of a number of proslavery zealots who readily agreed that if you put a slave beside a free laborer the slave would work less efficiently. But southern slaves were black, Ruffin argued, and blacks were oblivious to the incentives of free labor. They would work only under the compulsions of slavery. Moreover, they could work in tropical climates that defeated whites. Racial slavery thus made it possible for southern masters to wring prosperity from an otherwise unproductive people in an otherwise unproductive climate. Rather than repudiate the basic principle of the superior efficiency of free labor, the slaveholders followed the examples of Benjamin Franklin and Adam Smith by making an exception to the rule, in this case a racial exception.[17] Northern Democrats agreed. Free labor ideology was a perfectly reasonable doctrine, when applied to whites.

But Lincoln rejected the racial exception and so, as with his argument for the universal right to liberty, his version of free labor ideology involved the simultaneous attack on slavery and racism. There was nothing particularly original in Lincoln's defense of the superiority of free labor; that was standard classical economics. What made it startling was his claim that the rights of free labor applied to blacks and whites alike, that they were equally entitled to the bread they earned from the sweat of their brows. Free labor ideology became an antislavery argument only when abolitionists and politicians like Lincoln repudiated the racist exception to it. Once again Lincoln's argument against slavery had to be, at some level, an argument against racism. When it came to the natural rights of life, liberty, and the pursuit of happiness, Lincoln was at bottom a racial egalitarian.

The Rights of Citizenship

William H. Johnson was one of the small coteries that accompanied Lincoln from Springfield to Washington where Johnson, a black man, served as the president's valet. Lincoln had Johnson put on the Treasury Department payroll, though he worked exclusively for Lincoln in the executive mansion and accompanied Lincoln on several trips—to Antietam, for example, to visit McClellan after the battle. He also took the train with Lincoln to Gettysburg. They had by then become so close that there is speculation Johnson was the only person to have read a draft of the Gettysburg Address before it was actually delivered. On the ride back from Pennsylvania both Lincoln and his son began to exhibit symptoms of variola, a mild form of smallpox, and shortly thereafter Johnson got sick as well. There was a smallpox epidemic in Washington at the time, so Johnson may or may not have caught it from the president. But Lincoln took care of his valet during his illness, writing to the Treasury Department to ask that Johnson's pay be sent over as the man was too ill to pick it up himself. One day a reporter for the *Chicago Tribune* found Lincoln in Johnson's room dividing the pay up into different envelopes according to the man's instructions. But unlike Lincoln and his son, Johnson never recovered, and when he died the president took it upon himself to make the funeral arrangements. He ordered that Johnson be buried in the cemetery recently established at Arlington. He paid for a headstone out of his own pocket and chose the words that were engraved upon it: "William Johnson, Citizen."[18]

Ranking just below the natural rights promised by the Declaration of Independence was a large and amorphous body of legal rights and protections that are commonly referred to as the privileges and immunities of citizenship. In fact the concept of citizenship was legally underdeveloped before the Civil War. It was the climactic struggle over slavery in its final stage that forced the nation's lawmakers to confront the issue head-on. Before then the meaning of citizenship was obscure. The Constitution required that the privileges and immunities a citizen enjoyed in one state had to be respected by all the states, but it was not clear what this meant. State and national citizenships were not the same thing, but they seemed to be linked in some way, though precisely how no one could say for certain. Nor did the Constitution, or the major legal treatises of the antebellum period, specify precisely what the privileges and immunities of citizenship actually were. And even when a judge or a lawmaker did specify the rights of citizenship, the rights they cited were not clearly unique to citizens but were commonly granted to resident aliens as well. These included the right to own and convey property, the freedom to move about at will, the various freedoms of expression, in particular the freedom of religion, and the rights of due process, including habeas corpus, the right to sue, and the right to a jury trial. Citizenship did not include the privileges of sovereignty, the political power that flowed from those who were allowed to vote or hold office. Women and children were citizens, for example, but they could not vote or hold public office.[19]

It was slavery that threw off the strongest ray of clarity piercing the fog of citizenship in early America, yet this happened in a negative rather than a positive way. An ancient tradition, extending all the way back to Greece and Rome, all but defined a slave as a noncitizen. That tradition persisted in the United States, where it was so widely assumed that slaves had almost no rights that "rightlessness" can be thought of as the defining feature of American slavery. Slaves could not give speeches, publish books and newspapers, or assemble freely in public. They had no right to property—they "owned" only what their masters allowed them to own—and as they had neither the right to property nor the right to mobility it followed that the slaves had no right to convey property either. They had no right to form their own churches and they were able to worship only to the extent that their masters allowed it, or failed to notice it. Slaves could not sue or be sued except on the presumption that they were not in fact slaves. They had no right to a trial by jury, no right to face their accusers, and they could be imprisoned indefinitely without ever being charged with a crime.[20] On this matter, at least, virtually all Americans were agreed: Slaves were not citizens; they had none of the rights, privileges, and immunities that attached to citizenship. So it was that the clearest definitions of citizenship to be found in antebellum America often came from jurists in the act of specifying what it meant to be a slave.

The implications of slavery for the meaning of citizenship were complicated by the fact that slavery in America was racial; it was a status reserved to Africans and their descendants. Inevitably the question arose whether the stigma of noncitizenship that attached to blacks because they were slaves remained once a slave was freed. Did the racial identity that determined enslavement also determine citizenship? To put the matter more simply, could free blacks be citizens? The issue might easily have erupted in the immediate aftermath of the American Revolution, when thousands of blacks became free, but it did not. In fact most state courts, North as well as South, readily acknowledged that free blacks were entitled to most, if not all, of the rights of citizenship. As sectional tensions developed, however, the northern and southern courts went their separate ways on the citizenship rights of free blacks. In the North courts generally extended the privileges and immunities of citizenship to free blacks. Meanwhile southern courts reversed course and allowed the logic of slavery, with its presumption of noncitizenship, to delimit the rights of free blacks. By the 1850s the sectional divide had become a chasm. Northern courts maintained their long-standing recognition of black citizenship, but southern courts claimed that the stigma of race followed blacks out of slavery even after they had been freed. As a judge in Georgia put it in 1853, "the act of manumission confers no other right but that of freedom from the domination of the master, and the limited liberty of locomotion—it does not and cannot confer citizenship, nor any of the powers, civil or political, incident to citizenship." The reason for this, the judge explained, was that "the social and civil degradation, resulting from the taint of blood, adheres to the descendants of Ham in this country, like the poisoned tunic of Nessus."[21]

The sectional division within the state courts eventually made its way into federal court, although the federal judiciary tried for a long time to avoid the explosive issue. The obvious sticking point was the Constitution's requirement that each state respect the privileges and immunities of the citizens of the other states. Strictly speaking this would require either that the southern states recognize the citizenship rights of northern free blacks or that the northern states defer to the southern presumption of black noncitizenship. By the 1850s the citizenship rights of free blacks had become one of the smoldering issues in the developing sectional crisis. The conflagration erupted in 1857 when Chief Justice Roger B. Taney issued his controversial ruling in the case of *Dred Scott v. Sandford*.

Taney's decision wrote the proslavery jurisprudence of southern courts into the Constitution by declaring that blacks were not and never had been citizens of the United States. Technically, the only citizenship question before the High Court was whether Dred Scott was free and therefore a citizen of the state of Missouri. But Taney's decision made a hash of the difference between the rights of slaves and the rights of free blacks, and it obliterated the long-standing connection between state and national citizenship. Determined to prove that blacks were not citizens Taney concocted a novel concept of "national" citizenship that attached only to the descendants of those who had been state and national citizens at the time the nation was founded. As blacks had not been citizens of the states in either 1776 or 1789, they could not be citizens of the United States in 1857. After the founding states were free to extend some of the privileges and immunities of citizenship to whomever they chose, Taney ruled, but no state could ever, under any circumstance, grant citizenship to blacks.[22]

Nothing Taney said about citizenship made sense as either history or law. In the space of twenty pages he overturned the basic concept of birthright citizenship that had developed out of the Revolution. In its place Taney defined national citizenship as an inheritance bequeathed only to the descendants of those who had been citizens at the moment of the nation's founding. At the same time Taney opened an abyss between state and national citizenship, a constitutional firewall really, one that shielded the slave states from any possibility that free blacks might claim the privileges and immunities of U.S. citizenship. It was an outrageous decision. And if Taney hoped that by swinging his proslavery ax firmly enough he would silence all further discussion of the matter, he had seriously miscalculated.

Like most northerners, Lincoln had almost nothing to say about citizenship until the *Dred Scott* decision forced the matter out of the courts and into public discussion. But there were hints. The Fugitive Slave Act of 1850 had transferred jurisdiction of fugitive cases from northern courts to federal administrators and in the process it stripped accused runaways of the due process rights that states ordinarily granted them. In 1854 Lincoln said he would have preferred a statute that "did not expose a free negro to any more danger of being carried into slavery, than our present criminal laws do an innocent person to the danger of being hung."[23] At the very least this was an implicit recognition that free blacks were entitled to the same due process rights as white citizens. Like most Republicans in the 1850s Lincoln was cautious here, acknowledging that the Constitution did after all contain a fugitive slave clause and urging his fellow Republicans against calling for the repeal of the 1850 law lest it alienate too many swing voters.[24] He insisted nonetheless that the law "should have been framed so as to be free from some of the objections that pertain to it."[25] And as late as 1860 Lincoln repeated that the Fugitive Slave Act was "objectionable in some of its provisions" and even left open the possibility that it was unconstitutional.[26] This was scarcely a ringing endorsement of the citizenship rights of blacks, and the obscurity of Lincoln's language is an indication of his reluctance to broach the subject.

But the *Dred Scott* decision forced the issue. Lincoln was infuriated by the ruling and his reaction to it was uncharacteristically hot-tempered.

Two weeks after Taney published his decision Lincoln criticized the chief justice for insisting "at great length that negroes were no part of the people who made, or for whom was made, the Declaration of Independence, or the Constitution."[27] A year later, as he was formulating his thoughts for the upcoming Senate race against Stephen Douglas, Lincoln spelled out what he believed were the elements of a conspiracy to make slavery national and perpetual. "Study the Dred Scott decision, and then see how little even now remains to be done," Lincoln wrote. He reduced Taney's ruling to three major points, the first of which "is that a negro cannot be a citizen." The Court's purpose, Lincoln explained, was "to deprive the negro, in every possible event, of the benefit of that provision of the United States Constitution which declares that 'the citizens of each State shall be entitled to all privileges and immunities of citizens in the several States.' "[28] A few weeks later Lincoln restated his argument at the beginning of his famous House Divided speech. Here too Lincoln claimed to detect a proslavery conspiracy, a "piece of machinery so to speak—compounded of the Nebraska doctrine and the Dred Scott decision." The first of the "working points of that machinery" was, once again, Taney's assertion "that no negro slave, imported as such from Africa, and no descendant of such slave can ever be a citizen of any State, in the sense of that term as used in the Constitution of the United States."[29] Lincoln anticipated, correctly as it turned out, that his speech would set the terms for his upcoming series of debates with Stephen Douglas.

Douglas pounced. Lincoln says he is opposed to the *Dred Scott* decision because it "deprives the negro of the rights and privileges of citizenship," Douglas declared in their very first debate. He then unleashed a farrago of racist demagoguery by means of a series of rhetorical questions, all of them aimed at denying the citizenship of free blacks. "I ask you," Douglas shouted, "are you in favor of conferring upon the negro the rights and privileges of citizenship?" If you "desire negro citizenship, if you desire to allow them to come into the State and settle with the white man, if you desire them to vote on an equality with yourselves, and to make them eligible to office, to serve on juries, and to adjudge your rights, then support Mr. Lincoln and the Black Republican party, who are in favor of the citizenship of the negro."[30] There was no stopping him. "I hold that a negro is not and never ought to be a citizen of the United States," Douglas declared at Jonesboro. "I do not believe that the Almighty made the negro capable of self-government."[31]

Lincoln tried to silence his opponent by opening the next debate in Charleston with his single most egregious endorsement of racial discrimination, but when it came to racist invective Douglas could not be outdone. He shot back at Lincoln with a denial of black citizenship even more extreme than Taney's. The chief justice had claimed that blacks could not be citizens because their ancestors had been slaves. But Douglas proudly declared that "a negro ought not to be a citizen, whether his parents were imported into this country as slaves or not, or whether or not he was born here. It does not depend upon the place a negro's parents were born, or whether they were slaves or not, but upon the fact that he is a negro."[32] On and on Douglas went, bellowing forth his denunciations of Abraham Lincoln, the Republican Party, and black citizenship.

Lincoln withered beneath the assault. He pedaled backward, away from any endorsement of the citizenship rights. "I am not in favor of negro citizenship," Lincoln declared. He claimed that he had merely stated, as an empirical fact, that the *Dred Scott* decision denied the possibility that blacks could be citizens but that he had registered no specific objection to the Court's decision. His purpose had not been to endorse black citizenship but to demonstrate how the decision fitted into a larger pattern, a conspiracy, to make slavery national. This was technically true but substantively false. Anyone listening to or reading the House Divided speech would reasonably conclude that Lincoln was objecting to the Court's decision on black citizenship, not merely summarizing it. And there was more hairsplitting to come. A month later he gave himself a verbal escape hatch by paraphrasing Douglas's criticism in a curious way. Douglas complained that "I [Lincoln] had in a very especial manner" objected to the Supreme Court's ruling on black citizenship. Not so, Lincoln countered. He had not complained "especially" about that part of the decision. He had simply noted it, "without making any complaint at all," along with several other points made in the Court's decision. Hence Douglas's assertion "that I made an 'especial objection' (that is his exact language) to the decision on this account, is untrue in point of fact."[33]

It is often said in Lincoln's defense that he worded his racial remarks with extreme care, making it appear as though he were endorsing the racist sensibilities of his listener when, if you read the words carefully, he was actually committing himself to nothing. Here we have the same problem coming from the other direction: What appears on the face of it to have been a denunciation of Taney's ruling on citizenship was actually, Lincoln insisted, a neutral recitation of the facts. Once again, everything Lincoln said was true, in the narrowest conceivable sense. He did not "support" black citizenship, although unlike Douglas he did not *oppose* it either. He had not actually condemned the *Dred Scott* decision for denying black citizenship, although condemnation was implicit in the way he summarized it. Nor had he singled out the citizenship ruling for "especial objection" but had instead listed it as the first of three major parts of the decision, all of which when taken together suggested a conspiracy to make slavery national and perpetual. Like nearly every other Republican in America Lincoln was running for cover, trying to avoid the virtually radioactive political fallout of their implicit support for what most northern courts had long since decided: that blacks were entitled to the privileges and immunities of citizenship, in their states as well as their nation. On several occasions Lincoln actually did dispute Taney's citizenship ruling, but in a way that seemed calculated not to raise a racist ruckus. He pointed out, for example, that under Taney's preposterous rule immigrants who came to America after 1789 could never be national citizens. Nevertheless, Lincoln had learned his lesson. Not until he became president would he dare reopen the issue of black citizenship.

But reopen it Lincoln did, at the very moment he assumed the presidency. Lincoln inserted into his inaugural address an endorsement of black citizenship rights that could not be misunderstood by anyone familiar with the political struggles of the previous decade. As it had in the early 1850s the issue of black rights arose out of the controversy regarding the enforcement mechanisms of the Fugitive Slave Act. In his inaugural address Lincoln reaffirmed the government's constitutional obligation to facilitate the return of fugitive slaves. Nobody disputes this obligation, Lincoln declared. Then, having stepped so carefully around this very old wound, Lincoln began to pick relentlessly at the scab. There was, he pointed out, "some difference of opinion" about whether the constitutional obligation to return fugitives should be fulfilled by the states or by the national government. This was an understatement. What made the 1850 law so notorious to so many was precisely that it had taken jurisdiction away from the states. Lincoln was threatening to revise the 1850 law in a way that would restore the due process rights of free blacks in the North.[34]

In case anyone missed the larger meaning of his words, Lincoln spelled it out clearly in the next paragraph. In "any law upon this subject," he said, "ought not all the safeguards of liberty known in civilized and humane jurisprudence to be introduced, so that a free man be not, in any case, surrendered as a slave?" Beyond the matter of humane and civilized jurisprudence, Lincoln added, was the matter of citizenship itself. Even as we enforce the fugitive slave clause of the Constitution, he said, "might it not be well, at the same time, to provide by law for the enforcement of that clause in the Constitution which guarantees that 'The citizens of each State shall be entitled to all the privileges and immunities of the citizens in the several States?' "[35] Sitting behind Lincoln as he uttered these words were Chief Justice Roger Taney and Illinois Senator Stephen A. Douglas. Had Lincoln turned around and slapped both men in their faces his repudiation of them could not have been more startling.

What Lincoln hinted at in his inaugural address his administration formally proclaimed a year and a half later. In late 1862, with an emancipation policy about to be implemented, the citizenship status of the freed people became an urgent question. Lincoln's treasury secretary, Salmon P. Chase, sent a request to Edward Bates, the attorney general, asking whether, as a matter of policy, "colored men [are] citizens of the United States." Chase's letter was apparently prompted by an immediate issue. Federal licensing laws required that all masters of vessels plying the coastal trade be citizens, but many of those masters were black. If they were not citizens they could lose their licenses. But there was a longer history to Chase's question as well. The same issue had arisen back in 1821, and then Attorney General William Wirt had published an influential ruling that blacks were not citizens. Although it was not a judicial decision, Wirt's opinion may have been the most important official ruling on black citizenship before the *Dred Scott* case. So Chase was actually asking for much more than an answer to the relatively narrow question of whether blacks could be licensed or not.

In reply Bates produced an astonishing document, nearly thirty pages long, repudiating everything William Wirt and Chief Justice Taney had to say about black citizenship. In the first place, Bates ruled, there is nothing in the Constitution that so much as hints at gradations of citizenship, hence there can be no such thing as "full" as opposed to "partial" citizenship. Moreover, the Constitution "says not one word, and furnishes not one hint, in relation to the color or to the ancestral race" of citizens. Every person born free on American soil was, "at the moment of birth, prima facie a citizen."[36]

Taney had claimed that state statutes discriminating against blacks proved that they were not considered citizens. This could not possibly be true, the attorney general asserted, for among other things it would mean the laws prohibiting whites from marrying blacks excluded whites from citizenship. But Bates rejected any racial qualifications for citizenship, particularly the claim that blacks could not be citizens even if they had been born in the country. "As far as the Constitution is concerned, this is a naked assumption," Bates declared, "for the Constitution contains not one word upon the subject." Some people worried that if a black man can be a citizen he could also become the president, but those who object to black citizenship on that ground "are not arguing upon the Constitution as it is, but upon what, in their own minds and feelings, they think it ought to be." Anyone who was born free on American soil was a citizen, no matter what.

But the attorney general went still further in asserting the legal primacy of national over state citizenship. By tradition the nation recognized state citizenship while requiring other states to do the same. But Bates claimed something different. The privileges and immunities granted to citizens of the United States "cannot be destroyed or abridged by the laws of any particular state," Bates reasoned. On this point, he said, the Constitution "is plain beyond cavil." Citizenship in the United States is "an integral thing"; it cannot be "fractionalized," broken down into parts; it cannot mean one thing in one state and something else in another state. In sum, Bates concluded, blacks were full citizens of the United States and the privileges and immunities attaching to their citizenship could not be abridged by the states. If that were not enough, Bates closed his decision by flicking *Dred Scott* away like a piece of lint. Once the Supreme Court ruled that Scott was a slave there was no need for the justices to say another word, Bates declared, hence everything Taney had to say about citizenship was "of no authority as a judicial decision."

For all the rhetorical effervescence of Bates's opinion, its practical effect was limited. An attorney general's ruling serves as a statement of the administration's policy, but it has neither the force of statute nor the weight of judicial precedent. Bates's opinion almost certainly reflected the president's thinking, and it did have some effect. Chase's initial inquiry was prompted by a problem that required immediate resolution. Bates ruled that African Americans in command of vessels trading along the coast were citizens, and the issue was settled. There are also strong indications in Bates's ruling as well as his diary that the Lincoln administration began issuing passports to blacks, reversing the decision handed down a few years earlier by Caleb Cushing, the attorney general in James Buchanan's administration.[37]

But the Bates opinion was influential beyond its practical consequences. Antislavery radicals like Frederick Douglass quoted it extensively as they pressed their demand that the freed slaves be granted all the rights, privileges, and immunities of full citizenship. Charles Sumner and others were guided by the Bates decision when they moved to shore it up with a civil rights law and, later, a constitutional amendment. Such legal moves were a tacit recognition of the broad implications but insecure foundation of Bates's ruling. The next administration could overturn Bates as readily as he had overturned his predecessor. Fearing this possibility, Congress passed the Civil Rights Act of 1866, which gave the Bates ruling the force of statute law. But Lincoln's successor, Andrew Johnson, vetoed the bill, and although Congress overrode him, it realized that something even stronger than a statute was needed. The result was the Fourteenth Amendment, which completed the reversal of the *Dred Scott* decision begun by the Lincoln administration.

The Rights of States

By imposing an egalitarian citizenship nationwide the Lincoln administration seemed to vindicate the Democrats' assertion that Republicans were intent on destroying the rights of states. When he wasn't accusing Lincoln of favoring the "amalgamation" of the races, for example, Stephen Douglas charged that Lincoln would impose a uniform set of laws and customs across America, undermining the great principle of popular sovereignty that had traditionally left the states and territories free to organize their domestic institutions as they saw fit. Lincoln left himself open to this charge when he said that if slavery was wrong anywhere it was wrong everywhere, that the principles of the Declaration were national not local, that fundamental human equality meant that every citizen in America was entitled to the same basic rights. In his House Divided speech, when he said that the nation could not remain half slave and half free, that it would either become all one or all the other, Lincoln practically invited Douglas's attack. And because Lincoln did come out of a Whig tradition that favored a stronger central government, because as president he rode roughshod over the rights of states and individuals alike, because he presided over a significant and in some cases permanent increase in the size and power of the federal bureaucracy, historians have been content to let Douglas's accusation stand.

But even if we allow for the inconsistencies that inhere in being a politician, Lincoln was never the relentless centralizer Douglas made him out to be. Except for his claim to grandiose war powers, which shrank back down to size once the war ended, Lincoln always denied any impulse to meddle in matters that belonged rightfully to the states. True, he rejected the extreme states' rights dogma that reduced the Union to a mere compact of individual states or that rewrote the Declaration of Independence as though natural rights inhered in states rather than persons. Still, in every "fragment on government" he jotted down, every passing remark he made about the relative powers of individuals, states, and the nation, Lincoln was careful to respect the rights of states to determine their own "domestic" affairs. "I am for the people of the whole nation doing just as they please in all matters which concern the whole nation," Lincoln explained in 1858, "for those of each part doing just as they choose in all matters which concern no other part; and for each individual doing just as he chooses in all matters which concern nobody else."[38] There were a few obligations, basic but crucial, that belonged to the people as a whole acting through the national government. But some things were best left to individuals, others were the prerogative of communities, and still others belonged rightfully to states.

Slavery was unusual in this regard. The nation's founding principles condemned it as wrong everywhere, but the founders themselves made slavery an "exception" because they believed that "the actually existing state of things" made it "a necessity" to recognize its existence within the states. But although the federal government was obliged out of "necessity" to respect it, slavery was nevertheless a strictly local institution.[39] It did not even come under the protection of the constitutional right of property. One of Lincoln's objections to the *Dred Scott* decision was that it allowed masters to take their slaves into western territories "in disregard of the local laws to the contrary." The Supreme Court thereby overturned the long-standing legal principle whereby slavery was "confined to those states where it is established by local law."[40] When Douglas insisted that the states should be free to arrange their domestic institutions however they chose, "including that of slavery," Lincoln's short reply was: "I entirely agree with him." He held himself "under constitutional obligations" to allow the people in the states to regulate slavery "exactly as they please."[41] At issue was not slavery in the states, Lincoln said, but slavery in the territories.

So great was Lincoln's reluctance to interfere with the rights of states and localities that he was willing to respect slavery's existence beyond his strictly constitutional obligation to do so. He believed Congress had a constitutional right to abolish slavery in the District of Columbia, for example, but he thought it imprudent to do so unless abolition was submitted for ratification to the district's voters.[42] Lincoln did not know if Congress had the right to interfere with the domestic slave trade; he had never thought about it, he said. But if Congress did have the power, he added, "I should still not be in favor of the exercise of it."[43] Douglas was chasing phantoms. Notwithstanding "all his eloquence in behalf of the rights of States," Lincoln insisted, those rights "are assailed by no living man."[44]

Racial discrimination was even more clearly the prerogative of the states. The principles of fundamental human equality were universal, and the privileges and immunities of citizenship were national. But beyond these were a whole series of "domestic" regulations that had nothing to do with natural rights and were not among the privileges and immunities of citizenship. They included, most importantly, voting privileges, qualifications for officeholding, access to public education, the laws of marriage, and eligibility for jury service. It was all but universally agreed that such matters were not the federal government's business. Certainly Lincoln agreed. Who could vote, who could hold state office, who could marry whom, who could or could not attend public school, who could or could not serve on juries: These questions were answered in different ways by different state legislatures. In those answers the various states introduced into American law a vast mosaic of racial, ethnic, and gender discriminations. And in deferring to the states on these and other "domestic" matters, Lincoln necessarily deferred to discrimination as well.

In all his years of public service Lincoln made only two extended pronouncements about race relations—the first in his Peoria speech of 1854, the second at the opening of the Charleston debate four years later.[45] When critics demanded that he explain his position, Lincoln was inclined to quote one or both of the two statements he had already made. He also made dozens of fleeting remarks, including "darky" jokes, uses of the word *nigger*, brief statements to the effect that blacks and whites could not live together as equals, but most of these are too short or too ambiguous to support sustained analysis.[46] So the Peoria and Charleston statements have become the touchstones for every examination of Lincoln's views on race. They are among the most familiar and disturbing passages in the Lincoln canon. Here's what he said at Peoria:[47]

> My first impulse would be to free all the slaves, and send them to Liberia,—to their own native land. But a moment's reflection would convince me, that whatever of high hope, (as I think there is) there may be in this, in the long run, its sudden execution is impossible. If they were all landed there in a day, they would all perish in the next ten days; and there are not surplus shipping and surplus money enough in the world to carry them there in many times ten days. What then? Free them all, and keep them among us as underlings? Is it quite certain that this betters their condition? I think I would not hold one in slavery, at any rate; yet the point is not clear enough for me to denounce people upon. What next? Free them, and make them politically and socially, our equals? My own feelings will not admit of this; and if mine would, we well know that those of the great mass of white people will not. Whether this feeling accords with justice and sound judgment, is not the sole question, if indeed, it is any part of it. A universal feeling, whether well or ill-founded, can not be safely disregarded. We can not, then, make them equals.

This is as clear as mud. Lincoln would free the slaves, but not make them politically and socially the equals of whites. What does that mean? Fundamental human equality was the principle Lincoln always cited to justify his objection to slavery. The statement can make sense only if political and social equality were regulated at some level other than natural rights. But as Lincoln did not say what he meant by political and social equality there is no way to tell from the Peoria statement exactly what he had in mind. Here and there Lincoln dropped hints about what he was referring to; more often he simply repeated his vague support for the social and political inequality of blacks and whites. But he did not specify the forms of inequality until 1858, during his fourth debate with Douglas at Charleston, when Lincoln said this:[48]

> I will say then that I am not, nor ever have been in favor of bringing about in any way the social and political equality of the white and black races, [applause]—that I am not nor ever have been in favor of making voters or jurors of negroes, nor of qualifying them to hold office, nor to inter-marry with white people; and I will say in addition to this that there is a physical difference between the white and black races which I believe will for ever forbid the two races living together on terms of social and polit-ical equality. And inasmuch as they cannot so live, while they do remain together there must be the position of superior and inferior, and I as much as any other man am in favor of having the superior position assigned to the white race.

Here at last Lincoln said what he meant by social and political inequal-ity. He listed four specific areas in which he would support discrimination against blacks: voting, serving on juries, holding elective office, and "intermarriage" with whites. Each one of these was regulated by the states. None ranked among the natural rights; no one believed there was a natural right to vote, hold office, marry a white person, or sit on a jury. Nor were they among the traditional privileges and immunities of citi-zenship. None of the discriminations that Lincoln endorsed would deprive blacks of the right to own or convey property; to speak, publish, or assemble freely; to worship as they chose. Blacks might be excluded from the jury box, but they could not be denied the right to trial by jury, the right against self-incrimination, or the right to face their accusers. Nor could blacks be imprisoned unless formally charged with a crime. Natural rights and the privileges and immunities of citizenship were national, guaranteed by the Constitution to blacks and whites alike and therefore invulnerable to the wishes of the states. The discrimination that remained, the social and political inequality that Lincoln endorsed, was imposed by state legislatures.

To what extent was Lincoln's endorsement of racial discrimination the product of his prejudice and to what extent was it the product of his com-

mitment to the rights of states? Sometimes Lincoln came close to equating discrimination with states' rights. At Ottawa Lincoln denied that in
opposing slavery he "was doing anything to bring about a political and
social equality of the black and white races. It never occurred to me," he
added, "that I was doing anything or favoring anything to reduce to a
dead uniformity all the local institutions of the various states."[49] But the
fact that a state could discriminate did not mean that it should. Lincoln
would not, for example, endorse the kind of legislation that Massachusetts had recently passed discriminating against immigrants. Massachusetts had every right to pass the law, he said; it "is a sovereign and
independent state; and it is no privilege of mine to scold her for what she
does. Still," Lincoln said, "I am against its adoption in Illinois, or in any
other place where I have a right to oppose it."[50] Lincoln opposed state
laws discriminating against immigrants while supporting those against
blacks. So although discrimination was a prerogative of states' rights, it
was not merely a matter of states' rights.

Prejudice is the obvious explanation for Lincoln's readiness to endorse
racial and oppose ethnic discrimination, but it is probably not the entire
explanation. Hostility to immigrants was politically popular in Massachusetts but much less so in Illinois where intense antiblack racism was
more widespread. The distinctive patterns of social and political discrimination in the two states reflected the preferences of their respective voters. The racist statutes passed by the Illinois legislature were undoubtedly
the will of the state's voting majority, and in a democratic society the will
of the majority is not easily disregarded. Lincoln said as much at Peoria.
His own feelings, he said, "will not admit" the social and political equality of blacks, and even if they did, "we well know that those of the great
mass of white people will not." He readily conceded the possibility that
such "feelings" might be unsound and unjust. Nevertheless, a "universal
feeling, whether well or ill-founded, can not be safely disregarded. We
can not, then, make them equals."[51] No doubt Lincoln was caving in to
popular prejudices; no doubt he shared many of the prejudices himself.
But he believed in democracy, and in this case he was also deferring to the
clearly expressed will of the state's electoral majority.

It never seems to have occurred to Lincoln that the racial discriminations he endorsed might undermine the ability of blacks to pursue their
happiness or that they would diminish the privileges and immunities of
citizenship. He spoke eloquently of a society in which everyone had a

"fair chance in the race of life," but how fair could the race be in a society where black children were denied equal access to public school educations? Self-government, Lincoln often said, was the guiding principle of his political philosophy, but apparently he did not think the principle was compromised by state laws that excluded blacks from voting and holding elective office. Ever since 1821, when Missouri submitted a constitution that prohibited free blacks from moving into the state, opponents of slavery objected to such laws as a clear violation of every citizen's right to move freely from one state to another. But the only time Lincoln referred to such laws was in a private letter in which he expressed concern about Republicans who publicly opposed them. If he believed that state laws barring blacks from serving on juries in any way compromised the right to trial by jury, he kept the belief entirely to himself. There's an unnerving legalism about the distinction Lincoln drew between the equality of rights and citizenship and a state legislature's authority to discriminate. Free blacks could enjoy their natural rights and exercise the privileges and immunities of citizenship only within the states where they actually lived. When those states imposed a raft of legal discriminations on free blacks, they diminished the meaning of freedom and the value of citizenship.

Yet in restricting racial discrimination to the states Lincoln may have immunized his presidency from it. At one point in his 1858 campaign for the Senate Lincoln ridiculed Douglas for his obsession with the prospect of black voters, black jurors, and racial intermarriage. These, Lincoln said, are state matters, and if his supporters are so concerned about them, they should elect Douglas to the Illinois legislature and send Lincoln to the U.S. Senate. This helps explain a curious disjunction between the fact of Lincoln's racial prejudice and the significance of it. Freedom was a universal right, and citizenship was national; but discrimination was local. If the inequalities that Douglas was so anxious to preserve were enacted solely within the states, it should come as no surprise that they were of little or no consequence to the Lincoln administration in Washington. In addition to the restoration of the Union, the greatest achievements of his presidency, the policies that were of the most enduring significance, include emancipation, the enlistment of black troops, and the emphatic reassertion of black citizenship. These are best explained by reference to Lincoln's firm belief that blacks and whites were equally entitled to both natural rights and the privileges and immunities of citizenship.

It would be hard to name a single major policy implemented by the Lincoln administration that can be helpfully explained by reference to his racial prejudices. The most likely candidate is Lincoln's support for laws to facilitate the colonization of blacks outside the United States.[52] But Lincoln's record on this raises as many questions as it answers. For one thing, what he meant by "colonization" when he first spoke at length about it in 1852 seems very different from what he meant the last time he spoke publicly about it ten years later. By 1854 he had publicly admitted that it was both impractical and immoral to forcibly remove black Americans to Africa, yet he continued to endorse a voluntary migration to either Central America or the Caribbean. We can only speculate what it was that led him to believe that a mass emigration of four million blacks was a practical possibility, but I suspect he had two precedents in mind: the voluntary westward migration of millions of Americans and the voluntary immigration of millions of Irish and Germans. Both were matters of great public concern during his years as a practicing politician, and they may have left Lincoln with the sense that a similar pattern of voluntary mass migration was possible for blacks. One hint that this might be the case was the paradoxically egalitarian terms in which he spoke of black colonization. Where Stephen Douglas and most Democrats insisted that blacks were incapable of self-government, Lincoln spoke of a black colony that would provide the world with a second shining example of successful democratic republicanism. In addition, Lincoln spoke of such a colony as a place where blacks would be free to pursue the opportunities that were denied them in the United States by the entrenched prejudices of whites. Thus Lincoln's call for the voluntary emigration of blacks was grounded in a pessimistic assessment of the intractability of white racism more than his own racial prejudice. Although Lincoln stopped publicly advocating colonization in late 1862, he probably never stopped believing it was the best solution for all concerned.

One reason we can never be certain of what Lincoln had in mind is that colonization never blossomed into a major policy of his administration. The funds Congress appropriated for his plans were paltry, and Lincoln spent only a fraction of those. The plans that did exist were largely stillborn. The Chiriquí colony proposed for Central America collapsed before it got started. About five hundred voluntary migrants went to a different colony at Île à Vache, but most of those returned to America after a year or two. And that was it. To put those five hundred colonists in some perspective, there were fifty thousand casualties at Gettysburg, and four million slaves were emancipated. Even after due consideration is given to Lincoln's scheme of colonization, it remains unclear whether any of his adminstration's major policies are helpfully explained by reference to his racial prejudices. The best way to gauge the significance of Lincoln's views on race is to recognize that most of the discriminations he endorsed fell under the purview of the states.

In one crucial respect Lincoln's commitment to states' rights actually facilitated the most important policy of his administration, emancipation. Ever since John Quincy Adams made the argument in the 1830s, many Whigs—and later Republicans—believed that slavery was merely a state or "municipal" institution. In Adams's view, as in Lincoln's, slave "property" was entirely a creation of the states, and as such it did not fall under the protection of the constitutional right to property. The Constitution restrained the federal government from interfering with slave property out of necessity, but if the southern states seceded, the federal government was freed from its obligation to respect state-created slave property. In a case of open rebellion against the Union the war powers of the federal government could be used to emancipate the slaves, precisely because slavery was a state rather than a national institution. The same logic that led Lincoln to forswear any interference with slavery—that it was strictly a matter for the states to decide—doubled back during the war and became the legal basis for emancipation.

On the other hand, Lincoln's toleration of racial discrimination in the states contributed to the sharp disagreement that erupted between Lincoln and the Congress over their competing plans for Reconstruction. Congressional radicals were more willing than Lincoln to impose stringent conditions on the defeated Confederate states. They saw, long before the president did, that emancipation unaccompanied by political and civil rights would be meaningless at best and most likely murderous. If the freed people could not vote, serve on juries, or hold office as sheriffs, county commissioners, or justices of the peace, white southerners would be able to make the privileges and immunities of citizenship all but meaningless. Although he was moving in a radical direction before he died, it remained an article of faith for Lincoln that political and civil rights were established by the states.

The contradiction that so frustrated Stephen Douglas never disappeared. Lincoln was unfailingly eloquent on the universal right of all men and women to the fruits of their labor, he found his way toward a radical endorsement of citizenship rights for blacks, but not until the final years of his life did he begin to realize that for most black Americans a lifetime of hard work and the joys of citizenship could be undone by the toxic effects of racial discrimination in the states.

6

Lincoln and Colonization

Eric Foner

Abraham Lincoln, whose command of the English language surpassed that of nearly every other American president, did not produce a book during his lifetime (unless one counts the manuscript denying the divinity of the Bible that according to local lore, he wrote in New Salem, Illinois, in the 1830s and then destroyed at the urging of friends).[1] Lincoln did, however, put together two volumes of his speeches. One reproduced the Lincoln-Douglas debates. Less well known is his compilation of excerpts dealing with "negro equality."

During the 1858 Senate campaign in Illinois, Democrats persistently represented Lincoln as an abolitionist who favored "the equality of the races, politically and socially." All Republican speakers, his political adviser David Davis insisted, must "distinctly and emphatically disavow negro suffrage, negro holding office, serving on juries, and the like." William Brown, like Lincoln a former Whig member of the Illinois legislature, was running as the Republican candidate for his old seat. In October 1858, Brown asked Lincoln for material he could use to fend off Democratic charges. Lincoln assembled a scrapbook of passages that, he wrote, "contain the substance of all I have ever said about 'negro equality,'" beginning with excerpts from his celebrated Peoria speech of 1854 and ending with selections from the recent debates. Brown used the collection during the last weeks of the campaign, but both he and Lincoln lost their races. The volume remained in the possession of Brown's family until 1900, when a collector purchased it. It appeared in print three years later with the charmingly old-fashioned title *Abraham Lincoln: His Book*.[2]

In a letter to Brown, Lincoln explained his stance on racial equality. "I think the negro," he wrote, "is included in the word 'men' used in the Declaration of Independence," and that slavery was therefore wrong. But inalienable natural rights were one thing, political and social rights quite another. As Lincoln explained, "I have expressly disclaimed all intention to bring about social and political equality between the white and black races." This position distinguished Lincoln from the abolitionists, who advocated the incorporation of blacks as equal members of American society, and from Democrats like his rival Stephen A. Douglas, who insisted that the language of the Declaration applied only to whites. And what did Lincoln believe should become of black Americans when slavery ended? He included in his book a passage from the Peoria speech that envisioned their return to Africa, which he called "their own native land," even though by this time nearly all the slaves had been born in the United States.[3]

Lincoln's embrace of colonization—the government-promoted settlement of black Americans in Africa or some other location—was no passing fancy. He advocated the policy a number of times during the 1850s and pursued it avidly during the first two years of the Civil War. In his annual message to Congress of December 1862, Lincoln stated bluntly, "I cannot make it better known than it already is, that I strongly favor colonization." Gideon Welles, the wartime secretary of the navy, later wrote that Lincoln considered colonization "inseparable" from emancipation. Welles chided "historians, biographers," and other commentators for making "slight, if any, allusion to it." This remains the case nearly a century and a half after Lincoln's death. True, for scholars like Lerone Bennett, who see Lincoln as an inveterate racist, colonization serves as exhibit number one. For Lincoln's far larger cadre of admirers, however, no aspect of his life has proved more puzzling. Don Fehrenbacher calls Lincoln's zeal in promoting colonization the "strangest feature" of his career. Many historians find it impossible to reconcile Lincoln's belief in colonization with his strong moral dislike of slavery. They either ignore his advocacy of the policy or fall back on the explanation that as a consummate pragmatist Lincoln could not have been serious about the idea of settling the African American population outside the country.[4]

David Donald, who insists that until "well into his presidency" Lincoln really did believe in colonization, is one of the few recent scholars to take Lincoln at his word. Most others contend that Lincoln promoted colonization as a "public relations" strategy, a way of deflecting racist attacks on the Republican Party and his administration and defusing public resistance to emancipation. One problem with this explanation is that Lincoln's advocacy of colonization predated not only his presidency but his emergence as an antislavery politician. He had pretty much dropped out of politics when he spoke enthusiastically about colonization in his 1852 eulogy of Henry Clay.[5]

I.

A new look at Lincoln and colonization must begin by taking colonization seriously as a political movement that enjoyed remarkably broad support before and during the Civil War. Under the rubric of colonization, nineteenth-century Americans put forward a wide variety of programs, some voluntary, some compulsory, for removing free blacks and slaves from the country. Absurd as the plan may appear in retrospect, it seemed quite realistic to its advocates. Many large groups had been expelled from their homelands in modern times—for example, Spanish Muslims and Jews after 1492 and Acadians during the Seven Years' War. Virtually the entire Indian population east of the Mississippi River had been removed by 1840. The mass migration of peoples was hardly unknown in the nineteenth century. In the decade following the famine of the 1840s an estimated two million men, women, and children emigrated from Ireland. In 1850 the prospect of colonizing the three million American slaves and free blacks seemed less unrealistic than immediate abolition.

The notion of settling groups of New World blacks in Africa was a truly Atlantic idea, with advocates in the United States, the West Indies, Great Britain, and Africa itself. But as *Harper's Weekly* pointed out in 1862, nowhere else in the Western Hemisphere was it proposed "to extirpate the slaves after emancipation." Indeed postemancipation societies like Jamaica, Trinidad, and British Guiana desperately strove to keep the freed people from leaving the plantations. They supplemented their labor with immigrants, free and indentured, from Europe or Asia but never considered shipping the emancipated slaves en masse elsewhere.[6]

Colonization was hardly a fringe movement. "Almost every respectable man," Frederick Douglass observed, belonged to or supported the American Colonization Society. Henry Clay and Thomas Jefferson, the statesmen most revered by Lincoln, favored colonization. So, at one time or another, did John Marshall, James Madison, Daniel Webster, Andrew Jackson, Roger B. Taney, and even Harriet Beecher Stowe (whose abolitionist novel *Uncle Tom's Cabin* ends with the hero, George Harris, affirming his "African nationality" and emigrating from the United States). In an era of nation building, colonization formed part of a long debate about what kind of nation the United States was to be. It allowed its advocates to imagine a society freed from both slavery and the unwanted presence of blacks. Taking the nineteenth century as a whole, colonization needs to be viewed in the context of other plans to determine the racial makeup of American society, including Indian removal and, later, Chinese exclusion. As late as 1862 the House Committee on Emancipation and Colonization called for the removal of blacks so that "the whole country" could be occupied by whites alone.[7]

The idea of removing emancipated slaves has a long history. As early as 1715, John Hepburn, a New Jersey Quaker, published a tract advocating freeing the slaves, giving them an education, and returning them to Africa to promote the spread of Christian civilization. During the 1770s and 1780s blacks in Massachusetts and Rhode Island formulated plans for establishing an African settlement. The emigrants' virtue and industry, they argued, would refute racist assumptions about black incapacity, and by bringing Christianity, they would rescue Africans from the "heathenish darkness" in which they supposedly lived. In 1788, a year after helping to write the Constitution, James Madison proposed the creation of an African colony to promote manumission in the United States.[8]

Nearly all advocates of abolition in the revolutionary era Chesapeake, including Thomas Jefferson, believed that the end of slavery must be accompanied by the removal of the black population. Jefferson prefaced his famous discussion of blacks' physical and intellectual capacities in *Notes on the State of Virginia* with an elaborate plan for gradual emancipation and colonization. Children born to slaves after a certain date would be educated at public expense, supplied with "arms, implements of household and of the handicraft arts, seeds, pairs of the useful domestic animals," and everything else necessary for them to thrive as a "free and independent people," and transported to Africa. Simultaneously, ships would be dispatched to other parts of the world to bring to the United States an "equal number of white inhabitants." Jefferson acknowledged that it seemed pointless to go to all this trouble to "replace one group of laborers with another." But, he warned, without colonization the end of slavery would be succeeded by racial warfare or, worse, racial "mixture." To his dying day, Jefferson remained committed to colonization. In 1824 he proposed that the federal government purchase and deport "the increase of each year" (that is, children), so that the slave population would age and eventually disappear. Jefferson, who frequently waxed sentimental about the idea of family, acknowledged that some might object on humanitarian grounds to "the separation of infants from their mothers." But this, he insisted, would be "straining at a gnat."[9]

The first emancipation—the gradual abolition of slavery in the North—was not coupled with colonization. It seems to have been assumed that the former slaves would somehow be absorbed into society. But the rapid growth of the free black population in the early republic spurred believers in a white America to action. Founded in 1816, the American Colonization Society (ACS) at first directed its efforts at removing blacks already free. At the meeting in the nation's capital that launched the society, John Randolph of Roanoke insisted that the removal of this dangerous group would "materially tend to secure" the value of slave property. The ACS was initially called the American Society for Colonizing the Free People of Color of the United States. Nonetheless, colonizationists frequently spoke of abolishing slavery gradually, peacefully, and without sectional conflict. Upper South planters and political leaders whose commitment to slavery appeared suspect dominated the ACS. None was more adamant in linking colonization with abolition than Henry Clay.[10]

Although a slaveholder, Clay throughout his career condemned slavery as an evil while also insisting that precipitous emancipation would create an uncontrollable population of free blacks (whom he described as "a debased and degraded set," while disclaiming any desire to "wound their feelings"). Clay began his political career in 1799 by unsuccessfully urging the Kentucky constitutional convention to adopt a plan of gradual emancipation. Fifty years later the state again revised its constitution, and Clay, now one of the country's leading statesmen, put forward a detailed proposal. Beginning in 1855 or 1860, children born to slaves would become free at age twenty-five. Colonization of those emancipated was "absolutely indispensable" to the plan; otherwise "amalgamation—that revolting admixture, alike offensive to God and man," was sure to follow. Clay included a provision that until his scheme went into effect, owners would retain the right to sell slaves out of the state, thus suggesting that benefiting slaves and their children was not among his priorities. Nonetheless, the presentation of colonization as an adjunct of abolition by Clay and others helps explain why hostility to colonization became more and more intense in the Deep South.[11]

Gradual emancipation coupled with colonization formed one part of Clay's American System, his plan for regional and national economic development that he hoped would reorient Kentucky into a modern, diversified economy modeled on the free labor North. Slavery, he insisted, was why Kentucky lagged behind neighboring states in manufacturing and general prosperity. Clay succeeded James Madison as president of the ACS in 1836 and served until his own death sixteen years later. ("He is president of nothing else," quipped Frederick Douglass.) Lincoln was in the audience in Lexington, Kentucky, in November 1847, when Clay declared slavery "a great evil" and opposed the acquisition of new territory that might lead to its expansion but rejected freeing the slaves and allowing them to remain in the country as equals. In the speech, Clay called for the gradual end of slavery and identified the American Colonization Society as an organization of "unmixed benevolence." For almost his entire career Lincoln's outlook on slavery closely paralleled that of Clay.[12]

Recent literature has emphasized the complex, indeed contradictory appeals colonizationists used in generating support for their cause. Advocates of colonization portrayed blacks, sometimes in the same breath, as depraved and dangerous outsiders, Christian imperialists, a class wronged by slavery, potential trading partners, and redeemers of Africa. The one constant was that they could not remain in America. Leonard Bacon, pastor of the First Congregational Church of New Haven, wrote that racism condemned American blacks, free or slave, to irremediable and permanent "degradation." But in Africa they would be transformed into the carriers of modern civilization and Christianity and would achieve "real freedom" for themselves. Unlike Jefferson, most proponents of colonization believed in the mutability of human character. They insisted that blacks' status as slaves and unequal free persons arose from racism, not innate incapacity. Indeed colonizationists and abolitionists agreed on one thing: that black men and women had the capacity for improvement. As one colonization publication put it, "there is nothing in the physical, or moral nature of the African, which condemns him to a state of ignorance and degradation. . . . Light and liberty can, and do, under fair circumstances, raise him to the rank of a virtuous and intelligent being."[13] But those "fair circumstances" could never be achieved in America.

Their actual practice often contradicted colonizationists' claim to have the best interests of blacks at heart. They opposed efforts to expand free blacks' political and civil rights, fearing that such improvements in their condition would make them less willing to emigrate. It was best, declared Elias B. Caldwell, secretary of the ACS, to keep blacks "in the lowest state of degradation and ignorance" rather than encourage hopes of advancement in the United States. The ACS proved remarkably indifferent to the welfare of those it sent abroad. Emigrants suffered a high death rate from tropical disease. Long after it was clear that they had a better chance of survival if they settled at sites on high ground, the ACS regularly unloaded them at Monrovia, the malaria-infested coastal capital of Liberia.[14]

Of course some African Americans shared the perspective of the colonization movement. Almost every printed report of the ACS included testimonials from blacks who either had gone to Africa or were anxious to do so. The ACS relied heavily on such statements to develop support for its program. In 1815 the black sea captain Paul Cuffe settled small groups of black Americans in Sierra Leone. John Russwurm, who in 1827 founded *Freedom's Journal*, the nation's first black newspaper, abandoned it after two years and moved to Liberia. In his final editorial, he explained why: "We consider it a waste of mere words to talk of ever enjoying citizenship in this country; it is utterly impossible in the nature of things."[15]

It is often forgotten that between the Revolution and Civil War, more blacks left the United States under other auspices than via the ACS. From 1816 to 1860 the ACS transported to Africa around eleven thousand people, mostly slaves manumitted by their owners for the express purpose of removal to Liberia. But between fifteen and twenty thousand escaped slaves evacuated with the British at the end of the War of Independence. They ended up in Nova Scotia, Sierra Leone, the West Indies, and even the German state of Hesse (home of the notorious Hessians). During the 1820s several thousand black Americans emigrated to Haiti, whose government promised newcomers political rights and economic opportunity in the world's only independent black republic. The movement waned by the end of the decade, but the passage of the Fugitive Slave Act of 1850 created a crisis that led to the relocation of thousands of African Americans to Canada and rekindled interest in emigration to Africa.[16] When presented with a choice between slavery in the United States and freedom elsewhere, many blacks chose freedom.

Throughout the nineteenth century, however, most black Americans rejected both voluntary emigration and government-sponsored efforts to encourage or coerce the entire black population to leave the country. The similarities between the rhetoric of colonizationists and black emigrationists ought not to obscure the historical importance of the black mobilization against colonization that began immediately after the foundation of the ACS and continued through the Civil War. Indeed black hostility to colonization was one of the key catalysts for the rise of immediate abolitionism in the late 1820s and 1830s. The difference between colonization and abolitionism lay not only in their approach to getting rid of slavery but in their view as to whether blacks could hope to achieve equal citizenship in this country.

Recent work on the early republic has emphasized the persistence of abolitionist sentiment among both white reformers and free blacks. But the organized movements to eliminate slavery were white-dominated, gradualist, and linked to colonization. The militant abolitionism that emerged in the 1830s was different: immediatist, interracial, and committed to making the United States a biracial nation. This movement arose as the joining of two impulses: black anticolonization and white evangelicism and perfectionism. The founding of the ACS was quickly followed by a gathering of three thousand blacks in Philadelphia, who condemned the new society. The prominent black leaders James Forten and Richard Allen, who had supported Paul Cuffe's plan for emigration to Africa, were forced to reconsider their views because of the popular upsurge against colonization. The majority was "decidedly against me," Forten wrote. Through the attack on colonization, the modern idea of equality as something that knows no racial boundaries was born. In asserting their own Americanness, free blacks articulated a new vision of American society as a land of birthright citizenship and equality before the law, where rights did not depend on color, ancestry, or racial designation. They denied that racism was immutable, that a nation must be racially homogeneous, and that color formed an insurmountable barrier to equality. Antebellum black conventions regularly denounced colonization as a "gigantic fraud," an "evil trick," and the like. "We are Americans," declared the address of the Rochester Colored Convention of 1853. It spoke of blacks "not as aliens nor as exiles, but as American citizens asserting their rights on their native soil."[17]

David Walker's *Appeal*, a key document of radical abolitionism published in 1829, devoted its longest chapter to attacking the idea of colonization. America, Walker proclaimed, "is more our country, than it is the whites—we have enriched it with our blood and tears." He agreed with colonizationists that blacks lived in "abject" circumstances, but the cause was "the inhuman system of slavery," not innate incapacity or immutable prejudice. America, he proclaimed, could become an interracial society of equals. Walker confronted the most prominent advocates of colonization head-on. He devoted several pages to refuting Jefferson's musings on race in *Notes on the State of Virginia*. Jefferson had labeled blacks mentally inferior. "It is indeed surprising," Walker responded, "that a man of such great learning, combined with such excellent natural parts, should speak so of a set of men in chains." He blamed Jefferson for an increase in racism: "Mr. Jefferson's remarks respecting us, have sunk deep into the hearts of millions of the whites." Walker also cited Henry Clay's speech to the founding meeting of the ACS. Clay, he insisted, was not "a friend to the blacks. . . . [Slaves] work his plantation to enrich him and his family."[18]

The black response to colonization powerfully affected white abolitionists. In his influential pamphlet *Thoughts on African Colonization*, William Lloyd Garrison explained that his experience with the vibrant black communities of Baltimore and Boston inspired his conversion from colonization to abolition and racial equality. Like the ACS, Garrison compiled black statements—resolutions, addresses, letters—this time opposing colonization. The most potent objection to the idea, he wrote, was that it "is directly and irreconcilably opposed to the wishes of our colored population as a body." White abolitionists of the 1830s, most of whom had previously been sympathetic to colonization, now denounced the ACS for intensifying racial prejudice in America. Lewis Tappan, another former colonizationist who embraced immediate abolitionism, called on Henry Clay to recognize the ineffectiveness of the ACS.

"Slavery is rapidly increasing," he wrote to Clay in 1835. "Colonization has not, nor will it . . . diminish slavery. What is to be done? I answer, emancipate."[19]

II.

The assault by Walker, Garrison, Tappan, and others opened a chasm between militant abolitionism and the ACS. Colonizationists instigated and participated in the antiabolitionist riots that swept the North in the mid-1830s. Many foes of slavery abandoned the ACS. Nonetheless, while no longer the main embodiment of white antislavery sentiment, colonization survived as part of the broad spectrum of ideas relating to slavery and abolition. Before the Civil War, Lincoln lived in a world in which colonization was a significant presence. He grew up in Kentucky and southern Indiana and then lived in central Illinois among migrants from the Upper South. These were areas where the idea of colonization enjoyed considerable support. The Illinois Colonization Society, founded in 1830, attracted both genuine foes of slavery and those primarily concerned with ridding the state of free blacks. In 1833 a local colonization society was organized at Springfield, with numerous leading citizens as members, including John T. Stuart, soon to become Lincoln's first law partner. Several other close associates of Lincoln's, including David Davis and Orville H. Browning, were longtime advocates of colonization. So was William Brown, for whom Lincoln prepared his "book" in 1858.[20]

In January 1837, Browning, then a Whig state senator, presented to the Illinois legislature a report and resolutions affirming the right to property in slaves and condemning abolitionist agitation. The resolutions passed the House 77–6, with Lincoln as one of the dissenters. Six weeks later he and fellow legislator Dan Stone issued a "protest" against the resolutions, courageous for the time and place. What is often overlooked in this episode, known to all students of Lincoln, is that even though Browning's report affirmed the constitutional right to own slaves, it was essentially a defense of colonization, not slavery. It condemned the abolitionists primarily for undermining the efforts of colonization societies to liberate "that unfortunate race of our fellow men" from "thraldom" and return them "to their own benighted land." Lincoln's "protest" differed from the resolutions in affirming the right of Congress to abolish slavery in the nation's capital and in describing slavery as "founded on both injustice and bad policy." It concurred, however, with Browning's position that abolitionist efforts increased the evils of slavery rather than abating them. For many white Americans, including Lincoln, colonization represented a middle ground between the radicalism of the abolitionists and the prospect of the United States' existing permanently half slave and half free.[21]

Colonization organizations waxed and waned in Illinois during the 1840s and 1850s. Although some Democratic newspapers offered support, most members were Whigs "antagonistical to abolitionism," as one newspaper put it. In the 1850s Lincoln emerged as a public spokesman for colonization. His first extended discussion of the idea came in 1852, in his eulogy after Clay's death, delivered at a time when Lincoln's career in public office appeared to be over. Most eulogists hailed Clay as the Great Compromiser, the man who had almost single-handedly saved the Union in a series of sectional crises. Lincoln, by contrast, emphasized, indeed exaggerated, Clay's devotion to the "cause of human liberty." Lincoln hailed Clay for occupying a position between two "extremes": those whose assaults on slavery threatened the Union and those who looked to no end to the institution. He quoted some of Clay's procolonization speeches and embraced Clay's idea of gradual emancipation linked with returning blacks to their "long-lost fatherland." Anticipating his second inaugural address, Lincoln implied that the United States, like the ancient Egyptians, might one day suffer divine punishment for "striving to retain a captive people."

By 1853 Lincoln was closely enough identified with colonization that when the Reverend James Mitchell, a prominent colonization organizer from Indiana, came to Springfield seeking allies to promote the cause, a local minister referred him to Lincoln. Lincoln addressed the Illinois State Colonization Society's annual meetings in 1853 and 1855 (no record exists of the first speech, and only a brief outline of the second). In the year of his Senate race, 1858, Lincoln's was the first name listed among the eleven members of the society's Board of Managers. In his Peoria speech of 1854, Lincoln frankly confessed that he did not "know what to do" about slavery. His "first impulse," he said, would be to free the slaves and send them to Africa, but he admitted that the idea's "sudden execution" was "impossible." He read this passage to the audience during his first debate with Stephen A. Douglas in 1858.[22]

In some ways Lincoln's colonizationism proved quite different from that of others of his time. While encouraging blacks to emigrate, he never countenanced compulsory deportation. He said little about the danger of racial mixing, except when goaded by Democrats, he declared his opposition to interracial marriage and pointed out that the more slavery expanded, the more likely it was for "amalgamation" to occur. Unlike Jefferson, Lincoln did not seem to fear a racial war if slavery was abolished, and unlike other colonizationists, he expressed little interest in the Christianization of Africa. (Lincoln's own antislavery beliefs arose from democratic and free labor convictions, not religious perfectionism.) Lincoln never spoke of free blacks as a vicious and degraded group dangerous to the stability of American society. In his 1852 eulogy, he noted that Clay believed colonization would relieve slaveowners of the "troublesome presence of the free negroes." But later in the speech, when he spoke of the "dangerous presence" in the United States, it was not free blacks but slavery.[23]

In the mid-1850s, as Lincoln made the transition from Whig to Republican, Thomas Jefferson supplanted Clay as his touchstone of political wisdom. He referred repeatedly to Jefferson's belief in natural equality. Nonetheless, like Jefferson's, Lincoln's thought seemed suspended between a "civic" conception of American nationality, based on the universal principle of equality (and thus open to immigrants and, in principle, to blacks), and a racial nationalism that saw blacks as in some ways not truly American. He found it impossible to imagine the United States as a biracial society and believed that blacks would welcome the opportunity to depart for a place where they could fully enjoy their natural rights. "What I would most desire," he said in a speech in Springfield in 1858, "would be the separation of the white and black races."[24]

Springfield when Lincoln lived there in the 1840s and 1850s was a small city (its population had not reached 10,000) with a tiny black population (171 persons in 1850). Nonetheless, Lincoln could not have been unaware of the black presence. In the 1850s more than 20 black men, women, and children lived within three blocks of his house. He and his wife employed at least 4 free black women to work in their home at one time or another, and Lincoln befriended William Florville, the city's most prosperous black resident. But unlike Garrison and other white abolitionists, Lincoln had little contact with politically active free blacks before the Civil War and never criticized the state's notoriously discriminatory

Black Laws. When the black abolitionist H. Ford Douglas asked him to sign a petition for their repeal, Lincoln declined.

In 1848 the Black Baptist Association of Illinois sent the Reverend Samuel Ball of Springfield to visit Africa and report on prospects for emigration. On his return, Ball praised Liberia as "the brightest spot on this earth to the colored man." But when Ball died in 1852, only thirty-four black persons had emigrated from Illinois to Liberia under the auspices of national or local colonization societies during the previous twenty years. In 1858, local blacks held a public meeting to oppose colonization. "We believe," they declared, "that the operations of the Colonization Society are calculated to excite prejudices against us, and they impel ignorant or ill disposed persons to take measures for our expulsion from the land of our nativity. . . . We claim the right of citizenship in this, the country of our birth." Lincoln made no comment on the meeting. Later that year he put together his "book" reiterating his support for colonization.[25]

By the late 1850s the American Colonization Society seemed moribund. The *New York Herald* called its annual convention an "old fogy affair." In 1859, of a black population of four million, including nearly half a million free blacks, the ACS sent around three hundred to Liberia. "Can anything be more ridiculous," the *Herald* asked, "than keeping up such a society as this?"[26] Yet at this very moment the idea of colonization was experiencing a revival within the Republican Party. As in the days of Henry Clay, support centered in the border slave states and the lower Northwest.

The most avid Republican promoters of colonization were the Blair family—the venerable Francis P. Blair, once a close adviser of President Andrew Jackson's, and his sons Frank and Montgomery. They looked to Central America, not Africa, as the future homeland of black Americans and hoped that the promise of land and financial aid would make a colony attractive enough for a large number of blacks to settle there. Colonization was central to the Blairs' plan to speed the rise of the Republican Party and the progress of gradual, compensated emancipation in border states like Maryland and Missouri, where slavery was weak or in decline. In 1856, Frank Blair won election to Congress from St. Louis as an antislavery Democrat but soon switched parties, becoming the first Republican representative from a slave state. Montgomery played a prominent role in Maryland politics. The Blairs believed that the United States should be reserved for "the Anglo-Saxon race," while blacks would flourish in the tropics, to which they were suited by nature. They attacked slavery primarily for degrading nonslaveholding whites and retarding southern economic development.[27]

Republican endorsement of colonization, the Blairs insisted, would be "an enabling act to the emancipationists of the South." Colonization would refute the charge that abolition meant racial equality. It would have the added bonus of expanding the American commercial presence in the Caribbean (the region would become "our India") and blocking southern efforts to create a slave empire there. After the discovery of gold in California, Central America had attracted the interest of enterprising investors hoping to shorten the long sea voyage to the West Coast. In addition, in the mid-1850s the filibusterer William Walker conquered Nicaragua, established himself briefly as president, legalized slavery, and reopened the slave trade. Colonization, Frank Blair told Congress in 1858, would enable blacks—"a class of men who are worse than useless to us"—to secure American access to "the untold wealth of the intertropical region" while preventing "the propagation of slavery" there.[28]

During the late 1850s, Frank Blair tirelessly promoted the idea of colonization in speeches throughout the North and letters to prominent Republicans. He delivered a major address touting colonization as "the only solution to the Negro question" at Cooper Union in New York one month before Lincoln's celebrated oration at the same venue. Blair won the support of a number of Republican leaders and newspapers. His converts represented all wings of the party, but most represented the western states, where Republicans were particularly sensitive to the charge of favoring "negro equality." A variety of motives inspired these endorsements, including a genuine desire to assist blacks, racial prejudice, the hope of bolstering the efforts of Upper South Republicans, and cynical politics. After Ben Wade of Ohio endorsed the idea in a Senate speech, one constituent wrote: "I like this new touch of colonizing the niggers. I believe practically it is a d—n humbug. But it will take with the people."[29]

The Blairs made a special effort to enlist Lincoln in their cause. In February 1857, Frank Blair traveled to Springfield, where he met with "the leading men of the party," Lincoln doubtless among them. He advised them, he wrote his father, "to drop the negro and go the whole hog for the white man . . . the ground we have always taken here in St. Louis." In April, Lincoln and his partner William Herndon met in their law office with "one of the leading emancipationists of Missouri," probably Blair, and developed a plan to promote the Republican Party in the Upper South. Two months later, in a speech on the *Dred Scott* decision at Springfield, Lincoln called for "the separation of the races," adding that while the Republican Party had not officially endorsed the idea, "a very large proportion of its members" favored it. Such separation, he added, "must be effected by colonization." Lincoln noted that in biblical times, hundreds of thousands of Israelites had left Egypt "in a body."[30]

Like earlier colonizationists, the Blairs gathered endorsements from black leaders. The resurgence of interest in colonization among whites coincided with a rising tide of nationalism, as well as deep despair about their future in the United States, among blacks. With the Fugitive Slave Act threatening the freedom of northern blacks, the *Dred Scott* decision denying that they could be citizens, and the prospect of abolition as remote as ever, black emigration movements reemerged in the 1850s. Martin Delany advocated the creation of a new homeland for black Americans in the Caribbean, Central America, or Africa. Henry H. Garnet founded the African Civilization Society to bring about "the evangelicization" of the continent by black emigrants. James T. Holly, an Episcopal minister, called for emigration to Haiti. Like the Blairs, Delany envisioned mass emigration from the United States. Most black emigrationists of the 1850s, however, looked to a select group of migrants, a talented tenth, to bring to Africa, Haiti, or Central America the benefits of Christian civilization and American economic enterprise. Success abroad, they believed, would redound to the benefit of the descendants of Africa in "our own country and in other lands."[31]

Delany and Garnet endorsed the Blair plan. Their emigration efforts sparked a sharp debate within the black community. Black conventions, previously all but unanimous in opposition to colonization, now engaged in heated discussions of the future of the race in the United States. Early in 1861 the *Weekly Anglo-African* apologized to its readers for having devoted so much space to letters, pro and con, about emigration that "our usual editorial matter is crowded out." Even Frederick Douglass, the nation's most prominent black leader, seemed to modify his longstanding opposition to emigration. For two decades Douglass had reiterated his conviction that the colonization movement strengthened slavery and racism. "No one idea has given rise to more oppression and persecution to the colored people of this country," he wrote, "than that which makes Africa, not America, their home." But in January 1861, acknowledging that "the feeling in favor of emigration" had never been "so strong as now," Douglass offered guarded praise for the idea of migration to Haiti. He accepted an invitation to visit the island from James Redpath, the white abolitionist who headed the Haitian Emigration Bureau (funded by the government of Haiti). But at the last minute the trip was postponed. The Civil War had begun, portending, Douglass wrote, "a tremendous revolution in . . . the future of the colored race of the United States." "This," he added, "is no time for us to leave the country."[32]

III.

The outbreak of war may have ended Douglass's flirtation with emigration, but from the beginning of his administration, Lincoln made known his support for colonization. His cabinet included three strong advocates of the idea: Attorney General Edward Bates of Missouri, Secretary of the Interior Caleb B. Smith of Indiana, and Montgomery Blair, the postmaster general. Even before fighting began, Elisha Crosby, the new minister to Guatemala, departed for his post carrying secret instructions, "conceived by old Francis P. Blair" and endorsed by Lincoln, to secure land for a colony of blacks "more or less under the protection of the U.S. Government." He found the presidents of Guatemala and Honduras unreceptive. One asked why the Lincoln administration did not settle blacks in its own western territory, "a question," Crosby related, "which I must confess I found very difficult to answer."[33]

After fighting began, the Blairs' initiative continued. They hoped to use as guinea pigs the escaped slaves flooding into Fortress Monroe, Virginia, where General Benjamin F. Butler declared them "contraband of war" and refused to return them to their owners. "I am in favor of sending them straight to Hayti," Montgomery Blair wrote to Butler on June 8, 1861. "Suppose you sound some of the most intelligent, and see how they would like to go with their families to so congenial a clime." Around the same time, Blair approached Matías Romero, the Mexican chargé d'affaires in Washington, about the establishment of a black colony in the Yucatán. Romero forwarded the proposal to his government. But given that Mexico had recently surrendered one-third of its territory to the

United States, the prospect of further American intrusions on its soil aroused considerable opposition.[34]

Chiriquí, on the Isthmus of Panama, then part of New Granada (today's Colombia) seemed to offer the most promising prospect for colonization. On April 10, 1861, as the crisis at Fort Sumter reached its climax, Lincoln met at the White House with Ambrose W. Thompson, head of the Chiriqui Improvement Company, who claimed to have acquired several hundred thousand acres of land in the province in 1855. He had previously proposed to the Buchanan administration to establish a mail service between New York and California via his holdings. Now he touted the region's suitability for a naval station because of its fine harbor and rich coal deposits, which colonized blacks could mine. Lincoln, according to Secretary of the Navy Welles, was "much taken with the suggestion" and pressed Welles to look into the matter. The secretary responded that the navy had no interest in a coaling station in Chiriquí, that there was "fraud and cheat in the affair," and that he doubted blacks desired to become coal miners. Undeterred, Lincoln turned the matter over to Secretary of the Interior Smith. In October 1861 he authorized Smith to agree to a contract for "coal and privileges" in Chiriquí, which, Lincoln hoped, would not only benefit the federal government but help "to secure the removal of the negroes from this country." Lincoln also asked Ninian Edwards, his wife's brother-in-law, and Francis P. Blair, Sr., to look into the Chiriquí proposal. Both reported positively. Meanwhile Frank Blair urged his brother the postmaster general to press Lincoln to approve Thompson's plans: "it is very important that there shall be *no delay* in this affair." But in view of Welles's opposition, the project, for the time being, was shelved.[35]

As the question of emancipation moved to the forefront of political debate in late 1861 and 1862, discussion of colonization also intensified. In his annual message to Congress, delivered on December 3, 1861, Lincoln urged Congress to provide funds for the colonization of slaves freed under the First Confiscation Act as well as slaves that the border states might decide to free and to consider acquiring new territory for the purpose. A Washington newspaper suggested that the proposed black colony be called Lincolnia. The president also called for extending diplomatic recognition to Haiti and Liberia, partly to improve prospects for black emigration. Overall, commented the Washington correspondent of the

New York Times, the message took "the ancient ground of Henry Clay in regard to slavery . . . combined with the plan of Frank P. Blair, Jr." "No plan of emancipation," the reporter added, "unless accompanied by a practical scheme for colonization, will ever meet the President's assent."[36]

Colonization, the same writer observed in January 1862, was "rapidly gaining friends in Congress." And during the spring and summer of 1862, as Congress pressed ahead with antislavery legislation, colonization played an important part in its debates. The laws providing for abolition in the District of Columbia and the confiscation of the slaves of those who supported the Confederacy—important steps on the path toward general emancipation—both included provisions for the colonization of those willing to emigrate. The Senate, however, rejected a proposal to make colonization compulsory for those freed in the nation's capital. During 1862, Congress appropriated a total of six hundred thousand dollars to aid in the transportation of African Americans. Although Lincoln appears to have had little direct influence on congressional deliberations, proponents invoked the president's name in support of colonization. When he signed the District of Columbia emancipation bill, Lincoln noted that he was "gratified" that it included "the two principles of compensation and colonization." In April, in the midst of these debates, the House appointed a Select Committee on Emancipation and Colonization, six of whose eight members represented the four border slave states, Virginia, and Tennessee. Among them was Frank Blair, and its report, issued on July 16, repeated Blair's now-familiar mantra: Fear of "intermixture of the races" formed the main obstacle to abolition; removing blacks would stimulate white immigration so no labor shortage would result; blacks could never achieve equality in the United States; black emigrants would be the vanguard of an American empire in the Caribbean basin.[37]

In Congress the strongest support for colonization arose from border unionists and moderate Republicans from the Old Northwest. Radical Republicans, many of whom had long defended the rights of northern free blacks, generally opposed the idea, although some were willing to go along to placate the president and the border states. "The idea of removing the whole colored population from this country is one of the most absurd ideas that ever entered into the head of man or woman," declared John P. Hale, the Radical senator from New Hampshire. The fate of American blacks, he insisted, would be worked out in the United States.

Congressional and administration enactments in 1862 reflected these competing crosscurrents. Even while appropriating money for colonization, Congress established schools for black children in Washington, D.C., decreed that the same legal code should apply to blacks and whites in the city, and repealed the long-standing exclusion of blacks from militia service. In November, Attorney General Bates, a strong supporter of colonization, issued an opinion affirming the citizenship of free black persons born in the country (in effect overturning the *Dred Scott* decision).[38]

The disintegration of slavery in parts of the South occupied by the Union army reinforced the Lincoln administration's commitment to colonization. By 1862 thousands of "contrabands" were within Union lines. The army found them an increasing burden, the North did not want them, and Lincoln was not yet ready to enlist the males as soldiers. Lincoln had never been a proponent of manifest destiny; unlike the Blairs, he seemed uninterested in the prospect of an American empire in the Caribbean. But his focus in 1862 on promoting border emancipation as a way of undermining the Confederacy reinforced the importance of colonization. As early as September 1861 Lincoln's longtime friend Joshua Speed had warned him from Kentucky that public opinion would never countenance "allowing negroes to be emancipated and remain among us." "You might as well," Speed commented, "attack the freedom of worship in the North or the right of a parent to teach his child to read, as to wage war in a slave state on such a principle."[39]

When he launched his campaign for border emancipation in November 1861 by presenting a plan for gradual, compensated emancipation to Congressman George Fisher of Delaware, Lincoln did not mention colonization. He did, however, tell his old legislative colleague Browning, now representing Illinois in the U.S. Senate, that colonization "should be connected with it." Delaware opponents raised the cry that the end of slavery would lead to "equality with the white man," and Fisher quickly responded that colonization was part of the plan. Lincoln did not discuss colonization in his March 6, 1862, message to Congress in which he made his proposal for compensated emancipation public. But he seems to have concluded that unless coupled with colonization, his plan would go nowhere. According to the *New York Tribune*'s Washington correspondent, Lincoln frequently quoted the comment of Senator Garrett Davis of Kentucky that the state's unionists "would not resist his gradual emancipation scheme if he would only conjoin it with his colonization plan." But Lincoln's proposal for emancipation in the border went nowhere, even though in a last-ditch appeal on July 12 he assured members of Congress from border states that land could easily be obtained in Latin America for colonization and "the freed people will not be so reluctant to go."[40]

Numerous colonization schemes surfaced in the spring and summer of 1862. From Brazil, American Ambassador James Watson Webb, who as the procolonization editor of the *New York Courier and Enquirer* had helped whip up the city's antiabolition riot of 1834, proposed the creation of a joint stock company to settle black Americans along the Amazon River. A group of New Yorkers who claimed to own land in Costa Rica offered to sell it to the federal government. The Danish chargé d'affaires in Washington asked the administration to promote black emigration to St. Croix, whose sugar plantations had suffered from a "want of manual labor" since Denmark abolished slavery in 1848. (It may be doubted that many American freedmen desired to emigrate to an island whose laws required the laborer to "willingly obey" all orders of the employer and under no circumstances "presume to dictate what work he or she is to do.")[41]

The Chiriquí project now came back to life. In April 1862, Secretary Smith recommended that the government agree to a contract with Ambrose Thompson and advance three hundred thousand dollars to enable him to open Chiriquí's coal mines. Thus, he wrote to the president, would begin "a great national scheme which may ultimately relieve the United States of the surplus colored population." Lincoln seemed more enthusiastic about Smith's report than did any member of the cabinet. According to Welles, even Blair had "cooled off" regarding Chiriquí, if not colonization per se.[42]

In May the Reverend James Mitchell, the Indiana colonizationist Lincoln had met in 1853 and whom, the president had recently written, "I know, and like," published, at Lincoln's request, a rambling letter to the president. Destructive as it was, Mitchell warned, the war was nothing compared with the consequences if the races were not separated: the introduction of "the blood of nearly five million Africans into the veins of the Republic" and a "struggle between the black and the white race" that would "sweep over this nation." He believed blacks would leave voluntarily but added that it would be a good idea for the government to exert "a gentle pressure." The following month, at the recommendation of Secretary Smith, Lincoln appointed Mitchell commissioner of emigration under the Department of the Interior. Mitchell lobbied Congress on Lincoln's behalf.[43]

As talk of colonization increased, so did black opposition. To his dismay, Mitchell found newly freed blacks "to a great extent satisfied with their new liberties and franchises" and hoping for "further enlargement" in the United States. To counteract this reluctance to emigrate, Lincoln, for the first and only time, took the idea of colonization directly to blacks. Early in July he asked Mitchell to gather a group of blacks at the White House. The emigration commissioner conveyed the invitation to African Americans assembled at one of Washington's black churches. A long discussion followed, with many speakers stating that they could not commit their people "to any measure of colonization." But as it would be discourteous to refuse to meet with the president, a committee of five was appointed. On August 14, 1862, in Mitchell's words, "in the goodness of his heart, for the first time in the history of the country," an American president "received and addressed a number of colored men." What Lincoln said, however, made this one of the most controversial moments of his entire career.[44]

"You and we are different races," Lincoln told the black delegation. Because of white prejudice, "even when you cease to be slaves, you are yet far removed from being placed on an equality with the white race. . . . It is better for us both, therefore, to be separated." He offered a powerful indictment of slavery: "Your race are suffering in my judgment, the greatest wrong inflicted on any people." He refused to issue a similar condemnation of racism, although he also declined to associate himself with it. Racism, he said, was intractable; whether it "is right or wrong I need not discuss." Lincoln seemed to blame the black presence for the Civil War: "But for your race among us there could not be war." He offered removal as the remedy and touted Central America as an area of fine harbors and "rich coal mines" where even a small band of colonists might succeed. He urged blacks to "sacrifice something of your present comfort" by agreeing to emigrate. To refuse would be "extremely selfish." As the *New York Times*'s Washington correspondent observed, Lincoln's meeting with the black delegation "committed him more strongly than ever to the colonization policy as the surest solution of negro complications."[45]

A stenographer was present, and Lincoln's remarks quickly appeared in the nation's newspapers, as he undoubtedly intended. Edward M. Thomas, the delegation's spokesman, wrote to Lincoln that he found his remarks persuasive: "We were entirely hostile to the movement until all the advantages were so ably brought to our views by you." But the bulk of the antislavery public, black and white, along with many others, greeted the publication of Lincoln's remarks with dismay. "The scheme is simply absurd," wrote James Bowen, the police commissioner of New York City, "and is either a piece of charlatanism or the statesmanship of a backwoods lawyer, but disgraceful to the administration." Secretary of the Treasury Salmon P. Chase found the encounter shocking. "How much better," he remarked in his diary, "would be a manly protest against prejudice against color." A. P. Smith, a black resident of New Jersey, wrote the president: "Pray tell us, is our right to a home in this country less than your own, Mr. Lincoln? . . . Are you an American? So are we. Are you a patriot? So are we." Blacks considered it a "perfect outrage" to hear from the president that their presence was "the cause of all this bloodshed."[46]

Most indignant of all was Frederick Douglass. His vision of a society that had transcended the determinism of race stood as the polar opposite of the "pride of race and blood" that Lincoln, he wrote, had revealed. "Mr. Lincoln," Douglass complained, "assumes the language and arguments of an itinerant colonization lecturer, shows all his inconsistencies, . . . his contempt for Negroes and his canting hypocrisy." Douglass pointed out that blacks had not caused the war; slavery had. The real task of a statesman, he concluded, was not to patronize blacks by deciding what was "best" for them but to allow them to be free. Fourteen years later, when Douglass delivered his famous speech at the unveiling of the statue of Lincoln in Washington, the 1862 meeting still rankled. He could not forbear to mention the day when the president "strangely told us that we were the cause of the war . . . [and] were to leave the land in which we were born."[47]

Commenting on the meeting with the black delegation, a British newspaper observed, "If ever a public man was aware of the weight of his own words . . . President Lincoln must have been so." Yet Lincoln failed to consider that so powerful and public an endorsement of colonization might not only reinforce racism but encourage racists to act on their beliefs. Blacks reported that since the publication of the president's remarks they had been "repeatedly insulted, and told that we must leave

the country." The summer of 1862 witnessed a series of violent out-
breaks targeting blacks. Lincoln's meeting with the black delegation,
wrote the *Chicago Tribune*, "constitutes the wide and gloomy background
of which the foreground is made up of the riots and disturbances which
have disgraced within a short time past our Northern cities." The
"kindly" Lincoln, it went on, "does not mean all this, but the deduction
is inevitable."[48]

Heedless of this reaction, Lincoln pressed forward. Two weeks after
the meeting, he accepted an offer from Senator Samuel C. Pomeroy of
Kansas to organize black emigration parties to Central America. On
August 26, 1862, Pomeroy issued a public address to blacks, "sanctioned
by the President," inviting one hundred families to accompany him to
Chiriquí on October 1. Within a few days he had received more than
enough applications. Indeed Frederick Douglass wrote Pomeroy that his
two sons desired to be included, even though Douglass himself opposed
the idea. On September 11, even as the pivotal military campaign that culminated in the battle of Antietam unfolded, Lincoln authorized Secretary
Smith to sign an agreement with the Chiriquí company for the government to purchase land for the colonists and advance funds for the development of coal mines. The document envisioned the eventual dispatch of
ten thousand men, women, and children. By October, Pomeroy claimed
to have the names of more than thirteen thousand potential emigrants.
Even if he exaggerated, it seems evident that some black Americans found
emigration appealing. (Most appear to have been northern blacks, not
contrabands or recently emancipated slaves in the nation's capital.)[49]

Meanwhile Lincoln pressed the case for colonization with the cabinet.
He had broached the subject on July 21, eight days after he revealed to
Welles that he was considering general emancipation, but the members
agreed it "should be dropped." Then, on September 23, the day after issuing the Preliminary Emancipation Proclamation (which included a reference to colonizing the freed people), and again on the twenty-sixth, he
stated that he thought a treaty could be worked out with a government in
West Africa or Central America "to which the Negroes could be sent." It
was "distinctly understood," according to Welles, that emancipation and
colonization were linked. Attorney General Bates proposed compulsory
deportation, but Lincoln demurred: "[T]heir emigration must be voluntary and without expense to themselves."[50]

By the time of the cabinet discussion, numerous questions had arisen about the validity of the Chiriquí company's land grant, its grandiose accounts of the region's natural resources, and the attitude of the local government. Welles considered the company's leaders "scheming jobbers" and the entire plan "a rotten remnant of an intrigue of the last administration." Thaddeus Stevens informed Chase that the House Ways and Means Committee had determined that the area was "uninhabitable" and that in any event, the company "had not a particle of a title to an inch of it." The Smithsonian Institution reported that samples of Chiriquí coal examined by a leading scientist were worthless. If loaded onto naval vessels, the coal "would spontaneously take fire." Most important, Central American governments had been complaining to Secretary of State William H. Seward about public discussion of colonies on their soil. They had no intention, they made clear, of consenting. (Nicaraguans, the American ambassador reported, claimed descent from Spanish and Indians and "feel indignant at being ranked with the North American negro.") The cabinet agreed that colonization could not go forward without the agreement of the relevant governments. On September 24 the administration suspended Pomeroy's expedition.[51]

A strong nationalist with a powerful sense of America's destiny as a world power, Seward was at least as enthusiastic about the prospect of an American empire in the Western Hemisphere as the Blairs. But he had long had "grave doubts" about colonization, which is no doubt why Lincoln had previously circumvented his secretary of state in promoting the idea. Seward did not believe that any significant number of blacks would emigrate voluntarily and thought the United States needed all the workers it could find. "I am always for bringing men and States *into* this Union," he remarked, "never for taking any *out*." Lincoln and Seward had become very close; as Seward's secretary George Baker recalled soon after Lincoln's death, they "never disagreed in but one subject—that was the colonization of the negroes."[52]

Nonetheless, given Lincoln's desire to work out a colonization treaty, Seward on September 30 addressed a circular to the governments of Britain, France, the Netherlands, and Denmark, owners of colonial possessions in the Caribbean basin, offering to enter into agreements to colonize American blacks on their territory. Few of the governments seemed interested. By the end of October, Secretary Smith was forced to admit that the administration now had "no settled policy" regarding colonization. But a month later Lincoln was still writing to Chase that he hoped a Chiriquí contract could be arranged.[53]

If Lincoln had hoped that his embrace of colonization would reconcile opponents to emancipation, the elections of 1862 proved him wrong. Colonization rarely came up during political debates that fall. Republicans supported the emancipation policy on antislavery or military grounds. They said little about colonization, although many assured northern audiences that blacks naturally gravitated to warm climates and would leave the North for the South once slavery had been abolished. Democrats were not appeased by Lincoln's continuing references to colonization. They ridiculed the idea of compensated emancipation and colonization as unconstitutional, prohibitively expensive, and unworkable. Republicans' unwillingness to countenance compulsory deportation, they asserted, showed that colonization was a fraud. Instead, emancipation would unleash "a swarmy inundation of negro laborers and paupers" upon the North. Raising lurid racial fears paid electoral dividends: The Democrats captured the governorship of New York and gained thirty-four seats in the House of Representatives.[54]

In his annual message to Congress in December 1862, Lincoln reiterated his commitment to colonization. He asked for a constitutional amendment authorizing Congress to appropriate funds for the purpose, along with two others offering funds to states that provided for emancipation by the year 1900 and compensating owners of slaves who had gained freedom as a result of the war. Lincoln also claimed that the administration was continuing its efforts to sign treaties for the "voluntary emigration" of blacks and chided them for being unwilling to leave the country. Colonization, he maintained, would benefit whites: "Labor is like any other commodity on the market. . . . Reduce the supply of black labor by colonizing the black laborer . . . and . . . you increase the demand for and the wages of white labor." But at the same time he directly addressed white racial fears, offering an extended argument as to why if freed slaves remained in the United States, they would pose no threat to the white majority.

The December message was both a preparation of public opinion for the Emancipation Proclamation less than a month hence and a last offer to the border and Confederate states of a different path to abolition—gradual, compensated emancipation coupled with colonization. Lincoln's scheme would have had the government issue interest-bearing bonds to be presented to slaveowners, with the principal due when slavery ended in their states. He offered an elaborate set of calculations to prove that despite the economic value of slave property—over three billion dollars, an enormous sum—the growth of the white population through natural increase and immigration would make the burden of taxation to pay off the bonds less and less onerous as time went on. Lincoln was betting that the white population would grow faster than the black, an outcome that colonization would ensure. (This argument, however, seemed to contradict his assurance that by reducing the amount of available labor, colonization would raise whites' wages.) Without colonization, Lincoln said, the black population might grow faster than the white, dramatically increasing the cost of his plan.[55]

That Lincoln remained committed to colonization became apparent on December 31, 1862, the day before he issued the Emancipation Proclamation. With Senator James R. Doolittle of Wisconsin, one of the most avid proponents of colonization in Congress, present, Lincoln signed a contract with Bernard Kock to transport blacks to Île à Vache (Cow Island), eight miles off the coast of Haiti. Kock had persuaded the Haitian government to grant him the right to cut timber on the island. In the fall he had had a public letter to Lincoln printed extolling the resources of this "beautiful, healthy, and fertile island" and offering to assist in "your philanthropic idea of Colonization." Lincoln's commissioner of emigration, James Mitchell, lobbied on Kock's behalf. Less enthusiastic was Attorney General Edward Bates, who described Kock to Lincoln as "an errant humbug . . . a charlatan adventurer." But the president agreed that Kock would be paid fifty dollars each for transporting five thousand blacks to Cow Island. Doolittle and the Blairs were overjoyed. They believed, according to Elizabeth Blair Lee, the sister of Frank and Montgomery, "it is the beginning of the 2nd great Exodus."[56]

IV.

On January 1, 1863, blacks gathered in churches throughout the North and occupied South to await news of the Emancipation Proclamation. "I have never witnessed," the abolitionist Benjamin Rush Plumly wrote to Lincoln from Philadelphia, "such intense, intelligent and devout 'Thanksgiving.' " The mention of Lincoln's name "evoked a spontaneous benediction from the whole Congregation." "The Black people all trust you," Plumly reported. When a member of the congregation suggested that "you might be forced into some form of colonization," a woman shouted, " 'God won't let him,' . . . and the response of the congregation was emphatic." The process of deifying Lincoln as the Great Emancipator had begun.[57]

The Emancipation Proclamation represented a turning point in the Civil War and in Lincoln's own views regarding slavery and race. In crucial respects, it differed markedly from Lincoln's previous statements and policies. It was immediate, not gradual, contained no mention of compensation for slaveowners, and said nothing about colonization. For the first time it authorized the enrollment of black soldiers into the Union military (the Second Confiscation Act had envisioned using blacks as military laborers, not "armed service" as the Emancipation Proclamation provided). The proclamation set in motion the process by which in the last two years of the war 180,000 black men served in the Union army, playing a critical role in Union victory. It enjoined emancipated slaves to "labor faithfully for reasonable wages"—in the United States.[58]

After issuing the Emancipation Proclamation, Lincoln made no further public statements about colonization. But he did not immediately abandon the idea. On January 30, after meeting with an official of the Pennsylvania Colonization Society, he directed the Interior Department to advance money to a black minister who wanted to establish a settlement in Liberia. Early in February, Lincoln told William P. Cutler, a Radical Republican congressman from Ohio, that he was still "troubled to know what we should do with these people—Negroes—after peace came." (Cutler replied that he thought the plantations would continue to need their labor.) Meanwhile Ambrose W. Thompson tried to revive interest in his Chiriquí plan. He reminded Lincoln of his "address to the Negro committee" and blamed fear that blacks were to be "on a par with the white man" for Republican setbacks in the 1862 elections.[59]

Nothing came of Thompson's plans, but throughout the spring, John P. Usher, a proponent of colonization who had succeeded Smith as secretary of the interior, continued to promote various schemes. In April, he met with John Hodge, a representative of the British Honduras Company, "comprising . . . some of the leading banker capitalists, and merchants of London" and owner of "valuable lands" in desperate need of labor. Hodge hoped the administration would help him transport fifty thousand black indentured laborers to that colony or even "a much larger number." (If blacks were not interested, Hodge related, he would bring in "Coolies from India and China.") Lincoln gave Hodge permission to visit contraband camps in Virginia "to ascertain their willingness to emigrate." But Secretary of War Edwin M. Stanton refused, since the army was now recruiting able-bodied men for military service. "The mission failed," reported the New York Times, "and the gentleman went home."[60]

Thus in the spring of 1863 it was Secretary Stanton, not Lincoln, who called a halt to colonization efforts. "The recent action of the War Department," Usher commented ruefully, "prevents the further emigration from the U.S. of persons of African descent for the present." But as late as the fall of 1863 Usher was still using Interior Department funds to assist individual blacks who wished to leave for Africa, and James Mitchell was still working to organize "a proper body of discreet colored men" to undertake an emigration project.[61]

Meanwhile border unionists clung to the idea of colonization. In January and February 1863 congressmen from Missouri and Maryland introduced bills to provide funds for gradual, compensated emancipation in their states and the colonization of those freed. One such measure passed the House but never came to the Senate floor. The Blairs continued their propaganda effort, now using colonization as a weapon against radicals in the border and northern states who were calling for immediate and total abolition and the granting of civil equality to the former slaves. Such demands, Montgomery Blair declared in a June 1863 speech in New Hampshire, were a recipe for "blending the two colors to make a third." Blair anticipated Andrew Johnson's notorious speeches during Reconstruction by equating secessionists and abolitionists—the "Calhoun and [Wendell] Phillips Juntas"—both of whom, he claimed, opposed "the plan of Jefferson and Lincoln": emancipation and colonization. In a speech in the House in February 1864, Frank Blair excoriated those who wished to elevate blacks to equality with whites. He claimed that colonization was still the "humane, wise, and benevolent policy" of the president.[62]

By 1864, however, the influence of the border states was on the wane, and the Blairs' tirades, influential Republicans informed Lincoln, had made them "odious" to rank-and-file members of the party and done the president "immense harm," since they claimed to be speaking for the administration. In September, Lincoln asked Montgomery Blair to resign from the cabinet as part of an effort to win Radical support for his reelection.

The declining importance of the border was only one among many reasons why Lincoln's commitment to colonization faded in the last two years of the war. The service of black soldiers strongly affected his outlook. When the Emancipation Proclamation was issued, the black abolitionist H. Ford Douglas predicted that the progress of the war would "educate Mr. Lincoln out of his idea of the deportation of the Negro." Like Martin Delany, another prewar emigrationist, Douglas himself enlisted and was eventually commissioned as one of the few black officers. Lincoln would indeed come to believe that in fighting for the Union, black soldiers had staked a claim to citizenship and political rights in the postwar world. One of his secretaries, William O. Stoddard, wrote in July 1863 that "arming the negroes" was creating a "new race of freemen, who will take care of the South and of themselves too" when the war ended. In his famous letter to James C. Conkling defending his emancipation policy in August 1863, Lincoln contrasted the war's white critics with the black soldiers, who "have helped mankind on to this great consummation" of preserving the American republic.[63]

In addition, contact with articulate black spokesmen like Frederick Douglass, Martin Delany (whom Lincoln called "this most extraordinary and intelligent black man"), Sojourner Truth, Bishop Daniel A. Payne of the African Methodist Episcopal Church, and representatives of the propertied, educated free black community of New Orleans, seemed to broaden Lincoln's racial views. Simultaneously, the widespread interest in colonization members of Congress had evinced in 1862 evaporated. Republicans of all persuasions assumed blacks would form the South's agricultural labor force after the war had ended. When Congress in the spring of 1864 debated the Thirteenth Amendment abolishing slavery, no one supporting the measure promised to colonize the freed people.[64]

The fiasco at Île à Vache also contributed to the demise of colonization. Early in 1863, Secretary of State Seward convinced Lincoln to delay the implementation of the colonization contract he had signed with Bernard Kock on the eve of issuing the Emancipation Proclamation. In March, Kock transferred the contract to two Wall Street brokers, Paul S. Forbes and Charles K. Tuckerman, whom he convinced that Île à Vache was the perfect place to grow Sea Island cotton. They invested seventy thousand dollars in his scheme. Later that month Tuckerman met with Lincoln and persuaded him to approve a new contract with himself and Forbes for the transportation of five hundred blacks to the island. Tuckerman appointed Kock to oversee the project.[65]

On April 17, 1863, Kock and more than 450 men, women, and children embarked from Fortress Monroe. Reports soon began to filter back of destitution and unrest among the colonists. In the fall Usher dispatched an agent to report on conditions there. It turned out that Kock had declared himself "governor," taken the emigrants' money, and issued scrip printed by himself—at a profit of 50 percent—to be the sole currency on the island. When they disembarked, the settlers found three dilapidated sheds and no medical facilities. Funds that were supposed to have been used to build housing had instead been spent on "handcuffs and leg-chains and the construction of stocks for their punishment." The irate colonists soon drove Kock from the island. By the end of the year dozens had perished and others had left for the mainland of Haiti. In February 1864, Lincoln ordered Secretary of War Stanton to send a ship to bring back the survivors.[66]

Thus ended the only colonization project actually undertaken by the Lincoln administration. The *Chicago Tribune* entitled an editorial on the debacle "The End of Colonization." The disaster convinced Secretary Usher to abandon the entire policy. As he explained to Lincoln, despite "the great importance which has hitherto been attached to the separation of the races," colonization was dead. He viewed its demise philosophically: "Time and experience, which have already taught us much wisdom, and produced so many consequent changes, will, in the end, solve this problem for us also." Claiming that they had violated the contract, Usher refused to pay Tuckerman and Forbes the money due for transporting the colonists, although Lincoln's successor, Andrew Johnson, later appointed Tuckerman ambassador to Greece. The Senate launched an investigation, and in July 1864 Congress froze its previous appropriation for colonization. In the end only thirty-eight thousand of the six hundred thousand dollars had been spent, mostly to cover Pomeroy's expenses in 1862. (The action of Congress led Usher, who had never much liked Mitchell, to cut off the emigration commissioner's salary and evict him from his office. With the approval of Attorney General Bates, however, Lincoln retained Mitchell on the White House payroll.) On July 1, 1864, Lincoln's secretary John Hay noted in his diary, "I am glad that the President has sloughed off the idea of colonization. I have always thought it a hideous and barbarous humbug." This was not accurate, as Hay, whose opinions generally reflected Lincoln's, had strongly favored the idea in 1862.[67]

In 1863 and 1864, Lincoln for the first time began to think seriously of the role blacks would play in a postslavery world, what kind of labor system should replace slavery, and whether some blacks should enjoy the right to vote. In the Sea Islands reformers were establishing schools for blacks and aiding them in acquiring land. In the Mississippi Valley former slaves were being put to work on plantations. Lincoln expressed increasing interest in how these experiments fared. In August 1863 he instructed General Nathaniel P. Banks to include as part of wartime Reconstruction in Louisiana a system whereby "the two races could gradually live themselves out of their old relation to each other, and both come out better prepared for the new," mentioning especially "education for young blacks." In February 1864 he sent General Daniel E. Sickles to the Mississippi Valley to report, among other things, on "the colored people—how they get along as soldiers, as laborers in our service, on leased plantations, and as hired laborers with their old masters." Two months later he privately suggested to Governor Michael Hahn of Louisiana that the state's new constitution allow educated free blacks and black soldiers to vote. After winning a second term, Lincoln did try, one last time, at the Hampton Roads peace conference of February 1865, to revive the old idea of compensated emancipation and, it seems, alluded to the possibility of gradual abolition. He made no mention of colonization. "We shall hear no more of that suicidal folly," declared a contributor to the black-run *New Orleans Tribune*.[68]

The dream of a white America did not die in 1865, nor did black emigration efforts or proposals by white racists to expel the black population. But the end of slavery meant the end of colonization. It was Frederick Douglass who during the Civil War offered the most fitting obituary. In a reply to a letter by Montgomery Blair promoting colonization, Douglass dismantled one by one the arguments for the policy. There was no such thing as a people's being naturally fitted for a particular climate; blacks had adapted to America and, more, had become Americans, not Africans. The idea of colonization allowed whites to avoid thinking about the aftermath of slavery. It was an "opiate" for a "troubled conscience," Douglass wrote, which deflected attention from the work of emancipation and denied free blacks the incentive of citizenship to inspire self-education and hard work. Only with the death of colonization could Americans begin to confront the challenge of making this an interracial democracy.[69]

As for Lincoln, his long embrace of colonization suggests that recent historians may have been too quick to claim him as a supremely clever politician who secretly but steadfastly pursued the goal embodied in the Emancipation Proclamation or as a model of political pragmatism in contrast with the fanatical abolitionists. For what idea was more utopian and impractical than this fantastic scheme? Indeed, one Republican newspaper likened it to Charles Fourier's plan to construct a "paradise" on earth for mankind. "The future historian of the period," Harper's Weekly predicted in 1862, would find it difficult to decide which was "the more insane": the idea of a southern Confederacy or "the efforts of the loyal government" to export the South's labor force.[70] For a political pragmatist, Lincoln seriously misjudged the likelihood of the border states' adopting emancipation, even when coupled with colonization, and the willingness of most black Americans to leave the country of their birth. Even more profoundly, he overestimated the intractability of northern racism as an obstacle to ending slavery. In fact, for a variety of reasons, the majority of the northern public came to accept emancipation without colonization. Perhaps the much-maligned abolitionists, who insisted that slavery could be ended with the freed people remaining in the United States, were more realistic.

In the last speech before his death, Lincoln spoke publicly for the first time of suffrage for some blacks in the reconstructed South, notably the men "who serve our cause as soldiers."[71] Rejection of colonization after so prolonged an embrace had been necessary before Lincoln came to advocate even partial civil and political equality for blacks. He had come a long way from the views he brought together in 1858 in Abraham Lincoln: His Book.

7

Allies for Emancipation?:
Lincoln and Black Abolitionists

Manisha Sinha

Perhaps no other representation of emancipation has been more controversial than the Freedmen's Memorial Monument to Abraham Lincoln designed and built by the prominent nineteenth-century American sculptor from New England Thomas Ball. The sculpture of an upright Lincoln, benevolently and protectively extending his left hand over a kneeling slave, presents an isolated and one might argue distorted history of emancipation in the United States. Not only does the monument conjure the idea of blacks as passive recipients of the gift of freedom, but it also shows Lincoln as a superior, the great white father bidding his black children to arise from bondage. It is an imagery that made even Lincoln uncomfortable. On being greeted by newly freed slaves, some of whom fell before him, during his unofficial visit to the captured capital of the Confederacy, Richmond, on April 4, 1865, he is known to have murmured in embarrassment, "You must kneel to God only." The author of the Emancipation Proclamation was not an original advocate of abolition. In fact his journey to what he called "the central act of my administration, and the great event of the nineteenth century" was a relatively slow, though continuous, one.[1]

Many other historical actors played a part in the destruction of slavery; not the least of whom were the slaves. W. E. B. Du Bois, who in his masterpiece *Black Reconstruction in America* challenged the simple and ahistorical notion of emancipation as the act of a single man, first called attention to the so-called general strike of southern slaves during the Civil War, which crippled the war efforts of the Confederacy and forced the Lincoln administration to address directly the issue of slavery. Slaves, especially those who began streaming into Union lines from the early days of the Civil War, saw the Union army and Lincoln as their liberators before Lincoln and the Union army saw themselves in that role. This is the argument that has been brilliantly recapitulated by the historians involved in the Freedmen and Southern Society Project and their richly documented multivolume Freedom series. It would be misguided to derisively dub this interpretation the self-emancipation thesis or as endangering the place of Abraham Lincoln in the history of black emancipation and in American history generally. Rather it adds complexity, nuance, and fullness to a complicated story. Emancipation was a complex process that involved the actions of the slaves, the Union army, Congress, and the president.[2]

Historians have debated the relative roles of the slaves and Lincoln in the coming of emancipation. It is my purpose to shift the terms of this debate by drawing attention to a third group of emancipators; abolitionists, particularly African American abolitionists; and Radical Republicans. African Americans had demanded freedom from bondage as early as the American Revolution, and in the thirty years before the Civil War a strong interracial movement had called for the immediate abolition of slavery and for black rights. This essay highlights the largely forgotten role that abolitionists played in influencing the president's evolving views on slavery and race during the Civil War. It pays special attention to the relationship between Lincoln and black abolitionists. Finally, I discuss Lincoln's personal interactions with African American leaders, the first time that such interchanges took place between an American president and black Americans.

When Republicans assumed political power as state officials, congressmen, and members of a presidential administration, abolitionists gained access to government through their radical allies for the first time. Radicals like Charles Sumner and Thaddeus Stevens were influenced by abolitionists and were close to them in mind-set and views. Though not a majority, they were at the forefront of their party on abolition and black rights. Antislavery politicians such as John Quincy Adams, Joshua Giddings, and John P. Hale had long represented abolitionist concerns in Congress. However, Lincoln's election marked the rise of antislavery political power, a power that grew with the Civil War. Most historians acknowledge that Lincoln came under enormous pressure from abolitionists and radicals within his own party during the first two years of the war to act against southern slavery. Recently, some have also written about Lincoln's relationship with the great black abolitionist Frederick Douglass.[3] However, when it comes to the history of emancipation, the role of abolitionists has been somewhat undervalued.

In recent years the study of black abolitionism in the United States has come of age. Building on the foundational work of Benjamin Quarles and earlier black historians, scholars have drawn attention to the crucial role of African Americans in the rise of the antebellum abolition movement, with its emphasis on immediatism and black rights. We now know in detail the wide array of ideological weapons employed by African American abolitionists in their battle against slavery and racism. African Americans did not merely add an "experiential" side to abolitionist ideology in recounting their firsthand experiences with slavery and racism, nor were their arguments confined to emotional and sentimental "appeals to the heart." They were original thinkers on the problems of race, slavery, and democracy in antebellum America. Black abolitionists were guided not merely by narrow racial self-interest, as one historian of emancipation has argued, but by a vision of a truly democratic society without slavery, where African Americans would be accorded the rights of citizenship long denied to them. During the Civil War they were at the forefront of the struggle on key issues like emancipation, black citizenship, and the establishment of interracial democracy in the United States.[4]

Black and white abolitionists, as supporters and critics of the president, played a crucial role in influencing Lincoln and in goading him toward emancipation. When historians refer to Lincoln's evolving views on slavery and race during the Civil War and his capacity, to paraphrase the preeminent abolitionist leader William Lloyd Garrison, to grow in office, they must come to terms with the unprecedented access that abolitionists and African Americans gained to the White House on his election. Lincoln's famous ability to listen to all sides of the story may not have served abolitionists well when it came to border state slaveholders and northern conservatives, but it did bode well for their own role as the staunchest supporters of emancipation. Not only did black abolitionists strenuously advocate the cause of the slave, but they also forced the president to give up on his long-cherished plan of colonizing free blacks outside the country and to contemplate citizenship rights, including suffrage, for African Americans. Their influence on Lincoln must be gauged not only in terms of policy but in terms of ideology and philosophy, in their view of the Civil War as a revolutionary struggle against slavery, not just a war for the Union, a position that Lincoln came to accept in the last years of the war. He was not the "killer" of the abolitionist dream but one who helped realize it.[5]

I.

Lincoln of course was not an empty receptacle into which others poured their views or a man with no prior convictions simply guided by the unprecedented events of his presidency.[6] We know from the enormous scholarship on this most-written-about American statesman that he held at least two beliefs on slavery and race on the eve of becoming the president of the United States. He abhorred slavery as a moral blot on the American Republic, but he did not espouse racial equality. Lincoln came of political age during the sectional controversy over slavery. His earliest public views on slavery show what historian Mark Neely calls a "consistent antislavery record." In 1837, as a state representative, he refused to vote for a resolution condemning abolitionists. In a separate protest, along with a fellow representative from Sangamon County, he argued that "slavery is founded on both injustice and bad policy" but that abolitionism tended to "increase rather than abate its evils." As a one-term Whig congressman he opposed the popular Mexican War as a land grab for slavery, voted for the Wilmot Proviso, which prohibited the introduction of slavery to any territory to be acquired from Mexico, and proposed a plan for the gradual, compensated abolition of slavery in the District of Columbia.[7]

From the start Lincoln was antislavery but not an abolitionist. Like most nineteenth-century Americans, who revered the Union and Constitution, Lincoln did not sympathize with the abolitionist goal of immediate emancipation. But in viewing slavery as an unmitigated evil, Lincoln already shared crucial ground with abolitionists and Radical Republicans. As he admitted before the Civil War, "I have always hated slavery, I think, as much as any Abolitionist." He was, he recalled during the war, "naturally antislavery" and stated plainly (borrowing the words of the antislavery colonization clergyman from Connecticut Leonard Bacon) that if "slavery is not wrong, nothing is wrong."[8] In the 1850s Lincoln, a moderate, antislavery Republican, was committed only to free-soilism or the nonextension of slavery, the lowest common denominator in anti-slavery politics, along with a rather nebulous hope for its "ultimate extinction." But this was a position that he adhered to with great tenacity, as revealed in his refusal to compromise over the principle of nonextension after his election to the presidency with would-be Union savers, who wanted fixed guarantees for the perpetuity of slavery in the Constitution and its expansion to the western territories.

In his famous 1858 debates with Stephen Douglas, Lincoln repeatedly displayed his moral abhorrence of slavery, calling it a "monstrous injustice," and his belief that it contravened the founding principles of American republicanism. It was in the 1850s, when Lincoln made some of his most memorable speeches on slavery, that abolitionists, like the rest of the nation, started taking notice of him. Frederick Douglass commended Lincoln's "great speech" on a house divided and quoted from it extensively.[9] Lincoln's moral opposition to slavery and his view that slavery and freedom were essentially incompatible impressed abolitionists. Without his prior antislavery convictions, it is difficult to imagine how Lincoln would have come to accept the logic of emancipation during the Civil War.

The very fact, however, that Lincoln could view slavery as morally inexcusable and yet repudiate the minority abolitionist demand for its immediate end and black citizenship is adequate proof of his racialism. It was possible, as Eric Foner has pointed out, to be both antislavery and racially prejudiced in nineteenth-century America, a mix of attitudes held perhaps by most northern whites on the eve of the Civil War. But even when it came to the issue of race, Lincoln was probably ahead of a majority of his countrymen. In an 1857 speech on the *Dred Scott* decision, in which Chief Justice Roger Taney egregiously declared that a black man had no rights that a white person is bound to respect, Lincoln spent more time criticizing the decision for denying the humanity of African Americans than for repudiating both popular sovereignty and the Republican platform that the federal government had the constitutional power to restrict slavery in the territories.[10]

Just as there is ample historical evidence of Lincoln's antislavery views, we have abundant evidence of his views on race before the Civil War. Privately he belittled racist thought, and publicly he spoke of racial differences hedged with qualifications and moderation. Lincoln repudiated both racism and nativism as denying the founding creed of the American Republic. Even when he publicly stated that he was no racial egalitarian, Lincoln acknowledged that racial prejudice did not accord with fairness or rationality. In Illinois, with its large southern-born population and Black Laws that restricted the entry of blacks to the state, Lincoln was always on the defensive when it came to talking about race. Responding to Democrats' charge that "Black Republicans" advocated "racial amalgamation," Lincoln exclaimed, "I protest against the counterfeit logic which concludes that just because I do not want a black woman for a slave, I must necessarily want her for a wife. I need not have her for either. I can just leave her alone. In some respects she is certainly not my equal; but in her natural right to eat the bread she earns with her own hands without asking leave of anyone else, she is my equal, and the equal of all others."[11]

Given the tangled history of racial thought in the United States and the sexually charged racist rhetoric of his political opponents, it is striking that Lincoln pointedly singled out a black woman to articulate his ideas on racial equality. He also repeated the abolitionist accusation that slave women were subject to "forced concubinage" by slaveholders. He was not above portraying his Democratic opponents as the real amalgamationists and advocated a separation of races or colonization of African Americans. Commenting on Illinois's law against interracial marriage, he said, "I shall never marry a Negress, but I have no objection to anyone else doing so. If a white man wants to marry a Negro woman, let him do it, if the Negro woman can stand it." In each case, Lincoln turned the argument of his racist opponents upside down. It was not blacks who wanted to marry whites but white men who abused black women. Interestingly, the idea for the Freedmen's Memorial Monument to Lincoln began with a black woman from Virginia, Charlotte Scott, who started the fund drive for the memorial with the first five dollars she earned in freedom.[12]

Lincoln openly displayed his displeasure about having to deal with the issue of race. He highlighted the differences between Republicans and Democrats on race and charged Democrats with fostering racism. Republicans argued that "the negro is a man; that his bondage is cruelly wrong, and that the field of his oppression should not be enlarged. The Democrats deny his manhood; deny, or dwarf to insignificance, the wrong of his bondage; so far as possible, crush all sympathy for him, and cultivate and excite hatred and disgust against him."[13] Unlike Jefferson, whom Lincoln greatly admired as the author of the Declaration of Independence and for his antislavery views, and after whose party the Republicans had named themselves, Lincoln never in private or public expressed strong and crude racist sentiments against African Americans.

Lincoln reconciled his antislavery views with mainstream notions about race by arguing that the natural rights enumerated in the Declaration were applicable to black people but that this did not necessarily entail political and civil rights or social equality. His argument on race was constructed on the ground of self-interest, a justification that he had scorned many times as contrary to justice when it came to slavery, rather than on principle or any deeply held beliefs. But contrary to the *Dred Scott* decision, Lincoln argued that black citizenship was constitutional even though he personally was opposed to it. At the Charleston, Illinois, debate, Lincoln said he was "not in favor of negro citizenship" but immediately qualified that statement by saying that in his opinion, "different States have the power to make a negro a citizen under the Constitution of the United States, if they choose. . . . If the State of Illinois had that power, I should be opposed to the exercise of it."[14]

This was Lincoln's position on black rights on the eve of the Civil War, one that put him behind many abolitionists and Radical Republicans and led him to flirt continuously with the idea of colonization, but that put him far ahead of most hardened racists in the North and South who would expunge African Americans from the human family. Ironically, it was Lincoln's belief in a democratic America that made him an opponent of slavery as well as an advocate of colonization, because his ideal republic would not accommodate inequality. The events of the war would play their part in changing Lincoln's position on emancipation and black rights, but it was the spokesmen and women of black America who urged the president to heed "the better angels" of his nature and reevaluate his views on race, colonization, and black rights. Lincoln was not an incorrigible white supremacist, nor was he always an emancipationist.[15] Instead African American leaders, abolitionists, and Radical Republicans, who had long envisioned the establishment of an interracial democracy in the United States, played a crucial role in pushing the president to accept the logical outcomes of his own views on slavery and democracy: abolition, black rights, and citizenship. They challenged Lincoln on colonization and racial equality and broadened his commitment to democracy.

II.

For abolitionists, the election of Abraham Lincoln to the presidency in 1860 represented an antislavery triumph, but a limited one. As the black abolitionist weekly the *Anglo-African* put it, "It is the *existence* not the *extension* of slavery that is the issue." Abolitionists had a "love-hate" relationship with the Republican Party. In 1859, Garrison characterized the Republicans as a "timeserving, a temporizing, a cowardly party" but noted that it had "materials for growth." Similarly, Frederick Douglass felt ambivalent about the Republican Party but stressed its "antislavery tendencies" or "abolition element" as its defining feature. Unlike Douglass, some radical political abolitionists were more critical of the Republicans and Lincoln and nominated their own presidential ticket headed by the wealthy philanthropist Gerrit Smith. John S. Rock, the accomplished black physician and lawyer from Boston, best described the antislavery nature of the Republican Party in comparison to the abolition movement:

> The only class who avow themselves openly as the friends of the black man are the Abolitionists; and it would be well for the colored people to remember this fact. . . . I do not wish to be understood as saying that we have no friends in the Republican party, for I know that we have. But the most of those who sacrifice for our cause are among the Abolitionists. Next to them I place the Republicans, many of whom I have found more practically interested in our welfare than the rank and file of Abolitionists. But I place no one before the leading Abolitionists in this country— they who have spoken for the dumb, and who have braved the storms in their fury.[16]

Lincoln was personally far removed from the radical, interracial milieu of abolitionist activists before he became president even though his law partner and confidant William Herndon admired abolitionist leaders and subscribed to many of their newspapers. Some abolitionists were equivocal about their support for Lincoln because of the efforts of a majority of Republicans to disassociate their party from the advocacy of black rights. As conservative Republicans were fond of saying, theirs was a "white man's party," and their antislavery was motivated by their concern for whites and not for the welfare of black people. Thomas Hamilton complained in an editorial for the *Weekly Anglo-African*: "Where it is clearly in their power to do anything for the oppressed colored man, why they are too nice, too conservative, to do it." Since Republicans did not endorse black rights, African Americans must "rely on ourselves." Douglass, who had supported the Republican candidate John Frémont in the 1856 presidential election, was far more wary of Lincoln's candidacy. When New York State, which went heavily for the Republicans in 1860, defeated a black suffrage amendment to its constitution, Douglass noted angrily that for Republicans, "[t]he black baby of Negro suffrage was thought too ugly to exhibit on so grand an occasion." Similarly, H. Ford Douglas, the black abolitionist from Lincoln's home state of Illinois, criticized Republican "anti-slavery which wants to make the Territories free, while it is unwilling to extend to me, as a man, in the free States, all the rights of a man." He was especially critical of Lincoln's support of the Fugitive Slave Law and his refusal to endorse equal civil and political rights for African Americans. But even he thought that the Republican Party had the potential to become a great antislavery party.[17]

Lincoln's opponents, however, tried their best to put him in the same category as abolitionists in order to discredit him. As one Democratic newspaper in Illinois argued, "His niggerism has as dark a hue as that of Garrison or Fred Douglass." South Carolina secessionist Robert Barnwell Rhett claimed that Lincoln's running mate, Hannibal Hamlin, was a "mulatto" and had African blood. Southern and Democratic attempts to paint Lincoln and the Republican Party as being at par with African Americans and abolitionists, gained Lincoln many supporters among abolitionists who were critical of his party's moderate antislavery position. H. Ford Douglas, certainly no admirer of Lincoln, argued, "I love everything the South hates and since they have evidenced their dislike of Mr. Lincoln, I am bound to love you Republicans with all your faults."[18] Most African Americans and abolitionists ended up supporting Lincoln even though Republicans did not seek their support and indeed shied from them in their attempt to win over moderate and conservative northerners. The Republicans' electoral strategy in 1860 was geared to winning the conservative Lower North states rather than appeal to their secure base in the more antislavery Upper North.

Nevertheless, abolitionists, black and white, those who had voted for and those who did not vote for Lincoln, realized that his election marked a historic turning point in the progress of antislavery. Frederick Douglass rejoiced at the news of Lincoln's victory, noting, "Lincoln's election has vitiated . . . [the Southerners'] authority, and broken their power. . . . More important still, it has demonstrated the possibility of electing, if not an Abolitionist, at least an anti-slavery reputation to the Presidency." As Wendell Phillips, who had called Lincoln "the slave-hound from Illinois" for supporting the Fugitive Slave Law, enthused, "[F]or the first time in our history the *slave* has chosen a President of the United States. We have passed the Rubicon. . . . Not an Abolitionist, hardly an antislavery man, Mr. Lincoln consents to represent an antislavery idea." The Republican Party, he predicted, would soon be forced to come "to our position." After the secession of the Lower South, Garrison praised Lincoln's refusal to compromise on slavery nonextension. He wrote, "It is much to the credit of Mr. Lincoln that he has maintained his dignity and self-respect intact, and gives no countenance to any of the compromises." John S. Rock said that while Lincoln had been "more conservative than I had hoped to find him, I recognize in him an honest man, striving to redeem the country from the degradation and shame into which Mr. Buchanan and his predecessors have plunged it."[19]

With the outbreak of the Civil War in April 1861, political abolitionists like Douglass, Garrisonians such as Phillips, and Radical Republicans led by Charles Sumner immediately urged Lincoln to use his war powers to strike against slavery. As Douglass reminded his audience soon after the firing on Fort Sumter, "That great statesman John Quincy Adams, once told the Chivalry to their faces that the power to set the slaves at liberty was clearly implied in the war-making power." Abolitionists, including Garrisonian pacifists, supported the Union war effort. Garrison's desire for abolition outweighed his former commitment to nonviolence and his advocacy of disunion. With the exception of a few extreme nonresistant or antigovernment abolitionists like Stephen Foster and Parker Pillsbury, most abolitionists overcame antebellum schisms and united behind the Lincoln administration with the conviction that the war would prove to be the midwife of emancipation. As Rock argued, "This rebellion for slavery means something! Out of it emancipation must spring. I do not agree with those men who see no hope in this war. . . . There is nothing in it but hopes. Our cause is onwards."[20] They were doomed to disappointment.

During the first two years of the war the voices of abolitionists seemed to have hardly any impact on the president and his policies. Preoccupied with retaining the loyalty of the border slave states and engendering northern unity and support for the prosecution of the war, Lincoln insisted that his primary goal was the reconstruction of the Union, and he gave short shrift to the abolitionist agenda. Douglass criticized this policy: "What is the friendship of these so-called loyal slaveholders worth? The open hostility of these so-called loyal slaveholders is incomparably to be preferred to their friendship. They are far more easily dealt with and disposed of as enemies than as allies. From the beginning these Border States have been the mill-stone about the neck of the Government." Lincoln's revocation of John Frémont's and David Hunter's emancipation orders, the appearance of the president lagging behind Congress, and what was perceived as his general tardiness to move on the slavery question aroused strong criticism among abolitionists, black and white. James McCune Smith poured scorn on "an Administration, which with trembling knees and in the face of the enemy endeavored to pacify the South by returning Fugitive slaves." Phillips declared that his "patience" with Lincoln had been "exhausted." The Reverend Henry McNeal Turner, destined to become a prominent black leader during and after Reconstruction, wrote disconsolately of blacks hoping "to hear the Jubilee trumpet, *Arise, ye slaves, and come to freedom! But alas, alas, not yet*, is the echo." Turner referred to Lincoln as "the Presidential Pharaoh" for overturning Frémont's and Hunter's emancipation orders. The government's refusal to enlist black men in the Union army further dampened African American and abolitionist enthusiasm for the war. Douglass complained: "We are striking the guilty rebels with our soft, white hand, while we should be striking with the iron hand of the black man, which we keep chained behind us." While abolitionists and Radical Republicans from the outset championed a revolutionary war that would destroy slavery and the southern social order that rested on it, Lincoln had insisted that the war should not "degenerate into a violent and remorseless revolutionary struggle."[21]

Other actions, which did not garner so much attention, however, indicated that the president was not averse to the idea of emancipation. He approved of General Benjamin Butler's policy of designating runaway slaves as "contrabands" of war and of an opinion on black citizenship by Attorney General Edward Bates rescinding the *Dred Scott* decision. He signed the two Confiscation Acts that confiscated slaves used for military purposes by the Confederacy and all slaves of rebels, the acts abolishing slavery in the District of Columbia and the federal territories, and proposed plans for gradual and compensated emancipation for the border states. Most African Americans and abolitionists were pleased with these initial antislavery steps. As Philip A. Bell, editor of the black newspaper *Pacific Appeal*, observed, "We thought from President Lincoln's confiscation messages, his emancipation recommendations and other liberal actions, that it was his intention to strike at the root of the tree of strife." The Lincoln administration, pledged to enforce the suppression of the African slave trade, hanged the first slave trader for participating in the illegal trade and extended diplomatic recognition to the black republics of Haiti and Liberia. Douglass wrote happily, "I trust I am not dreaming but the events taking place seem like a dream."[22]

African Americans hailed the news of emancipation in the capital especially as a portent of general emancipation. According to the *Christian Recorder*, the official organ of the African Methodist Episcopal Church and one of the few black newspapers published throughout the Civil War, it was a "great moral victory" that "gild[s] the future with hope." At a jubilee meeting presided over by black abolitionist Amos G. Beman, the "colored citizens of New Haven" thanked the radicals in Congress, the "philanthropic Christian statesmen—Messrs. Hale, Sumner, Wilson and Wade, of the Senate—Messrs. Lovejoy, Potter and Stevens, of the House," and "our honored President," in "whom we have the most implicit confidence," for the emancipation act of the District of Columbia. Similarly, another meeting of the "people of color" at Terre Haute, Indiana, led by the Reverend T. Strothers, expressed its gratitude to members of Congress for their "zeal in battling for the downfall of slavery" and "the President of the United States, in all his actions since his inauguration, and through the war which is going on in our country, up to the present time, a man acting with discretion, and aiming to do what is just and right to all men, and having the fear of God before him."[23] African Americans saw the president and the radicals in Congress as working toward a common goal.

To abolitionists it seemed that the president's "face was turned toward Zion, but he seemed to move with leaden feet." They urged him to move faster against slavery, and their calls culminated in Horace Greeley's famous "the Prayer of Twenty Millions" demanding abolition. By the summer of 1862 Lincoln had already decided to issue an emancipation proclamation. It was not simply that he was wisely biding his time and waiting for northern antislavery sentiment to mature in order to move on emancipation. He himself had to be convinced of the failure of his appeasement of border state slaveholders and northern conservatives and of the military necessity to free the slaves and enlist black men. As Douglass observed, "He is tall and strong but he is not done growing, he grows as the nation grows." The emancipationist arguments of abolitionists and Radical Republicans, especially those who shared a personal relationship with the president like Senator Charles Sumner of Massachusetts, made headway when border state slaveholders proved to be obdurate regarding Lincoln's proposals for gradual, compensated emancipation and colonization and the war reached a military stalemate. Harriet Tubman, abolitionist heroine of the Underground Railroad and future scout for the Union army, argued that God would not let Lincoln beat the South until he did the right thing and abolished slavery. Douglass made these arguments forcefully when he pointed out that slavery was "a tower of strength" for the Confederacy. Abolition, then, was a moral and military necessity, necessary to win the war and save the Union. As Phillips argued, "Let them feel that *we* can *criticize & demand* as well as the Border States & Conservative side." But even when abolitionists were critical of Lincoln's policies, they believed that their words could move him because he was basically antislavery. Douglass noted astutely, "A blind man can see where the President's heart is." Most accepted Garrison's judgment that while abolitionists should criticize the president and Congress for being slow to move on emancipation, they must be supported as political allies.[24] Abolitionists realized that Lincoln's presidency and the war presented them with a golden opportunity to make their case for emancipation anew.

During the Civil War, the long-reviled abolitionist movement gained new respectability in the eyes of the northern public. Viewed as "zealous crackpots," they now appeared "as prophets who had tried to save their country before it was too late." Abolitionist leaders who had braved mob violence as disunionists and fanatics until the very eve of the war, acquired public authority as influential proponents of emancipation as the war dragged on. They revived their earliest tactics and deluged Congress with petitions as they had not done since the 1830s. The crucial difference was that an antislavery party now controlled Congress, and their petitions were read with respect rather than gagged as incendiary documents. In April 1862, Sumner in the Senate and William Kelley in the House of Representatives presented to Congress a petition for abolition signed by fifteen thousand women and more than seven hundred feet long. The petition campaign reached a crescendo in 1863, when Elizabeth Cady Stanton and Susan B. Anthony of the Women's Loyal National League organized a massive drive for the passage of the Thirteenth Amendment to the Constitution, abolishing slavery throughout the United States.[25]

Abolitionists wrote, spoke, published, and organized new societies for emancipation, like the 1861 Emancipation League in Boston, whose purpose was "to insist that all slaves who become practically freed by our advancing armies, or by any power of Congress or the President, shall never be restored to bondage, and that no State now in rebellion be recognized as [a] member of the Union, except on the condition of emancipation." The abolitionist Washington Lecture Association in the capital organized a series of emancipation lectures. The president and his wife attended several of these lectures, as did leading members of Congress. George Cheever delivered two sermons in the House of Representatives and an abolitionist lecture at the Smithsonian. Phillips, Douglass, and the fiery young abolitionist orator Anna Dickinson were in demand throughout the North for their speeches proposing emancipation. In March 1862 Phillips made a triumphant visit to Washington. He was introduced by Sumner to the Senate, and Greeley's *New York Tribune* reported: "The attentions of Senators to the apostle of Abolition were of the most flattering character." He dined with the Speaker of the House, Galusha Grow, lectured three times at the Smithsonian, and had a private interview with Lincoln. Phillips left with a very favorable impression of the president after having berated him publicly so often for being a laggard in the cause of abolition. Abolitionists, who had been political outsiders as radical agitators throughout the antebellum period, now walked the halls of power as influential advocates for the slave. As Mary Grew of the Philadelphia Female Anti-Slavery Society, one of the oldest interracial female abolitionist societies, wrote in 1862, "It is hard to realize the wondrous change which has befallen us abolitionists. After thirty years of persecution . . . abolitionists read with wonder . . . respectful tributes to men whose names had hitherto been used as a cry to rally a mob." In James McPherson's words, "Abolitionism had arrived."[26]

Lincoln also became the first American president to receive African

Americans in the White House. African Americans had served as domestic workers in the White House since the inception of the Republic, but they had never before been consulted on matters of state. By providing black leaders and abolitionists with access to government, Lincoln set a precedent long before Theodore Roosevelt asked Booker T. Washington to dine in the White House. As John H. Rapier, a black army surgeon, wrote, "Did you ever see such nonsense? The President of the United States sending for a 'Nigger' to confer with him on the state of the country!" What appears to be a minor point assumes significance when one recalls the politically marginal place African Americans inhabited in antebellum America. Over 90 percent of the black population was enslaved, and an overwhelming majority of free blacks could not vote and lacked any political voice. The abolition movement provided the only space for black Americans to be heard outside the confines of their communities. Black orators, authors, newspapers, intellectuals, conventions and organizations, antislavery agents, and fugitive slaves put their distinctive stamp on the abolition movement, especially in marrying the cause of abolition with that of equal rights for African Americans. For black abolitionists, as much as their white counterparts, a Republican presidency meant having for the first time the opportunity to pressure the federal government to act on abolition. Perhaps no other black abolitionist leader was more influential in this regard than Frederick Douglass, who used his monthly magazine and speeches to proclaim his views on abolition, black rights, and military service. When Lincoln met Douglass, he acknowledged having read of him and his criticisms of his slowness to act on emancipation. He assured Douglass that while he had come to emancipation relatively slowly, he would never retreat from a position once he had taken it.[27] African Americans who struggled to have their voices heard both within and outside the abolition movement had gained the president's ear.

Lincoln's ability to meet with African Americans without condescension impressed black leaders. It also enabled him to listen to the opinions of black abolitionists on important occasions. Douglass, the most prominent black leader of his generation, pointed out how he was cordially and respectfully received by Lincoln, who addressed him as "Mr. Douglass." He said Lincoln received him just as "one gentleman receive[s] another" and he "treated me as a man." Bishop Daniel A. Payne of the African Methodist Episcopal Church, who called on Lincoln to urge him to sign the District of Columbia Emancipation Act in April 1862, compared his gracious reception by Lincoln with the cold and stiff formality of John Tyler, for whose servant he had preached a funeral sermon. Payne told him that "the colored citizens of the republic" had been praying for him since the day he assumed office. Elizabeth Keckley, dressmaker and confidante of Mary Todd Lincoln's, arranged for Sojourner Truth, the famous black female abolitionist speaker, to meet Lincoln. Truth claimed that she had "never been treated with more kindness and cordiality than I was by the great and good man, Abraham Lincoln," who signed her autograph book "For Aunty Sojourner Truth A. Lincoln." Both Keckley and Truth, like many other black women abolitionists, such as Mary Ann Shadd Cary, Harriet Jacobs, and Frances Ellen Watkins Harper, were active in contraband relief and successfully solicited the Lincolns' support for their efforts. At the second inaugural, when guards tried to stop Frederick Douglass from entering the White House, Lincoln personally intervened and greeted his "friend, Douglass" warmly. On Lincoln's death, Mary Todd Lincoln made sure that some of his prized personal possessions went to Sumner and abolitionists, including African Americans such as Douglass, Henry Highland Garnet, and Keckley.[28]

As president Lincoln also allowed the local black community to use White House grounds for public celebrations and received black delegations graciously on more than one occasion. In August 1864 he received a delegation of "colored men of Baltimore" who presented him with a handsomely bound edition of the Bible. The engraving on its front cover showed Lincoln striking the chains from the slaves. On presenting the Bible, the Reverend S. M. Chase of the delegation remarked, "Towards you, sir, our hearts will ever be warm with gratitude. We come to present you with this copy of the Holy Scriptures as a token of respect for your active participation in furtherance of the cause of emancipation of our race." Lincoln admired the Bible, shook hands with the entire delegation, and said that he had always believed that "all mankind should be free."[29] African Americans not only pushed for emancipation but also continually reminded Lincoln of the momentous nature of his decision to free the slaves.

While black abolitionists formed one part of the chorus of voices that pressured Lincoln to act on emancipation, they played a crucial role in opposing his ideas on colonization. The president had long advocated the notion of colonizing all free blacks outside the country. Lincoln's support for colonization was not merely a clever tactic to win support for emancipation but a belief predating the Civil War on how to solve the country's so-called race problem. In fact he argued that it would be impossible to free the slaves without some plan to colonize free blacks. Unlike Jefferson, though, Lincoln's support for colonization was not based on a strong racial antipathy toward blacks. In his first annual message to Congress in December 1861, Lincoln recommended colonizing free and freed blacks to "some place, or places, in a climate congenial to them."[30]

But black abolitionism had come of age in the 1820s by opposing the American Colonization Society, founded in 1816. One black protest meeting in 1831 declared that colonization was "a plan to deprive us of rights that the Declaration of Independence declares are the 'unalienable rights' of all men. . . . We are natives of the United States . . . and we feel that we have rights in common with other Americans." With a few exceptions, this sentiment against colonization had not changed, even though a sizable minority had advocated emigration outside the United States in the 1850s. No other aspect of Lincoln's policies garnered more abolitionist criticism than his attempt to marry emancipation with colonization in the early years of the war. As Garrison, who was usually well disposed toward the president, wrote in the *Liberator* of Lincoln's colonization schemes, "Can anything be more puerile, absurd, illogical, impertinent, and untimely!" Americans, John S. Rock argued, were content to have the black man as a slave, but the moment he is free he is "instantly transformed into a miserable and loathsome wretch, fit only to be colonized somewhere near the mountains of the moon, or eternally banished from the presence of all civilized beings. . . . [I]t is the emancipated slave and the free colored man whom it is proposed to remove—not the slave: this country and climate are perfectly adapted to negro slavery; it is the free black that the air is not good for! What an idea! A country good for slavery, and not good for freedom!"[31]

Well aware of abolitionist antipathy toward colonization, Lincoln invited five African Americans, four of whom were contraband or former slaves and none of whom was prominent in black abolitionist circles, to persuade them to support his plans for the colonization of black Americans in August 1862, on the eve of issuing his preliminary Emancipation Proclamation. While acknowledging black suffering under slavery, Lincoln denied African Americans the hope of racial equality in the United States. Edward M. Thomas, leader of the delegation, wrote that Lincoln's

arguments laid out the advantages of emigration and changed the delegates' hostility to the idea of colonization. But a public meeting at the
black Union Bethel Church subsequently was so hostile to Lincoln's plans
that the delegates dared not attend it. In their final reply to Lincoln, the
delegates wrote that they thought it "inexpedient, impolitic and inauspi-
cious to agitate the subject of the immigration of the colored people of
this country anywhere."[32]

The reaction among black abolitionists was even more hostile. In his
strongest criticism of the president, Douglass wrote that "Mr. Lincoln
assumes the language and arguments of an itinerant Colonization lecturer, showing all his inconsistencies, his pride of race and blood, his contempt for Negroes and his canting hypocrisy." He was "a genuine
representative of American prejudice and negro hatred." Frances Ellen
Watkins Harper, the black abolitionist orator, responded: "The President's dabbling with colonization just now suggests to my mind the idea
of a man dying with a loathsome cancer, and busying himself about having his hair trimmed according to the latest fashion." She recommended
that Lincoln should be "answered firmly and respectfully, not in the tones
of supplication and entreaty, but of earnestness and decision, that while
we admit the right of every man to choose his home, that we neither see
the wisdom nor expediency of our self-exportation from a land which
has in great measure [been] enriched by our toil for generations, till we
have a birth-right on the soil, and the strongest claims on the nation for
that justice and equity which has been withheld from us for ages." She
ridiculed the idea of any country being able to "part with four millions of
its laboring population."[33]

Dismay at Lincoln's colonization plans percolated down the black
community. In a letter addressed to the colored people of the United
States, "Payne" warned that "a crisis is upon us" because unlike before,
when "associations of white men" recommended colonization, "the
American Government has assumed the work and responsibility of
colonizing us in some foreign land within the torrid zone, and is now
maturing measures to consummate this scheme of expatriation." Black
Philadelphians sent an Appeal to the President poignantly stating: "Many
of us have our own house and other property, amounting in the aggregate
to, millions of dollars. Shall we sacrifice this, leave our homes, forsake our
birth-place, and flee to a strange land, to appease the anger and prejudice
of the traitors now in arms against the Government?" But they addressed

Lincoln as an ally, ending with the statement, "In the President of the United States we feel and believe that we have a champion." Even when criticizing Lincoln's colonization plans, many African Americans did not doubt his good intentions. One black writer argued, "The misdirected goodness of great men's hearts would often plunge the world into grief and lamentation, because great men are not always wise, neither do they understand all things." The most stinging rebuke of the president's plans came from black abolitionist George B. Vashon. "No feeling of selfishness, no dread of making sacrifices (as you intimate) detain" black Americans "in the land of their birth," he wrote to Lincoln. "They are fully conscious of the hatred to which you have adverted, they endure its consequences daily and hourly; tremblingly too perhaps lest the utterances of their Chief Magistrate may add fuel to the fire raging against them."³⁴ In short, black people warned that Lincoln's colonization proposals would not solve the problem of race in America but were a symptom and a spur to racial prejudice.

Strong black opposition to colonization did not deter Lincoln from experimenting with questionable plans to colonize African Americans in Chiriquí (Panama), Liberia, and Haiti. But African American noncompliance and abolitionist pressure forced the president to give up on colonization as a viable option for freed people. As H. Ford Douglas put it, "This war will educate Mr. Lincoln out of his idea of the deportation of the Negro."³⁵ Lincoln's eventual abandonment of colonization after he had decided to free the slaves was a triumph of abolitionism, particularly black abolitionism. Black abolitionists had played no small part in uncoupling colonization from emancipation in his mind.

By 1863, having decided to emancipate the slaves using his war powers and abandoning colonization, gradualism, and compensation, Lincoln had come to abolitionist ground. It marked, Douglass argued, the end of border state influence and the acceptance of abolitionist ideas. Despite its legalistic prose and the omission of slaves in the border states of the Union and the Union-held parts of the Confederacy, the proclamation was a truly revolutionary act that spelled the doom of human bondage in the American Republic. Abolitionists knew that slavery would not survive in Missouri once it had been destroyed in Mississippi. When implemented by military victory, emancipation was also the single largest confiscation of property, albeit human property, in the history of the United States. Garrison called it "an important step in the right direction, and an act of immense historic consequence." Douglass, like Lincoln, dubbed it "the greatest event of our nation's history, if not the greatest event of the century."[36] Uncompensated, immediate abolition from being the goal of a small radical movement had become national policy.

Abolitionist celebrations and "jubilee meetings" took place across the North on New Year's Day 1863. At the interracial abolitionist celebration in Tremont Temple, Boston, Rock noted that Lincoln had "exceeded our most sanguine expectations." Several abolitionist celebrations took place in New York City with the biggest one in Cooper Union, where Lincoln had delivered his famous 1860 speech. Blacks in Leesburg, Ohio, passed a resolution stating that Lincoln's name "will ever be gratefully remembered by the colored race of America." For black abolitionists, the president became permanently identified with the moment of liberation, living on as an icon of black freedom in African American celebrations of emancipation in years to come. Marking the Day of Jubilee or Jubilo, veteran black abolitionist William Cooper Nell observed, "New Year's day—proverbially known throughout the South as 'Heart-Break Day,' from the trials and horrors peculiar to sales and separations of parents and children, wives and husbands—by this proclamation is henceforth invested with new significance and imperishable glory in the calendar of time." Former slaves throughout the Union-held South celebrated with as much fervor. From Beaufort, South Carolina, came this wish to the president: "We never expect to meet you face to face on earth, but may we meet in a better world than this: this is our humble prayer." Abolitionists and, more generally, black Americans' euphoric reception of the Emancipation Proclamation helped make it a defining moment in the war. Henry McNeal Turner argued that emancipation marked the start of "a new era, a new dispensation of things."[37]

Even though some radicals and abolitionists tried to replace Lincoln as the Republican standard-bearer in 1864, in the end most rallied behind him and contributed to his victory. Nearly all black abolitionists remained cool to the movement to replace Lincoln on the Republican ticket. As Rock put it, "There are two parties, the one headed by Lincoln is for freedom and the republic, the other headed by McClellan is for despotism and slavery." According to J. W. C. Pennington, Lincoln was "the only American President who has ever given any attention to colored men as citizens." His reelection was the "best security" for "negro freedom and African redemption." Pennington went on to assert that he thought "nine-tenths of my colored fellow citizens" agreed with him. Democratic race-baiting, calling Lincoln "Abraham Africanus I" and "A general agent for the Negroes," and accusing the Republican Party of promoting "miscegenation" or racial intermixture, again endeared Lincoln to African Americans. Black support for the president was cemented by Lincoln's determination not to repudiate his proclamation and to work resolutely for a constitutional amendment that would forever prevent the resurrection of slavery in the Union. Confronted with the prospect of electoral defeat in 1864, Lincoln even summoned Douglass to the White House and proposed a plan for spiriting slaves to Union lines so that the greatest numbers of them would be legally free.[38]

Lincoln's reelection allowed him to work for emancipation in his preferred constitutional manner. The Thirteenth Amendment to the Constitution, which Lincoln assiduously promoted, became his dying legacy for the nation. The passage of the amendment, he thought, was "a fitting and necessary conclusion to the final success of the Union cause." On the passage of the amendment, the Reverend Henry Highland Garnet became the first black man to address Congress, on Lincoln's fifty-sixth birthday. Garnet called on the "rulers of this great nation" to "Emancipate, Enfranchise, Educate, and give all the blessings of the gospel to every American citizen."[39] After emancipation, Lincoln also came to appreciate that African Americans were an integral part of the American Union and that sooner or later the government and nation would have to address the issue of black citizenship and rights.

By this time Lincoln had come to share the abolitionist and African American view of the Civil War as a providential, apocalyptic event that would not only end slavery but redeem the American Republic and vindicate its founding principles. The black abolitionist insistence on tying the cause of the slave and black rights with that of American democracy influenced Lincoln's overall conception of the war. Lincoln had always argued that slavery was an undemocratic institution based on tyranny. During the Civil War abolitionists had successfully made black freedom indispensable to the preservation of American democracy. According to Douglass, the history of slavery clearly showed that "the friends of slavery are bound by the necessity of their system . . . to subvert all liberty, and pervert all the safeguards of human rights." Lincoln would immortalize in the 1863 Gettysburg Address the abolitionist conception of the war as the second American Revolution, representing a "new birth of freedom" in the Republic.[40]

The abolitionist understanding of the war gave meaning and purpose to the conflict in a way that simply a war for the Union never could.

Lincoln, like the abolitionists, also came to understand the war as a chastisement for the nation's departure from its founding principles and the sin of slavery. While not influenced by religion to the extent that some recent biographers have claimed, Lincoln began to view the Civil War as a divine intervention in human history, an event directed by a power greater than him. The carnage, no doubt, made him meditate on its possible meaning, which came to parallel closely the abolitionist conception of the Civil War. Lincoln eloquently gave words to this abolitionist understanding of the war in his second inaugural address. Remembered chiefly for the platitude "with malice toward none, with charity for all," he said more memorably, "Fondly do we hope—fervently do we hope—that this mighty scourge of war may speedily pass away. Yet if God wills that it continue, until all the wealth piled by the bondsman's two hundred and fifty years of unrequited toil shall be sunk, and until every drop of blood drawn from the lash, shall be paid by another drawn with the sword, as was said three thousand years ago, so still it must be said 'the judgments of the Lord, are true and righteous altogether.' " So moved was Douglass by the president's words that he quoted the above passage in its entirety in his eulogy for Lincoln.[41]

III.

Even more than emancipation, it was in regard to black rights and citizenship that Lincoln "grew" during the war. Abandoning his antebellum position that blacks were entitled to no more than natural rights, he came to contemplate political and civil rights for them. The failure of colonization as well as black military service pushed Lincoln to reevaluate his position on African American rights. Moreover, strong African American, abolitionist, and Radical Republican demands for equality influenced Lincoln's evolution on this issue. More than any other factor, it was the contributions of African American soldiers to Union victory that made Lincoln amenable to the idea of black citizenship.

Black abolitionists had advocated the recruitment of black soldiers at the very start of the war. The antebellum exclusion of African American men from the state militias was symptomatic of their exclusion from the duties and rights of republican citizenship. Black abolitionists such as William Cooper Nell had pointed in vain to black military service during the Revolutionary War and the War of 1812 in their efforts to combat racial discrimination. With the onset of the Civil War, black abolitionists were quick to realize that military service would allow African Americans not only to strike a blow against slavery but also to demand citizenship rights. As Douglass put it, "Once let the black man get upon his person the brass letters, U.S.; let him get an eagle on his button, and a musket on his shoulder and bullets in his pocket, and there is no power on earth which can deny that he has earned the right to citizenship in the United States."[42] The administration's policy of excluding black men from military service was thus particularly upsetting to African American leaders. But once Lincoln decided to emancipate the slaves, his view of black military service also changed. The exigencies of the war and the shortage of manpower as the conflict dragged on led the Lincoln administration and Congress to recruit African Americans, including slaves, and grant freedom to those who served and their families.

The enlistment of black men, supported and led by abolitionists, raised the question of racial equality. The all-black Fifty-fourth Massachusetts was quickly recruited under the auspices of the abolitionist Governor John Andrew. The wealthy manufacturer and abolitionist George L. Stearns, a staunch advocate of black military service, hired prominent black abolitionists such as Douglass, William Wells Brown, Charles Lenox Remond, John Mercer Langston, Henry Highland Garnet, and Martin Delany as recruiting agents. By the end of the war, about two hundred thousand African Americans had served in the Union army and navy. Despite initial inequalities in pay and rank, black abolitionists supported recruitment of black soldiers but demanded equal rights, including the equalization of pay scales. In his broadside, "Men of Color, To Arms!" Douglass argued that "action," rather than "criticism, is the plain duty of the hour." But he added that he could not recruit more black men "with all my heart" as long as inequalities persisted.[43]

Protests over racial inequalities in the Union army prepared African Americans and abolitionists for the long fight for equality and citizenship rights. Rock noted, "[T]he colored soldier has the destiny of the colored race in his hands." The protest that inequality in pay sparked among African American soldiers was evident in the outpouring of letters they sent to the *Christian Recorder*, a newspaper that was distributed widely among black regiments during the Civil War. The editors reported that they were "continually getting letters from our noble and brave colored soldiers" over this issue. Black soldiers were paid ten dollars a month, from which three dollars were deducted for their uniforms, while white soldiers were paid thirteen dollars a month with an additional allowance of three dollars for their uniforms. In protest, some black regiments refused their pay, causing considerable hardship to themselves and their families. As one black soldier writing under the pseudonym Wolverine wrote, "It is not the money . . . that we are looking at! It is the principle; that one that made us men when we enlisted." Daniel Walker of the famous Fifty-fourth Massachusetts proudly asserted, "We have fulfilled all our agreements to the Government, and have done our duty wherever we have been, but thus far the government fails to fulfill their part of the contract, by not paying us." Black men should now be treated as equal citizens and soldiers, they argued.[44]

The federal government soon got wind of the storm brewing over inequality in pay. James Henry Gooding of the Fifty-fourth Massachusetts sent a letter to Lincoln asking for a soldier's pay for performing a soldier's duty. Black soldiers, the letter reminded the president, were poor, and their families could ill afford doing without their salaries. Seventy-four soldiers from the Fifty-fifth Massachusetts signed a letter to Lincoln warning of more "stringent measures" if their demands were not heeded. When asked to intervene, Lincoln felt that he could not act "upon grounds of moral right without regard to his Constitutional powers." Congress, where Sumner and his fellow senator from Massachusetts, Henry Wilson, led the fight for equal pay, passed an act equalizing pay scales retroactively from January 1, 1864, and to all those who had been free in April 1861 from the time of their recruitment. Abolitionist officers of black regiments soon got around the law by devising oaths for soldiers claiming that they had owed no man their labor since the time of their recruitment. Thomas Wentworth Higginson led a crusade for equal pay, deluging northern newspapers and politicians with letters until Congress passed a law in March 1865 granting retroactive pay to all black regiments from the time of their enrollment.[45]

Initially, African Americans were also barred from officer ranks. Douglass's desire for an officer's commission in the Union army came to naught. Ethio, for instance, asked for colored "chaplains, officers, sutlers, matrons, nurses, teachers, recruiters, contractors, traders, surgeons" and argued that blacks should not be confined to serving only as soldiers in the Union army. "All that we ask is to give us a chance, and a position higher than an orderly sergeant," wrote John H. W. N. Collins, a black orderly sergeant. In the last two years of the war, however, not only were pay scales equalized, but African Americans were also commissioned as officers. The most famous instance was the black abolitionist leader Martin Delany, commissioned as a major in the Union army. Another black abolitionist and Lincoln critic, H. Ford Douglas, received an officer's stripes. And Henry McNeal Turner, along with several dozen other African Americans, served as chaplains in the Union army. By the end of the war around a hundred African Americans had served as officers. A majority of them however were with the Louisiana Native Guards, a militia composed of the state's free "gentlemen of color" that predated the war.[46]

Douglass's first meeting with Lincoln was about the issues of pay and officer rank for African Americans as well as Confederate atrocities against black Union soldiers. The president assured Douglass that he would sign any commission for a black officer recommended by the secretary of war. Lincoln would also issue a retaliatory order against the Confederate policy of enslaving and killing black Union army soldiers, despite his misgivings about punishing the innocent for the crimes of others and letting the war descend into a brutal bloodletting on all sides. While the Lincoln administration did not retaliate for the Fort Pillow massacre of black Union troops, it did suspend the exchange of prisoners with the enemy because of the Confederacy's refusal to exchange black Union prisoners of war. For the most part, Lincoln had decided that "having determined to use the Negro as a soldier, there is no way but to give him all the protection given to any other soldier."[47]

Black heroism at the battles of Fort Wagner, Milliken's Bend, and Port Hudson impressed both the president and the northern public at large. "T.S.W." of the First United States Colored Troops (USCT), wished "to know, whether, after doing such daring exploits, we do not deserve the rights and privileges of the United States of America." Lincoln, like his military commanders, came to believe that "the emancipation policy, and the use of colored troops, constitute the heaviest blow to the rebellion; and that at least one of these important successes could not have been achieved when it was, but for the aid of black soldiers." Indeed Lincoln adopted nearly all the abolitionist arguments on the value and significance of black military service. When peace arrives, he wrote, "there will be some black men who can remember that, with silent tongue, and clenched teeth, and steady eye, and well-poised bayonet, they have helped mankind onto this great consummation; while, I fear, there will be some white ones, unable to forget that, with malignant heart, and deceitful speech, they have strove to hinder it." Black Union army soldiers returned the compliment. At its Christmas celebration in 1863, the Seventh Regiment of the Corps d'Afrique passed a resolution: "We cannot express in words our love for the President of the United States, as language is too weak to convey the estimation in which we hold him."[48] Not surprisingly, black Union army veterans were the largest contributors to the Freedmen's Monument to Lincoln.

Lincoln soon came to sympathize with the idea that one could not deny citizenship rights to black soldiers who had fought on behalf of the Union. According to the precepts of republicanism, in which Lincoln, abolitionists, and the soldiers themselves were well versed, one deserved the rights of citizenship after performing the duties of citizenship. In fact Lincoln had suggested as early as the 1830s that even women, if they paid taxes or bore arms in defense of their country, should be given the right to vote. (While later suffragists used this remark to portray Lincoln as a champion of female suffrage, he was never involved in the women's rights movement, unlike black abolitionists such as Douglass.) The national black convention in Syracuse in October 1864, presided over by leading abolitionists like Douglass, Wells Brown, George T. Downing, Garnet, and John Mercer Langston, issued an "Address of the Colored National Convention to the People of the United States," demanding suffrage. It read in part, "Are we good enough to use bullets, and not good enough to use ballots? May we defend rights in time of war, and yet be denied the exercise of those rights in time of peace? Are we citizens when the nation is in peril, and aliens when the nation is in safety? May we shed our blood under the star spangled banner on the battlefield, and yet be debarred from marching under it at the ballot box?"[49]

Black soldiers themselves made the case for citizenship best. J. H. Hall of the Fifty-fourth Massachusetts asked why blacks were "not recognized as true and lawful citizens" after having "performed our duty as soldiers, and maintained our dignity and honour as citizens." As they had fought to "maintain a Republican government," he wrote, "we want Republican privileges." Hall concluded, "All we ask is the proper enjoyment of the rights of citizenship, and a free title and acknowledged share in our own noble birthplace, which we are ready and willing to defend while a single drop of blood courses through our veins." And R. M. Smith of the Third USCT reminded white Americans that "the black man has proved himself a patriot, a hero, and a man of courage. He is preparing by education, to be a true and worthy citizen of the United States." Thomas Webster of the Forty-third USCT thought that since black soldiers were "fighting as hard to restore the Union as the white man is," they should at least have "equal rights with a foreigner."[50]

The demands and protests of abolitionists and radicals also caused Lincoln to begin to come to terms with black suffrage. Throughout the war black and white abolitionists continued to fight for equality and against discrimination in the North. Over Garrison's opposition, the American Anti-Slavery Society under the leadership of Douglass and Phillips voted to continue the fight for equal rights in 1865. Douglass demanded "the most perfect civil and political equality," that black men should "enjoy all the rights, privileges and immunities enjoyed by any other members of the body politic." Abolitionists' work, he said, would not be done until "the colored man is admitted in good and regular standing into the American body politic." In a resolution written by Phillips, the Massachusetts Anti-Slavery Society declared that the black man had "an equal share with the white race in the management of the political institutions for which he is required to fight and bleed, and to which he is clearly entitled by every consideration of justice and democratic equality." Abolitionist and black demands helped make African American citizenship a cornerstone of Radical Reconstruction.[51]

Lincoln came under increasing fire from African Americans, abolitionists, and Radical Republicans for not making black suffrage a precondition for the reconstruction of southern states. For Phillips, African American voters would form the foundation of a regenerated South. Sumner spent long hours with the president trying to convince him to act on black suffrage. These criticisms and conversations may have influenced Lincoln as black demands for the vote also made their way to the White House. As early as November 1863 New Orleans's politically active free blacks asked the military governor for the right to vote. In February 1864 they received an emissary from the Lincoln administration who asked that they inform the president of their demands. They replied that they wanted schools, the ballot, and equality before the law and expressed their "unbounded and heartfelt thanks to the President of the United States." By April they had drawn up a petition with a thousand signatures asking for the right to vote because they were free, owned property, and had served in the War of 1812 and in the Union army. Lincoln received their two representatives, Jean Baptiste Roudanez and Arnold Bertonneau, but is reported to have said, "I regret, gentlemen, that you are not able to secure all your rights and that circumstances will not permit the government to confer them upon you." The two delegates were feted by abolitionists in Boston, including Garrison and Douglass, and their visit must have made some impression on the president. Soon after, Lincoln penned his famous letter to Louisiana's governor, Michael Hahn, suggesting that "the very intelligent, and especially those who have fought gallantly in our ranks" be given the franchise. It would help, "in some trying time to come, to keep the jewel of liberty within the family of freedom." By this point he had enough interactions with black abolitionists to realize that African Americans did boast a "very intelligent," learned, and politically active leadership. A month later Lincoln received a delegation of black North Carolinians who asked him to "[g]rant unto your petitioners that greatest of privileges, when the State is reconstructed, to exercise the right of suffrage." According to the *Anglo-African*, he assured them "of his sympathy and earnest cooperation."[52]

Lincoln's wartime reconstruction plans were geared to end the war speedily and successfully. His 1863 Proclamation of Amnesty and Reconstruction called for the reunion of rebel states if at least 10 percent of the population swore loyalty to the government and accepted abolition. It did not include black suffrage, which Lincoln left to the discretion of the military-led state governments. Even radicals in Congress who proposed their own plan for reconstruction in the Wade-Davis bill of 1864 did not include black suffrage in their plans at this stage, though they granted African Americans specific legal protections and civil equality. In the year before his death Lincoln came to acknowledge that at least some black Americans were entitled to the right to vote. He was assassinated before he could incorporate these beliefs in any permanent plan for reconstruction. In his last public speech, justifying his plans for the reconstruction of Louisiana under his 10 percent plan, Lincoln said he would "prefer" if suffrage was conferred on the "very intelligent" and "those who serve our cause as soldiers." The state's constitution, he argued, opened the public school system for blacks and whites and empowered the legislature "to confer the elective franchise on the colored man." He stated the same ideas informally from the balcony of the White House to a crowd gathered below on the eve of his assassination. In the audience was his assassin, John Wilkes Booth, the proslavery Confederate sympathizer and actor, who pledged to kill him for his championship of "nigger citizenship. That is the last speech he will ever make."[53]

African Americans mourned the death of the president as a genuine loss to the cause of black freedom and equality. For Douglass, Lincoln's death was "a personal as well as a national calamity; on account of the race to which I belong and the deep interest which that good man ever took in its elevation." The *Christian Recorder* noted: "Humanity has lost a friend, and the colored man one not easily replaced." Similarly, in an editorial for the *New Orleans Black Republican*, S. W. Rogers wrote, "The greatest earthly friend of the colored race has fallen by the same spirit that has so long oppressed and destroyed us. In giving us our liberty, he has lost his own life. Following the rule of the great and glorious in the world, he has paid the penalty of Apostleship. He has sealed with blood his Divine commission to be the liberator of a people." More than any other group, African Americans played a major role in anointing Lincoln with martyrdom for their cause. A freedmen's meeting on Hilton Head Island, South Carolina, resolved that in his "proclaiming *Liberty* to our race," Lincoln's career was crowned by "a blessed immortality, sealed by his blood, and embalmed him in the memory of future generations." Martin Delany, the father of black nationalism, mourned the death of "the humane, the benevolent, the philanthropic, the generous, the beloved, the able, the wise, great and good man, the President of the United States, ABRAHAM LINCOLN, the just." He recommended that "every individual of our race" contribute one penny each to build a monument to Lincoln as "a tribute from the black race."[54]

By the time of his death Lincoln's views on slavery and racial equality had evolved significantly, and black abolitionists had played no small part in pushing him along this path. If some men are born great, some acquire greatness, and others have greatness thrust upon them, Lincoln surely belonged to the second category. In his speech at the unveiling of the Freedmen's Monument, Douglass gave the best assessment of Lincoln's role as a bridge between abolitionism and public opinion, a corrective to the version of emancipation represented by the monument. "Viewed from genuine abolition ground, Mr. Lincoln seemed tardy, cold, dull, and

indifferent; but measuring him by the sentiment of his country, a sentiment he was bound as a statesman to consult, he was swift, zealous, radical and determined." Lincoln, Douglass pointed out, was preeminently
"the white man's President." But "while Abraham Lincoln saved for you
a country, he delivered us from bondage," he told his audience, and "in
doing honor to the memory of our friend and liberator, we have been
doing the highest honor to ourselves and those who come after us." For
Douglass, Lincoln, as the author of the Emancipation Proclamation, was
not just an ally for emancipation but at "the head of a great movement,
and was in living and earnest sympathy with that movement."[55]

Abolitionists, especially black abolitionists, had played a crucial role in
the coming of emancipation and in challenging Lincoln to abandon colonization and accept black rights. Their ideas on interracial democracy and
equal citizenship, largely forgotten in the history of emancipation, forced
both the president and the nation at large to accept the consequences of
abolition and helped set the agenda for reconstruction. The radical egalitarianism of black and white abolitionists pushed Lincoln and the Republican Party, initially committed to only the nonextension of slavery, to
adopt the twin abolitionist goals of immediate, uncompensated emancipation and black rights. Precisely because Lincoln had come around to
these ideas during the war, his historical legacy would be inextricably
bound with their struggle for freedom and the movement to abolish slavery. But it had been the pioneering efforts and ideas of black abolitionists
crystallized in the broader interracial abolition movement that had helped
initiate and shape the process of emancipation and introduced the idea of
an interracial democracy under the presidency of Abraham Lincoln.

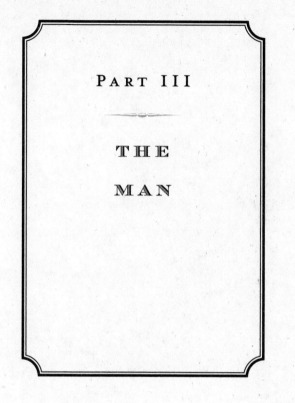

PART III

THE

MAN

8

Lincoln's
Sacramental Language

ANDREW DELBANCO

I.

A half century ago, on the occasion of the one hundred fiftieth anniversary of Abraham Lincoln's birth, Jacques Barzun added something fresh to Lincoln studies, never an easy achievement. Ever since Harriet Beecher Stowe, in 1864, called Lincoln's "state papers . . . worthy to be inscribed in letters of gold," a long list of writers, critics, and historians has lined up to echo her judgment. But by crediting him with breaking "the monopoly of the dealers in literary plush," Barzun was saying something new.[1]

The novelty was the idea that Lincoln exerted a transforming effect not only on race relations, or the power of the federal government, or the rise of the Republican Party but on the development of American literature. It was Lincoln, according to Barzun, who purged our language of its nineteenth-century flourishes and attuned it to the twentieth-century ear, which preferred austerity and brevity to elegance and pomp. This new Lincoln was a protomodern stylist who sprang from nowhere as if by virgin birth, a self-bred genius without foreground or precedent, whose "morbid regard for truth and abnormal suppression of aggressive impulses suggest that he hugged a secret wound." Out of those secret torments he fashioned "a style . . . unique in English prose and doubly astonishing in the history of American literature, for nothing led up to it."

Fifty years ago conditions were favorable for making the case. It was America's high Freudian moment, a time of peculiar receptivity to the psychologically fraught genius who somehow turned his demons into art.[2]

Edmund Wilson, for example, although he had no particular taste for Lincoln (he described him, perhaps with unconscious self-reference, as "cold and aloof" with "the conviction of his own superiority"), defined the true artist as one "whose genius becomes purer and deeper in ratio to his isolation." Elected to the presidency with a bare plurality of the vote, condescended to by allies and vilified by enemies, left alone with his conscience to make the fateful decisions of war, Lincoln fit the bill. Barzun's phrase for him was "artist saint."[3]

Like the writer with whom he was most often compared, Mark Twain, Lincoln was also the beneficiary fifty years ago of a sea change in literary taste. Formal poets such as Henry Wadsworth Longfellow and James Russell Lowell were losing their reputation to the street-talking Walt Whitman (progenitor of the Beats) and the gnomic Emily Dickinson. The rank order of American novelists was undergoing similar revision.[4] Formality and prolixity (James Fenimore Cooper, Henry James) were going out; economy and plain speech (Stephen Crane, Sherwood Anderson, along with Twain) were coming in. Ernest Hemingway's proclamation, first issued in 1935, that "all modern American literature comes from one book by Mark Twain called *Huckleberry Finn*" had become so much a matter of consensus that writing in the same year as Barzun, Norman Podhoretz declared *Huckleberry Finn* the "key to the very essence of the American imagination."[5]

Lincoln and Twain seemed natural counterparts, and there was a certain historical warrant for making the connection. Born in the border states (Twain in Missouri, Lincoln in Kentucky), both had come east to persuade the gatekeepers of American culture to let them in.

Lincoln's moment came in February 1860 in the Great Hall of the Cooper Institute in New York City, where he addressed a capacity crowd, including such New York intellectuals as Horace Greeley and the venerable William Cullen Bryant. "No former effort in the line of speech-making had cost Lincoln so much time and thought," his friend William Herndon later remarked. The result was a kind of legal brief in which Lincoln argued that the founding fathers had always envisioned the future United States as a "confederacy of free states."[6] At one point, drawing out with mocking languor the words *gur-reat pur-rinciple* with which the portly Senator Douglas liked to describe his doctrine of popular sovereignty, the lean and lanky Lincoln turned the risk that his audience would laugh at him into an occasion for their laughing with him. The kingmakers were impressed.

By the middle of the twentieth century America's leading intellectual historian, Perry Miller, was describing Lincoln and Twain as spiritual siblings, "two inspired raconteurs [who] used comedy . . . to mask a black melancholy that coiled around the base of their spirits," and by the time Garry Wills, in 1993, credited Lincoln with having "created a political prose for America, to rank with the vernacular excellence of Twain," the twin canonization had long been complete.[7] Today Lincoln's literary prestige, like Shakespeare's, is so great that he seems less a writer than a virtual anthology of quotable *sententiae* ("You can fool some of the people all of the time . . .") that turn up in speeches and columns by politicians and pundits of all stripes all the time. One recent book about the perils of e-mail—an unlikely occasion, it would seem, for summoning the words of a long-ago president—makes its point with an inverted allusion to Lincoln's first inaugural address: "Email," the authors tell us, "has a tendency to encourage the lesser angels of our nature."[8]

Now that we have reached Lincoln's bicentennial, it seems a good moment to ask whether Lincoln is still with us as an actual historical figure who wrote and spoke in the world or only as the object of dutiful homage and clever appropriation. To put the question another way, Are we still able to hear his voice as his contemporaries heard it?

II.

There are reasons to think not. Many forces of estrangement have pushed Lincoln farther from us than from our predecessors. Among these forces perhaps the most potent is our disconnection from the culture of oratory in which he was formed. Americans of fifty years ago were still faintly in touch with it. They could remember the Four Freedoms speech of Franklin Roosevelt and, through the transatlantic medium of radio, the wartime speeches of Winston Churchill, of whom Edward R. Murrow famously said that he "mobilized the English language and sent it into battle." But in our age of the sound bite, it is almost impossible to grasp what public speaking once meant in America.

Perhaps the closest analogy is to a big-time sporting event or, as Garry

Wills has suggested, a rock concert. Nineteenth-century America was a speechmaking nation, a culture of sermons, orations, and lectures at private as well as public ceremonies, in big-city theaters as well as small-town meeting halls. Until the telegraph came into use in the 1850s, no public speaker had any means better than paper and print for transmitting what he said and not even rudimentary means for amplifying his voice while saying it. Speechmaking was a test of stamina that required the histrionic skills of an opera singer or a revival preacher. While listening to a famous evangelist preach outdoors in eighteenth-century Philadelphia, Benjamin Franklin did some quick calculations and concluded that the man must have been audible to some thirty thousand people, which "reconciled me," he wrote, "to the ancient histories of generals haranguing whole armies, of which I had sometimes doubted." Nearly a century later, during Lincoln's youth, it was not unheard of for an orator to talk till he dropped, as when one Connecticut congressman, known for his corpulence and vitriol, fainted at the climax of his own speech and had to be carried out of the hall and resuscitated in the open air.[9]

Lincoln himself was capable of this kind of marathon performance and was never known to swoon. His speech on the recently passed Kansas-Nebraska Act, delivered in the fall of 1854 at Peoria, Illinois, lasted three hours and, in the written form known to us, amounts to seventeen thousand words. But of course any speech, especially a lengthy one, loses something in translation to the page, and the loss is compounded by the passage of time. What may be effective emphasis to those who hear it can become, to those who read it years later, reiterative and repetitious. As Douglas Wilson points out in an excellent recent book, *Lincoln's Sword: The Presidency and the Power of Words*, Lincoln's "basic sense of language, like the poet's, is aural; he hears it" rather than sees it on the page.[10] In this respect he was thoroughly a man of his time, a time when, as Emerson put it, "the speech of man to men" was considered the "most flexible of all organs, of all forms."[11]

We get a hint of what oratory meant to Lincoln by following his back-and-forth with the printer who, in the aftermath of the attack on Fort Sumter in the spring of 1861, helped prepare for publication his first presidential message to Congress. The two men engaged in what Douglas Wilson aptly calls a "battle of the commas" as the printer removed those he thought superfluous and, with perfect reciprocity, the author restored them. But we can follow this battle only if we grasp the distinction (archaic to us) between the grammatical comma, which mattered to the editor, and the rhetorical comma, which mattered to the author.[12] The whole spectacle is all the more striking because it took place at a time when grammatical rules were relatively loose and even spelling could be a matter of personal taste. A few years earlier, when Lincoln's contemporary Herman Melville came upon "a surprising profusion of commas" in the page proofs of his latest book, he was happy to leave their fate to the printing house: "I hope that some one who understands punctuation better than I do, will give the final hand to it."[13]

Lincoln cared about commas not because they were syntactically necessary but because they were his way of signaling a pause that lent gravity to the next phrase. "The people of Virginia," he wrote in his first message to Congress, "have thus allowed this giant insurrection to make its nest within her borders; and this government has no choice left but to deal with it, *where* it finds it."[14] The comma preceding that italicized *where* serves no syntactical function, but by breaking the tempo of the clause, it intensifies the warning that there will be no safe zone for treason. What was said (by Edmund Ruffin) nearly a hundred years earlier about that avatar of orators Patrick Henry is equally true of Lincoln: "His pauses, which for the length might sometimes be feared to dispel the attention, riveted it the more by raising the expectation."[15]

Lincoln, in other words, was a speakerly writer, a writer who understood, as Perry Miller put the matter, that "language as printed on the page must convey the emphasis, the hesitancies, the searchings of language as it is spoken." Herndon reports that Lincoln often read aloud in order better to absorb the meaning of what he was reading.[16] A confirmed believer in the spoken word, he stood with Emerson against those, including Emerson's fellow transcendentalist Henry D. Thoreau, who regarded "language heard" as "brutish" compared with the written word, which, as Thoreau put it, is much to be preferred as "a reserved and select expression too significant to be heard by the ear."[17] In everything Lincoln wrote, whether or not composed for oral delivery, one senses that the words move from his mind via his ear en route to the page. In this sense, the published versions of his speeches are always and only approximations of what and how he spoke.

With these complications in mind, Douglas Wilson opens his book by revisiting a touchstone moment on which Barzun lingered in his 1959 essay, the farewell speech that Lincoln delivered in February 1861 from the rear platform of the train that was about to take him east out of Springfield to assume the presidency. Barzun made much of a small phrase—*these people*—in Lincoln's valedictory remarks: "To this place, and the kindness of these people, I owe everything." But "why '*these* people' "? Barzun wanted to know. "Why not 'you people,' whom Lincoln was addressing from the train platform, or 'this place and the kindness of *its* people' "? Barzun's explanation was ingenious and disclosed a genuine truth: that Lincoln had a "peculiar relation to himself" as if he were standing apart at a long overseeing distance, observing himself and "these people" as passive agents in the hands of God, or fate, or Providence.

It was an intriguing idea, but it was based on a wrong premise. As far as we know, Lincoln never said "these people" on that last day in Springfield. As Wilson points out, "the linchpin of Barzun's observation—the word 'these'—was not, of course, in the reports of the spoken address but appears only in Lincoln's written revision." In fact a manuscript of the speech survives in "train-shaken handwriting"—proof, or at least good evidence, that Lincoln composed the published version on the moving train after it had left the station and that what he wrote represented a revision of what he had said extemporaneously, or from notes, on the platform. Such textual instabilities (to borrow a term from literary theory) are among the things about Lincoln that readers fifty years ago simply did not know, at least not to the degree that we know them now.

We also know more about Lincoln's collaborations with other writers. We know, for example, how strong a hand his secretary of state and former rival for the Republican nomination, William H. Seward, had in drafting Lincoln's first inaugural address. Following the lead of Thomas Jefferson's first inaugural ("We are all Federalists, we are all Republicans"), Seward introduced a conciliatory tone into a speech that, in its early drafts, had been a "no-nonsense" challenge to the secessionist South.[18] This kind of evidence reveals a Lincoln who had not yet fully evolved from an apprentice deferring to seasoned advisers into an authoritative master—just the sort of evidence (if presidents may still be said to evolve) that, in our age of the digital draft and the delete button, may be denied to future historians.

Here is Seward's rough draft of how the speech might end:

I close. We are not we must not be aliens or enemies but ~~countrym~~ fellow countrymen and brethren. Although passion has strained our bonds of affection too hardly they must not ~~be broken they will not~~, I am sure they will not be broken. The mystic chords which proceeding from ~~every ba~~ so many battle fields and so many patriot graves ~~bind~~ pass through all the hearts and ~~hearths~~ all the hearths in this broad continent of ours will yet ~~harmon~~ again harmonize in their ancient music when ~~touched as they surely~~ breathed upon ~~again~~ by the ~~better angel~~ guardian angel of the nation.

And here is the conclusion of the speech as Lincoln eventually delivered it:

> I am loath to close. We are not enemies, but friends. We must not be enemies. Though passion may have strained, it must not break our bonds of affection. The mystic chords of memory, stretching from every battle-field, and patriot grave, to every living heart and hearthstone, all over this broad land, will yet swell the chorus of the Union, when again touched, as surely they will be, by the better angels of our nature.

The more personal note of "I am loath to close," the pared-down simplicity of "We must not be enemies," the intensified echo of "heart" by "hearthstone," the strengthened theme of shared memory, and, most of all, the shift from the image of a heavenly angel guarding the nation to the idea that America's public struggle is replicated in each American's private struggle between anger and charity—all this turns the speech from a political statement into a work of art.[19]

Any consideration of Lincoln as a writer must come to terms with many such acts of collaboration—as, for instance, in the Gettysburg Address when he echoed (who knows how consciously?) Theodore Parker's phrase "government of all, for all, and by all" and turned it into "government of the people, by the people, for the people." One scholar has gone so far as to say that "Lincoln's literary skill is most readily observable in those instances when he took someone else's prose and molded it to his own use."[20] In this case, the addition of the definite article and the triple substitution of bisyllabic "people" for the single syllable "all" slows down the phrasing, heightens the stresses on the preceding prepositions "of . . . by . . . for," and makes the whole statement more ringing and resonant.[21] By playing variations on a borrowed theme, as he had done in the first inaugural, he turns melody into music.

And then there is the question of how to read the words that Lincoln sequestered among his private papers—words, that is, that he wrote but, after consulting with himself, never sent to the intended recipient. Here, for example, is an unsent letter to General George Meade following the battle of Gettysburg, in which the president expresses his frustration. "I do not believe you appreciate the magnitude of the misfortune involved in Lee's escape," he wrote to Meade ten days after the battle, and in the next rebuke—"He was within your easy grasp"—we can almost hear him howling. With rising anger, he goes on: "And to have closed upon him would, in connection with our other late successes [a reference to Grant's victory at Vicksburg], have ended the war. As it is, the war will be prolonged indefinitely. Your golden opportunity is gone, and I am distressed immeasurably because of it."[22] But in the aftermath of a battle that had cost scores of thousands of lives and left the field drenched in blood amid the stink of unburied corpses, Lincoln clearly regretted these formulations. Nothing, he knew, had been "easy" at Gettysburg. There is sometimes as much to be learned about a writer's literary instincts from the words he suppresses as from the words he allows to go forward over his name.

Finally, there is the awkward problem that we have become more aware that some of the things Lincoln is supposed to have said—quips, aphorisms, tart retorts—he probably never did say. About a decade ago, in a book entitled *Recollected Words of Abraham Lincoln*, Don E. Fehrenbacher and Virginia Fehrenbacher compiled a rich sampling of Lincoln apocrypha—"utterances recalled piecemeal by hundreds of his contemporaries" that had previously been "scattered about in diaries, letters, newspaper interviews, and reminiscent writing of various kinds"—and grouped the entries according to the likelihood of their authenticity. It comes as a disappointment to learn that Lincoln probably never said about a vain politician that "if he had known how big a funeral he would have had, he would have died years ago."[23] One wishes—against the evidence—that he really did describe General Benjamin Butler as so pleased with himself that he could "strut while sitting down." The authority in this case is Carl Sandburg, an estimable but not, alas, a reliable source.[24]

III.

Yet if much has happened over the past fifty years to complicate our sense of Lincoln's literary achievement, we also have some advantages over previous generations (to borrow a phrase from David Donald) in "getting right" with him. For one thing, the context in which he lived was strikingly like our own. It was a time of government paralysis that seemed to be leading toward a breakdown of public trust in the Republic itself. It was a time of breakneck technological change that rendered traditional forms of discourse and communication obsolete. Over the course of Lincoln's lifetime, military technology advanced from the wooden warship to the ironclad, from smooth-barreled muskets to bored-barrel rifles capable of rapid loading, from cannonball guns to artillery that delivered shrapnel-filled shells with long-range accuracy. With the advent of photography—that "marvellous" invention, as Oliver Wendell Holmes called it in the gruesome year 1863—it was suddenly possible to preserve not only "the first smile of infancy and the last look of age" but the "wrecks of manhood thrown together in careless heaps" on the killing fields at Antietam, thanks to the lethal efficiency of the new weapons.[25]

When Lincoln was born in 1809, it took two men working at a small-town newspaper several hours to turn out a hundred single-sided sheets; by the time he died in 1865 two workers, with the use of multiple-cylinder printing presses, could produce thousands of eight-page folded papers in an hour.[26] And most amazing, deployment of the telegraph meant that war news or words uttered in a local legislative chamber could be disseminated to millions of people in a matter of minutes. In our thinking about Lincoln in the present, it helps to keep in mind that technologies of the past that seem primitive now—crank-started automobiles, mimeograph machines, cathode-ray television—were marvels to those who first experienced them.

Lincoln was adept at exploiting the new technologies of his own day (he was, for example, a careful manager of his own photographic portraits), and if the means for transmitting words was changing, so, he knew, was the audience who received them. He lived, as we do, in an age of large-scale immigration. Within a decade of his death, in the centen-

nial year of the Republic, 1876, the percentage of the American population that was foreign-born was larger than in the bicentennial year, 1976.
Especially in the industrializing cities, "men . . . who have come from
Europe," as he put it in Chicago during the senatorial campaign of 1858,
"or whose ancestors have come hither and settled here" were a rising
political force. Extension of the franchise was hastening the decline of
what the historian David Hackett Fischer has called the culture of "deference"—a political culture, that is, in which public speech had been
mainly an insider discourse belonging to people of learning and high
social status, to whom the broader public was expected to listen in a spirit
of deferential consent.[27]

One way to understand Lincoln's growth as a writer is to listen as he
adjusts to the new audience. Although (or perhaps because) he was not
born into privilege, he littered his early speeches with what Edmund Wilson called "the old-fashioned ornaments of forensic and Congressional
rhetoric."[28] In the 1838 address to the Springfield Lyceum, for instance,
every phrase seems to reach for a decorous image: "Let reverence for the
laws, be breathed by every American mother, to the lisping babe, that
prattles on her lap." This was a conventional paean to the law, full of
pieties like those dished up by any number of contemporaries, especially
Whigs.[29] Its tone was didactic. Its theme was the anarchic force of the
mob and the sacrosanct value of the law. If this were the style by which
we remembered Lincoln, his memory would be much dimmer than it is.

But as the sectional crisis deepened and especially as events of the
1850s—the Fugitive Slave Law, the Kansas-Nebraska Act, the *Dred Scott*
decision, John Brown's raid—made ever more glaring the contradiction
between law and conscience, the old platitudes became insupportable.
With slavery unjust but legal in the South and the act of harboring a fugitive slave just but illegal in the North, "law and order," as one incensed
New Englander put it in 1851, were lining up "on the wrong side" of the
great moral question of the day. As the day of reckoning approached, Lincoln became an entirely different kind of writer.[30]

His tone changed. He learned how to sound conversational without
being casual, as if talking seriously to himself with welcoming awareness
that he was being overheard. It was a new public style that James Russell
Lowell called "familiar dignity."[31] Take, for example, this moment in the
first inaugural address, when Lincoln is still hoping that war can be

averted: "Suppose you go to war, you cannot fight always; and when, after much loss on both sides, and no gain on either, you cease fighting, the identical old questions as to terms of intercourse are again upon you." This sentence goes straight to the heart of the matter in a way that anyone who has ever quarreled with a friend or spouse—everyone, that is—will immediately understand. "A husband and wife may be divorced," he says, "and go out of the presence, and beyond the reach of each other; but the different parts of our country cannot do this." Yet if the style is blunt and plain, the content is by no means banal; it is the same point that Max Weber was to make sixty years later in a famous essay in which, following the World War I armistice, he wrote of the bitterness of concluding a war with a return to "status quo peace."[32]

At a time when virtually no one in America could see an end to the impasse over slavery, obfuscation was the coin of the realm, especially with respect to the issue of race. But Lincoln had a talent for cutting through obfuscation, and through the 1850s his talent grew. Sometimes he employed it in ways that strike us today as tawdry or even pandering, as when he replied to Stephen Douglas's fearmongering about the danger of racial mixing: "The Judge regales us with the terrible enormities that take place by the mixture of races. . . . Why, Judge, if we do not let them get together in the Territories they won't mix there."[33] Even as he concedes the premise that close contact between the races should be avoided (the sexual implication is never far from the surface), Lincoln undercuts the indignation that Douglas brings, however sincerely, to the question, and with a leavening dash of humor, he wins the rhetorical skirmish.

His humor of course has been anthologized, imitated, praised, and even plagiarized as one of the defining aspects of his character, but it was much more than merely an attractive or entertaining feature of his style. It was a means of establishing personal rapport with strangers in public. Better than any American politician before or since, Lincoln understood humor as a form of communication that forges a partnership between speaker and hearer in which the former initiates the joke until the latter "gets it" and thereby closes the circle. He understood how a joke establishes intimacy through a feeling of confidential sharing that breaks down the hierarchy of the speaker/hearer relation. And if humor served the public Lincoln, it was also important—even desperately important (this is where Perry Miller saw the affinity with Twain)—for the private Lincoln. "If it were not for these stories, jests, I should die," he is reported by Herndon to have said, "they give me vent—are the vents of my moods and gloom."[34]

It is a mistake to confuse Lincoln's humor with levity. He could be at his most serious when joking. Consider these remarks in the spring of 1865 to the 140th Indiana Regiment: "While I have often said that all men ought to be free, yet I would allow those colored persons to be slaves who want to be, and next to them those white persons who argue in favor of making other people slaves." After waiting out the applause, he adds with a flourish that is partly a punch line and partly a twisting of the knife, "I am in favor of giving an opportunity to such white men to try it on for themselves."[35]

For some, Lincoln the jokester was simply a boor whose "vulgarity," as Mary Chesnut wrote in her diary shortly before his inauguration, was "beyond credence."[36] In her view, his main claim to literary distinction was as a master of malapropism: "We are always picking up some good thing of the rough Illinoisan's saying. Lincoln objects to some man—'Oh, he is too *interruptious*'; that is a horrid style of man or woman, the interruptious. I know the thing, but had no name for it before." Yet even Mrs. Chesnut's disdain contains, in spite of herself, a grudging respect for Lincoln's gift at articulating something she has felt without being able to find quite the right word to express it.

And if he spoke with wit, he also read with wit—as, for example, when he gives close attention in the last debate with Douglas to the Constitution itself, noting the absence of frank words such as *negroes* (in the three-fifths clause) and *slavery* (in the fugitive slave clause) in favor of the euphemisms *persons* and *service*. This "covert language" of the Constitution, he says, "was used with a purpose," not so much to disguise the fact of slavery in the present as to ensure that in the future, "after the institution of slavery had passed from among us . . . there should be nothing on the face of the great charter of liberty suggesting that such a thing as negro slavery had ever existed among us."[37] Lincoln read the Constitution as implicitly prophetic rather than culpably complicit and thereby managed to capture the embarrassment of the founders without indicting them for their failure to abolish the source of their embarrassment.

In the first message to congress, as Douglas Wilson points out, we see the same sharpness of interpretation when he zeroes in on the consequential difference between the terms *secession* and *rebellion* as employed by leaders of the Confederacy. "Secession," he writes, is a "sugar-coated" word, an "ingenious sophism" that attempts "an insidious debauching of the public mind" in an effort to persuade the people of the South that wrecking the Union was anything more than rebellion pure and simple. Here, in remarks delivered at the Baltimore Sanitary Fair in the spring of 1864, is another example of his alertness to how much depends on what a grammarian would call word usage:

> The world has never had a good definition of the word liberty, and the American people, just now, are much in want of one. We all declare for liberty; but in using the same *word* we do not all mean the same *thing*. With some the word liberty may mean for each man to do as he pleases with himself, and the product of his labor; while with others the same word may mean for some men to do as they please with other men, and the product of other men's labor. Here are two, not only different, but incompatable [sic] things, called by the same name—liberty. And it follows that each of the things is, by the respective parties, called by two different and incompatable names—liberty and tyranny.
>
> The shepherd drives the wolf from the sheep's throat, for which the sheep thanks the shepherd as a *liberator*, while the wolf denounces him for the same act as the destroyer of liberty, especially as the sheep was a black one. Plainly the sheep and the wolf are not agreed upon a definition of the word liberty; and precisely the same difference prevails today among us human creatures, even in the North, and all professing to love liberty. Hence we behold the processes by which thousands are daily passing from under the yoke of bondage, hailed by some as the advance of liberty, and bewailed by others as the destruction of all liberty. Recently, as it seems, the people of Maryland have been doing something to define liberty; and thanks to them that, in what they have done, the wolf's dictionary, has been repudiated.

Notwithstanding his delight in using it for light purposes, Lincoln respected language as an ultimately serious business, a battleground on which Americans were contesting their most basic convictions.

According to his friend Joseph Gillespie, he "despised ornament or display." William Herndon agreed: "Abstractions [and] glittering generalities" drove him to rage. This allergy to literary exhibitionism put Lincoln at odds with the norms of public discourse, as anyone knows who has read his "chaste" (Garry Wills's word) Gettysburg Address side by side with Edward Everett's plush oration delivered that same afternoon. Everett's speech was laden with classical reference (it begins by invoking the battle of Marathon) and belonged, as Wills has shown, to the ancient tradition of the Periclean funeral oration. It was an impressive but conventional performance at a time when "clergymen, orators, versifiers, and novelists" decorated their speeches and writings with passages from the worthies of classical and English literature. This was true in the South as well as the North, in private as well as in public. We find, for instance, the daughter of a Louisiana planter paraphrasing in the pages of her diary Satan's words in Milton's *Paradise Lost* ("It is better to reign in hell than serve in heaven") as she declares her preference for "Death in the confederacy, rather than bliss in the Union!"[38] In an age when formal schooling depended a great deal on memorization, literature was not something to be looked up or looked into; it was something one carried in one's memory, where it waited to be tapped.

In Lincoln's writing, public or private, this sort of allusiveness is scarce—partly, no doubt, because of the limits of his formal education. Yet as Wills has stressed, he was a kind of natural classicist. He used the exordium as a gesture of solidarity with opponents ("all the protection which, consistently with the Constitution and the laws, can be given, will be cheerfully given to all the States . . . as cheerfully to one Section, as to another"). He used balanced antinomies ("We shall *lie down* pleasantly, dreaming that the people of *Missouri* are on the verge of making their State *free*; and we shall *awake* to the *reality*, instead that the *Supreme* Court has made *Illinois* a *slave* State") and stepped reiterations ("Fondly do we hope, fervently do we pray"). But since these rhetorical techniques were more instinctive than instructed, his writing conveys a feeling of intrinsic energy released from within rather than of design imposed from without. It meets the standard, in Thoreau's phrase, of growing "from within outward, out of the necessities and character of the indweller." There is no posturing or evasion; we feel the author's character revealed in the author's language. One measure of the revelation is the fact that the voice in his personal writings (letters, private memoranda) is fundamentally the same as the voice in his public writings.

Take, for example, the "Fragment on Slavery," a note to himself composed, most likely, in 1854:

If A. can prove, however conclusively, that he may, of right, enslave B.—
why may not B. snatch the same argument, and prove equally, that he
may enslave A?—

You say A. is white, and B. is black. It is *color*, then; the lighter, having
the right to enslave the darker? Take care. By this rule, you are to be slave
to the first man you meet, with a fairer skin than your own.

You do not mean *color* exactly?—You mean the whites are *intellectually*
the superiors of the blacks, and, therefore, have the right to enslave them?
Take care again. By this rule, you are to be slave to the first man you meet,
with an intellect superior to your own.

But, say you, it is a question of *interest*; and, if you can make it your
interest, you have the right to enslave another. Very well. And if he can
make it his interest, he has the right to enslave you.

This remarkable piece of writing may, in fact, have been another instance
of borrowing (there is a similar formulation in a book by the antislavery
Kentucky minister John Fee, published in 1851), but whatever its precedents, it manifests a fusion of thought and feeling so complete that it is
impossible to distinguish the one from the other.[39]

What T. S. Eliot said of poetry—that we feel in it a "direct sensuous
apprehension of thought, or a recreation of thought into feeling"—is
true of Lincoln's prose. Despite his concessions to prevailing racial attitudes ("there is a physical difference between the two [races], which in my
judgment will probably forever forbid their living together upon the
footing of perfect equality . . ."),[40] it is impossible to draw a sharp line
between Lincoln's rational arguments against slavery as a threat to white
people and his feeling of outrage at the plight of black people. Here is his
speech on the *Dred Scott* decision:

All the powers of earth seem rapidly combining against him. Mammon is
after him; ambition follows, and philosophy follows, and the Theology
of the day is fast joining the cry. They have him in his prison house; they
have searched his person, and left no prying instrument with him. One
after another they have closed the heavy iron doors upon him, and now
they have him, as it were, bolted in with a lock of a hundred keys, which
can never be unlocked without the concurrence of every key; the keys in
the hands of a hundred different men, and they scattered to a hundred

different places; and they stand musing as to what invention in all the dominions of mind and matter, can be produced to make the impossibility of his escape more complete than it is.[41]

This is writing of the highest order—vivid without contrivance, indignant without self-reference, dramatic without melodrama—which never descends into demagoguery but rises to moral sublimity. It is hard to think of another political figure in our history whose literary power comes anywhere close.

IV.

"The dogmas of the quiet past," Lincoln wrote in his second annual message to Congress, "are inadequate to the stormy present. As our case is new, so we must think anew, and act anew. We must disenthrall ourselves, and then we shall save our country."[42] In this belief he stood with Melville (with whom he may have disagreed about punctuation, but with whom he agreed on more fundamental things), who had written not long before that "those who are solely governed by the Past stand like Lot's wife, crystallized in the act of looking backward, and forever incapable of looking before."[43] Lincoln is best understood in the pragmatist tradition that leads from Melville, Whitman, and Emerson to William James and John Dewey, writers who believed that the human mind, by conceiving a hitherto unconceived future, has the power to bring it into existence. Language was of ultimate importance to him because he understood that it is by means of language that we begin the process of converting imagination into actuality.

Yet there is an obvious difference that makes Lincoln unique among the great American writers. Unlike his literary peers, he was a man who possessed formidable political power—the power, that is, to make or refrain from war, the power (as he finally concluded, pressed by the exigencies of war) to emancipate slaves or keep them in bondage. He had always insisted that the founders intended that slavery be placed "where the public mind shall rest with the belief that it is in the course of ultimate extinction."[44] One of the most moving aspects of his career is his deepening awareness that at stake in the war was not only the preservation of the Union—which, as he said in his famous letter to Horace Greeley in the summer of 1862, he would save "without freeing *any* slave" or "by freeing *all* the slaves" or "by freeing some and letting others alone"—but the fate of the slaves themselves. With the paramount purpose in mind of saving the Union, for which he needed the loyal slave states and the support of northerners hostile to anything that smacked of abolition, he had been slow to do much to hasten the "ultimate extinction" of slavery. But as the war went on, he came under increasing pressure from his own generals to treat slaves as contraband. Once he declared partial abolition in the Emancipation Proclamation of January 1863 (slavery remained untouched in the loyal slave states) and then, over the coming months, approved the formation of black regiments in the Union army, he understood that his own "policy of emancipation, and of employing black soldiers" had given "to the future a new aspect." Against those who had predicted otherwise, he noted in December 1863, that "no servile insurrection, or tendency to violence or cruelty, has marked the measures of emancipation and arming the blacks." And he thanked *all* the soldiers, black and white, to whom "the world must stand indebted for the home of freedom disenthralled, regenerated, enlarged, and perpetuated."[45]

The war had changed everything. Reading Lincoln and thinking about his life are to be reminded of how hard it is to grasp that the people we study as historical actors did not know the future, which, to us, is the past. It is not hard to understand this fact in a notional sense. But really to comprehend it—to know it viscerally—requires emptying our minds as far as possible of knowledge that could not be foreknown (Lee's retreat from Gettysburg, for example, which, as Lincoln received bulletins from the battlefield, he could certainly not have counted on, given what had happened at Fredericksburg and Chancellorsville). It is no small challenge to think ourselves into the prospective ignorance that Lincoln and his contemporaries had to cope with as they tried to discern the future.

When, for example, he wrote in April 1864 to the Kentucky newspaper editor Albert Hodges that "I claim not to have controlled events, but confess plainly that events have controlled me," he was not thinking abstractly about some theological doctrine of predestination (though he may have been inclined toward such an idea) but concretely about the contingencies of history. Perhaps he was thinking of what would have happened had Colonel Robert Anderson not moved his troops three years earlier under cover of darkness from the vulnerable Fort Moultrie to the bastion of Fort Sumter in Charleston Harbor, where only starvation or a sustained barrage could dislodge him; or perhaps he was thinking what would have happened if the volleys of Confederate shells fired the previous summer at the Union defenders on Cemetery Ridge on the third day of fighting at Gettysburg had hit their targets rather than exploded behind Union lines. If the shells had found their mark, would Lee have prevailed? Would the will of the North have been broken? Would there have been a stampede for president toward McClellan, who was likely to have pursued a "status quo peace"? Such questions invite us into the inescapable maze of counterfactual history, and wandering that maze must be something like what it was to live through these events without foresight.

Lincoln's writing can only be understood in this context of radical uncertainty under pressure from onrushing events. Better than any contemporary, he saw that old ways of using language had to give way to new conditions. One feels the pressure building in his speeches throughout the 1850s, but it was the war itself that changed everything for everyone, starting with the "civilized" rules of warfare as they had been hitherto understood. General Sherman, for instance, regarded as a fiend by the people through whom he sent his army on a mission of organized pillage in order (from his point of view) to supply themselves on their march from Atlanta to Savannah, was outraged by the enemy's use of land mines to slow his advance. "This was not war, but murder," he wrote in his memoir, "and it made me very angry." A few months earlier an enlisted man in the First Tennessee Regiment described Yankee sharpshooters as "shameful and cowardly" as they picked off his comrades who had stepped out from cover to aid the enemy wounded.[46] The fact is that Lincoln and his contemporaries were living at a time of overwhelming moral confusion on every question from the norms of the battlefield to relations between the races. Nathaniel Hawthorne put it mildly when he described the "social system" as "thoroughly disturbed."[47]

It was not until well after the war that American writers fully realized what had happened to their nation and their culture. In a chapter entitled "The Chastening of American Prose Style," Edmund Wilson described one effect—the effect on literary style—of this realization. Here, from John W. De Forest's 1867 novel, *Miss Ravenel's Conversion from Secession to Loyalty* (De Forest had served as a captain in the Union army) is an example of what he had in mind:

I had just finished breakfast, and was lying on my back smoking. A bullet whistled so unusually low as to attract my attention and struck with a loud smash in a tree about twenty feet from me. Between me and the tree a soldier with his great-coat rolled under his head for a pillow lay on his back reading a newspaper which he held in both hands. I remember smiling to myself to see this man start as the bullet passed. Some of his comrades left off playing cards and looked for it. The man who was reading remained perfectly still, his eyes fixed on the paper with a steadiness which I thought curious, considering the bustle around him. Presently I noticed that there were a few drops of blood on his neck, and that his face was paling. Calling to the card players, who had resumed their game, I said, "See to that man with the paper." They went to him, spoke to him, touched him, and found him perfectly dead. The ball had struck him under the chin, traversed the neck, and cut the spinal column where it joins the brain, making a fearful hole through which the blood had already soaked his greatcoat. It was this man's head and not the tree which had been struck with such a report. There he lay, still holding the New York *Independent*, with his eyes fixed on a sermon by Henry Ward Beecher. It was really quite a remarkable circumstance.

With its utter lack of adornment and its ironic juxtaposition of random death with the pious words the dead man had been reading when the bullet struck—words that doubtless attributed every event, no matter how small, to the omnipotent will of God—this bit of postwar prose gives a retrospective clue to Lincoln's literary achievement.

What it tells us—contra Barzun—is that it is not quite right to affiliate him with later writers who recoiled from "literary plush" and adopted in its place the plain style of journalistic reportage in which description, as in the last sentence of the passage quoted above, supplants interpretation and has a clipped tone of ironic detachment. Most American writers stepped back from the Civil War into this kind of reticent bemusement. "The subsidence of that great convulsion," as Henry James wrote with typical obliqueness, "has left a different tone from the tone it found." The old literary conventions, no less than racial or religious attitudes, had been shaken, if not destroyed, by the war, and most American writers had little to say about what, exactly, would come in to take their place. Even Melville, in his poems about young men marching off to battle with dreams of glory ("far footfalls died away till none were left"), trailed off into bewilderment as he described them coming back "not as they filed two years before, / But a remnant half-tattered, and battered, and worn / Like castaway sailors, who—stunned / By the surf's loud roar / . . . at last crawl, spent, to shore."

In *Patriotic Gore*—the title captures his point—Edmund Wilson followed the lead of such Civil War writers as De Forest and Ambrose Bierce in trying to "remove the whole subject [of the Civil War] from the plane of morality." The contest between North and South was, to Wilson, no different from the behavior of sea slugs eating and excreting each other. Ideas and ideals (Union, Freedom) were decorative words pasted onto a brutal struggle for power and domination. A variant of this view has been put forth more recently by Louis Menand in a book about the rise of pragmatism that argues that the Civil War not only "discredited the beliefs and assumptions of the era that preceded it" but discredited belief itself.[48]

There is much to be said for this reading of American literary and spiritual history. But Lincoln does not fit into it. In Lincoln we encounter, by contrast, a mind searching for transcendent meaning in the carnage and asserting that meaning for both sides. Like his great eulogist Walt Whitman, who saw the collective face of democracy in the faces of the dying boys, northerners and southerners alike, whom he nursed and mourned in the hospital wards, Lincoln was appalled by the coming of the war and by what it wrought when it came. From his first message to Congress, in which he asserted that what "ballots have fairly, and constitutionally, decided" must not be appealed "back to bullets," to his second inaugural, he saw the war as a "mighty scourge" inflicted by God as punishment equally on North and South for the collective sin of slavery.

He was, in short, a believer. His faith was in the transcendent principle of human equality. He believed, moreover, that all Americans had an innate feeling for this principle; that is why he abandoned the old oratorical mode of speaking from an Olympian position of privileged knowledge and spoke, instead, to what he believed his hearers already knew. "I have never had a feeling politically," he said on the steps of Independence Hall in Philadelphia en route to his first inauguration, "that did not spring from the sentiments embodied in the Declaration of Independence." He believed that these sentiments were shared by all people, including white people who lived in the South and who could "no more divest themselves" of their "human sympathies . . . than . . . of their sensibility to physical pain." He was sure that these people had a "sense of the wrong of slavery" and of "humanity in the negro." He was equally sure that the idea of equality was present a priori in the hearts of America's most recent immigrants:

> We have . . . among us perhaps half of our people . . . who have come from Europe—German, Irish, French, and Scandinavian—men that have come from Europe themselves, or whose ancestors have come hither and settled here, finding themselves our equals in all things. If they look back through this history to trace their connection with those [revolutionary] days by blood, they find they have none, they cannot carry themselves back into that glorious epoch and make themselves feel that they are part of us, but when they look through that old Declaration of Independence they find that those old men say that "We hold these truths to be self-evident, that all men are created equal," and then they find that that moral sentiment taught in that day evidences their relation to those men, that it is the father of all moral principle in them, and that they have a right to claim it as though they were blood of the blood, and flesh of the flesh of the men who wrote that Declaration (*loud and long continued applause*) and so they are.

Again and again, Lincoln insisted that the Declaration finds "all men . . . equal upon principle" and pointed out (as he had done privately in the "Fragment on Slavery") that "making exceptions to it" raises the slippery slope question of "where will it stop. If one man says it does not mean negro, why may not another say it does not mean some other man?"[49]

Lincoln's achievement as a writer was to communicate his faith that the Declaration is America's scripture. This achievement was sealed and "symbolized," as Robert Bellah has written, by his own words and, ultimately, by his martyrdom.

V.

The question of Lincoln's literary status today is therefore the question of whether his "symbolic and sacramental" language (Robert Lowell's phrase) retains anything like the force it once exerted on the American imagination.[50] This is of course an unanswerable question because we have only crude methods for answering it. But surely there is reason—despite the bicentennial flood of new editions, collections, biographies, conferences, television specials, exhibitions, and so on—to doubt it.

Starting in the iconoclastic 1960s, Lincoln's prestige as the Great Emancipator came under attack from historians who, for many good reasons, gave new emphasis to the role of the slaves in achieving their own liberation. By the 1990s attendance at the Lincoln Memorial was declining, and the Freedmen's Monument (it exists in two versions, in Boston and Washington), which shows the president standing beside a kneeling former slave, was being denounced for making the black man look as if he were "shining Lincoln's shoes."[51] Today the downturn in Lincoln's reputation would seem to have been arrested, if not reversed. David Donald's biography (published in 1995) and Doris Kearns Goodwin's narrative account of Lincoln's political wizardry (*Team of Rivals* [2005]), both reached the best seller lists. Yet if Lincoln retains a certain iconic significance, he has lost his commanding presence—especially, one suspects, for students and young adults. It is not so much that his stature has been diminished (that has happened to virtually all the erstwhile icons of American history) as that he has become less a vital figure than a shadow or abstraction. For Americans of urbane sophistication, he seems to exist today mainly in the affectless twang of fictional or half-fictional caricatures, like Forrest Gump and Garrison Keillor, who inhabit a postmodern limbo somewhere between authenticity and irony, with Honest Abe hovering vaguely in the background.

Fifty years ago the claim that Lincoln made an important difference to our literature had plausibility and even a certain inevitability. Urbane intellectuals were still able to imagine—if not fully to share—Walt Whitman's frame of mind when, while working as a nurse in a Union hospital, he walked past the White House under the spell of the man who lived there, musing on the luminous purity of the "White House of future dreams and dramas." But today, after Watergate, and Monica, and the Election of the Hanging Chads, it seems doubtful that there is a poet left in America who imagines "dreams and dramas" in the White House as anything more than fantasies or farce—though as I write (April 2008), another Illinoisan has surprised many Americans who never thought they would find hope through politics again.

Still, the reasons for our estrangement run deeper than politics. When

Barzun asked, "Does not every schoolchild learn that the Gettysburg Address is beautiful, hearing this said so often that he ends up believing it?" he was making an assumption that we no longer make, at least not with impunity. He was assuming that Lincoln was a looming presence to America's schoolchildren and the central symbol of what, a few years later, Bellah called America's civil religion. He was also assuming that "the beautiful" is an aesthetic truth as timeless and self-evident as the political truth that Lincoln found in the Declaration. This assumption more or less prevailed from Lincoln's time (when Emerson, in a statement applicable to Lincoln, asserted that "the whole secret of the teacher's force lies in the conviction that men . . . want awakening . . . to a perception of beauty") to Barzun's time. But it is not clear that it has survived the postmodern skepticism that was already on the rise when Barzun wrote and that is only now abating.

Some of this skepticism is well placed. There are good reasons, in our age of proselytizing for American-style "democracy" as God's gift to the world, to be wary of all forms of providential politics even when marked, as Lincoln's was, by humility. ("It may seem strange that any men should dare to ask a just God's assistance in wringing their bread from the sweat of other men's faces; but let us judge not that we be not judged.") Although he had opposed American jingoism at the time of the Mexican War, he was, as he made clear in the closing lines of the Gettysburg Address, a strong believer in America's manifest destiny as the beacon to mankind. In this too he agreed with Melville, who wrote in 1850 that "we cannot do a good to America but we give alms to the world."

And then there is the difficult question—the sort of question Lincoln posed about the word *liberty*—of what exactly he meant by equality and whether his meaning retains force for us today. In his first message to Congress, he answered this question with a definition that has by now an archaic ring to it. We would call it equality of opportunity: "[T]he leading object of government is, to elevate the condition of men—to lift artificial weights from all shoulders—to clear the paths of laudable pursuit for all, to afford all, an unfettered start, a fair chance, in the race of life." With this passage in mind (there are many others of substantive equivalence), it is tempting to wonder what Lincoln would say about the whole cluster of questions that still attaches to the issues of race and class in contemporary America, where the "artificial weights" seem to grow heavier and the task of clearing the paths more complex and daunting.

He cannot of course help us with these questions, and it is no doubt absurd—or at least ahistorical—to imagine a dialogue with him about them. Yet as we face them on our own, it may be worth pausing on the astonishing fact that we once had a president whose eloquence on behalf of equality as he understood it is still able to move us.

9

Lincoln's Religion

RICHARD CARWARDINE

"Lincoln often if not whol[l]y was an atheist," insisted one of his friends and political associates, James H. Matheny, in 1870. Recounting conversations held and overheard during a quarter of a century's close acquaintance, he told how the young Lincoln had been "Enthusiastic in his infidelity": He had "call[ed] Christ a bastard," "ridiculed the Bible" as self-contradictory and irrational, and written "a little Book on Infidelity." Holding convictions that "bordered on absolute Atheism," he learned to be discreet: "as he grew older he . . . didn't talk much before Strangers about his religion, but to friends—close and bosom ones he was always open & avowed—fair & honest, but to Strangers he held them off from Policy." During the 1850s, as "a rising man" politically, he had "played a sharp game" on the Christian community and duped pious voters into believing he was "a seeker after Salvation &c in the Lord."[1] Matheny lined up with other close associates convinced that Lincoln had been no Christian. They included Lincoln's law partners William H. Herndon and John T. Stuart, and his "particular friend" Ward Hill Lamon.[2] They took one side of a posthumous tug-of-war over the soul of the sixteenth president.

Contending with them were those who insisted—in the words of his fellow lawyer Isaac N. Arnold—that Lincoln "believed in the great fundamental principals [sic] of Christianity."[3] The not entirely edifying controversy in which the protagonists engaged followed a torrent of sanctifying sermons that, in the shadow of Lincoln's Good Friday assassination, canonized the Great Emancipator and Savior of the Union and hid a more complicated, because more human, truth. The controversy took off after the appearance of the first substantial biography, the work of a pious New England Republican, Josiah G. Holland. Eulogistic and sentimental, *The Life of Abraham Lincoln* presented "a true-hearted Christian man," "who thought more of religious subjects than of all others, who had an undying faith in the providence of God" and who would "always be remembered as eminently a Christian President." Herndon deemed the portrait preposterous and, with rebuttal in mind, set about collecting and recording material from anyone who would provide biographical information.[4]

One of the many whom Herndon interviewed was Judge David Davis, Lincoln's campaign manager in 1860 and later one of his Supreme Court appointees. Davis responded in a way that counseled caution in any examination of his friend's faith. "I don't Know anything about Lincoln's Religion," he told Herndon, "don't think anybody Knew. The idea that Lincoln talked to a stranger about his religion or religious views . . . is absurd to me." It would have been entirely out of character: "I Know the man so well: he was the most reticent—Secretive man I Ever Saw—or Expect to See."[5] Windows into men's souls are rarely transparent, and Lincoln kept his veiled more than most. His taciturnity in this and other intimate matters, his preference for keeping his own counsel, and the relative paucity of his written private reflections: All these have acted to conceal his religion, opening the way to claim and counterclaim and offering scope for most faith traditions to embrace him as one of theirs. Quakers have pointed to his Virginia forebears, Baptists to his parents' faith, Episcopalians to their officiating at his wedding, Presbyterians to the ministers under whom he regularly sat, and Spiritualists to their séances at the White House. In addition, Methodists, Unitarians, Universalists, and Catholics—not to mention Freemasons—have found, or invented, reasons to clasp him to their bosoms.[6]

This combination of self-serving claims and exiguous, contradictory evidence makes it only too tempting to dismiss the search for Lincoln's soul as an unprofitable exercise, of marginal significance when compared with the better-documented reality of Lincoln the party organizer, pragmatic leader, and shrewd strategist. It is these political themes that have dominated scholarly lives of the sixteenth president. More often than not, the reflective Lincoln, capable of serious thought about ultimate concerns, has remained hidden in the biographical shadows.[7] Yet we doubly misread the political Lincoln if we take his religion too lightly. First, his evolving ideas about faith are significant for what they tell us about the values and principles that shaped his vision, complemented his ambition, and drove his politics. Secondly—and perhaps even more important—Lincoln's sensitivity, though not subjection, to public opinion gave him a keen understanding of its cultural sources, which included the powerful influence of religion, especially mainstream Protestantism.

Recent scholarship on American religion during the early decades of the Republic has abundantly demonstrated the increasing and powerful role of evangelical Protestants in shaping both private lives and the public sphere and has rescued the historiography of the immediate postrevolutionary generations from the once-prevailing "Calvinist consensus." Not only did the proportion of churched evangelicals in the overall population increase at least twofold during the first half of the nineteenth century, but the denominations that dominated this surge, which is often described as a "second great awakening," were those that in 1776 had lacked numbers and standing: the Methodists (who had become the largest single denomination by the time Lincoln reached early manhood) and the Baptists. Nathan Hatch has emphasized the populist and initially countercultural character of these "upstart" churches, which were agents of a widespread antiauthoritarian revolt; others have just as forcefully stressed the churches' assiduous institution building, revealed in an increasingly "sacralized" landscape of new and expanded meetinghouses. Both reflecting and reinforcing elements in the wider culture, the most successful denominations validated "Arminian" doctrines of human agency, self-reliance, self-improvement, and moral enterprise and so challenged theological notions of "inability" associated with the prevailing Calvinism of the previous century.[8]

By the 1850s relatively few Americans lacked a degree of loyalty toward one Christian denomination or another, and at least four in every ten were members of, or in attendance at, a disparate range of evangelical churches. Thanks in particular to the scholarship of Mark A. Noll, we now understand this powerful evangelical subculture to have been instrumental in fusing commonsense philosophy, Protestant religion, and republicanism—religious and civil freedom—into a creed that fed and invigorated American nationalism.[9] This was also a creed that in the early and middle years of the nineteenth century drew on long-standing and still-developing ideas of God's special plan for what had now become the United States.[10] Related to this sense of mission was a widespread millennialist conviction about moral and social improvement. This found a variety of expressions, not least in order to accommodate conflicting understandings of the theological significance of slavery; from the 1830s, northern reformers' antislavery aspirations and faith in the moral benefits of a free labor economy were increasingly matched, among southern divines, by a proslavery millennialist manifesto for the amelioration of bondage, the strengthening of benevolent Christian paternalism, and the moral improvement of the slaves. Collectively, these ideas drew church leaders, particularly evangelicals, toward the sphere of politics and even into active campaigning, with considerable significance for political agendas and electoral mobilization.[11]

Lincoln's own faith—to the extent that it is possible to discern it—was cut from a different cloth from that of mainstream Protestants. He was certainly no evangelical. But as this essay will explain, his religious unorthodoxy did not make him any less attentive to mobilizing the progressive elements of contemporary Protestantism, first on behalf of the prewar Republican Party and then of the wartime unionist coalition.

Lincoln's Faith

"The truth about Mr. Lincoln," declared Herndon and his cobiographer, Jesse K. Weik, "is that he read less and thought more than any man of his standing in America, if not in the world. He possessed originality and power of thought in an eminent degree."[12] Yet if he did not read widely, he read and reread familiar texts until they were burned into his memory. And the two texts from which he quoted with greatest appetite, and at will, were the Bible and Shakespeare.

Through his own efforts he acquired a command of the King James Bible that colored his rhetoric and conversation. The habit of scripture reading, encouraged by his mother, was never lost. Although his mother's cousin Dennis Hanks recalled that "Lincoln didnt read the Bible half as much as said," nonetheless, Hanks conceded, "he did read it."[13] He made the scriptures a formidable weapon. "It is a pleasure to be able to quote lines to fit any occasion," he told a young boy in Springfield; "the Bible is the richest source of pertinent quotations."[14] An Illinois Presbyterian minister, walking past a group of citizens clustered around Lincoln as he entertained them with a flow of anecdotes, called out as he passed: "Where the great ones are there will the people be." Quickly Lincoln replied, "Ho! Parson a little more Scriptural; 'Where the carcass is there will the eagles be gathered together.'"[15]

Deep familiarity with the Bible is not of course evidence of a religious faith, but Lincoln's immersion in the scriptures—alongside his keen appetite for Shakespearean soliloquies saturated with anxious self-examination and moral wrestling—points to a man for whom profound private reflection on ethical matters was an essential part of his being.[16] Continuous religious inquiry was a natural ingredient of his broader intellectual quest. The weight of evidence points to an evolution in his views as an adult. As a young man in New Salem, freed from the hard-shell, hyper-Calvinist milieu of his Baptist parents' faith and practice, Lincoln found a stimulus in deistic rationalism, but after taking on professional and family responsibilities in Springfield, he encountered and ruminated on a more intellectual Protestantism. Then, when he was president, the circumstances of war ensured an even more profound, pressing engagement with the meaning of life and death.

The claim that the Lincoln of New Salem was an atheist is as implausible as it is beyond proof. Rather he was drawn to Tom Paine's *Age of Reason* and other deist works, including Constantin de Volney's *Ruins*, attracted by their rationalist critique of the scriptures. Equally, he warmed to Robert Burns's poetry, including his satire on Calvinist self-righteousness.[17] The story that Lincoln wrote an essay questioning the Bible as divine revelation is plausible; it is certainly consistent with what we know of his views at this time. But Lincoln's skepticism easily embraced belief in a Creator. Isaac Cogdal, a long-standing acquaintance, did not dispute that Lincoln had written an essay denying the inspiration of scripture, but insisted that his friend still "believed in God—and all the great substantial groundworks of Religion." This, though, was not a quixotic or impulsive God or one who consigned souls to endless punishment.[18]

When he moved to Springfield, Lincoln for the first time counted among his neighbors college-trained ministers capable of engaging intelligently with unorthodox views. After marrying Mary Todd, he worshiped occasionally in the Episcopal church. Then, following the death of three-year-old Eddie in 1850, the grieving family joined the First Presbyterian Church, whose Old School pastor, James Smith, had conducted the funeral ceremony. Mary entered into full membership, and the Lincolns rented a pew, though Lincoln himself attended irregularly. Smith was an intellectual Scot ready to engage seriously with the corpus of leading freethinkers. In *The Christian's Defense*, a substantial work of theology, Smith used historical and natural sciences in the service of orthodox Christianity. He gave a copy to Lincoln, who, he maintained, gave the arguments a "searching investigation." In consequence, Smith claimed, Lincoln avowed "his belief in the Divine Authority and the Inspiration of the Scripture." Lincoln also read Robert Chambers's analysis of Christianity and evolutionary science and the writings of liberal theologians.[19]

The weight of evidence points, however, to a Lincoln more in sympathy with Unitarian, not Trinitarian, doctrines. His son Robert wrote of knowing nothing of Smith's having "converted" his father to a Christ-centered belief. Jesse Fell, a Bloomington lawyer and liberal Christian who had "repeated Conversations" with Lincoln on religious subjects, insisted that during his Springfield years Lincoln "did not believe in what are regarded as the orthodox or evangelical views of Christianity." Together they discussed the Unitarianism of William E. Channing and Theodore Parker, whose works Lincoln read and admired for their liberalism and rationality. "His religious views were eminantly practical," Fell insisted, "and are Sumed up on these two propositions, 'the Fatherhood of God, and the Brotherhood of Man.'"[20]

Whether or not Lincoln moved closer to conventional Trinitarian Christianity during these years, all were agreed that he was not, in Mary Lincoln's words, "a technical Christian"; he had, she said, "no hope—& no faith in the usual acceptation of those words." Springfield's New School Presbyterian minister, Albert Hale, regretted that Lincoln was not "born of God." But most insisted that he was "*naturally* religious," whatever his shortcomings over ceremonials and creeds. "He would ridicule the Puritans, or swear in a moment of vexation; but yet his heart was full of natural and cultivated religion," declared one of his closest associates, Leonard Swett. Even those who doubted his piety did not question the moral integrity of a man known not to drink, smoke, or gamble.[21]

On one feature of Lincoln's thought all were agreed. Lincoln described himself as a lifelong fatalist, and none demurred. "What is to be will be," he told Congressman Isaac Arnold, in words he often repeated to Mary Lincoln: "I have found all my life as Hamlet says: 'There's a divinity that shapes our ends, Rough-hew them how we will.'" Herndon recalled many conversations in which Lincoln had asserted that "all things were fixed, doomed in one way or the other, from which there was no appeal" and that "no efforts or prayers of ours can change, alter, modify, or reverse the decree." The predestinarian ethos of Lincoln's hyper-Calvinist Baptist upbringing undoubtedly molded this view of fate; throughout his life he alluded to the determining power of "Divine Providence." According to Herndon, Lincoln believed that all conscious human action was shaped by "motives,' self-interested, rational, and predictable responses to surrounding conditions "that have somewhat existed for a hundred thousand years or more." There was thus no freedom of the will; as Lincoln put it himself in 1846, he had sometimes (but no longer) argued the case "that the human mind is impelled to action, or held in rest by some power, over which the mind itself has no control." Such views were anathema to mainstream Christians, who viewed this "doctrine of necessity" as a godless creed that denied moral responsibility. Lincoln, though, continued mainly to present his deterministic faith in a religious language that invoked an all-controlling God.[22]

This only residually Calvinist faith, with its elements of Universalism and Unitarianism, helped shape Lincoln's approach to slavery as a morally charged political issue. He regarded the Declaration of Independence, in which he grounded his arguments during the 1850s, as a near-sacred statement of universal principles, one consistent with his belief in a God who had created all men equal and pursued his relations with humankind on the principles of justice. The scriptural basis for the Declaration lay in the book of Genesis: If mankind were created in the image of God, then "the justice of the Creator" had to be extended equally "to all His creatures, to the whole great family of man." The Republic's founders had declared that "nothing stamped with the Divine image and likeness was sent into the world to be trodden on, and degraded, and imbruted by its fellows."[23]

God's words to Adam, "In the sweat of thy face shalt thou eat bread," provided Lincoln with the text for his theology of labor: the burden and duty of work and the individual's moral right to enjoy its fruits.[24] God's arrangement of the human form expressed that theology, which demanded that blacks receive the education and path to self-improvement denied them by slavery: "[A]s the Author of man makes every individual with one head and one pair of hands, it was probably intended that heads and hands should cooperate as friends; . . . that that particular head, should direct and control that particular pair of hands[;] . . . that each head is the natural guardian, director, and protector of the hands and mouth inseparably connected with it; and that being so, every head should be cultivated, and improved, by whatever will add to its capacity for performing its charge."[25]

Whatever Lincoln's religious views on the eve of his presidency, there is little doubt that his wartime experience encouraged an increasing profundity of faith and a new religious understanding, which pulled him somewhat closer to the historic Calvinism that had profoundly shaped most of northern Protestantism.[26] Not only did he feel a sense of personal responsibility for a war of unimagined savagery, but the conflict brought him trials closer to home, the deaths of friends and close colleagues and, above all, the loss through typhoid of a favorite son, Willie, in February 1862. He attended public worship more habitually than in his life before, at the Old School Presbyterian Church on Washington's New York Avenue. He found in his darkest nights increasing solace in the scriptures; on one occasion Elizabeth Keckley, Mary Lincoln's seamstress and intimate, curious to see what particular passages were absorbing the Bible-reading president, crept behind him and found him deep in the book of Job. Before the war Lincoln regarded superintending Providence as a remote power that operated according to the laws of the universe, but under the pressure of events he exchanged that Providence for an active and more personal God, an intrusive and judgmental figure, one more mysterious and less predictable than the ruling force it superseded.

Lincoln later remarked that "from the beginning" he had seen that "the issues of our great struggle depended on the Divine interposition and favor. If we had that all would be well." His proclamation for a national day of fasting and prayer, after the defeat at Bull Run, prayed for the intervention of a justly vengeful God to support of Union arms. When Orville Browning urged his friend to strike against slavery as the means of securing divine assistance, Lincoln replied, "Browning, suppose God is against us in our view on the subject of slavery in this country, and our method of dealing with it?" Browning was much impressed by a reply "which indicated to me for the first time that he was thinking deeply of what a higher power than man sought to bring about by the great events then transpiring."[27]

Lincoln invoked the concept of a mysterious, unknowable God actively intervening to shape events in his remarks during the summer of

1862 to a visiting delegation of Quakers urging emancipation: "Perhaps
. . . God's way of accomplishing the end which the memorialists have in
view may be different from theirs." In a remarkable private expression of
his thinking—his "meditation on the divine will," most probably composed during 1863 or 1864—Lincoln wrote: "In great contests each party
claims to act in accordance with the will of God. Both *may* be, and one
must be wrong. God can not be *for*, and *against* the same thing at the same
time." There followed, however, not a statement of unionist certainty
but a startling hypothesis: "In the present civil war it is quite possible that
God's purpose is something different from the purpose of either party.
. . . I am almost ready to say this is probably true—that God wills this
contest, and wills that it shall not end yet." God *chose* to let the contest
begin. "And having begun He could give the final victory to either side
any day. Yet the contest proceeds."[28]

These were the words of a man whose changing ideas on divine intervention indicated some movement toward the evangelical mainstream,
but whose hesitancy over equating the Union cause with God's will, or
with Christian holiness, set him apart from it. This was just one aspect of
his ambivalence in the face of orthodoxy. Lincoln shared most Protestants' understanding of his dependence on, and responsibilities to, a
higher power. He spoke at various times of his "firm reliance upon the
'Divine arm,'" of seeking "light from above," and of being "a humble
instrument in the hands of our Heavenly Father." Even more significant,
he began to use the possessive pronoun—"responsibility to my God,"
"promise to my Maker"—in ways that suggested a belief in a more personal God. Yet he showed more humility than did most Protestant
preachers. "I hope," he told a delegation from the Chicago churches, "it
will not be irreverent for me to say that if it is probable that God would
reveal his will to others, on a point so connected with my duty, it might
be supposed he would reveal it directly to me; for . . . it is my earnest
desire to know the will of Providence in this matter. *And if I can learn what
it is I will do it!*" But in the absence of miracles or direct revelation, he had
to use the only means available, observation and rational analysis.[29]

Lincoln's evolving religious understanding fused with his developing
emancipation policy during the spring and summer of 1862. At the landmark cabinet meeting on September 22, Lincoln explained—in Gideon
Welles's account—how he had vowed before the battle of Antietam that
he would read victory as "an indication of Divine will, and that it was his

duty to move forward in the cause of emancipation"; not he but "God had decided this question in favor of the slaves." Lincoln's religious transformation suggests his need for new sources of philosophical support at a time when the old ones were losing their power. The majority of evangelical Protestants could easily accommodate emancipation within their familiar millennial doctrine, but Lincoln had to seek out a new theological framework of his own. The man who had once "ridiculed the Puritans" came to stand during wartime on the same ground as the earnest antislavery Protestants who pressed him, even if they had got there by different intellectual routes.[30]

Lincoln, Religion, and Antebellum Political Mobilization

Lincoln's prewar political experience in Illinois left him in no doubt of the significance of religion in electoral politics and the capacity of churches to mobilize opinion beyond their walls. As a Whig and then Republican organizer-campaigner he knew all about the state's cultural fault line between, on the one side, those settlers from slave states south of the Ohio who located in the south and center of Illinois and, on the other, later arrivals originating from New England and the wider Northeast, who settled to the north. This clash was additionally fed by the religious antagonism between the rough, pioneer gospel preachers, generally from the South, and a new breed of college-trained, more sophisticated ministers, mostly from the North. These conflicting outlooks coexisted in the central counties of the state. In Springfield's First Presbyterian Church, Lincoln was surrounded by conservatives with the strongest ties to the South, while the antislavery origins of the Second Presbyterian Church reflected the more radical outlook of settlers from New England and its diaspora.[31]

Lincoln's personal experience testified to the politician's need to respect the religious sensibilities of voters and to the role of religious identity in shaping political discussion and electoral configurations. Failing to secure the Whig nomination for the congressional seat in 1843, he explained: "[I]t was everywhere contended that no Christian ought to go for me, because I belonged to no church, [and] was suspected of being a deist." These influences, he judged, "were very strong" and "levied a tax of considerable per cent upon my strength throughout the religious community." Three years later, his nomination now secured, he ran for Congress against the formidable Methodist circuit rider Peter Cartwright. Discovering that the Democrats were defaming him as "an open scoffer at Christianity," Lincoln arranged for the publication of a handbill. It is a document as remarkable as it is curious, one by which he sought to repair or limit the political damage without compromising his intellectual integrity. Couching his statement negatively, he declared: "I am not a member of any Christian Church"; "I have never denied the truth of the Scriptures"; "I have never spoken with intentional disrespect of religion in general, or of any denomination of Christians in particular"; "I have, entirely left off [arguing the 'doctrine of necessity'] for more than five years"; "I do not think I could myself, be brought to support a man for office, whom I knew to be an open enemy of, and scoffer at, religion"; "I . . . do not think any man has the right . . . to insult the feelings, and injure the morals, of the community in which he may live." Lincoln described this as "the whole truth, briefly stated, in relation to myself, upon this subject." But it was scarcely full disclosure. He avoided any statement of positive belief: "[T]he higher matter of eternal consequences," he judged, should remain an issue between man and his Maker alone.[32] His caution can reasonably be seen both as a mark of what he considered properly a private affair and as a measure of the cultural grip of religion.

Lincoln was ill at ease with religious sectarianism but recognized that interdenominational conflict was an inseparable part of the experience of Illinoisans and that religious loyalties and antagonisms helped shape their choice of party. The pious could be found in all parties, but some denominations steered more strongly in one political direction than another. Reform-minded, New School Calvinists tended to the Whigs; Democrats' particular strength lay among Catholics, antimission Baptists, and "ritualist" Protestants. Many Methodists, Baptists, and Old School Calvinists rallied to Whiggery, though many others in these churches, especially the southern-born, remained loyal to a Democratic Party explicit in its Jeffersonian tolerance of religious pluralism.

The fragmenting of the Whig Party nationally and locally during the early and mid-1850s did little to alter the broad picture of a political universe significantly tempered by religious sensibilities. Indeed, in the aftermath of the Kansas-Nebraska Act, the Republican Party that captured much of the Whig vote (whether directly or via the unstable nativist

Know-Nothing Party) was even more evidently the inheritor of the millennialist, antislavery reformism of New School Protestants in particular. Lincoln himself fully recognized the ethical-religious dimensions of the legislation. His Peoria speech acknowledged that "lovers of liberty" appalled by a great moral wrong expected their political leaders to address their ethical concerns.[33] Implicit in much of Lincoln's subsequent course was his recognition that the moral constituencies brought into focus by the events of 1854 needed effective and articulate political leadership. Whether through a continuing Whig Party or the emergent Republican coalition, Lincoln acted over the next six years in a way that sought to clarify and publicize the lines dividing what he saw as the two fundamental moral constituencies in the nation, those who saw slavery as wrong and those who either did not care or praised it as a positive good.

The poison of slavery "as a moral, social and political evil" provided Lincoln with his most potent themes from his 1854 speeches in Springfield and Peoria, to his striking effort at the Cooper Union in 1860, but nowhere did he address the ethical dimension more powerfully than in the last three joint debates with Stephen A. Douglas in 1858. At Galesburg, Quincy, and Alton it was the moral case, not the socioeconomic argument, that provided his rhetorical power. All men, regardless of color, possessed the natural rights set down in the Declaration of Independence. "I hold that . . . [the negro] is as much entitled to these as the white man. . . . [I]n the right to eat the bread without leave of anybody else which his own hand earns, he is my equal and the equal of Judge Douglas, and the equal of every other man." Jefferson's document "meant to set up a standard maxim for free society, which should be . . . revered by all; . . . constantly labored for, and even though never perfectly attained, constantly approximated, and thereby . . . augmenting the happiness and value of life to all people of all colors everywhere." Douglas and Roger B. Taney had recently reinterpreted the Declaration's "sacred principles" in order "to dehumanize the negro—to take away from him the right of ever striving to be a man."[34]

Aiming to blur the line between "the men who think slavery a wrong and those who do not think it wrong," Douglas—Lincoln declared—had created an ethical fog, deeming there to be some middle ground between the forces of slavery and freedom and "blowing out the moral lights around us." He practiced "a false statesmanship that undertakes to build up a system of policy upon the basis of caring nothing about *the very thing that every body does care the most about.*" But true statesmanship involved confronting voters with clear choices. At Alton Lincoln declared that "the real issue . . . is the eternal struggle between these two principles— right and wrong—throughout the world. They are the two principles that have stood face to face from the beginning of time; and will ever continue to struggle. The one is the common right of humanity and the other the divine right of kings."[35]

For many of those who heard them, these speeches took on the character of moral discourses, even political sermons. If Lincoln himself avoided any hint of evangelical self-righteousness, he still occasionally deployed scriptural language and allusion, sometimes for humorous effect, but more usually to offer Christian encouragement for sustaining the principles of his chief text, the Declaration of Independence. "The Savior, I suppose, did not expect that any human creature could be perfect as the Father in Heaven; but He said, 'As your Father in Heaven is perfect, be ye also perfect.' He set that up as a standard, and he who did the most towards reaching that standard, attained the highest degree of moral perfection. So I say in relation to the principle that all men are created equal, let it be as nearly reached as we can." The Declaration's principles were inspired by "truth, and justice, and mercy, and all the humane and Christian virtues."[36]

Recognizing the mainly Protestant sources of antislavery energy, Lincoln argued a progressive moral case in the confidence that his words would resonate within church communions. Though cool toward the moral absolutism of the abolitionists, he still presented his case in terms that would stir up the antislavery moderates of the mainstream churches. His fusion of Jeffersonian principles with occasional scriptural precepts, set in the context of a Whig-Republican ethic of self-improvement, delighted those antislavery Christians who blended the Enlightenment idealism of the founding fathers with New Testament theology. Lincoln's religious correspondents in 1858 encouraged him to use "a little more *positive* language . . . so that everyone, no matter how humble or unintelligent he is, can and must see & feel that you are *right*, & that he [Douglas] is *wrong!*," and to hold on to "high ground . . . up to the standard of the Christianity of the day." The contest was "no less . . . than for the advancement of the kingdom of Heaven or the kingdom of Satan." The Quaker correspondent who praised Lincoln for being "fairly mounted on the eternal invulnerable bulwark of *truth*" against an opponent who had "the devil on his side" left the senatorial candidate in no doubt of his ability to reach and inspire Republicans of this stripe.[37]

In 1860, running for the presidency, Lincoln again benefited from his and his party's capacity to touch an ethical-religious nerve. The Republicans' campaign, promising an end to slavery's further expansion, achieved its ideological force from its blend of the economic, the political, and the moral: Free soil and free labor, under threat from an aggressive and unscrupulous "slave power," were not only an economic good but essential means of moral advance. Crusading Republicans rallied millennialist Protestants by setting the antislavery battle in a gospel context; the irrepressible conflict between free and slave labor was "Christ's doctrine of righteousness conflicting with evil." Though Lincoln remained publicly silent following his nomination, his published speeches provided a staple of the Republican propaganda diet. At the same time, parading as the party of sound Christian values, Republicans presented their candidate as a figure of sound Protestant faith and firm piety. As his biographers explained, "He is a regular attendant upon religious worship, and though not a communicant, is a pew-holder and liberal supporter of the Presbyterian church in Springfield, to which Mrs. Lincoln belongs"; he had "always held up the doctrines of the Bible, and the truths and examples of the Christian religion, as the foundation of all good." His promoters kept him clear of the taint of "infidelity," so electorally troublesome for him in the 1840s, and projected him as the rescuer of the nation "from the rule of a Godless . . . Administration." Lincoln himself never sought openly or directly to exploit religious sectarianism for electoral gain, but these scruples did not afflict Republican campaigners, who readily played on popular anti-Catholicism and branded Stephen Douglas, married to a Catholic wife, with the mark of the Beast.[38]

Republican voting patterns had a more than random relationship to religious and church affiliations and the ethnic identities with which they were interwoven. Antislavery reformers rallied to Lincoln as an incorruptible representative of a particular variety of progressive Protestantism, represented by Quakers, Freewill Baptists, Wesleyan Methodists, and Free Presbyterians. The larger Protestant denominations within the free states lacked the same degree of political consensus—indeed Lincoln lamented the opposition he faced from the majority of church ministers in Springfield itself—but across the North as a whole Republicans significantly extended their influence within evangelical communions. Unlike

John C. Frémont in 1856, Lincoln ran impressively among German Reformed and other German Protestant voters and made electorally significant accessions from the American Party and—to a lesser extent—from the northern Democracy. Although his Republican Party did not command a monolithic evangelical vote, it did regiment the moral energies of evangelical churches more effectively than ever before in the cause of political antislavery and purification. Lincoln's candidacy, far from being at odds with the party's Protestant morality, served its purposes well. Republicans were both more and less than "the Christian party in politics," but in the eyes of northern antislavery voters they deserved that label more than any previous major party. Combining constitutional conservatism and ethical earnestness, Lincoln gave the Republicans a standard-bearer who admirably met the needs of a party that embraced both political pragmatists and high-minded crusaders.[39]

Lincoln and Religious Nationalism

The Civil War was not, of course, a war about religion; its object was not to exterminate a religious infidel or impose religious uniformity. It was, rather, a war about national integrity and, by 1863, the future of slavery. Yet it can properly be described as a holy war, for both sides believed they were engaged in a fight to prevent what one called the "perversion of our *holy religion*" and another the victory of "pro-slavery atheism."[40] Religion shaped the moral framework within which death and suffering, triumph and disaster could be explained or accommodated. Men and women of all conditions—rich and poor, white and black, young and old, slave and free, on the battlefield or the home front—found in their religion consolation, resolve and inspiration. Some of the most vivid images of the conflict are those of a sanctified war, whether it be five thousand of Sherman's troops, accompanied by regimental bands, singing the doxology as they marched through Georgia, or the Confederate president's baptism and confirmation in the Episcopal Church, or Union coins newly engraved with the words "In God we Trust," or thousands of Confederate troops accepting complete immersion in mass baptisms.[41]

Abraham Lincoln's own evolving language and ideas encourage the integration of religious thought, impulses, and institutions into the wider history of the Civil War. His first inaugural address, delivered in March 1861 to a Union fractured by the withdrawal of seven states intent on an independent Confederacy, is a statement of both constitutional reassurance and political determination: The Union was no threat to the institutions of the South; it was perpetual and indivisible; as president he was impotent to negotiate its destruction. Although he noted that each party believed it had "the Almighty Ruler of nations, with his eternal truth and justice" on its side, and although he made an appeal for patience to allow for the workings of "intelligence, patriotism, Christianity, and a firm reliance on Him, who has never yet forsaken this favored land," Lincoln's speech was essentially a secular appeal to rational interest and designed to defuse an acute political crisis.[42]

Four years later, with the Confederacy fast crumbling, Lincoln used a quite different language in a seven-hundred-word speech designed to promote a magnanimous postwar reconciliation: "With malice toward none; with charity for all; with firmness in the right, as God gives us to see the right, let us strive on to finish the work we are in; to bind up the nation's wounds." These words brought to a climax a second inaugural address in which Lincoln inquired into the religious meaning of the war. His recourse to the scriptures and focus on God's mystery gave the speech the character of a sermon. Lincoln's sympathy for the moral predicament of the South had never blinded him to the wrongness of slavery. But whatever his distaste for Confederate theology, he worried about self-righteousness: "[L]et us judge not that we be not judged." The Union's victory, when it came, would have been secured at such cost that there could be only one logical explanation: "The Almighty has His own purposes." Working through human history, God had delivered "this terrible war" to punish both North and South for their involvement in slavery. "Woe unto the world because of offences!"; "Fondly do we hope—fervently do we pray—that this mighty scourge of war may speedily pass away," but if God—omnipotent, inscrutable, and mysterious—"wills that it continue, until all the wealth piled by the bond-man's two hundred and fifty years of unrequited toil shall be sunk, and until every drop of blood drawn with the lash, shall be paid by another drawn with the sword, as was said three thousand years ago, so still it must be said 'the judgments of the Lord, are true and righteous altogether.'"[43]

Lincoln's second inaugural, naturally, had no less political a purpose than did his first; it was designed to prepare Union loyalists for an inclusive, nonpunitive plan of presidential reconstruction of the South. But it also reflects Lincoln's evolution as a religious thinker and his understanding of the power of religious ideas and institutions to inspire Americans in a struggle to which he himself attached a providential meaning. Lincoln's wartime ideas of God and the nation, as publicly expressed, are striking for their kinship with those of the Union's powerful mainstream churches.

Lincoln's second inaugural was by no means his only public theological foray. Between the summer of 1861 and the autumn of 1864 he issued nine separate proclamations appointing days of national fasting, humiliation, and prayer and of thanksgiving, many of them prompted by moments of despair or elation occasioned by battlefield events. In addition, several of his public letters and responses to visiting clergy provided the public with a strong sense of the president's understanding of the workings of what he variously called "Almighty God," "our beneficent Father who dwelleth in the Heavens," "the Divine Majesty," "the Almighty and Merciful Ruler of the Universe," "Divine Providence," "the Supreme Being," "the Father of Mercies," and "the Great Disposer of events." Collectively these writings anticipate the key themes of the second inaugural, as well as pursue other ideas besides. Three major lines of thought present themselves: Every nation was a moral being with duties, God's purposes were wise and mysterious, and the American Union, under God, promised to be an agent of moral and political transfiguration.

Lincoln's Calvinistic frame of thought prompted him to conceive of the Almighty as the ruler of nations as well as of men, to identify nations as moral entities equally as capable of transgressions against the divine law as the individuals who composed them. Thus, he explained, "nations like individuals are subjected to punishments and chastisements in this world." The calamity of civil war, the sacrifices, and the suffering had to be seen as punishments "inflicted upon us, for our presumptuous sins, to the needful end of our national reformation." Americans had a duty to "confess our national sins," to repent, and to pray for God's clemency. In his proclamations Lincoln did not specify what those sins were, beyond the nation's neglect of God: "[W]e have forgotten . . . the gracious hand which . . . enriched and strengthened us; and we have vainly imagined

. . . that all these blessings were produced by some superior wisdom and virtue of our own. . . . [W]e have become too . . . proud to pray to the God that made us!" But "those nations only are blessed whose God is the Lord."⁴⁴

Beyond the confines of the proclamations, however, and well before the second inaugural, Lincoln made clear his conviction that the nation's continuing trials related specifically to its perpetuating the wrong of slavery. As he told the Kentucky editor Albert Hodges in April 1864, "If God now wills the removal of a great wrong, and wills also that we of the North as well as you of the South, shall pay fairly for our complicity in that wrong, impartial history will find therein new cause to attest and revere the justice and goodness of God." God's punishment of the nation for slavery, Lincoln frequently reflected, was part of the Almighty's purposes, which were, he declared, "mysterious and unknown to us." He offered no clearer and more memorable statement of his views than in two remarkable letters to Eliza P. Gurney, of the Society of Friends. "If I had had my way," he said, eighteen months into a conflict to which he could see no imminent conclusion, "this war would have been ended before this, but we find it still continues; and we must believe that [God] permits it for some wise purpose of his own." Two years later, shortly after William Tecumseh Sherman had transformed the Union's military prospects by taking Atlanta, Lincoln told her: "The purposes of the Almighty are perfect, and must prevail, though we erring mortals may fail accurately to perceive them in advance. We hoped for a happy termination of this terrible war long before this; but God knows best, and has ruled otherwise. . . . Surely He intends some great good to follow this mighty convulsion, which no mortal could make, and no mortal could stay."⁴⁵

However mysterious God's purposes, then, and however disobedient the nation, there was reason to believe that a purified Union would emerge from the fiery trial of war. Lincoln's thanksgiving proclamations marveled at the "the gracious gifts of the Most High God" who had delivered "fruitful fields," productive industry, an increasing population, and reasons "to expect continuance of years with large increase of freedom." At the dedication of the Gettysburg cemetery, he memorably reformulated this idea in a nonscriptural rhetoric of salvation and renewal: For loyal unionists the great task was to "resolve that these dead shall not have died in vain—that this nation, under God, shall have a new birth of freedom—and that government of the people, by the people, for the people, shall not perish from the earth."[46]

Lincoln's theology in the second inaugural—with its humility and remarkable absence of self-righteousness—stands in some contrast with the theology of the mainstream Union pulpits, mostly confident that God was on their side. Lincoln himself privately hinted at this when he told Thurlow Weed that he believed the speech was "not immediately popular," adding: "Men are not flattered by being shown that there has been a difference of purpose between the Almighty and them."[47] Yet for much of the time Lincoln and the loyal northern clergy spoke a common theological language, and this would be a matter of considerable political, not just theological, significance. Lincoln's call in April 1861 to put down the rebellion generally drew northern pulpits onto a common platform. Prewar conservative conciliators, both Protestant and Catholic, and radical higher-law evangelicals now united to defend "this one country of freedom" and support "a great people's war for Christian democracy." This was a unity qualified by a few principled pacifists—Quakers and Mennonites—and by guarded Dissenters, but the vast majority of northern clergy trumpeted their support for a war to prevent national annihilation. One editor doubted if in the history of the world so many pulpits had thundered against rebellion as on the last Sunday of the first month of the war.[48]

Those pulpits then, and during the rest of the conflict, helped crystallize ideas about the nature and meaning of the American nation. Theirs was an overwhelmingly Protestant and evangelical vision. Through torrents of rhetoric, ministers of the mainstream churches—above all, Methodist, Baptist, Presbyterian, Congregationalist, and Episcopalian—strove to make sense of unfolding events. Nations, they knew, had a primary and essential place in God's moral economy. He worked through them to achieve his purposes and was the supreme arbiter of their affairs. Every nation's days were numbered, but no nation would die until its purposes were realized. And none doubted that God had chosen the American Union for special favor and a particular role. Its people enjoyed "the richest inheritance of civil and religious freedom ever bequeathed to any nation in ancient or modern times" and were guided by "the best government that was ever constituted since the world began." America's mission would see it "conquer the world." This was no conventional lust for conquest; as a latter-day Israel, America's role was to serve, by example, the welfare of the whole human race. This made the rebellion of the South not only political treason against the secular nation but profanity, or treason against God.[49]

If the Confederacy represented "the vilest treason ever known since the great secession from heaven"—dispatching Jefferson Davis to the same quarters as Lucifer—then the question arose: Why was God putting the *whole* nation through this time of trial? For many the war was part of a testing process of discipline characteristic of America's history. As Israel had been chastised, to purge corruption, so the rigors of the early colonial settlements and the Revolution itself had helped "purify" the American nation. The crisis of civil war marked an advanced stage in this program of cleansing from sin. And what, above all, explained the nation's paroxysm was its complicity in the peculiar institution. As the Chicago clergy told Lincoln at the White House in September 1862, the Almighty had "bared his arm in behalf of the American slave" and now commanded the nation's rulers as he once had ordered Pharaoh: "Let my people go!"[50]

Yet whatever punishment God might mete out, there were no grounds for despair. Out of the severity of war, the Presbyterian William Shedd believed, would come "a solid and well-compacted growth" as men of the "most diverse social, political, and religious sentiments[,] . . . of all classes, conditions, and opinions . . . rallied with the unanimity of a single mind." Moreover, this consolidated America would be a transfigured nation. In a startling image, a Connecticut Congregationalist fused Christ and the Union: "I rejoice to be with the nation, when in its Gethsemane it sweats its great drops of blood, and on its Calvary it is crucified by its own children. . . . Our children and children's children will speak of 1861, as we speak of 1776. . . . And when the nation shall have . . . covered the continent; when it shall have overmastered the monster of slavery, and . . . when it shall stand up . . . transfigured with Divine beauty for the doing of God's will, men will give thanks to God for this great and sore trial."[51]

These words remind us that many antislavery Protestants who would not have considered themselves abolitionists before the war soon saw that the logic of events would turn the conflict into an assault on slavery. Within weeks they judged that the army had the right to liberate the slaves to weaken an enemy, who was using them to dig trenches, build fortifications, and work artillery. Many applauded when General Ben Butler declared the runaway slaves of disloyal masters to be "contraband of war" and sang alleluias when General John Frémont risked proclaiming free the slaves of all Missouri rebels. Eventually, conservative Protestants too saw Lincoln's Emancipation Proclamation of January 1863 as a legitimate weapon of war, given that the rebels had refused to return to the Union on terms that protected slavery. By the summer of 1864 even Old School Presbyterians had concluded that to preserve "our national life . . . slavery should be at once and for ever abolished."[52] The shifting balance of voices within northern Protestantism, however, found little echo within the Union's Catholic communion, whose overwhelming conservatism, though it did not compromise the church's broad-based loyalty in the face of rebellion, translated into deep hostility to "the incompetent, fanatic, radical administration of Abraham Lincoln" once his Emancipation Proclamation had turned the conflict into "a war of races."[53]

The logic of Protestant evangelicals' understanding of events culminated in the certainty that, as one Episcopalian insisted, "God is with us; . . . the Lord of Hosts is on our side." Without question, God was against the rebels. How could he possibly "smile upon rebellion, treason, and a nationality with slavery as its corner-stone"? a Methodist editor asked. A few preachers warned against hubris and self-righteousness. As Charles Fowler put it, "The only way to get God on *our side* is to get on *his side*." But usually this appetite for self-criticism coexisted with a belief in the North's moral superiority, engaged as it was in a "sacred cause . . . hallowed with . . . [the] blood" of its "best and noblest sons." The North's sins were stains that could be washed away; the Confederacy's were systemic evils removable only by destroying the body itself. "It is not merely war between sections, between North and South, between Abraham Lincoln and Jefferson Davis," explained one Methodist minister. "It is war between God on one side, a gigantic wrong on the other."[54]

Sitting under the preaching of Phineas D. Gurley in the New York Avenue Presbyterian Church, and bombarded by scores of church petitions, Lincoln was wholly familiar with the religious nationalism and political theology of Protestant loyalists.[55] If unionist Protestants were commonly more confident than Lincoln that God was on their side, in other respects the themes of the president's public theology harmonized well with their own. His originality lay rather more in his memorable expression of an idea than in the idea itself. Both he and they knew that nations had a place in the Almighty's moral economy; both conceived of an interventionist God; both understood the Union, under divine Providence, to amount to more than a glorious experiment in liberty and republicanism; both understood slavery to compromise that design.

This broad congruence between Lincoln's public theology and that of religious loyalists had rich meaning for the wartime politics of the Union. Mainstream Protestants embraced Lincoln as one of them; Lincoln worked constructively to mobilize the churches behind the war effort. Among the complex of ingredients that made for the Union's eventual victory, none was more important than its capacity to sustain popular patriotism, despite the enormous cost in human suffering. The North's superiority in resources and the administration's success in preventing the internationalizing of the war were essential for the nation's preservation but were in themselves inadequate for victory. Without a sustained and regenerating patriotism during this bloody trial the Lincoln administration would have capsized on the rocks of war weariness. The White House understood the importance of harnessing a range of voluntary organizations to this end. They included the political parties and the Federal army, but none was more potent as a moral influence than the nation's religious and philanthropic institutions. Of these, none could match the power of the millions of evangelical Protestants who constituted the country's most formidable religious grouping.

Lincoln thus strove to maintain good relations with church leaders of every major faith, Protestant, Catholic, and Jewish. He aimed at broad religious representation in the appointment of hospital and army chaplains. He met a full gamut of religious visitors who came to lecture him, offer opinions, seek appointments, or merely pay their respects. They included nationally renowned preachers, well-placed editors of mass-circulation papers, and distinguished abolitionists. There were representatives of the agencies devoted to the well-being of soldiers, the United States Sanitary Commission and the United States Christian Commission. Lincoln held meetings with Sabbatarians, temperance men, and Covenanters who sought a Christian amendment to the Federal Constitution. He kept his door open for the Catholic archbishop John J. Hughes, who was on close terms with Secretary of State William H. Seward, and who, at the president's request, visited Europe as an ambassador for the Union cause in 1861–62. Some critics missed the political import of Lincoln's time-consuming meetings with "preachers" and "Grannies," but he himself fully understood their value.[56]

For their part, thousands of Union clergy saw in Lincoln a president who warranted respect, even admiration, not simply ex officio but because they found in him qualities to be extolled. His was not charismatic power, properly understood, and there was no personal cult of Lincoln. Yet popular perceptions of Lincoln mattered in sustaining the Union administration as a whole. And those perceptions were shaped to an extent by preachers who used their position to review the president's qualities and to place him within the divine economy. Scrutinizing Lincoln's character and demeanor, loyal clergy mostly provided a counterweight to popular impatience over the Union's snaillike progress on the battlefield and over what was deemed the paralysis of the administration itself. In sermons, tracts, and newspapers Protestant ministers told of the president's admirable moral qualities, the honesty, determination, integrity, and unflinching patriotism of a resolute leader.

In a quintessential example of loyal preaching, the Methodist George Peck delivered a two-hour sermon on Nehemiah's rebuilding of Jerusalem and the wartime efforts of his enemies to stop it by sending messengers who mischievously called for negotiations. The preacher ingeniously turned Nehemiah into "the president of the country" beset by secessionist rebels who sought to secure by an armistice what they had failed to achieve by open assault. Peck did not mention Lincoln, but his coded argument was clear, delivered as it was during the summer of 1864, when Lincoln faced a growing demand from peace Democrats and fainthearts in his own party to respond to peace feelers supposedly emanating from the Confederate high command. Nehemiah is a surrogate for Lincoln: "a man of great executive ability," of "great courage, great prudence, and a profound knowledge of human nature"; "a man of much prayer, and great faith in God," whose "*puritan* rule" elicited the contempt of "*secessionists*" who "don't pray much" but "curse and swear and never work"; "a man of a thousand," whom "[n]either force nor fraud, threats nor flattery, could jostle . . . a hair's breadth."[57]

The approving association of Lincoln with what his critics disparaged as "puritanism"—that is, the conscience-driven evangelicalism of New England and its diaspora—derived in part from the president's setting aside more days for national religious observance, including the first ever national thanksgiving, than any of his predecessors, many of whom had jibbed at a practice that seemed to trespass on the separation of church and state. Devout unionists particularly rejoiced in the unique language Lincoln used in his Proclamation of Thanksgiving in July 1863, shortly after two simultaneous military triumphs on the Fourth of July, at Vicksburg and Gettysburg, had blissfully confirmed the direct intervention of the Almighty in the Union's affairs. Here he invoked "the influence of the Holy Spirit to subdue the anger . . . [and] change the hearts of the insurgents." Bishop Charles McIlvaine rushed to thank Lincoln "[e]specially . . . for what has never come into a Proclamation from that high seat of authority before, a solemn recognition of the being & influences of '*the Holy Spirit*.'"[58]

Although Lincoln continued to disappoint those hoping he would confess Christ as his personal Savior, many observers perceived in Lincoln a capacity for reverence and "deep religious feeling." Jonathan Turner remarked that people "seem . . . to imagine that he is a sort of half way clergyman." Many represented him as an instrument of the divine will, operating under Providence to become, after George Washington, "the *second saviour of our country*." As freedom became a reality, African Americans regarded the president-emancipator as an Old Testament prophet, a Joshua fighting the battle of freedom. Most vividly of all, a Chicago Methodist believed he had located "the true theory & solution of this 'terrible war'" in the remark of one of the city's lawyers: "*You may depend upon it, the Lord runs Lincoln*."[59]

Together, Lincoln's cultivation of loyalist religious constituencies and their reciprocal confidence in him contributed signally to the larger mobilization of nationalist sentiment. Cadres of Protestants operated well beyond their conventional domain, recruiting volunteer soldiers for the Union and Christ, energizing the aid agencies that served the Union's fighting men, ministering as field chaplains to inspire the troops with the nation's millennial purposes, and participating as organizers in the home front politics of national defense. Union evangelicals engaged in urgent drumbeating on behalf of the Lincoln administration. When the issue was the very existence of the nation, there could be no middle ground. With remarkable consistency, Protestant spokesmen lined up to defend the administration's conscription measures, its tolerance of arbitrary arrests, and its strong-arm action against draft resisters and dissenters.

These staunch loyalists nonetheless saw themselves as political harmonizers, engaged in pulling behind the war effort those of different denominations, ethnicities, and party traditions, meeting on the common platform of national unity. They may have had the self-image of "large tent" patriots, but in reality, with elections continuing on a largely unaltered schedule in the wartime Union, party politics became even more polarized and cutthroat than in time of peace. A minority of war Democratic leaders accepted the embrace of Lincoln's Union-Republican administration but their party remained independent, separate, and strong in the country at large. The continuing Democratic leadership ministered to a variety of popular concerns, playing on deep racial antipathies and the consequences of emancipation, attacking the president and his state-level allies for their assault on civil liberties, blaming the lack of military progress on the administration's incompetence, and exploiting a deepening war weariness to call for a peace that would reverse the revolution and restore the old slaveholding Union. Their religious reading of events contested the administration's implicit claim that it was yoked to the Almighty. The Democratic newspaper editor in Lincoln's Springfield reflected sarcastically on August 4, 1864: "To-day is 'Massa Linkum's' day of fasting, humiliation and prayer. . . . [T]he nation has ample reason for fasting, because Lincoln has made food so high; for humiliation at the disgraces his . . . imbecile policies have brought upon us; and for prayer that God, in his goodness, will spare us a second term of *such* a president." The *Chicago Times* proposed a prayer for general use: "We know, oh our Father, that this wicked . . . war was produced by unrighteous demagogues . . . and that it is continued by such men as Mr. Lincoln and Mr. Davis . . . , not for the good of the country, but for narrow and ungodly partisan ends. . . . Make us to know that it is only by the retirement from power of such men as Mr. Lincoln and Mr. Davis, and the filling of their positions by wise and patriotic men, that we can ever obtain that peace for which we are now supplicating. Amen!"[60]

For all the determined earnestness of their language, however, antiadministration clergy and their lay sympathizers remained a self-conscious minority within mainstream northern Protestantism. The reality was that most of the North's politically active Protestants either were deeply committed to Lincoln's administration or, as radical critics, had nowhere else, electorally, to go. The 1864 campaign arguably witnessed the most complete fusing of religious crusade and political mobilization in America's electoral experience. Ministers engaged in a fervent round of ward meetings, election speeches, sermons, addresses to troops, and editorializing. Religious tract society agents distributed campaign literature. Churches became Union-Republican clubs. The president's reelection was due in large part to the extraordinary mobilization of support by those who saw themselves as agents of God and of Lincoln, the leaders of the Protestant churches.

Lincoln more than once humorously remarked of a vain and recently deceased Illinois politician that had he realized how big an event his own funeral would turn out to be would have died years earlier.[61] In the light of Lincoln's own premature death, the joke has a cruel irony. His assassination prompted throughout the loyal Union a display of public grief previously unprecedented in American history. The president as martyr—a latter-day Moses in leading his people out of bondage, Christ-like in falling victim on Good Friday—now played out a unique role in the sanctification of American nationalism. "Black Easter" was part of the providential plan to purify the nation and inaugurate the kingdom of God. A Brooklyn Presbyterian typically rejoiced that "A martyr's blood has sealed the covenant we are making with posterity," guaranteeing "the rights of men, the truth of the Gospel, the principles of humanity, the integrity of the Union, the power of Christian people to govern themselves, the indefeasible equality of all creatures of God . . . , no matter what may be the color of their skin."[62] On this reading, an unlikely, "infidel" politician of the 1830s had—through his Christian martyr's blood—secured the transfiguration of the nation.

10

Abraham Lincoln:
The Family That Made Him,
the Family He Made

Catherine Clinton

Abraham Lincoln remains the most studied person in American history. Yet blank pages within his personal narrative continue to haunt and tempt scholars. The meanings that can be teased out of accounts of Lincoln's youth continue to fascinate.[1] Our understanding of his fraught relationship with his father and with women—his mother and stepmother, sister and sisters-in-law, sweethearts and his own wife, as well as wives of friends and surrogate daughters—may benefit from important recent work on southern honor and the nineteenth-century family and renewed interest in his personal psychology.

Lincoln was a new man of the prairie. He would not cling to the conventions of his father's generation but pioneered a new path, one that commingled several traditions. He was a courtier, overgenerous to women and remembered for both kindness and being a "true gentleman." But while charitable and courteous, he both abhorred and ignored aristocratic pretensions. His courage and honesty recommended him, while the "niceties" escaped him. Whatever Lincoln lacked in terms of form, he surely made up for with content.

No other significant relationship in his adult life is more ambiguous and debated than that with Mary Todd. Their family life has been examined more in children's literature than scholarly tomes.[2] But the family that created him is just as complicated and contradictory as the family he created. And both remain central to understanding the man and the myths he generated.

Certainly the popular image of Lincoln as a backwoods boy, a child of humble origins, is built on verifiable evidence. Lincoln learned during his formative years that he was very much on his own and had to rely on his own skills and wits. He learned to distrust those whose lives were shaped by comfort and privilege, realizing that while these advantages did not make the man, lack of them could prevent the man from developing into what he might have been. Even if close kin were men of slave property and standing, this did not necessarily translate into any particular views about slavery. He was born into a fluid age, a time when families might separate and fragment, as so many did, dramatically, during the American Civil War.

Lincoln was born in 1809, the second child and first son of Nancy Hanks and Thomas Lincoln, on a farm near the village of Hodgenville, Kentucky. Thomas Lincoln was a handsome man with a stocky build, nearly six feet tall, with black hair and gray eyes. He had known the woman who became his wife for many years before they married. Nancy was twenty-three, seven years younger than her husband, dark-haired and hazel-eyed with a delicate build.[3] Despite exaggerated Lincoln lore, the family cabin was considerably better than a manger; nonetheless, the baby made his appearance on a bed of corn husks laid over poles. Nancy Hanks had married Thomas three years before and given birth to daughter Sarah in 1807.[4] Seeking better prospects, Thomas took his pregnant wife and daughter away from their hardscrabble life in Elizabethtown, Kentucky, where he was a carpenter striving to get ahead.

He sought independence for his young family, which is why he relocated in 1808 to a cabin at Sinking Creek.[5] The Lincoln farm failed to thrive. In keeping with the restless pattern of the age, the family of four relocated to Knob Creek, a region Nancy Lincoln knew well, having spent time at the home of her grandparents nearby. Thomas moved near his wife's family, as was often the custom of the country.

The National Park Service has recently renovated its site at the Lincoln Birthplace, providing a genealogy for Abraham Lincoln. The wall chart traces Lincoln's paternal line back to Lincolnshire in the fifteenth century.[6] But the record for Nancy Hanks is considerably briefer.[7] Discussions of Lincoln's maternal heritage may have been left deliberately vague.[8] Lincoln offers only a brief mention in his autobiography: "My mother, who died in my tenth year, was of a family of the name of Hanks."[9]

Nancy Hanks was uncertain about her family origins. In 1783 she was the first child born to Lucey Hanks, but the identity of Nancy's father remains a mystery. Lucey's second child, Sarah, was born in Kentucky, four years after Nancy, also without any identifiable father.[10] Nancy Hanks's mother did wed in 1791, and following her marriage to Henry Sparrow, she gave birth to eight children, two of whom became clergymen.[11]

However, at some point Nancy became aware—perhaps painfully so—that she was not like her Sparrow half brothers and sisters. Nancy Hanks was abandoned by her mother, sent to live with others, passed around within a network of relatives' households.[12] Lucey's sister Elizabeth and her husband, Thomas Sparrow (brother of Lucey's husband), took in not only Nancy Hanks but also Dennis Hanks, who was the illegitimate son of one of Lucey's other sisters, also named Nancy Hanks.[13]

Reconstructing Lincoln's ancestry remains complicated, and to track down exact truths remains impossible. To speculate on the various scenarios sheds little direct light on Lincoln's life. However, exploring facets of family honor, a theme strongly emphasized in recent literature on the nineteenth-century South, may provide some insight into Lincoln's complex personal character.

First and foremost, Lincoln learned about the haves and have-nots within a family during his most impressionable years. He was taught the consequences of dishonor, which differed greatly depending on whether the lapse was by a man or a woman. He discovered what abandonment could mean, what the abdication of duty and responsibility might wreak. Some might be given property and privilege, education and place, while others, deprived of resources, fared differently. Some might be given a name, while others, through no fault of their own, were subject to shame.

Lincoln was part of a new generation that grew up in the wake of the American Revolution, fomenting a revolution in attitudes toward child rearing and family relations that has inspired a rich scholarly literature.[14] One recent scholar described the transition as follows: "A patriarch's family had to have a 'family name,' a local history of prestigious forefathers, unbroken lines of patronage and dependency, for him to claim the patriarchal mantle. However, the social and cultural rupture of the Revolution, followed by the failed patriarchalism of the post-Revolutionary generation, left the antebellum generation defining anew their relationship to the past."[15] In many ways, Lincoln's life reflected these new directions.

During his own personal development, Lincoln found that nothing could be taken for granted, especially sacrifices that might have seemed part of the natural order, like a mother's care or a father's pride. Lincoln's circumstances powerfully shaped his character. He deplored bullies and those who took advantage to assert their own powers. He empathized with those, like his mother, who had been cheated by circumstance, with those less fortunate than others who enjoy privileges from birth. Lincoln inherited and embraced a strong ethic of charity. He consistently sided with those who strove to improve themselves and the lives of others.[16]

There is every reason to believe Lincoln was deeply affected by his mother's religious principles: "I remember her prayers and they have always followed me. They have clung to me all my life."[17] His parents adhered to the concept of grace earned through conversion, a tenet of the Baptist faith. Even if Lincoln did not subscribe to the practice of formal membership within his parents' church, he may have absorbed its evangelical humanism. In any case he certainly knew his Bible.

His own contemporaries furiously debated Lincoln's faith and religious inclinations.[18] His best friend in Springfield, Joshua Speed, called him a "skeptic," and the best man at his wedding, Joseph Matheny, believed that Lincoln was "enthusiastic in his Infidelity."[19] In the first half of nineteenth century, more than 80 percent of Americans regularly attended services, while less than 50 percent were formal members of churches. Lincoln fitted this profile in that he was married by an Episcopal minister and then irregularly attended services at a Presbyterian church—even paying pew fees, as his wife was a church member—although he never officially joined any congregation. Historian Vernon Burton suggests that Lincoln democratically stood with the sinners rather than the "smugly saved."[20]

Smugness was certainly something Lincoln abhorred, especially in the clergy. Any "stain" on his mother's name did not affect Lincoln's own feelings for her, as he proclaimed: "[A]ll that I am or ever hope to be I owe to her."[21] Lincoln never advertised what he suspected or knew about his mother's origins with illegitimacy, a delicate subject in mid-nineteenth-century America. His effusive language about Nancy Lincoln as an "angel" suggests that he emphasized her goodness and purity as compensation for lingering suspicions about her bastardy.

His friend and biographer Ward Lamon recalled that the usually voluble Lincoln was pointedly circumspect: "The lives of his father and mother, and the history and character of the family before their settlement in Indiana, were topics upon which Mr. Lincoln never spoke but with great reluctance and significant reserve."[22] When asked directly by his law partner William Herndon about his ancestry, Lincoln confessed that his maternal grandfather was a "well bred Virginia farmer or planter" but gave no name.[23] Bastardy and secrecy were embedded within his family history and played a role in shaping his psyche.

Like Shakespeare's Richard III, in the Elizabethan play he much admired,[24] Lincoln brooded over questions of legitimacy and illegitimacy, inheritance and privilege. As an adult he may have followed the onstage trials and tribulations of the English monarchy with enthusiasm, but as a child, grappling with his own family's tangled web within a southern culture obsessed with family origins, he found that these issues triggered a different emotional response.

Because of his mother's illegitimacy, Lincoln appears to have imbibed lessons of charity and forgiveness, traits that others commented on for the rest of his life.[25] As a young man he was always courtly to women, and he retained an unusually high regard and esteem for them throughout his life. His sentimentality and empathy were legendary. Thus, lessons learned about his mother's roots critically influenced his moral education.

Lincoln's thirst for book learning also remains legendary.[26] Education was not just an end unto itself but offered a step up the ladder, which young Abraham desperately desired. It was democracy in action. In any case, Nancy Hanks Lincoln was more educated than her husband and a driving force behind her son's ambitions to better himself. As Dennis Hanks recalled, it was Nancy who taught her children their "ABCs, using Webster's spelling book and reading the Bible."[27] Thus, though her birth was "low," she raised the standard within the family circle.

By contrast, Thomas Lincoln, as his son suggested, "grew up literally without education."[28] His own lack of education does not completely explain Thomas Lincoln's disdain for intellectual pursuits. He seems to have viewed his children as units that might be marked for utility and did not want any interference with extracting value. These kinds of calculations did nothing to endear him to any of Lincoln's household.

Imagining that his only remaining child was escaping his control seemed to throw Thomas Lincoln into one of his periodic foul moods, causing him more gloom than usual. He had come to depend on this son and sought out his company. He was not a drunk, he did not beat Abraham, yet Thomas Lincoln's contempt might inflict equal damage. Boys looked to their fathers for inspiration. Abraham Lincoln was no different. But his inspiration came from the knowledge that his father was the disinherited second son.

Lincoln was influenced by his father's mercurial moods. Whether Thomas's darkness was a medical condition or induced by circumstances, Lincoln's father succumbed to blue spells, and upon occasion, friends feared for his sanity.[29] Perhaps some of his melancholy was induced by his unstable economic status.

A teenager when his own father died, Thomas Lincoln had received only a small portion of his father's estate. The bulk of family property was inherited by his brother Mordecai in 1786. While his brother built on his good fortune, Thomas became an itinerant laborer. At one point he was working alongside slaves for his uncle Isaac, a wealthy landholder in Tennessee. He had been on his own for nearly a decade when he met and married Nancy.

The birth of a son was greeted by the couple as a significant landmark. Thomas named the boy after his father, killed in an Indian attack. Nancy was prideful about her son, who grew so rapidly that it was hard for his mother to keep him in clothes.[30] Keeping her son in books soon proved equally challenging. He rapidly surpassed the family patriarch, first in reading and then in height. When just a child, Abraham learned to read the Bible, and he often read it aloud to his father. His familiarity with religious texts was not unusual, but Lincoln quoted frequently and lyrically from biblical stories, the Psalms, the entire New Testament, almost always from memory, for his entire life.

Lincoln began his formal education at local "blab schools" where children read their lessons aloud. This proclivity for oral expression, for reading aloud and being read to, was something Abraham Lincoln never outgrew.[31] At times Lincoln was a merry child playing pranks, like sitting in a tree and trying to aim a full load from his bowels into a mate's hat below.[32] But he was also remembered as a somber and contemplative boy with his nose buried in a book. But since most of these memories cannot be linked to a particular year, it is impossible to determine if they predated one of the signal events of his childhood, the death of his mother.

Death was a frequent visitor to antebellum families; mortality rates were high, and few families escaped either the death of a parent or—more commonly—a child. Lincoln himself remembered his mother's taking him to the grave of his baby brother, who died in infancy, not surprising in an age where young children accounted for 40 percent of mortality.[33]

The death of Nancy Hanks Lincoln followed the family's move to Pigeon Creek, Indiana. Lincoln remembered the transition to Indiana as "pinching times." At first, they lived in a half-faced camp (a three-sided cabin). But in the autumn of 1817, within a year of resettlement, Nancy's foster parents, Thomas and Elizabeth Sparrow, joined them with eighteen-year-old Dennis Hanks in tow. This reunion signaled faith in this new settlement and the promise of economic autonomy.

Things took a turn for the worse when an outbreak of "milk sickness" arrived in the summer of 1818. Abraham's mother began nursing those stricken. Both the Sparrows were consumed by the fever and did not survive. Then Nancy fell ill herself. Dennis Hanks remembered: "She knew she was going to die and called up the children to her dying side and told them to be good and kind to their father, to one another, and to the world. . . ."[34] This must have been a severe trial for the young boy: to have his beloved mother bid farewell, resting such responsibilities on his young shoulders. Her deathbed wish was for Lincoln to fulfill family duties, which he took extremely seriously. Nancy was buried a few months shy of her thirty-fifth birthday in a coffin made by her husband, fastened with pegs whittled by her son. It was a year before a minister was able to offer a proper memorial service at her burial site, a not uncommon delay on remote frontiers.

Both Abraham (age nine) and his sister, Sarah (eleven), were devastated by their mother's death, believing Nancy irreplaceable. Thomas Lincoln needed help to raise his motherless children and felt the loss *required* a replacement. He decided to go to Kentucky to find a new spouse in 1819. He left his children with Dennis Hanks, isolated and alone on his Indiana farm, for several months. This period sadly typified children "left behind," in almost every sense of these words.

In light of the depths to which the family had sunk, Nancy's children may have welcomed even an interloper into their frontier squalor. They were perhaps surprised at the appearance of a widow with three children. But evidence indicates that Sarah and Abraham were pleased at how their father's new wife addressed their material needs.

When his stepmother, Sarah Bush Johnston Lincoln, arrived, she immediately sought improvements, like scrubbing her stepchildren clean, so they might appear "more human."[35] She had been an industrious wife and widow, sending her daughter to a local academy back in Kentucky. But she gave up life in a city and set out for the prairie with Thomas Lincoln. The new Mrs. Lincoln brought along "luxuries" to their rustic domain, including knives, forks, and spoons. She also brought with her a sense of domestic purpose and order that conveyed itself to her stepchildren. She insisted that Thomas install a floor, a window, a sleeping loft, as well as a new roof and door. The remodeled cabin allowed Sarah Bush Lincoln to care for all her children. The blended family thrived. Later in life Lincoln referred fondly to these particular boyhood years.[36]

Many accounts mentioned Nancy Lincoln's submission to her husband; she did not cross him.[37] By contrast, Lincoln's stepmother made demands on her husband, and we know she championed Abraham's cause to Thomas. Although illiterate, Sarah Bush Lincoln sensed young Abraham's potential and enrolled him in classes taught by a local schoolmaster about a mile from the Lincoln cabin. When the school closed, the Lincoln children were sent farther afield. However, Lincoln's father insisted that farmwork took precedence over school. He might "slash" his son for neglecting his chores while absorbed in reading.[38] Abraham's formal education was sporadic and woefully brief; according to Lincoln himself, the aggregate "did not amount to one year."[39]

Like many young men of his generation, Lincoln sought out teachers. Horace Mann suggested that "children should take a larger part in directing their own education. Motivation should come from a sense of inward duty rather than fear of reprisal or desire for accolades."[40] Abraham Lincoln was a living example of this new breed of pupil.[41] Twenty-first-century scholars have moved away from the neat categories (the evangelical, moderate, and genteel) outlined by Philip Greven in his pioneering classic *The Protestant Temperament*.[42]

Lincoln's sense of home and family was dealt another blow with his sister's marriage and then her death in childbirth. When her brother was seventeen, Sarah married a neighbor boy named Grigsby and moved a few miles away. Sarah and Abraham had been extremely close, and this physical separation, although a natural development and a happy circumstance for Sarah, was a difficult transition for Lincoln. Left behind, Abraham was found wanting when weighed on the scales of his father's affections.[43]

By this time Abraham was ready to break free of his father's parental grip. He even asked a neighbor to recommend him for a job on a riverboat. But until he came of age, Lincoln was indebted to his father, who was aging, blind in one eye, and indifferent to the hardship he imposed on his intellectually gifted son. Abraham was perhaps unwilling to desert the household early because of his affection for his stepmother, who had shown unusual kindness to him. Sarah Bush Lincoln maintained an affectionate relationship with Abraham throughout his difficulties with his father and even after her husband's death.[44]

When his sister, Sarah Lincoln Grigsby, died in childbirth in January 1828, Abraham Lincoln was plunged into a consuming grief shortly before his nineteenth birthday. Once again he felt abandoned. With his sister gone, life on the Indiana farm frontier appeared even bleaker.

Then, in 1830, Lincoln's father decided to emigrate to Decatur, Illinois, two hundred miles away. Perhaps recognizing it was his last chance to exploit his strapping son's labor, Thomas Lincoln made plans to move. Once the Lincolns laid claim to their land in Illinois, Abraham spent the spring and summer engaged in the hard work of homesteading, fencing in fifteen acres of land along the Sangamon River and using four oxen to "broke the prairie."[45] No longer the spindly adolescent, Abraham weighed nearly 215 pounds and had reached his full height of six feet four inches. He was a grown man, eager to break free.

Lincoln always seemed to empathize with those held in check, those prevented from pursuing their talents and dreams. This sense of empathy may have helped make him the ideal champion of free labor and someone who had an emotional connection to the concept of emancipation.

Lincoln left his father's farm behind in 1831 and struck out on his own, moving to New Salem, Illinois. He found the town full of engaging people who warmly welcomed him into the community, where his talents and ambitions were applauded and nurtured.[46] This was a new and welcome change from the indifference to which he had become accustomed.

Within two years of his arrival—"a friendless, uneducated, penniless boy," as he later characterized himself—twenty-three-year-old Abraham Lincoln audaciously put himself forward as a candidate for the state legislature. Even though Lincoln lost this bid, he won the overwhelming majority of the votes in his new hometown.[47] The contest displayed his ability to shine when he was given the support he craved. It also showed that he had found a new home and was able to knit together a circle of friends who treated him like the favorite son he was to become. Friends in many ways replaced kin.

Lincoln became particularly close to Mentor Graham, who claimed to be his teacher, and with Graham's wife. Graham's daughter later commented, "Lincoln loved my mother and would frequently ask her for advice on different questions. . . ."[48] This advice would often be about young women Lincoln hoped to court. Several New Salem matrons apparently enjoyed mothering him. He boarded with Elizabeth Abell, a neighbor of his close friend Bowling Green's, in a "sort of home intimacy."[49]

Stories about his upbringing rarely mention his father; Abraham was hardly a chip off the old block. Instead many of Lincoln's cronies chronicled the intensity of disaffection between father and son. This became more evident as Lincoln moved from New Salem to Springfield and distanced himself from his father's Illinois farm. From an early age Lincoln, by preference or necessity, cast his emotional net wide, reaching out to a community that would nurture and support his desire to overcome the challenges he was dealt. He may never have forgotten his roots, but he was clearly interested in leaving the past behind, determined to escape Thomas Lincoln's fate. Young Lincoln found others to idolize during his formative years. When Bowling Green died in 1842, he was so choked up at the funeral that Lincoln was unable to finish the eulogy he was delivering.

But the death of this father figure did not turn Lincoln's attentions to his own aging parent in decline.

When Lincoln emancipated himself from his father's household, he left his stepbrother John Johnston behind. This stepson would have to deal with Thomas Lincoln's relentless demands for loyalty and labor. Johnston got his stepfather involved in a partnership in a gristmill in the 1840s, which burdened them with debt. He wrote to Lincoln on more than one occasion, asking for a handout.[50] Lincoln visited his father's home when he was out riding the Eighth Judicial Circuit, although not often. His stepbrother wrote in May 1849 that Thomas was dying and "craves to see you." Lincoln dropped everything to go to his father's bedside, even though this family visit may have cost him an appointment with the Land Office.[51]

But when another cry for help came from the Thomas Lincoln household in the winter of 1850–51, Abraham Lincoln at first did not even respond to his stepbrother's pleading. Then, when another relative sent word the situation was dire, he begged off, using his wife's health as an excuse. Other scholars have pointed out that Lincoln could have made the trip if he had wanted.[52] It is more telling that his wife had just given birth to their third child, and neither Lincoln's wife nor any of the children had made a pilgrimage to meet Thomas Lincoln. Not Thomas, not Sarah, or any of the assorted Coles County relatives had made a visit to the Lincoln home in Springfield. In the wake of this deathbed request, Lincoln felt obliged to have his stepbrother tell his father, "[I]f we could meet now, it is doubtful whether it would not be more painful than pleasant."[53]

Thomas Lincoln died shortly thereafter, and Lincoln did *not* attend the funeral. Lincoln's feelings about his father's death, and even about his father generally, remain a topic rich with speculative interpretations. He did name his last child after his father in 1853, in a sort of nod to the family tradition; Abraham himself was named after his father's father, who also had a strained relationship with his son.

Lincoln had broken free of his father during his years in New Salem, making his own way in the world, with hopes of creating his own family. He was keenly interested in women but seemed unable to put his best foot forward in the realm of romance. During his time in New Salem, Lincoln became close to one particular young woman, Ann Rutledge, who apparently had as sensitive a soul as his own. She also allegedly had a fiancé when she and Lincoln became romantically entangled. They became close when she was "unavailable," perhaps one of the factors that sparked their intimacy. When she died in August 1835, he exhibited deep despair. One acquaintance recalled, "He made a remark one day when it was raining that he cold not bare [*sic*] the idea of its raining on her Grave."[54]

The death of his mother, the death of his sister, and the sad circumstances surrounding the death of Ann Rutledge opened floodgates of grief. Each of the three women with whom he had become intimate had been taken from him. As he became more and more withdrawn, more emotionally reticent, his relationships with women became even more challenging. Melancholy broke over the young man in fresh and engulfing waves.

David Donald has suggested that during his New Salem days (and perhaps into his early Springfield period) Abraham Lincoln formed attachments "to older, married and hence unavailable, women."[55] Many of these women made it their business to try to find Lincoln a wife.[56] Clearly, Lincoln was weighed down by thoughts of both *how* and *with whom* he might cast his lot. Lincoln knew because of "honor and conscience in all things," he would be forced to hold to his end of any bargain he might make. His inability to relate to women in the easygoing manner he managed with men hampered him, as did his poor, ruffian manners and looks.

But eventually he selected a mate. Abraham Lincoln married in 1842 and started his own family by 1843. His law practice and career as a legislator did not recommend him for marriage as much as his own desperate longing to find a wife. By the time he met Mary Todd for the first time around 1839 in Springfield, Illinois, Lincoln was a mature thirty but still uncomfortable in the realm of romance, where he was considerably less mature. He may have been engaged to Ann Rutledge, and he may have courted a Kentucky belle named Mary Owens, but his skills at romance were pitiable. Lincoln would rather have faced a hostile crowd than a lone, unattached woman.

By contrast, Mary Todd was considerably skilled at parlor politics, a flirt in three states (Kentucky, Illinois, and Missouri) by the time she and Lincoln wed in her sister's parlor in November 1842. But the details of their courtship remain full of mystery.[57] Scholars disagree on the source of the couple's attraction or even if there ever was a loving relationship. Some describe it as a union of mutual convenience rather than a love match. There are those who challenge not just the couple's affection for each other but all of Lincoln's relationships with women.[58]

The road to matrimony may have been littered with obstacles, but once the ceremony concluded, the couple entwined their fates and mutually pledged to make a success of their union. Mary Lincoln was not just the wife, a domestic partner, but served as her husband's sounding board for every speech. Mary Lincoln was deeply partisan and blindly loyal, and she held fierce grudges.

It is quite impossible to determine the truth of any marriage, and there will always be more than two sides to the story, especially in a small town like antebellum Springfield, Illinois, where everyone was exposed to everyone else's private affairs. But it is safe to say that by all appearances, the couple were devoted to each other and remained faithful. If either had strayed, gossips would have focused upon this scandal, and it would have wormed its way into interviews about the great man after Lincoln's death. His devotion to his wife embodied the era's concept of honor.

The Lincolns were an unusual match, even apart from their tempestuous and troubled courtship. Did the disapproval of Mary's relatives become an obstacle when the couple first became romantically involved? Would this family objection have been a severe impediment to someone like Lincoln, not just a bump on the highway of romance? Regardless, Mary Todd had determined her own unusual fate and decided that Lincoln should be her husband. Finally, in the fall of 1842, with an inscription of "Love is eternal" on her wedding ring, Mary Todd married Abraham Lincoln.[59] Mary intended for their courtship to be thus remembered: his crisis and her fidelity.[60]

Mary clung to the notion that she was the only one to whom her husband had ever truly been attached. She had been courted by many attractive prospects over the years, spurning advances by Patrick Henry's grandson, by politician Edwin Webb, and unnamed others. Her station in life afforded her contact with a wide range of eligible suitors. She had ample opportunity to travel—back to Kentucky or to other family in Missouri or Illinois. But she remained in Springfield and did not abandon hope over a difficult period, finally being rewarded with a husband, Abraham Lincoln.

What was it that propelled these two together, with such dramatic interventions and interuptions? One of Mary's Kentucky sisters visited their home for six months in 1854–55 and suggested a warm, intellectually compatible relationship: "I heard him say he had no need to read a book after Mary gave him a synopsis. He had great respect for her judgement and never took an important step without consulting her."[61] This kind of union was a textbook case for couples in the nineteenth century.[62] Mary and Abraham in many ways exemplified the new companionate marriage.

Prior to the nineteenth century, many genteel women might have selected a mate on the basis of an exchange or consolidation of property. Marital partners were often selected on the basis of what they might bring to the altar. Marriages were arranged as a contract between two consenting families, but over time women exercised increasing control over the selection of a mate. It was, as one antebellum woman confided, "a day to fix my fate." But fifty years after the American Revolution, marital patterns shifted to reflect new priorities, ones that included romantic love as well as family and financial considerations. Individual desire shaped the choices of young couples. Again, Abraham and Mary were emblematic of this historic shift.

Lincoln saw in his wife a permanent solution to the loss of mother love, while Mary too sought strong emotional support, having lost her mother at an early age. They used pet names and exhibited tokens of affection. Mary was one of the few who could conjure Lincoln from his periodic bouts of melancholy, while Lincoln was able to soothe his wife when her fear of thunderstorms or some other episode tripped her into hysteria. They helped heal each other's wounds.

Mary Lincoln's most powerful gift to her husband, however, was the prospect of fatherhood, a role he keenly relished. She became pregnant within weeks of their marriage. As Mary's due date grew near, Abraham Lincoln may have been thinking of the tragic death of his sister, Sarah, in childbirth. Mary had the vivid example of her own mother's death following childbirth nearly twenty years before. Naturally, both were apprehensive that "the happiness of the conjugal relation was obliged to be bought at so dear a price."[63]

Nine months after their wedding, on August 1, 1843, Robert Todd Lincoln arrived. With parenthood, both Lincolns felt new priorities, and Mary carved out for herself, to a greater extent, a new identity. After their child was born, Lincoln rarely called his wife by her pet name, Mollie, although he still might affectionately refer to her as Puss, joking about her as a feline in front of intimates. After she bore him the first of four sons, Lincoln reverently addressed his wife as Mother. Mary had always, in the Victorian style of the day, referred to her husband as Mr. Lincoln, but following their son's arrival, she most often addressed him as Father. Mary fondly recalled her memory of him bending over to peer at their newborn, staring with awe and affection.

The baby was prudently named after his grandfather Todd. There had been two previous Robert Todd namesakes (one by each of his wives) who had not survived. None of Mrs. Lincoln's siblings had paid their father this tribute yet. Mary sensed an opportunity and seized it. She always curried her father's favor and now was a particularly important juncture. Her father's generosity helped the couple move out of a boardinghouse and into their own home.

During a speaking tour on behalf of the Whig candidates in 1844, Lincoln returned to Indiana, his former home, where both his mother and sister were buried. This nostalgic journey included encounters with old friends with whom he was happy to catch up and, in some sense, face his past. This experience prompted an outburst of verse. Indeed love of poetry was something he and Mary shared. They often read poetry aloud to each other, and both penned verses. Lincoln's compositions occasionally appeared (unsigned) in the local paper. Lincoln's sentimental visit to his childhood home, he described "aroused feelings in me which were certainly poetry." Marriage and having his own children in many ways opened up a new vein of emotional depth, one that poured out in rhyme.[64]

Both Lincolns doted on their children. Neither was much of a disciplinarian, but apparently Mary was even worse than her husband at handling her boys. She was extremely indulgent where her toddlers were concerned. Lincoln was unperturbed, if not lax, about child rearing, and confessed, "It s my pleasure that my children are free, happy and unrestrained by parental tyranny. Love is the chain hereby to bind a child to its parents."[65]

Robert was joined by his brother Edward Baker on March 10, 1846. This brought even more responsibilities and challenges for the mother in a growing family, especially as Lincoln was making a run for Congress later that summer. Lincoln was elected to Congress, and Mary decided that she and their two boys would accompany Mr. Lincoln to Washington, an unusual decision, which did not work out. She was forced to leave early and return to family in Kentucky with Eddie and Robert in tow. Several stories stem from this period that demonstrate that the Lincolns were viewed as parents who let their children ride roughshod over them, not a hard impression to make in a Washington boardinghouse full of politicians.

While they were on a trip to Kentucky, Eddie Lincoln became ill, and after fifty-two days of suffering, his body gave up the struggle on February 1, 1850. The boy died in Springfield a few weeks shy of his fourth birthday. His death certificate blamed chronic consumption.[66] Whatever the cause, their son's death was a terrible blow. Lincoln suffered stoically, writing three weeks after his toddler's funeral with poignant simplicity: "We miss him very much."[67]

While Lincoln mourned with reticent dignity, his wife found herself overwhelmed by grief, suffering severe spells of weeping and a lack of appetite. Fearing for his wife's recovery, Lincoln sought out Dr. James Smith, a Presbyterian cleric, not a physician. The reverend proved an effective counselor and got Mrs. Lincoln through a difficult period. She penned verse to commemorate her boy's death: "Bright is the home to him now given/ for of such is the Kingdom of Heaven."[68] Although she might not have felt Christian resignation at the time, she trusted that she might grow into piety under Smith's tutelage. Mary officially joined Smith's church in 1852.[69] Abraham Lincoln seemed to appreciate Reverend Smith's pastoral care and enjoyed theological discussions with him.

Burying Eddie was one of the hardest things the Lincolns had ever done. For each of them, the death of a loved one represented the return of a dark shadow. Lincoln's penchant for melancholy might have allowed him to sink into gloom, but apparently he reined in his emotions and forged ahead with legal work. His professional zeal was a crucial necessity to rebuilding his law practice after his time in Congress.

In spring and summer of 1850, Robert was an only child again, a most puzzling and painful time for the precocious six-year-old. Both parents tried to preoccupy themselves with other matters. Soon Mary was pregnant again. Although the Lincolns did not intend to forget their most treasured lost child, they wanted to climb out of the deep trench of sorrow into which his death lowered them. The couple joyfully greeted the birth of William Wallace Lincoln four days before Christmas in 1850. His safe arrival proved a godsend for the entire family and lifted the gloom. Two years later the family greeted the birth of Thomas Lincoln, Abraham's father's namesake, who was nicknamed Tad by his father.

The tragic death of eleven-year-old Willie Lincoln in February 1862 has been told with moving simplicity in Civil War literature, children's books, and Lincoln biographies.[70] William Wallace Lincoln represented the dearest hopes of both his parents. He was a studious and affable boy and an especially good example for his younger brother, Tad. A White House visitor commented, "[H]is self-possession—aplomb, as the French call it—was extraordinary." His resemblance to his father was common praise, and because of this, it was often assumed he was his father's favorite child.[71] So the death of Willie Lincoln had a tremendous impact on the family.

Parental indulgence was exercised in excess where Tad was concerned, as both Lincolns mourned an irreplaceable loss. (Although there was a rumor of Mrs. Lincoln's pregnancy during her years in the White House, she did not replace Willie with a baby.) After his brother's death, Tad and his father made even more frequent excursions to Stuntz's toy shop on New York Avenue. Lincoln confided: "I want to give him all the toys I did not have and all the toys that I would have given the boy who went away."[72]

Tad became overindulged, demanding and obtaining favors through his father's intercession. Lincoln issued a flurry of "official requests" on his son's behalf, including a letter to the secretary of the navy for a sword, to the secretary of war to find him some flags, and finally to an army captain, asking him to locate "a little gun that he can not hurt himself with."[73]

Tad had always been crazy about military matters—pistols and parades at the top of his list. Tad's favorite toy soldier was dressed like a Zouave, a gift from the Sanitary Commission of New York, a doll he named Jack. This toy soldier provided endless fun, as he was caught sleeping at his post with regularity, often "shot at sunrise," and then buried near the rosebushes, despite protests of the White House gardener. At one point Tad burst into his father's office and sought a pardon. Lincoln played along, only granting clemency after a mock trial, with a reprieve written on official paper. (Apparently Jack couldn't stay out of trouble and was found guilty and hanged from a tree at a family friend's home shortly thereafter.)[74]

Tad's obsession with military matters had a darker side. Once he became alarmed about safety at the White House and requisitioned arms for the house staff and drilled them to stand guard duty. His brother Robert was furious about this incident, but the president seemed to sense the anxiety in his younger son and temporarily allowed this charade, dismissing the armed servants once Tad was tucked away in bed.[75] Tad had been scolded for pointing a gun at a playmate and dressed down for firing a gun at the house of his playmates, where he accidentally shot out a window. Yet his begging allowed all to be forgiven, and he was finally given his own firearm.[76]

One of the most serious breaches between the Lincolns erupted just weeks before war's end, when Robert Lincoln convinced his father to help him enlist. As soon as war broke out, Robert had thought about joining the army. But his mother objected, and his father went along with her. After his Harvard graduation in June 1864, Robert was extremely agitated and refused to live in Washington, where his lack of uniform made him feel both conspicuous and embarrassed. When he finally joined the army in January 1865, his mother was angry. Her husband and older son had conspired against her. Mrs. Lincoln was devastated that the president would allow Robert to enter military service over her objections.

Lincoln of course had been placed in an impossible situation. He was the commander in chief, who not only demanded that thousands of young men volunteer for the military but also enforced a draft. The deaths of tens of thousands weighed heavily, while his own son sat out the war. His wife wanted to preserve their son at all costs. She could not bear to have him carried away like the two other boys she had lost. But the situation became a matter of honor, of paternal integrity, and Lincoln finally consented: His son could follow his conscience and enlist.

As president Lincoln used his influence, appealing directly to General Grant on January 19, 1865, writing that his son wanted to "see something of the war before it ends."[77] Grant kindly responded, "I will be most happy to have him in my Military family," and welcomed Robert Lincoln to his own staff as a captain.[78] The president's son served near the front where many of the final battles were fought.

Mary felt betrayed. Even though Robert emerged from the war unscathed, his enlistment created a strong undercurrent of resentment within the private quarters of the White House. Lincoln had been willing to respect his son's feelings and his needs and to take on paternal responsibilities in a way his own father had not.

Lincoln responded to his son's sense of honor and duty, perhaps recalling his own days on the frontier, when he had joined the Illinois militia during the Black Hawk War. Lincoln was willing to risk his older boy, to untether the chains of love he wrapped around his remaining sons. It was a gamble he won when Robert returned from military duty safe and sound.

Mary spent the weeks after her son's enlistment in terror and dread. She exulted over Lee's surrender, knowing Robert would be coming home. Yet it was a joy short-lived when he came back to the White House on the very day his father was shot. While the nation was robbed of a president who would be immortalized as the savior of the Union, Mary, Robert, and Tad lost the man they all called Father.

PART IV

POLITICS

AND

MEMORY

11

The Theft of Lincoln in Scholarship, Politics, and Public Memory

DAVID W. BLIGHT

Since at least the attempt to steal Abraham Lincoln's body from his newly constructed tomb shortly after he was buried in Springfield, Illinois, in 1865, a myriad of appropriations, uses, inventions, and reinventions—thefts—of the sixteenth president's meaning and memory have ensued in American popular culture, in formal politics, in scholarship, and in public memory. The South's Lost Cause and the Confederate Legend, replete with ancestor worship, racist ideology, and a tenacious version of history that writes slavery out of the story of the Civil War, is a persistent and probably eternal myth in American culture. But the Lincoln Legend, in different forms, is perhaps as equally tenacious in the hands of its persistent advocates and its detractors.

Commercially, the Lincoln image has never been more popular it appears; he now appears on television advertisements for an insurance company that places the stovepipe-hatted one on a golf course as a source of security and wisdom and in a piece selling anti–foot odor ingredients, where his nose on the penny is turned up in disgust. The Brunswick Billiards Tables were advertised on the televised Women's National Billiards Championships with Civil War–era photos of the president, period music, and the plea "Be a Lincoln" and "buy a Brunswick." A pharmaceutical company has now used Lincoln's image on huge posters in airports and train stations, sitting knowingly, giving advice to use a certain sleeping pill. Any day now we may see Lincoln's famous melancholia used to sell a new brand of antidepressant. H. L. Mencken warned sardonically of this never-ending trend in our culture in 1922, the year the Lincoln Memorial was unveiled. Lincoln, he said, "becomes the American solar myth, the chief butt of American credulity and sentimentality." Lincoln, according to Mencken, had been rendered a "mere moral apparition" by so much symbolic use, "a sort of amalgam of John Wesley and the Holy Ghost . . . fit for adoration in the chautauquas and Y.M.C.A.'s."[1] And that was only 1922!

Lincoln has long been infinitely malleable. He can be dour, pained, tragic, sorrowful or the humorist and the raunchy storyteller; he can be everyman or the prince of our democracy. He can be the distant intellectual political theorist who reimagined American race relations or the racist demagogue who held back progress in race relations until only total war "forced" him into "glory," as Lerone Bennett has argued in a recent book. As the poet Carl Sandburg famously put it, Lincoln was a "man of both steel and velvet, who is as hard as rock and as soft as drifting fog, who holds in his heart and mind the paradox of terrible storm and peace unspeakable." Lincoln could do it all, and we still make him do so. He can serve as everyone's aid or tool in one struggle over historical memory after another. We all seem to keep him handy to use as we see fit. The reformer Ida Tarbell's remark still holds up well. Lincoln, she wrote, "is companionable as no public mind that I've ever known. . . . You feel at home with him, he never high hats you and he never bores you, which is more than I can say of any public man living or dead with whom I have tried to get acquainted. . . . I have kept him always on my work bench."[2]

Lincoln lovers and vilifiers alike need to use and reuse his words and his image. Is this because we are bereft of political poetry in our own time? Are we without thinkers and leaders to find the language to match the crises of our own bloodied and distracted era? Why couldn't Americans find any other poet of our own age to write and speak at the first anniversary of the September 11 attacks on New York? Did the Gettysburg Address really fit that commemorative moment, or was it simply too risky to leave such an occasion to the partisan whims of the speech writers serving such inarticulate leaders as George Pataki and George W. Bush?

All presidents try to assume the mantle of Lincoln when they need him. One of the most eye-popping misuses of Lincoln came from former President Ronald Reagan at the 1992 Republican National Convention.

As the Reagan revolution seemed under threat from the Democratic chal-
lenger Bill Clinton, the retired president trotted out four maxims that he
claimed were cherished principles of Abraham Lincoln's:

> You cannot strengthen the weak by weakening the strong.
> You cannot help the wage earner by pulling down the wage payer.
> You cannot help the poor man by destroying the rich.
> You cannot help men permanently by doing for them what they
>   could or should do for themselves.

Television cameras captured the thrilled faces and wild cheers of the
Republican delegates as they watched their beloved Reagan draw Lincoln
securely into their moral worldview. Lincoln, through Reagan's charm,
would make them, as Rosalynn Carter once put it, "comfortable with
their prejudices." The problem, however, was that Lincoln had never
uttered any of these aphorisms. When members of the press pointed this
out, Reagan's aides assured them that the president had, well . . . done his
own "research." He had taken the quotations from *The Toastmaster's Treasure Chest* by Herbert V. Prochnow. Prochnow had in turn taken them
from a 1916 book, *Lincoln on Private Property*, by William John Henry
Boetcker. Boetcker had made them up. His little book had been reprinted
in many editions through the years and been passed down through
Republican clubs. In this embarrassing misappropriation of Lincoln,
Reagan was only beginning a new chapter in his party's spurious late-
twentieth-century effort to persuade voters that they were still the "party
of Lincoln."[3]

The political right, however, has had no monopoly on misquoting
Lincoln. A favorite that seems to have nineteenth-century roots and a
good deal of staying power (appearing in the *Lincoln Encyclopedia* in 1950)
is alleged to have been written in a letter by Lincoln to a Colonel Thomas
Elkins, November 21, 1864: "I see in the near future a crisis approaching
that unnerves me and causes me to tremble for the safety of my country
. . . corporations have been enthroned and an era of corruption in high
places will follow, and the money power of the country will endeavor to
prolong its reign by working upon the prejudices of the people until
all wealth is aggregated in a few hands and the Republic is destroyed."
Lincoln never wrote these words either. As Lincoln scholar Thomas

Schwartz reports, the president's son Robert had earlier attempted to put this one to rest by suggesting that the quotation likely came from a séance in a small town in Iowa in the 1890s.[4]

Lincoln always seems to be there when we need him, relevant or not. As recent as September 2006 in "Bush and Lincoln," in the *Wall Street Journal*, former Speaker of the House Newt Gingrich argued that President Bush had not yet committed to a strategy of total "victory" and unconditional surrender in our current "World War III" against radical Islam and terror. In order to do so, Bush, claimed Gingrich, must model his approach on Lincoln's war strategy to defeat the Confederacy adopted in roughly the late summer of 1862. Other than the implication that Bush needs some of Lincoln's wisdom and the courage to commit to true social sacrifice and mobilization for war, it is not clear how we connect the dots between Baghdad and Second Manassas, Antietam, and the Preliminary Emancipation Proclamation in this reach to stamp Lincoln's gravitas onto the disaster in Iraq. In the same week in the *Wasington Post*, E. J. Dionne suggested in "The Rise of the Lincoln Democrats" that a "quiet counter-realignment" had been taking place in what he calls the "Lincoln states" of the Northeast and the Midwest. Moderate suburban Republicans, claimed Dionne, in states like Pennsylvania, New Jersey, Ohio, Minnesota, and Wisconsin, frightened off by the conservative wing of the current Republican Party, would swing the House of Representatives to the Democrats in the fall 2006 elections. Dionne was on to something, but why these states need to be called Lincoln states remains unclear. Bill Clinton carried many of these same voters twice, and Franklin Roosevelt attracted their parents or grandparents four times. But it is Lincoln's prestige, symbol, or imprimatur that Dionne, like so many others, reaches for to get our attention. I am reminded of the headline that appeared in the *Chicago Defender* in the 1936 election, urging blacks to shift their allegiance to FDR: ABRAHAM LINCOLN IS NOT RUNNING IN THIS ELECTION![5]

One should exercise some restraint in casting aspersions on our current-day Lincoln thieves, since this process has ever been thus. Historian David Donald demonstrated this poignantly in his famous 1947 essay "Getting Right with Lincoln." By the twentieth century, Donald showed, for American politicians of all parties, Lincoln could be "everybody's grandfather." Donald had his own favorite Lincoln to advance, and he has spent a distinguished career sustaining the image and the man he had first written about with irony sixty years ago, the towering political figure characterized by his "essential ambiguity" and his "enormous capacity for growth."[6]

Despite all the efforts to pin Lincoln down ideologically, psychologically, religiously, legally, linguistically, sexually, and morally, the Lincoln of change, growth, and contradiction (even a self-described malleability) makes possible his endurance as symbol and as scholarly subject. And despite the considerable labors of devotees of the political theorist Leo Strauss, who crave a principled and consistent Lincoln to advance conservative agendas, his power over us derives from his splendid inconsistency. Certainly this is what has made Lincoln so useful to opposite ends of the political spectrum, to African Americans trying to preserve a usable past, and to right-wing ideologues, some of whom now find it politically impossible to operate without getting right, in their own peculiar way, with an emancipationist memory of the Civil War. There are many ways to "love" Lincoln. My own favorite comes from W. E. B. Du Bois. "I love him," Du Bois wrote in 1922 after expressing disgust at the nation's continuing adoration of Robert E. Lee, "not because he was perfect, but because he was not and yet triumphed. . . . The world is full of folk whose taste was educated in the gutter. The world is full of people born hating and despising their fellows. To those I love to say: See this man. He was one of you and yet became Abraham Lincoln." Like so many others, including Sandburg, Du Bois was drawn to Lincoln's embodiment of paradox. "There was something left," he said of Lincoln, "so that at the crisis he was big enough to be inconsistent—cruel, merciful, peace-loving, a fighter, despising Negroes and letting them fight and vote, protecting slavery, and freeing slaves. He was a man—a big, inconsistent, brave man."[7]

Du Bois's is the Lincoln of my own taste, choice, and use. Not a flavor of the month, but one for all time. But the revival of Lincoln scholarship and Lincoln memory in the past decade or so has given us many new variations on this theme, and we need to take notice of the political potential in the new thievery. As the bicentennial of Lincoln's birth nears in 2009, and the United States Lincoln Bicentennial Commission plans its extensive commemorations, we shall see only more grist for this mill. In the past few years excellent books on Lincoln have emerged from liberal academic historians, libertarian pseudohistorians, a sexuality expert, legal scholars, literary theorists, political theorists, journalists, and psychologists. Many recent books have added notably and surprisingly to our knowledge of Lincoln as a thinker and writer, but many also sustain a trend that might be called Lincoln triumphalism practiced by a select group of devoted Lincoln scholars.[8]

One of the most celebrated works of the Lincoln establishment is Allen Guelzo's *Lincoln's Emancipation Proclamation: The End of Slavery in America*. Guelzo, however, seems so determined to protect Lincoln from critics that one wonders why the Emancipation Proclamation needs such a vehement defense in the early twenty-first century.

It takes nothing away from the many recent good books on Lincoln to suggest that they (especially Guelzo's) may be efforts to defend Lincoln from those critics who have tried to take the mantle of Great Emancipator away from him and crush it in a wave of myth busting from left and right. Lerone Bennett's *Forced into Glory* (1999) spent more than six hundred pages trying to demonstrate that Lincoln was a white supremacist first and always and that traditional scholarship, political rhetoric, and the industry of memory and hero worship over time had created "the biggest attempt in recorded history to hide a man. . . ." Lincoln's defenders, claimed Bennett, had managed to turn "a racist who wanted to deport all blacks into a national symbol of integration and brotherhood" and had "fooled all the people all the time." But his selectively researched polemic gained great traction in black communities; its argument, strained as it is, has a new staying power at the grassroots, nonacademic level of historical interest, a phenomenon no one should ignore. Bennett's book gained little respect in academic circles, however, and garnered few mainstream reviews. Yet Guelzo also does not advance the debate over whether Lincoln alone freed the slaves or whether some slaves, by their own bravery, actually should be judged as "self-emancipated." Guelzo declares the self-emancipation thesis not worthy of the time of day. The "self-emancipation thesis," says Guelzo, "asks too great a suspension of disbelief."[9] Numerous books and some slave narratives have demonstrated that slaves' volition in this story is more than worthy of our attention.[10]

It is as though Bennett had stolen the Great Emancipator from the halls of academe and some Lincoln scholars had simply taken him back. Whether the two communities are even aware of each other's theft is another matter, since Bennett's and Guelzo's respective readers and advocates rarely speak to each other. The crucial questions about Lincoln on race and emancipation (as well as colonization schemes launched by his administration) are far more complicated than polemical debate can settle.

Lincoln the emancipator is one example of the intersection between scholarship and public memory that will forever witness volatile collisions. This is largely because it still very much matters how slavery ended in America and how its aftermath in law, society, politics, and social psychology still infuses our national memory with its most vexing dilemmas. As long as we have a politics of race in America, we shall have a politics of memory over Lincoln, the Civil War, and how and why black freedom came.

Another community of historical writing on Lincoln and the Civil War emanates from the right wing, some of it white supremacist and neo-Confederate and some of it staunchly libertarian, antistatist, even utopian, where Lincoln hating is the stand-in for the hated "big government." Two books stand out among a crowded subfield of neo-Confederate, prosecession, largely ersatz scholarship. The first is Charles Adams's *When in the Course of Human Events: Arguing the Case for Southern Secession* (2000); the second, Thomas J. DiLorenzo's *The Real Lincoln: A New Look at Abraham Lincoln, His Agenda, and an Unnecessary War* (2002).[11]

Why pay attention to these books? The simple answer is that they sell well, better than some canonical works on Lincoln and the Civil War of recent years that might be considered part of a liberal orthodoxy forged around the books of James McPherson, Eric Foner, and others. But more important, along with such recent books as *The Politically Incorrect Guide to American History*, by Thomas E. Woods, Jr., given huge publicity by Fox News, MSNBC, and other media outlets, and which had a stint on the *New York Times* best seller list, these works provide a historical undergirding for a broadening conservative and libertarian attack on the actual legacies of the original Republican Party, the Progressive movement, the New Deal regulatory state, the Great Society, and the civil rights movement.[12] Moreover, carefully researched, well-written academic history (even by those authors who reach broad audiences) is merely one more target of Lynne Cheney's network of enthusiasts who love Whiggish happy, redemptive American history. Their real targets are the "liberal elites" that allegedly control the academy, brainwash generations of students, and too often remain in their cocoons, scorned and irrelevant to the ways history is used in the civic arena.

In a recent essay in *Reviews in American History*, Daniel Feller took on the Adams and DiLorenzo books, as well as a third, by Jeffrey Rogers Hummel, *Emancipating Slaves, Enslaving Free Men: A History of the American*

Civil War. Feller points out that the Library of Congress catalogs my book *Race and Reunion: The Civil War in American Memory* (2001) right next to Tony Horwitz's *Confederates in the Attic* (2002) and Adams's defense of secession (with mine apparently in the middle). "Though Adams and Blight sit adjacent on the shelves," writes Feller, "the gulf between them, both in viewpoint and audience, is nearly bottomless. Contemplating that gulf provokes some disturbing thoughts."[13] In this essay I have at least tried to peer across this disturbing gulf.

Adams, an economist by training, is self-described as the "world's leading scholar on the history of taxation." DiLorenzo teaches (also economics) at Loyola College in Maryland and has been active in the League of the South. Both authors consider the slavery issue a mere pretext for the larger reason Lincoln and Republicans went to war: to advance the centralized, leviathan state. Both authors despise Lincoln, and they argue that the war's greatest legacy is federal "tyranny" over the states and especially over individual liberty. Secession was not only understandable but right and holy. And Lincoln's war was vicious and "criminal." It was a war waged, in Adams's and DiLorenzo's view, for increased taxation, higher tariffs, and business profits. Adams compares Lincoln's ruthlessness in prosecuting a war with unconditional surrender to that of Stalin and Hitler in World War II. Adams considers Lincoln a virulent racist and calls the second inaugural "psychopathic," a mere cover for his larger motive, the total destruction of southern civilization. During Reconstruction, according to Adams, the Union Leagues were the terrorist wing of the Republican Party and the Ku Klux Klan a harmless, necessary veterans' organization. Three of Adams's chapters had first been published in the white supremacist magazine *Southern Partisan.*[14]

This is all standard Lost Cause dogma of a fairly extreme brand, and it could have been written in 1890 or 1913 by any number of first- or second-generation ex-Confederates. But as Feller writes, it is not merely a "brainless rant." It has all the usual scholarly apparatus, footnotes and bibliographical essay. Adams's work is a screed full of some wild roundhouses, but it also reads much like a monologue on Fox News or a Grover Norquist press release about the condition of the American polity circa 2004. It is history serving a political persuasion, facts spun into a compelling narrative for the scorned and rebuked, white Christian conservatives of America who believe their faith in God, country, and righteousness is somehow under attack. Adams's history, like Norquist's lobbying, offers nourishment for the new Federalists and state rightists who believe government and taxation to be America's great domestic enemies.[15]

DiLorenzo's book is even more extreme, and perhaps more beguiling, in its sheer hatred of Lincoln. *The Real Lincoln* may be taking some of its cues from a book of the same title published in 1901 by Charles L. C. Minor. That book, at the high tide of Lost Cause writing, trashed Lincoln as unheroic, un-Christian, and a vulgar buffoon, a kind of counter-example to the noble Christian soldier Robert E. Lee. But primarily DiLorenzo uses and twists Lincoln's presidency into a libertarian manifesto for this age of conservative ascendancy. DiLorenzo's Lincoln provoked the Civil War to bring into being the modern "welfare-warfare state." Rather than the Great Emancipator, the sixteenth president should be remembered as the "great centralizer."[16]

What mainstream America celebrates in Lincoln's conception of the Civil War as the "rebirth" of freedom, DiLorenzo sees as the "death of federalism." His Lincoln is the dictatorial godfather of big government.[17] Leaders of secession were the Civil War's real heroes, according to DiLorenzo, because their cause had nothing to do with slavery—only with resisting federal tyranny. DiLorenzo's real complaint is the economic legislation passed by the Lincoln administration and the Civil War Congress: protective tariffs, the Morrill Act (subsidized land-grant colleges), federal subsidies to railroads, nationalized currency, the income tax, the Homestead Act, and, most egregious of all, emancipation by military force (the theft of individual property) and the huge extensions of federal power in the Fourteenth and Fifteenth Amendments.

There is no likelihood that the DiLorenzos of the right will make significant numbers of Americans reject Lincoln, but much of the argument looks like only a slightly angrier, heightened version of the campaign manual of movement conservatives during the George W. Bush administration. They can never appear to hate Lincoln—and do not need to—but they do tend to hate government and are very much interested in confirming judges and passing legislation that would roll back the activist-interventionist government, and the beginnings of the regulatory state, that the original Republicans created.

Today's Republicans, however, cannot agree among themselves about the legacy of their party's first president. The libertarian assault on Lincoln makes all the more ironic the Republican National Committee's recent well-funded, glitzy campaign to reclaim once again the mantle of the "party of Lincoln," to portray itself as the true party of "civil rights." Early in 2005, just as President Bush was inaugurated for his second term, the Republican Party's Policy Committee, then led by California Congressman Christopher Cox, produced a multicolor calendar that it distributed by the thousands to African American churches and other civic groups across the country. Called the "2005 Republican Party Freedom Calendar," it featured on its cover a majestic image of the Lincoln Memorial statue and twelve photographs of African American and other minority Republicans in American history. The calendar's subtitle leaves no doubt of its long-range historical claims: "Celebrating a Century and a Half of Civil Rights Achievement by the Party of Lincoln."[18]

Congressman Cox's introduction offers a particular and curious version of history. It declares the Republican Party "the mightiest force for individual liberty in the history of the world" and "the most effective political organization in the history of the world in advancing the cause of freedom by staying true to its founding principles." And Cox makes clear to the black audience he hopes to reach who the enemy was and is. "We started our party," he says, "with the express intent of protecting the American people from the Democrats' pro-slavery policies that expressly made people inferior to the state." "Today," he continues, "the animating spirit of the Republican party is exactly the same as it was then: free people, free minds, free markets, free expression, and unlimited individual opportunity."[19] Libertarians in the guise of free-soilers! It is a little hard to imagine the Bush White House of 2006–08, stumping for "intelligent design" in biology classrooms and against embryonic stem cell research in medical laboratories, as proponents of our collective "free minds" and "free expression." But the "party of Lincoln" has come to mean many things to many people.

Cox and his staff were determined to create an ideological enemy of both past and present. "Leading the opposition to these ideas 150 years ago" (free markets and free minds), Cox continued, "just as today, was the Democratic party. Then, just as now, their hallmarks were politically correct speech; a preference for government control over individual initiative (and of course slavery was the most extreme form of government control over individual initiative); and an insistence on seeing people as members of groups rather than as individuals." I know of no one who ever accused Stephen A. Douglas of using politically correct speech, but early-twenty-first-century Republicans are careful to invoke the symbol of Ronald Reagan (an odd kind of right-wing correctness of speech in our own era), as Cox did in this calendar, as the great spokesman of "the only country on earth to be based not on race or nationality, but on an ideal." For black audiences, not to mention millions of whites and others with historical memories, these are odd claims to make for Reagan, the most racially divisive president in modern American history. But the "Freedom Calendar" leaves one impression above all others: Black voters, and whites who need to feel better about being Republicans, should draw a clear, uninterrupted line from Harriet Tubman and Frederick Douglass to Condoleezza Rice and Colin Powell, and American history ought to be seen as a consistent struggle of the Republican Party to sustain a society where the "individual is master and the government is servant." This sophistry has many parallels and antecedents. After President Franklin Roosevelt had captured a majority of the black vote in 1936 (the first time a Democrat had ever done so), he remarked with derision: "Does anyone maintain that the Republican party from 1868 to 1938 (with the possible exception of a few years under Theodore Roosevelt) was the party of Abraham Lincoln?" With even more derision, we might say today: "Does anyone really believe that the Republican Party from 1964 to 2004 was the party of Abraham Lincoln?"[20]

It is easy to simply laugh away such slippery, ahistorical versions of the past century and a half of American political history. But incredulity is hardly enough against the realization that millions of Americans either believe this story or are blissful in their ignorance. However, this sleight of hand history of the Republican Party (sinless, indeed, righteous on race) has not yet swayed even a few percent more African Americans to vote for Bush-era Republicans. Evidence that the facile "calendar" strategy backfired appeared when Ken Mehlman, then the party chairman, went to the NAACP annual convention in July 2005 in Milwaukee largely to apologize for the Republican record on race and civil rights, especially its notorious "southern strategy," begun under Richard Nixon, but manipulated by no one more adroitly than Ronald Reagan and to a lesser extent by President George H. W. Bush. Mehlman pleaded guilty to the Republicans' "trying to benefit politically from racial polarization." "I am here today . . ." he told the suspicious NAACP delegates, "to tell you we were wrong." Meanwhile, on the same day, July 14, 2005, President Bush was speaking to "business leaders" at the Indiana Black

Expo, emphasizing gains for African Americans in education, faith-based initiatives, and private enterprise. "Racial polarization" would seem to be a thing of the distant past, rendered no longer operative by a passive voice from a Republican leadership eager to make the past fit its present. In his speech to the NAACP Mehlman used the phrase "party of Abraham Lincoln" no fewer than six times.[21] Whether a Lincoln currency still buys anything among African Americans who know something about the recent history of civil rights remains doubtful.

Further evidence that the Republicans will need something more serious to truly attract black allegiance, especially in the wake of Hurricane Katrina, appears in President Bush's July 2006 speech to the annual convention of the NAACP, an organization he had snubbed for four years. Bush's speech writers placed a remarkable document in his hands. This time it was based on the history of the last forty years. He called the civil rights movement a "second founding" of the United States and the movement's leaders the new "founders." He acknowledged racism to be the "stain we have not yet wiped clean." And the only reference to the "party of Lincoln" was in an open admission of his party's failures in race relations. "I understand that many African Americans distrust my political party," said Bush. "I consider it a tragedy that the party of Abraham Lincoln let go of its historic ties to the African American community. For too long my party wrote off the African American vote, and many African Americans wrote off the Republican party."[22] So much for the calendar strategy and the selling of nonsense as history. Only a short time after launching the calendar effort and its related kind of outreach to black voters, the official Republican Party all but admitted the implausibility of its own arguments.

It is as though in thus reaching out, Bush's aides decided that for this symbolic moment at least it was time to disown part of the political heritage of his biological father (G. H. W. Bush) as well as his political father (Reagan). No matter how malleable, no matter how ambiguous, perhaps deep in the legacies of the original father of the Republican Party there is one ghost that will not down: Lincoln possessed a genuine sense of tragedy, and from it he learned and grew. Whether President Bush has a sense of the tragic, or of history generally, is open to debate. Whether his party will ever overcome its late-twentieth- and early-twenty-first-century politics of racial resentment remains to be seen.

We could attribute all this simply to the twisted ways politicians use history. But this broad manipulation of history is of course nothing new. The various thefts of Lincoln from the right, and even to some extent in mainstream scholarship, are part of a larger distortion of the story of emancipation in the First Reconstruction and the story of the civil rights revolution in the Second Reconstruction. It is a bold attempt by the conservative movement to gain control of the master narrative of American history in order to reverse many of the gains of both revolutions.

The New Right has abandoned the racism of the Old Right and found a new narrative in "color-blindness" as the true meaning of the long struggle for racial justice. Color-blind conservatism gave us the most ardent state rightist on the Supreme Court in Clarence Thomas, and it has now put the ardent black libertarian Janice Rogers Brown on the U.S. Court of Appeals. Color-blind conservatism has fashioned a master narrative in which American history is a morality tale of progress from the Emancipation Proclamation to the Fourteenth Amendment to the 1964 Civil Rights Act to Secretaries of State Powell and Rice, all as legacies, somehow, of the "party of Lincoln." In the America of the early twenty-first century, we can all feel as if we freed the slaves, we all participated in the Underground Railroad, we all cheered for the civil rights movement (even if a few of us got "polarized").

As Republicans try to steal the meaning of American history and ride Lincoln's coattails while hating the government he imagined, they are seeking what all insurgent political movements need, a *warrant of the past*. That warrant is one of the chief prizes in all political contests. Whether Karl Rove, Ken Mehlman, Lynne Cheney, and their friend and sometime silent partner President Bush can win this struggle over storytelling remains a pivotal question for Americans. Millions of them care and read about Lincoln, and as the sixteenth president's bicentennial nears, the concept of the "party of Lincoln" may get more scrutiny than the creators of the "Freedom Calendar" ever intended.

As he considered Karl Rove's immediate legacy in recent American political history, the Bush administration's critic Frank Rich chose George Allen's "macaca moment" (his reference to a dark-skinned Asian American in his campaign audience in 2006) as "a single symbolic episode to encapsulate the collapse of Rovian Republicanism." Rich captured in a phrase the nature of the Republican Party's attempted theft of the past and of the "monochromatic whiteness at the dark heart of Rovian Republicanism."[23]

The modern GOP possesses a history it hardly wishes to know, and that past, recent and long term, has everything to do with why not a single black Republican serves today in the United States Congress. As the 2009 Lincoln bicentennial arrives, the Republicans will likely scramble once again to assume the mantle of the "party of Lincoln." But their founder had a warning for them. In his annual message to Congress, December 1, 1862, Lincoln famously said: "Fellow-citizens, we cannot escape history. We of this Congress and this administration, will be remembered in spite of ourselves."[24]

Contributors

DAVID W. BLIGHT is Class of 1954 Professor of American History at Yale University. His book *Race and Reunion: The Civil War in American Memory* (2001) earned a number of awards, including the Frederick Douglass Prize, the Lincoln Prize, and the Bancroft Prize. His most recent book, *A Slave No More: Two Men Who Escaped to Freedom, Including Their Narratives of Emancipation*, was published in 2007.

RICHARD CARWARDINE is Rhodes Professor of American History at the University of Oxford. Among other books he has written, *Evangelicals and Politics in Antebellum America* (1993) and *Lincoln: A Life of Purpose and Power* (2003), which won the Lincoln Prize in 2004. He is currently working on a study of religion in American national construction during the first century of the Republic, and is organizing a collaborative project on Lincoln's international legacy.

CATHERINE CLINTON is a Chair Professor of U.S. History at Queen's University, Belfast. Her numerous publications include *The Plantation Mistress: Woman's World in the Old South* (1982) and *Harriet Tubman: The Road to Freedom* (2004). Her biography of Mrs. Lincoln will be published in 2009.

ANDREW DELBANCO is Levi Professor in the Humanities and director of American studies at Columbia University. His books include *Melville: His*

World and Work (2005) and, as editor, *The Portable Abraham Lincoln* (1992), to be published in a revised edition in 2009.

ERIC FONER is DeWitt Clinton Professor of History at Columbia University and has served as president of the American Historical Association, Organization of American Historians, and Society of American Historians. He is the author of many books, including *Free Soil, Free Labor, Free Men: The Ideology of the Republican Party Before the Civil War* (1970); *Reconstruction: America's Unfinished Revolution, 1863–1877* (1988), winner, among other awards, of the Bancroft Prize; and, with Joshua Brown, *Forever Free: The Story of Emancipation and Reconstruction* (2005).

HAROLD HOLZER, cochairman of the U.S. Abraham Lincoln Bicentennial Commission and senior vice president for external affairs at The Metropolitan Museum of Art, is the author, coauthor, or editor of thirty books on Lincoln and the Civil War. He received a Lincoln Prize for *Lincoln at Cooper Union: The Speech that Made Abraham Lincoln President* (2004). His latest book is *Lincoln President-Elect* (2008).

JAMES M. MCPHERSON is George Henry Davis '86 Professor of American History Emeritus at Princeton University, where he taught from 1962 to 2004. He won the Pulitzer Prize in history in 1989 for *Battle Cry of Freedom: The Civil War Era* and the Lincoln Prize in 1998 for *For Cause and Comrades: Why Men Fought in the Civil War*. His most recent book is *This Mighty Scourge: Perspectives on the Civil War* (2007).

MARK E. NEELY, JR., McCabe Greer Professor of the History of the Civil War Era at Pennsylvania State University, has written widely on Lincoln and his era. Among his works are *The Abraham Lincoln Encyclopedia* (1981) and *The Fate of Liberty: Abraham Lincoln and Civil Liberties* (1991), winner of the Pulitzer Prize. His current project deals with nationalism in the Civil War.

JAMES OAKES is Graduate Humanities Professor and professor of history at the Graduate Center, City University of New York. He is the author of *The Ruling Race: A History of American Slaveholders* (1982), *Slavery and Freedom: An Interpretation of the Old South* (1990), and *The Radical and the Republican: Frederick Douglass, Abraham Lincoln, and the Triumph of Antislav-*

ery Politics (2007), winner of the Lincoln Prize. He is currently writing a history of emancipation during the Civil War.

MANISHA SINHA is associate professor of Afro-American studies and history at the University of Massachusetts, Amherst. She is the author of *The Counterrevolution of Slavery: Politics and Ideology in Antebellum South Carolina* (2000) and the coeditor of the two-volume *African American Mosaic* (2004) and *Contested Democracy* (2007). She is currently working on a forthcoming book on African Americans and the abolition movement, 1775–1865 (Harvard University Press).

SEAN WILENTZ is the Sidney and Ruth Lapidus Professor in the American Revolutionary Era at Princeton University. He is the author and editor of numerous books, including *The Rise of American Democracy: Jefferson to Lincoln* (2005), which was awarded the Bancroft Prize. His latest work is *The Age of Reagan: A History 1974–2008* (2008).

Notes

～～～⌒⌒～～～

A. LINCOLN, COMMANDER IN CHIEF by James M. McPherson

1. Roy P. Basler, ed., *The Collected Works of Abraham Lincoln*, 9 vols. (New Brunswick, N.J., 1953–55), 1: 509–10.
2. T. Harry Williams, *Lincoln and His Generals* (New York, 1952), vii.
3. Colin R. Ballard, *The Military Genius of Abraham Lincoln: An Essay* (London, 1926); T. Harry Williams, *Lincoln and His Generals*; Kenneth P. Williams, *Lincoln Finds a General: A Military Study of the Civil War*, 5 vols. (New York, 1949–59); Allan Nevins, *The War for the Union*, 4 vols. (New York, 1959–71).
4. Mark E. Neely, Jr., *The Abraham Lincoln Encyclopedia* (New York, 1982); Don E. Fehrenbacher, *Lincoln in Text and Context: Collected Essays* (Stanford, Calif., 1987); Gabor S. Boritt, ed., *The Historian's Lincoln: Pseudohistory, Psychohistory, and History* (Urbana, Ill., 1988); Merrill D. Peterson, *Lincoln in American Memory* (New York, 1994).
5. Basler, ed., *Collected Works*, 8: 332.
6. Michael Burlingame and John R. Turner Ettlinger, eds., *Inside Lincoln's White House: The Complete Civil War Diary of John Hay* (Carbondale, Ill., 1997), 20: diary entry of May 7, 1861.
7. Basler, ed., *Collected Works*, 3: 268; 7: 23; 8: 151.
8. Karl von Clausewitz, *On War*, trans. and ed. Michael Howard and Peter Paret (Princeton, 1976), 87–88.
9. *War of the Rebellion . . . Official Records of the Union and Confederate Armies*, 128 vols. (Washington, 1880–1901), ser. I, vol. 34, part 3: 332–33. Hereinafter OR.
10. Allen Thorndike Rice, ed., *Reminiscences of Abraham Lincoln by Distinguished Men of His Time* (New York, 1888), 391–92.
11. *Chicago Tribune*, Sept. 16, 1861, quoted in Thomas J. Goss, *The War Within the Union High Command: Politics and Generalship During the Civil War* (Lawrence, Kan., 2003), 42.
12. OR, ser. 3, vol. 2: 401–02; Abraham Lincoln to Edwin M. Stanton, Jan. 12, 1863, in Basler, ed., *Collected Works*, 6: 55.
13. Goss, *War Within Union High Command*, xv.
14. Lincoln to Frémont, Sept. 2, 1862, Lincoln to Orville H. Browning, Sept. 22, 1861, Basler, ed., *Collected Works*, 4: 506, 532.
15. Gideon Welles, "The History of Emancipation," *Galaxy*, 14 (Dec. 1872), 842–43.

16. For the platform, see Edward McPherson, *The Political History of the United States During the Great Rebellion*, 2nd ed. (Washington, 1865), 406–07.

17. Basler, ed., *Collected Works*, 5: 357.

18. Lincoln to Andrew Johnson, March 26, 1863, Basler, ed., *Collected Works*, 6: 149–50.

19. Ibid., 6: 410; 7: 500, 507.

20. *Personal Memoirs of U. S. Grant*, 2 vols. (New York, 1885–86), 2: 122.

21. Basler, ed., *Collected Works*, 5: 34–35.

22. Lincoln to McClellan, Feb. 3, 1862, ibid., 5, 118–19. For Johnston's apprehension of just such a campaign plan as Lincoln proposed, see Johnston to Jefferson Davis, Nov. 22, 1861, *OR*, ser. I, vol. 51: 1072–73.

23. Basler, ed., *Collected Works*, 5: 182; McClellan to his wife, April 8, 1862, Stephen W. Sears, ed., *The Civil War Papers of George B. McClellan* (New York, 1989), 234.

24. Lincoln to McClellan, Apr. 9, 1862, Basler, ed., *Collected Works*, 5: 185.

25. Ibid.

26. Lincoln to Sherman, Dec. 26, 1864, ibid., 8, 181.

27. Lincoln to McClellan, Oct. 13, 1862, ibid., 5, 461; Francis P. Blair [Sr.] to Montgomery Blair, Nov. 7, 1862, in William F. Smith, *The Francis Preston Blair Family in Politics*, 2 vols. (New York, 1933), 2: 144.

28. Basler, ed., *Collected Works*, 4: 95.

29. Ibid., 5, 85 n.; Lincoln to Buell (copy to Halleck), Jan. 13, 1862, ibid., 98.

30. *OR*, ser. I, vol. 46, part 1: 11; Burlingame and Ettlinger, *Inside Lincoln's White House*, 193, diary entry of Apr. 30, 1864.

31. Lincoln to Hooker, June 10, 16, Basler, ed., *Collected Works*, 6: 257, 281.

32. Lincoln to Halleck, July 7, 1863, ibid., 6: 319.

33. *OR*, ser. I, vol. 27, part 3: 519; Howard K. Beale, ed., *Diary of Gideon Welles*, 3 vols. (New York, 1960), 1: 370; Burlingame and Ettlinger, *Inside Lincoln's White House*, 62, diary entry of July 14, 1863.

34. Lincoln to Meade, July 14, 1863, Basler, ed.,*Collected Works*, 6: 328.

35. Lincoln to Henry W. Halleck, Sept. 19, 1863, ibid., 6: 467.

36. Quoted in Shelby Foote, *The Civil War, A Narrative: Fort Sumter to Perryville* (New York, 1958), 430.

37. Lincoln to McDowell, May 25, 28, 1862, Basler, ed., *Collected Works*, 5: 235, 246.

38. Henry W. Halleck to Buell, Oct. 19, 1863, *OR*, ser. I, vol. 16, part 2: 627. See also Lincoln to McClellan, Oct. 13, 1862, Basler, ed., *Collected Works*, 5: 460–61.

39. Rufus Ingalls to Montgomery Meigs, Oct. 26, 1862, *OR*, ser. I, vol. 19, part 2: 492–93; Lincoln to Nathaniel Banks, Nov. 22, 1862, Basler, ed., *Collected Works*, 5: 505–06.

40. James S. Rusling, *Men and Things I Saw in Civil War Days* (New York, 1899), 16–17; Washburne to Lincoln, May 1, 1863, Abraham Lincoln Papers, Robert Todd Lincoln Collection, Library of Congress.

41. Lincoln to Flag Officer Louis M. Goldsborough, May 7, 10, Basler, ed., *Collected Works*, 5: 207, 209; William Keeler to his wife, May 9, 1862, in Robert W. Daly, ed., *Aboard the USS "Monitor," 1862: The Letters of Acting Paymaster William Frederick Keeler* (Annapolis, Md., 1964), 113, 115; Salmon P. Chase to Janet Chase, May 11, in John Niven, ed., *The Salmon P. Chase Papers*, vol. 3: *Correspondence, 1858–March 1863* (Kent, Ohio, 1996), 193–97; quotation from 197.

THE CONSTITUTION AND CIVIL LIBERTIES UNDER LINCOLN
by Mark E. Neely, Jr.

1. I want to thank Eric Foner, William Blair, and Sylvia Neely for offering valuable advice and useful criticisms of earlier drafts of this article.

2. See, for a recent example, James F. Simon, *Lincoln and Chief Justice Taney: Slavery, Secession, and the President's War Powers* (New York, 2006), 190.

3. Carl Brent Swisher, *The Oliver Wendell Holmes Devise History of the United States Supreme Court*, vol. 5: *The Taney Period, 1836–1864* (New York, 1974), 846–48.

4. *War of the Rebellion. A Compilation of the Official Records of the Union and Confederate Armies*, 128 vols. (Washington, 1880–1902), ser. II, vol.1: 575–77.

5. Mark E. Neely, Jr., "'Seeking a Cause of Difficulty with the Government': Reconsidering Freedom of Speech and Judicial Conflict Under Lincoln," in Phillip S. Paludan, ed., *Lincoln's Legacy* (Urbana, Ill., 2008). Lincoln's order about the writ appears in Roy P. Basler, ed., *The Collected Works of Abraham Lincoln*, 9 vols. (New Brunswick, N.J., 1953–55), 4: 347. The OR prints the decision headed "Before the Chief Justice of the Supreme Court of the United States, in chambers." *War of the Rebellion . . . Official Records of the Union and Confederate Armies*, 128 vols. (Washington, 1880–1902), ser. II, vol. 1: 577. See also the work by Carl Brent Swisher cited in note 3 for the point about the decisions in chambers. Swisher states that Merryman was arrested for involvement in burning railroad bridges around Baltimore a month earlier.

6. Daniel Farber, *Lincoln's Constitution* (Chicago, 2003), 158. The habeas corpus clause appears in Article I, Section 9.

7. Don E. Fehrenbacher, "Roger B. Taney and the Sectional Crisis," *Journal of Southern History*, 43 (November 1977): 555–66. See also Swisher, *Oliver Wendell Holmes Devise History of the United States Supreme Court*, vol. 5: *The Taney Period, 1836–64*, 945, 951.

8. Clinton Rossiter, ed., *The Federalist Papers* (New York, 1999), 553.

9. Maeva Marcus, ed., *The Documentary History of the Supreme Court of the United States, 1789–1800*, vol. 4: *Organizing the Federal Judiciary: Legislation and Commentaries* (New York, 1992), 69.

10. *Ex parte Merryman*, 1, http://web.lexis-nexis.com . . . , accessed Sept. 28, 2004.

11. Marcus, ed., *Documentary History of the Supreme Court of the United States, 1789–1800*, 4: 71.

12. Akhil Reed Amar, *The Constitution: A Biography* (New York, 2005), 122.

13. Basler, ed., *Collected Works*, 5: 436–37.

14. Ibid., 6: 264.

15. Ibid., 6: 263.

16. Ibid., 6: 302.

17. Ibid., 6: 303.

18. Ibid., 6: 451.

19. Ibid., 6: 451–52.

20. Farber, *Lincoln's Constitution*, 190. Farber made the observation in passing, but without investigating the question of Taney's specific powers as a Supreme Court justice (as opposed to the power of judges in general to issue writs of habeas corpus) and without investigation of the Judiciary Act and the constitutional question. In other words, Taney's position on jurisdiction says more about Taney than Lincoln; Farber seems to have it the other way around.

21. The perennial question of constitutional history is well stated and answered in regard to the antebellum slavery question by Don E. Fehrenbacher in *The Dred Scott Case: Its Significance in American Law and Politics* (New York, 1978). Civil liberties during the war fitted the same interpretation. Yet in other matters in the war, the Constitution powerfully shaped events. See Mark E. Neely, Jr., *The Union Divided: Party Conflict in the Civil War North* (Cambridge, Mass., 2002), 35–36, 118–19, 194–96.

22. Douglas Wilson, *Lincoln's Sword: The Presidency and the Power of Words* (New York, 2006), 86.

23. Basler, ed., *Collected Works*, 6: 263–64.

24. Ibid., 6: 265.

25. Ibid., 6: 262–64.

26. James G. Randall, *Lincoln the President: Midstream* (New York, 1953), 226.

27. David Herbert Donald, *Lincoln* (New York, 1995), 443. The position of the *Chicago Tribune* perhaps most nearly fitted Donald's description of the reaction of Unionists to the Corning letter; see issues of June 17 and 18, 1863.

28. *New York Tribune*, June 15 and 16, 1863.

29. *New York Evening Post*, June 15, 1863.

30. Phillip Shaw Paludan, "'The Better Angels of Our Nature': Lincoln, Propaganda, and Public Opinion in the North During the Civil War," in Stig Förster and Jörg Nagler, eds., *On the Road to Total War: The American Civil War and the German Wars of Unification, 1861–1871* (Cambridge, Mass., 1997), 368. On this subject I benefited from the paper presented by James Flook entitled "Quelling Dissent: Lincoln's Response to the Vallandigham Arrest" and the subsequent discussion at the meeting of the Society for Military History at Frederick, Maryland, Apr. 22, 2007.

31. Paludan, "Better Angels of Our Nature," 369.

32. Ibid., 371 and n.

33. The chronology is very clear in E. B. Long, *The Civil War Day by Day: An Almanac, 1861–1865* (orig. pub. 1971; New York, n.d.), 366–67. On the evolution of the text of the Corning letter see Douglas Wilson, *Lincoln's Sword: The Presidency and the Power of Words*, 163–79.

34. Earl Schenck Miers, ed., *Lincoln Day-by-Day: A Chronology, 1809–1865* (orig. pub. in various dates and vols.; 3 vols. in one, Dayton, 1991), 3: 189. Lincoln had the Corning letter in presentable enough shape to read it to the cabinet for advice over a week earlier, on June 5. The cabinet at that time assumed that he was thereafter going to revise it for publication. Basler, ed., *Collected. Works*, 6: 261 n.

35. Michael F. Holt, "An Elusive Synthesis: Northern Politics During the Civil War," in James M. McPherson and William J. Cooper, Jr., eds., *Writing the Civil War: The Quest to Understand* (Columbia, Mo., 1998), 123–24, makes the crucial point about "misreading" the 1862 elections.

36. Frank L. Klement, *The Limits of Dissent: Clement L. Vallandigham and the Civil War* (orig. pub. 1970; New York, 1998), 229.

37. Jay Monaghan, *Lincoln Bibliography, 1839–1939*, 2 vols. (Springfield, Ill., 1943), 1: 54–55, 59–60; Mark E. Neeley, Jr., "The Civil War and the Two-Party System," in James M. McPherson, ed., *"We Cannot Escape History": Lincoln and the Last Best Hope of Earth* (Urbana, Ill., 1995) 93–94.

38. Basler, ed., *Collected Works*, 8: 52.

39. But he did fire off one more volley of a similarly contentious nature for the Ohio gubernatorial campaign later the same month, a letter of June 29, 1863, to Matthew Birchard and others, who had sent Lincoln a copy of the resolutions of the Ohio State Democratic Convention. Basler, ed., *Collected Works*, 6: 300–06.

40. Ibid., 8: 101.

41. Mark E. Neeley, Jr., *The Fate of Liberty: Abraham Lincoln and Civil Liberties* (New York, 1991), 48, 168–69.

42. Ibid., 6: 8.

43. Samuel R. Curtis to Abraham Lincoln, Dec. 17, 1862, Abraham Lincoln Papers, Library of Congress, microfilm edition, reel 45. See also Curtis to Lincoln, Dec. 20, 1862, ibid., about reliance on enrolled militia and civil laws in the state.

44. Franklin A. Dick to Abraham Lincoln, Dec. 19, 1862, ibid.

45. John O'Fallon to Abraham Lincoln, Jan. 5, 1863, ibid., reel 47. On O'Fallon, see Louis Gerteis, *Civil War St. Louis* (Lawrence, Kan., 2001), 15, 22, 44. The "secession" mayor was Daniel G. Taylor, who had run on an anti-Republican "Union" ticket in 1861. Ibid., 90.

46. Charles Drake to Abraham Lincoln, Jan. 22, 1863, Lincoln Papers, reel 47. See also A. G. Edwards to C. Gibson, Jan. 24, 1863 (about business rather than politics), Jan. 24, 1863, Lincoln Papers, reel 48.

47. Basler, ed., *Collected Works*, 8 : 217.

48. Grenville M. Dodge to Abraham Lincoln, Jan. 16, 1865, Lincoln Papers, reel 90.

49. William E. Parrish, *A History of Missouri*, vol. 3: *1860–1875* (Columbia, Mo., 1973), 92, and on Willard Hall, 31–32.

50. Michael Fellman, *Inside War: The Guerrilla Conflict in Missouri During the American Civil War* (New York, 1989), 10 (for the frank use of the term *coup d'état*).

51. Parrish, *History of Missouri*, vol. 3: 90–91.

52. William A. Hall to Abraham Lincoln, Jan. 19, 1865, Lincoln Papers, reel 91.

53. Basler, ed., *Collected Works*, 8 : 308.

54. William C. Harris, *Lincoln's Last Months* (Cambridge, Mass., 2004).

55. Basler, ed., *Collected Works*, 8 : 319.

56. Ibid., 8 : 319 n–320 n.

57. Ibid., 6 : 627.

58. *Chicago Tribune*, March 3, 1865.

59. Richard Franklin Bensel, *The American Ballot-Box in the Mid-Nineteenth Century* (New York, 2004), 217–53. The vote totals come from *The Tribune Almanac and Political Register for 1865* (New York, 1865), 67.

60. Basler, ed., *Collected Works*, 6 : 266.

61. See his Annual Message to Congress, of Dec. 6, 1864, ibid., 8, 150–51. He calculated the total gain in voting in the North and did not call attention to the anomalous decline in voting in the border states, where military interference at the polls was a major issue.

62. John Pope to Thomas Fletcher, March 13, 1865, in *OR*, series I, vol. 48, part 1 : 1070–1071, 1072; April 12, 1865, in ibid., part 2, 80.

63. Basler, ed., *Collected Works*, 6 : 269.

64. To Lincoln his movement seemed slow, or so he said in the Corning letter: "[T]horoughly imbued with a reverence for the guarranteed rights of individuals, I was slow to adopt the strong measures, which by degrees I have been forced to regard as being within the exceptions of the constitution, and as indispensable to the public Safety." Basler, ed., *Collected Works*, 6 : 264.

ABRAHAM LINCOLN AND JACKSONIAN DEMOCRACY by Sean Wilentz

1. Roy P. Basler, ed., *The Collected Works of Abraham Lincoln*, 9 vols. (New Brunswick, N.J. 1953–55), 4 : 184; 3 : 85; Don E. Fehrenbacher and Virginia Fehrenbacher, *Recollected Words of Abraham Lincoln* (Stanford, Calif., 1996), 37, 507. The last two quotations were recalled by, respectively, John Minor Botts and Robert C. Winthrop.

2. David Donald, *Lincoln Reconsidered: Essays on the Civil War Era* (orig. pub. 1956; New York, 1961), 187–208. Donald, who was ahead of his time, focused on Lincoln's Whiggish opposition to expanded presidential powers outside of matters directly related to his position as commander in chief. Studies emphasizing different aspects of Lincoln's Whig background include Kenneth M. Stampp, *The Era of Reconstruction* (New York, 1965); Daniel Walker Howe, *The Political Culture of the American Whigs* (Chicago, 1979); Gabor S. Borritt,

Lincoln and the Economics of the American Dream (Memphis, Tenn., 1978); Allen C. Guelzo, *Abraham Lincoln: Redeemer President* (Grand Rapids, Mich., 1999); Richard Carwardine, *Lincoln: A Life of Purpose and Power* (New York, 2003).

3. The flat equation sometimes drawn between northern Whigs and antislavery, and northern Democrats and proslavery (or doughface acquiescence over slavery) has never accorded with the evidence. As Ulysses S. Grant, a man of self-declared Whig leanings, recalled, "Opposition to slavery was not a creed of either political party. In some sections more anti-slavery men belonged to the Democratic party, and in others to the Whigs." See Grant, *Personal Memoirs of U. S. Grant* (1885–86), in *Grant: Memoirs and Selected Letters* (New York, 1990), 143.

4. Basler, ed., *Collected Works*, 2: 543, 545; 3: 79, 89, 93, 329, quotations on 2: 545; 3: 93.

5. For a strong statement of some of these themes, see Stephen B. Oates, "Abraham Lincoln: Republican in the White House," in John L. Thomas, ed., *Abraham Lincoln and the American Political Tradition* (Amherst, Mass., 1986), 98–110. The question of the continuities and discontinuities of Whiggery in the 1850s also harkens back to an old debate sparked by Thomas B. Alexander. "Persistent Whiggery in the Confederate South, 1860–1877," *Journal of Southern History*, 27 (Aug. 1961): 305–29. Alexander's effort to explain the politics of certain southern political figures during Reconstruction on the basis of their old Whig loyalties did not stand up very well, mainly, critics showed, because party lines and ideas changed so much after 1854.

6. Basler, ed., *Collected Works*, 1: 114, 162, 178, 226; 4: 49.

7. Thomas Ford, *A History of Illinois* (Chicago, 1854), 290; Basler, ed., *Collected Works*, 1: 48.

8. Robert H. Wiebe, "Lincoln's Fraternal Democracy," in Thomas, ed., *Abraham Lincoln*, 11–30; quotations on 16.

9. Carwardine, *Lincoln*, 59 (quotation).; Basler, ed., *Collected Works*, 1: 315.

10. Basler, ed., *Collected Works*, 2: 323; 1: 338.

11. Joseph Neilson, *Memories of Rufus Choate* (Boston and New York, 1884), 350–51; Rufus Choate, "Letter to the Whigs of Maine, August 9, 1856," in Samuel G. Brown, ed., *Works of Rufus Choate with a Memoir of His Life* (Boston, 1862), II, 215; Basler, ed., *Collected Works*, 3: 375. Cf. [Josiah Quincy], *The Duty of Conservative Whigs in the Present Crisis: A Letter to the Hon. Rufus Choate, by a Conservative Whig* (Boston, 1856).

12. Basler, ed., *Collected Works*, 3: 339.

13. Ibid., 1: 74–76, 110–11; Leonard L. Richards, *"Gentlemen of Property and Standing": Anti-Abolition Mobs in Jacksonian America* (New York, 1970). On the connections between Lovejoy's killing and the lynching in St. Louis of the black man, Francis McIntosh—described by Lincoln as a "horror-striking" episode—see Sean Wilentz, *The Rise of American Democracy: Jefferson to Lincoln* (New York, 2005), 465–67.

14. Basler, ed., *Collected Works*, 1: 75; William M. Wiecek, *The Sources of Antislavery Constitutionalism in America, 1760–1848* (Ithaca, N.Y., 1977), 202–27. Wiecek generally takes a dim view of what he calls the moderates' "abolition manquée," even though it was the moderates' political success that sparked the southern secession that led to emancipation.

15. Basler, ed. *Collected Works*, 2: 1–9; *Congressional Globe*, 30th Congress, 2nd session, 212; *New-York Daily Tribune*, July 1, 1848; *True Democrat* [Cleveland], June 10, 1848.

16. For a more extended account of these developments, see Wilentz, *Rise*, 549–59, 594–601, 610–32.

17. *American Freeman* [Milwaukee], Aug. 23, 1848.

18. Frederick Robinson, *Address to the Voters of the Fifth Congressional District* (n.p., n.d. [1862]), 11.

19. Wilentz, *Rise*, 626 (quotation); *Congressional Globe*, 25th Congress, 3rd session, Appendix, 175; *New-York Daily Tribune*, July 25, 1856.

20. Herndon quoted in Guelzo, *Redeemer President*, 4; Merrill D. Peterson, *The Jefferson Image in the American Mind* (orig. pub. 1960; Charlottesville, Va., 1998), 162–64, 198–209; Basler, ed., *Collected Works*, 3: 374–76; 2: 532. It remains all the more important to note that Lincoln's sudden embrace of Jefferson ran against the grain of Merrill Peterson's portrayal of how American political leaders of every stripe found some way to align their views with the Jeffersonian legacy. For Lincoln, getting right with Jefferson occurred only after he had abandoned Whiggery for the antislavery Republicans.

21. Which is not to overlook that Lincoln's and Jefferson's outlooks remained fundamentally different in many ways. See especially Guelzo, *Redeemer President*, especially 3–25.

22. See especially Peterson, *Jefferson Image*, 99–109, 162–226.

23. Basler, ed., *Collected Works*, 2: 60, 384.

24. Ibid., 2: 346.

25. Don E. Fehrenbacher, *The Dred Scott Case: Its Significance in American Law and Politics* (New York, 1978), quotation on 456a; Douglas, *Kansas, Utah, and the Dred Scott Decision. Remarks of the Hon. Stephen A. Douglas, on Kansas, Utah, and the Dred Scott Decision* (Chicago, 1857), 5.

26. *New York Daily-Tribune*, March 7, 1857; Richard H. Sewell, *Ballots for Freedom: Antislavery Politics in the United States, 1837–1860* (New York, 1976), quotation on 301; Basler, ed., *Collected Works*, 2: 401.

27. Ibid., 2: 402.

28. Ibid., 2: 494–95.

29. Ibid., 3: 28, 243, 278.

30. Ibid., 4: 92–93, n.1, 237, 341; William H. Herndon and Jesse W. Weik, *Herndon's Lincoln: The True Story of a Great Life* (Chicago, 1889), 3: 478. The connections between Lincoln and Jackson were not lost on ordinary supporters. "Withal, I am an *uncompromising Union Man*. I despised *Nullification* in 1832, as I do the *Rebellion* now. I stand by the Administration in their noble efforts to save the Union . . . ," a native South Carolinian, relocated to New Jersey, wrote the president in 1864, to show his proadministration bona fides. "I approved of Andrew Jackson's course in 1832, and, I approve of Abraham Lincoln's course now. I prepared the article 'And. Jackson on States Rights' to strengthen your administration in the judgement of people in this section of the country." Paul T. Jones to Abraham Lincoln, Apr. 11, 1864, Abraham Lincoln Papers, Library of Congress.

31. James D. Richardson, ed., *A Compilation of the Papers and Messages of the Presidents*, 2 vols. (orig. pub. 1897; Washington, 1910), 2: 1209. Basler, ed., *Collected Works*, 4: 270.

32. Ibid., 6: 269.

33. Ibid., 3: 147.

34. The painting was widely reproduced as a lithograph by the Dupuy Company of Pittsburgh (Blythe's home), entitled *President Lincoln Writing the Proclamation of Freedom*.

35. Benjamin P. Thomas, *Abraham Lincoln: A Biography* (New York, 1952), 456–57.

36. Addison C. Gibbs to Lincoln, Sept. 24, 1863, Abraham Lincoln Papers, Library of Congress. My thanks to Eric Foner for alerting me to this letter.

VISUALIZING LINCOLN: ABRAHAM LINCOLN AS STUDENT, SUBJECT, AND PATRON OF THE VISUAL ARTS by Harold Holzer

1. Lincoln identified Clay as his "beau ideal" of a statesman at the first Lincoln-Douglas debate at Ottawa, Illinois, on Aug. 21, 1858; four years earlier, at an Oct. 16, 1854, speech at Peoria, he called Jefferson "the most distinguished politician of our history." Roy P. Basler, ed., *The Collected Works of Abraham Lincoln* 9 vols. (New Brunswick, N.J., 1953–55), 3: 29, 2: 249.

2. Henry C. Whitney, *Life on the Circuit with Lincoln* (Boston, 1892), 45–46.

3. Basler, ed., *Collected Works*, 4: 235.

4. Quoted in Noble E. Cunningham, Jr., *Popular Images of the Presidency: From Washington to Lincoln* (Columbia, Mo., 1991), 19, 287 n. 52.

5. Abner Ellis recollection in Douglas L. Wilson and Rodney O. Davis, eds., *Herndon's Informants: Letters, Interviews, and Statements About Abraham Lincoln* (Urbana, Ill., 1998), 174.

6. *Art in the United States Capitol* (Washington, 1976), 138, 142. The two Trumbull canvases were acquired in 1824 and 1822, respectively.

7. The author is indebted to the Civil War Institute, Gettysburg College, for inviting him to publish his first thoughts on these themes in *Standing Tall: The Heroic Image of Abraham Lincoln*, 43rd Annual Fortenbaugh Memorial Lecture (Gettysburg, Pa., 2004). The discussion of Washington as Lincoln's boyhood hero was first offered at the National Endowment for the Humanities' "Heroes of History" Lecture at Ford's Theatre, Oct. 18, 2004. For more on Greenough, see Wayne Craven, *Sculpture in America*, rev. ed. (Newark, Del., 1984), 107–08; Christopher A. Thomas, *The Lincoln Memorial & American Life* (Princeton, 2002), 119–20.

8. For a photograph of the statue, see Dorothy Meserve Kunhardt and Philip B. Kunhardt, Jr., *Twenty Days* (New York, 1965), 116; Craven, *Sculpture in America*, 108–09. The Metropolitan Museum owns a bare-shouldered ca. 1832 marble bust of Washington by Greenough, which the sculptor thought so successful "in pleasing my countrymen that I think of getting up a statue of him." See Thayer Tolles, ed., *American Sculpture in the Metropolitan Museum of Art*, vol. 1: *A Catalogue of Works by Artists Before 1865* (New York, 1999).

9. William Scott, *Lessons in Elocution; or, A Selection of Pieces in Prose and Verse for the Improvement of Youth in Reading and Speaking . . . to Which Are Prefixed Elements of Gesture* (Boston, 1811), 33–36.

10. Basler, ed., *Collected Works*, 4: 114, 89.

11. Bates Lowry and Isabel Barrett Lowry, *The Silver Canvas: Masterpieces from the J. Paul Getty Collection* (London, 1998), 19.

12. Basler, ed., *Collected Works*, 4: 39. Lincoln was referring to the photograph made in New York by Mathew Brady on the day of his Cooper Union address, Feb. 27, 1860.

13. William C. Darrah, *Cartes de Visite in Nineteenth Century Photography* (Gettysburg, Pa., 1981), 8–9.

14. Rufus Rockwell Wilson, ed., *Memories of Lincoln by Thomas D. Jones* (New York, 1934), 5.

15. Leonard Wells Volk, "A Lincoln Life-Mask and How It Was Made," in Rufus Rockwell Wilson, ed., *Intimate Memories of Lincoln* (Elmira, N.Y., 1945), 243–44.

16. Quoted in Donald Charles Durman, *He Belongs to the Ages: The Statues of Abraham Lincoln* (Ann Arbor, Mich., 1951), 3.

17. For pictures of Volk's heroic Lincoln statues, see ibid., 13, 15.

18. See Harold Holzer, Gabor S. Boritt, and Mark E. Neely, Jr., *The Lincoln Image: Abraham Lincoln and the Popular Print* (New York, 1984), 35, 72. The first of these images, the Thomas Sinclair sheet music cover "Lincoln Quick Step," surrounded a handsome lithographed portrait of Lincoln with images of flatboat piloting and rail-splitting, along with close-up images of an ax, a maul, and oars.

19. Mark A. Plummer, *Lincoln's Rail-Splitter: Governor Richard J. Oglesby* (Urbana, Ill., 2001), 42.

20. "Johnson" to William H. Herndon, ca. 1865–1866, in Douglas L. Wilson and Rodney O. Davis, eds., *Herndon's Informants: Letters, Interviews, and Statements About Abraham Lincoln* (Urbana, Ill., 1998), 463.

21. David Donald, *Lincoln Reconsidered: Essays on the Civil War Era* (New York, 1961), 162–63.

22. The key twentieth-century studies are: Frederick Hill Meserve, *The Photographs of Abraham*

Lincoln (New York, 1943); Stefan Lorant, *Lincoln: A Picture Story of His Life*, rev. ed. (New York, 1969), based on books issued in 1941, 1952, and 1957; Charles Hamilton and Lloyd Ostendorf, *Lincoln in Photographs: An Album of Every Known Pose* (Norman, Okla., 1963), later rev. 1969 and 1998.

23. Donn Piatt, *Memories of Men who Saved the Union* (New York and Chicago, 1887), 29–30.

24. Quoted in Hamilton and Ostendorf, *Lincoln in Photographs*, 139.

25. Charles Alfred Barry, reminiscences in the Boston Transcript, n.d., reprinted in Rufus Rockwell Wilson, ed., *Intimate Memories of Lincoln* (Elmira, N.Y., 1945), 308.

26. Hamilton and Ostendorf, *Lincoln in Photographs*, 17. The authors suggest that the photograph was made at the request of a different sculptor, Henry Kirke Browne, but a careful examination of the pose strongly indicates its similarity to Volk's full-length statuettes, issued in both beardless and bearded versions through the 1860s.

27. Hicks's recollections were published in Allen Thorndike Rice, ed., *Reminiscences of Lincoln by Distinguished Men of His Time* (New York, 1886), 593–607.

28. Ibid., 602.

29. "Portrait painter" J. C. Wolfe boarded on Monroe Street, on the Springfield public square, the year he painted the portrait. See C. S. Williams, *Williams' Springfield Directory: City Guide and Business Mirror for 1860–61* (Springfield, Ill., 1860), 144. See also Harold Holzer, "Lincoln Heard and Seen: A Crucial Letter and Life Portrait Finally Surface," *American Heritage* (Feb.–March 2005), 16.

30. Thomas M. Johnston to C. H. Brainard, July 23, 1860, original in the Lincoln Museum, Fort Wayne, Indiana.

31. John G. Nicolay to Therena Bates, Aug. 26, 1860, Nicolay Papers, Library of Congress.

32. Basler, ed., *Collected Works*, 4: 102.

33. Jones's reminiscences, originally published in the *Cincinnati Commercial* on Oct. 18, 1871, were reprinted in Thomas D. Jones, *Memories of Lincoln*, ed. Rufus Rockwell Wilson (New York, 1934).

34. Francis B. Carpenter, *Six Months at the White House with Abraham Lincoln: The Story of a Picture* (New York, 1867), 35.

35. Quoted in Rufus Rockwell Wilson, *Lincoln in Portraiture* (New York, 1935), 167.

36. See Gabor S. Boritt, Mark E. Neely, Jr. and Harold Holzer, "The European Image of Abraham Lincoln," *Winterthur Portfolio*, 21 (Summer–Autumn 1986), 164–65, 179, 180, 182.

37. Lloyd Ostendorf, *Lincoln's Photographs: A Complete Album* (Dayton, Ohio, 1998), 88.

38. John W. Forney to Lincoln, Dec. 30, 1861, Abraham Lincoln Papers, Library of Congress.

39. Basler, ed., *Collected Works*, 4: 240.

40. Quoted in "Lincoln's Growth as Portraits Tell It," *New York Times Magazine*, Feb. 7, 1932.

41. Wilson, *Lincoln in Portraiture*, 179.

42. Michael Burlingame and John R. Turner Ettlinger, *Inside Lincoln's White House: The Complete Civil War Diaries of John Hay* (Carbondale, Ill., 1997), 109.

43. Jones, *Memories of Lincoln*, 15.

44. *Art and Artists of the Capitol*, 197.

45. Carpenter, *Six Months at the White House*, 269.

46. Ibid., 28. The *Washington Chronicle* editor John Wein Forney reported that Lincoln said on the day he signed the proclamation: "If my name ever goes into history it will be for this act. . . ." See Carpenter, *Six Months at the White House*, 269.

47. P. J. Staudenraus, ed., *Mr. Lincoln's Washington: The Civil War Dispatches of Noah Brooks* (New York, 1967), 361–63.

48. Carpenter, *Six Months at the White House*, 9, 11–12, 25.

49. For a glance at the Carpenter sketchbook, see Harold Holzer and Mark E. Neely, Jr., *Mine Eyes Have Seen the Glory: The Civil War in Art* (New York, 1990), 74–75.

50. Carpenter did believe, he said, in "allegory," and he positioned the most liberal members of the cabinet to the left-hand side of the canvas, the conservatives to the right, with Lincoln mediating from the middle.

51. "American Painters: Their Errors as Regards Nationality," *Photographic and Fine Art Journal* (Aug. 1857; rep. from the *Cosmopolitan Art Journal*), 232; Carpenter, *Six Months at the White House*, 28; for advertisement, see addendum to book, *The Publications of Hurd and Houghton, New York*, 4.

52. "Carpenter's Great National Picture," promotional appendix to Henry J. Raymond, *The Life and Public Services of Abraham Lincoln . . .* (New York, 1865), n.p.

53. Its dedication was reported in the *New York Times*, Feb. 13, 1878; see also Harold Holzer, Gabor S. Boritt, and Mark E. Neely, Jr., "Francis Bicknell Carpenter (1830–1900): Painter of Abraham Lincoln and His Circle," *American Art Journal*, 16 (Spring 1984): 78.

54. Glenn V. Sherwood, *Labor of Love: The Life & Art of Vinnie Ream* (Hygiene, Colo., 1997), 163, 175–76.

55. Mark E. Neely and Harold Holzer, *The Lincoln Family Album: Photographs from the Personal Collection of a Historic American Family* (orig. pub. 1990; rev. ed. Carbondale, Ill., 2006), 102.

56. Artist Charles Wesley Jarvis also copied one of the photographs, but though several historians later claimed the artist had also, like Wilson, enjoyed life sittings, this has never been proved. See Wilson, *Lincoln in Portraiture*, 279; Mark E. Neely, Jr., "Recent Acquisitions," *Lincoln Lore*, no. 1709 (July 1980): 1.

57. See, for example, Meserve, *The Photographs of Abraham Lincoln*, plate 100. Lorant and Ostendorf agreed with the attribution to Apr. 10, although Ostendorf revised it to Feb. 5 for the final edition of his work.

58. William J. Sims, "Matthew Henry Wilson: 1814–1892," *Connecticut Historical Society Bulletin*, 37 (Oct. 1972): 109–111.

59. For the Prang adaptation, see Holzer, Boritt, and Neely, *The Lincoln Image*, 143.

60. Carpenter, *Six Months at the White House*, 232–33.

61. Henry C. Whitney, *Life on the Circuit with Lincoln . . .* (Boston, 1892), 599–601. Whitney was convinced Lincoln deserved the grandest celebrations in art, quoting Milton on the title page of his book: "A pillar of state; deep on his front engraven,/Deliberation sat, and public care;/. . . Drew audience and attention, still as night,/Or summer's noontime air."

NATURAL RIGHTS, CITIZENSHIP RIGHTS, STATES' RIGHTS, AND BLACK RIGHTS: ANOTHER LOOK AT LINCOLN AND RACE by James Oakes

1. Roy P. Basler, ed., *The Collected Works of Abraham Lincoln*, 9 vols. (New Brunswick, N.J., 1953–55), 3: 214.

2. Ibid., 2: 501.

3. Ibid., 3: 216.

4. Ibid., 2: 539.

5. Ibid., 2: 234.

6. Ibid., 3: 84. Emphasis added.

7. Ibid., 2: 405.

8. Ibid., 3: 504.

9. Ibid., 3: 312, 315.

10. Ibid., 2: 264.

11. Ibid., 3: 445–46.

12. Ibid., 2: 222–23.

13. Ibid., 3; 399.

14. Ibid., 2: 500–01.

15. The classic exploration of this theme in Republican Party ideology is Eric Foner, *Free Soil, Free Labor, Free Men: The Ideology of the Republican Party Before the Civil War* (New York, 1970).

16. Basler, ed. *Collected Works*, 2: 405.

17. James Oakes, "The Peculiar Fate of the Bourgeois Critique of Slavery," in Winthrop D. Jordan, ed., *Slavery and the American South* (Jackson, Miss., 2003), 29–48. Flummoxed by the persistent prosperity of slavery, which by their economic theory should have been declining instead of expanding, Franklin pointed to the exceptional conditions that made free labor in the American colonies temporarily more expensive than slave labor, and Smith resorted to tautology. Slavery was always more expensive than free labor, he said, except on tropical plantations where it was not.

   On the ubiquity of classical economic thought in the antebellum South, see Lawrence Shore, *Southern Capitalists: The Ideological Leadership of an Elite, 1832–1885* (Chapel Hill, N.C., 1986); Joyce Chaplin, *An Anxious Pursuit: Agricultural Innovation Modernity in the Lower South, 1730–1815* (Chapel Hill, N.C., 1993); Michael A. Morrison, *Slavery and the American West: The Eclipse of Manifest Destiny and the Coming of the Civil War* (Chapel Hill, N.C., 1997).

18. Johnson's story appears in several books, the most recent of which is Gabor Boritt, *The Gettysburg Gospel* (New York, 2006), 170. For a concise review of the issues discussed in this section, see Joseph R. Fornieri, "Lincoln and Negro Citizenship," *Lincoln Lore: The Bulletin of the Lincoln Museum*, no. 1885 (Summer 2006), 6–17.

19. The literature on citizenship in early America is vast. The analysis in this and subsequent paragraphs derives primarily from the following: James H. Kettner, *The Development of American Citizenship* (Chapel Hill, N.C., 1978; William M. Wiecek, *The Sources of Antislavery Constitutionalism in America, 1760–1848* (Ithaca, N.Y., 1977), 154–71; Rogers M. Smith, *Civic Ideals: Conflicting Visions of Citizenship in U.S. History* (New Haven, 1997); William J. Novak, "The Legal Transformation of Citizenship in Nineteenth Century America," in Meg Jacobs, William J. Novak, and Julian Zelizer, eds., *The Democratic Experiment: New Directions in American Political History* (Princeton, 2003), 85–119.

   Kettner's pathbreaking book demonstrated that the "development" of citizenship in antebellum America was propelled by the legal conflict over slavery, in particular by its implications for the status of free blacks. Wiecek confirms the relationship between the struggle over slavery and the legal meaning of citizenship. Smith traces the persistent tradition of "ascriptive hierarchy" that countered the universalistic implications of revolutionary liberalism. Novak's provocative essay argues that it was not citizenship that determined status in early America but status, derived from long-established common law categories, that determined citizenship rights. But Novak too confirms that citizenship was pushed to the foreground by the slavery controversy. Except for his inexplicable failure to cite Kettner's major book, Novak's extensive notes are an outsdanding guide to the bibliography.

20. I develop this point more extensively in James Oakes, *Slavery and Freedom: An Interpretation of the Old South* (New York, 1990).

21. Quoted in Thomas D. Morris, *Southern Slavery and the Law, 1619–1860* (Chapel Hill, N.C., 1996), 372.

22. *Dred Scott v. John F. A. Sanford*, 60 U.S. (Howard), 393. Like most historians, my understanding of the *Dred Scott* decision is profoundly influenced by one extraordinary book: Don E. Fehrenbacher, *The Dred Scott Case: Its Significance in American Law and Practice* (New York, 1978). See in particular his analysis of Taney's ruling of citizenship, 335–64. Ket-

tner, *Development of American Citizenship*, 300–33, puts the decision into a crucial context of citizenship law. Kenneth M. Stampp, *America in 1857: A Nation on the Brink* (New York, 1990), 82–109, is both a lucid summary of the case and a cogent analysis of its political context.

23. Basler, ed., *Collected Works*, 2: 233 n.

24. Lincoln's concerns about the political wisdom of calling for repeal of the Fugitive Slave Law were expressed in an 1859 exchange of letters with Salmon P. Chase of Ohio. See ibid., 3: 384, 386.

25. Ibid., 3: 41.

26. Ibid., 3: 514.

27. Ibid., 2: 403.

28. Ibid., 2: 453.

29. Ibid., 2: 462, 464.

30. Ibid., 3: 9.

31. Ibid., 3: 112.

32. Ibid., 3: 177–78. See also 268, 274.

33. Ibid., 3: 179, 299–300.

34. Ibid., 4: 264.

35. Ibid.

36. All quotations of Bates in this and subsequent paragraphs are taken from *Opinion of Attorney General Bates on Citizenship* (Washington, 1863).

37. Decisions about granting passports to blacks seemed to follow automatically from decisions regarding black citizenship. In 1856 Congress first authorized the secretary of state to issue passports to "citizens of the United States." *Statutes at Large . . . 34th Cong., 1st Sess.*, 60. A year later the Supreme Court, in *Dred Scott v. Sanford*, declared that blacks were not, never had been, and never could be citizens of the United States. On June 22, 1859, Attorney General Jeremiah S. Black affirmed that a "passport cannot be issued to any other than a citizen of the United States." J. Hubble Ashton, ed., *Official Opinions of the Attorneys General of the United States* (Washington, D.C., 1866), 9: 350–52. Bates issued his opinion that blacks were citizens in August 1862, and one month later, on September 25, 1862, he hinted in his diary that blacks were entitled to passports. "Among our colored people who have been long free, there are many who are intelligent and well advanced in arts and knowledge, and a few, who are ebucated [*sic*] and able men. These are free to go where they please, in foreign countries though it has been guessed by some of our politicians, who are wiser that the constitution, that this government has no power to grant them passports for their protection, in foreign parts." Howard K. Beale, ed., *Diary of Edward Bates, 1859–1856* (Washington, D.C.: 1933), 263–64. The evidence is thus indirect, but it suggests that an earlier decision not to grant passports to blacks was revered by the Lincoln administration. During the 1864 presidential campaign African American editors often mentioned the granting of passports to blacks as one of the reasons for supporting Lincoln's reelection.

38. Basler, ed., *Collected Works*, 2: 452.

39. Ibid., 2: 452.

40. Ibid., 3: 78, 80.

41. Ibid., 3: 116.

42. Ibid., 3: 254–55.

43. Ibid., 3: 42.

44. Ibid., 3: 277.

45. I'm not counting a third statement, Lincoln's condescending lecture on colonization delivered to a group of handpicked blacks he called into the executive mansion in Aug. 1862,

because as disgraceful as it was, it was not a general statement of Lincoln's views on racial equality and was not intended as such. The meeting was, in David Blight's words, Lincoln's "worst racial moment." Yet paradoxically, Lincoln's only extended allusion to racial inequality during the meeting was framed as a blistering attack on white racism.

46. For example, bigots were frequently the *targets* of Lincoln's racially inflected jokes, and nearly every time he used the word *nigger*, Lincoln was paraphrasing someone else, usually a racist critic, Stephen Douglas most often. Lincoln rarely explained why he pined for racial separation or why whites and blacks could not live together as equals, but when he did, his explanations tended to focus on intractable white racism rather than innate black inferiority. Finally, when Lincoln did assert that blacks and whites were not equal, he listed the same set of inequalities that he said elsewhere differentiated every human being from every other one. Not surprisingly, given this plethora of ambiguities, most of Lincoln's brief utterances on race have lent themselves to extravagantly different interpretations.

47. Basler, ed., *Collected Works*, 2: 255–56.

48. Ibid., 3: 145–46.

49. Ibid., 3: 19.

50. Ibid., 3: 380.

51. Ibid., 2: 256.

52. Eric Foner's essay in this volume, "Lincoln and Colonization," contains the most thorough survey of Lincoln's views and proposals.

LINCOLN AND COLONIZATION by Eric Foner

I wish to thank Melinda Lawson, Mark Neely, James Oakes, and Manisha Sinha, who read an earlier draft of this essay and offered many helpful suggestions.

1. Douglas L. Wilson and Rodney O. Davis., eds., *Herndon's Informants* (Urbana, Ill., 1998), 13, 61.

2. David Davis to Abraham Lincoln, August 3, 1858, Abraham Lincoln Papers, Library of Congress; J. McCan Davis, *Abraham Lincoln: His Book* (New York, 1903).

3. Roy P. Basler, ed., *Collected Works of Abraham Lincoln*, 9 vols. (New Brunswick, N.J., 1953–55), 2: 255; 3: 327–28.

4. Ibid., 5: 534–35; Albert Mordell, ed., *Civil War and Reconstruction: Selected Essays by Gideon Welles* (New York, 1959), 250; Lerone Bennett, *Forced into Glory: Abraham Lincoln's White Dream* (Chicago, 2000); Don E. Fehrenbacher, "Only His Stepchildren: Lincoln and the Negro," *Civil War History*, 20 (Dec. 1974): 307. In William Lee Miller's study of Lincoln's moral leadership, *Lincoln's Virtues: An Ethical Biography* (New York, 2002), 354, colonization receives a brief mention three-quarters of the way through the book. In her eight hundred-page work on Lincoln and his cabinet, *Team of Rivals: The Political Genius of Abraham Lincoln* (New York, 2005), Doris Kearns Goodwin says almost nothing about colonization. Michael Lind, *What Lincoln Believed: The Values and Convictions of America's Greatest President* (New York, 2005) follows Bennett in stressing Lincoln's commitment to colonization.

5. David Herbert Donald, *Lincoln* (New York, 1995), 166–67. For examples of scholars who state that Lincoln did not really believe in colonization, see Peter J. Parish, *The American Civil War* (New York, 1975), 240–42, and G. S. Boritt, "The Voyage to the Colony of Lincolnia: The Sixteenth President, Black Colonization, and the Defense Mechanism of Avoidance," *Historian*, 37 (Aug. 1975): 619–32. Works that explain colonization as nothing

more than a political strategy include Stephen B. Oates, *Abraham Lincoln: The Man Behind the Myths* (New York, 1984), 101; Richard Striner, *Father Abraham: Lincoln's Relentless Struggle to End Slavery* (New York, 2006), 149–50, 181, 185; Michael Vorenberg, "Abraham Lincoln and the Politics of Black Colonization," *Journal of the Abraham Lincoln Association*, 14 (Summer 1993): 24; and Adam I. P. Smith, *No Party Now: Politics in the Civil War North* (New York, 2006), 56, which calls Lincoln's plan "a vital weapon in the public relations battle" preceding emancipation.

6. *Harper's Weekly* (April 5, 1862); Eric Foner, *Nothing But Freedom: Emancipation and Its Legacy* (Baton Rouge, La., 1983), 8–23. For decades, the only full-length book on colonization was P. J. Staudenraus, *The African Colonization Movement 1816–1865* (New York 1961). But a number of important works have appeared of late, notably Eric Burin, *Slavery and the Peculiar Solution: A History of the American Colonization Society* (Gainesville, Fla., 2005) and Claude A. Clegg III, *The Price of Liberty: African Americans and the Making of Liberia* (Chapel Hill, N.C., 2004). An important contribution to the renewed interest in colonization was David Brion Davis, "Reconsidering the Colonization Movement: Leonard Bacon and the Problem of Evil," *Intellectual History Newsletter*, 14 (1992): 3–16.

7. Philip S. Foner, ed., *The Life and Writings of Frederick Douglass*, 5 vols. (New York, 1950–75), 1: 310; 37th Congress, 2d Session, House Report 148, *Report of the Select Committee on Emancipation and Colonization*, 148.

8. David Brion Davis, *Challenging the Boundaries of Slavery* (Cambridge, Mass., 2003), 64–65; Floyd J. Miller, *The Search for a Black Nationality; Black Emigration and Colonization 1787–1863* (Urbana, Ill., 1975), 4–5; H. N. Sherwood, "Early Negro Deportation Projects," *Mississippi Valley Historical Review*, 2 (March 1916): 484–94; W. Bryan Rommel-Ruiz, "Colonizing the Black Atlantic: The African Colonization Movements in Postwar Rhode Island and Nova Scotia," *Slavery and Abolition*, 27 (Dec. 2006): 350–54.

9. Thomas Jefferson, *Notes on the State of Virginia* (Philadelphia, 1788), 154, 199–202; Merrill D. Peterson, ed., *Thomas Jefferson: Writings* (New York, 1984), 1484–87.

10. Isaac V. Brown, *Biography of the Rev. Robert Finley*, 2nd ed. (Philadelphia, 1857), 103–15; Paul Goodman, *Of One Blood: Abolitionism and the Origins of Racial Equality* (Berkeley, 1998), 14–18; Douglas R. Egerton, "Averting a Crisis: The Proslavery Critique of the American Colonization Society," *Civil War History*, 43 (June 1997): 147; Daniel W. Howe, *The Political Culture of the American Whigs* (Chicago, 1984), 136.

11. Harold D. Tallant, *Evil Necessity: Slavery and Political Culture in Antebellum Kentucky* (Lexington, Ky., 2003), 1–5; James F. Hopkins, ed., *Papers of Henry Clay*, 10 vols. (Lexington, Ky., 1959–91), 9: 779–80; 10: 674–80, 844–46.

12. Foner, ed., *Douglass*, 1: 310; Robert V. Remini, *Henry Clay: Statesman for the Union* (New York, 1991), 491–92, 508; Hopkins, ed., *Clay Papers*, 8: 812; 10: 372–76.

13. Hugh Davis, "Northern Colonizationists and Free Blacks, 1823–1837: The Case of Leonard Bacon," *Journal of the Early Republic*, 17 (Winter 1997): 651–75; Burin, *Peculiar Solution*, 22.

14. Leon Litwack, *North of Slavery: The Negro in the Free States, 1790–1860* (Chicago, 1961), 22–23; Clegg, *Price of Liberty*, 68–69.

15. Dickson D. Bruce, Jr., "National Identity and African-American Colonization, 1773–1817," *Historian*, 58 (Autumn 1995): 15–28; Clegg, *Price of Liberty*, 22–25; Sandra S. Young, "John Brown Russwurm's Dilemma: Citizenship or Emigration," in Timothy P. McCarthy and John Stauffer, eds., *Prophets of Protest: Reconsidering the History of American Abolitionism* (New York, 2006), 90–114.

16. Burin, *Peculiar Solution*, 169; Simon Schama, *Rough Crossings: Britain, the Slaves, and the American Revolution* (London, 2005); Brenda G. Plummer, *Haiti and the United States: The Psychological Moment* (Athens, Ga., 1992), 27–31.

17. Matthew Mason, *Slavery and Politics in the Early American Republic* (Chapel Hill, N.C., 2006); Robert P. Forbes, *The Missouri Compromise and Its Aftermath: Slavery and the Meaning of America* (Chapel Hill, N.C., 2007), 28–29, 219, 251; Young, "Russwurm's Dilemma," 101; Clegg, *Price of Liberty*, 35; Leonard I. Sweet, *Black Images of America 1784–1870* (New York, 1976), 39; Foner, ed., *Douglass*, 2: 255.

18. Herbert Aptheker, *One Continual Cry: David Walker's Appeal to the Colored Citizens of the World* (New York, 1965), 72–91, 109–15.

19. William Lloyd Garrison, *Thoughts on African Colonization* (Boston, 1832), 5; Hopkins, ed., *Clay Papers*, 8: 773.

20. Leonard P. Richards, *"Gentlemen of Property and Standing": Anti-Abolition Mobs in Jacksonian America* (New York, 1970), 21–36; Charles N. Zucker, "The Free Negro Question: Race Relations in Antebellum Illinois, 1801–1860," (unpub. diss., Northwestern University, 1972), 191; Merton L. Dillon, "The Antislavery Movement in Illinois, 1809–1844" (unpub. diss., University of Michigan, 1951), 132–51; Paul M. Angle, *"Here I Have Lived": A History of Lincoln's Springfield 1821–1865* (New Brunswick, N.J., 1935), 52; Willard L. King, *Lincoln's Manager: David Davis* (Cambridge, Mass., 1960), 51; *Springfield Journal* in *Daily Missouri Republican* (St. Louis), Feb. 7, 1858.

21. *Journal of the House of Representatives of the Tenth General Assembly of the State of Illinois* (Vandalia, 1836), 238–41, 309; *Journal of the Senate of the Tenth General Assembly of the State of Illinois* (Vandalia, 1836), 195–98; Basler, ed., *Collected Works*, 1: 75.

22. Kenneth J. Winkle, *The Young Eagle: The Rise of Abraham Lincoln* (Dallas, 2001), 254–55, 265; Basler, ed., *Collected Works*, 2: 131–32, 255–56, 298–99; 3: 15; John C. Briggs, *Lincoln's Speeches Reconsidered* (Baltimore, 2005), 113–27; Emma Lou Thornbrough, *The Negro in Indiana Before 1900* (Indianapolis, 1957), 82–87; interview with James Mitchell, *St. Louis Daily Globe-Democrat*, Aug. 26, 1894; *Springfield Journal* in *Daily Missouri Republican* [St. Louis], Feb. 7, 1858.

23. Basler, ed., *Collected Works*, 2: 132.

24. Ibid., 2, 521. On civic and racial nationalisms, see Eric Foner, *Who Owns History?: Rethinking the Past in a Changing World* (New York, 2002), 151–57.

25. Donald, *Lincoln*, 167; Kenneth J. Winkle, " 'Paradox Though It May Seem': Lincoln on Antislavery, Race, and Union, 1837–1860," in Brian Dirck, ed., *Lincoln Emancipated: The President and the Politics of Race* (DeKalb, Ill., 2007), 19; C. Peter Ripley, et al., ed., *The Black Abolitionist Papers*, 5 vols. (Chapel Hill, N.C., 1985–93), 5: 91–92; Richard E. Hart, "Springfield's African-Americans as a Part of the Lincoln Community," *Journal of the Abraham Lincoln Association*, 20 (Winter 1999): 48–53; *African Repository*, May 1848, 158; Zucker, "Free Negro Question," 206.

26. *New York Herald*, Jan. 12, 1860.

27. Eric Foner, *Free Soil, Free Labor, Free Men: The Ideology of the Republican Party Before the Civil War* (New York, 1970), 268–72; Francis P. Blair, Jr., *The Destiny of the Races of This Continent* (Washington, 1859), 7–8.

28. Blair, *Destiny of Races*, 24; Sharon H. Strom, "Labor, Race, and Colonization: Imagining a Post-Slavery World in the Americas," in Steven Mintz and John Stauffer, eds., *The Problem of Evil: Slavery, Freedom, and the Ambiguities of American Reform* (Amherst, Mass., 2007), 264; Robert E. May, *Manifest Destiny's Underworld: Filibustering in Antebellum America* (Chapel Hill, N.C., 2002); *Congressional Globe*, 35th Congress, 1st Session, 293.

29. William E. Parrish, *Frank Blair: Lincoln's Conservative* (Columbia, Mo., 1998), 66–80; Foner, *Free Soil*, 276–78; Richard H. Sewell, *Ballots for Freedom: Antislavery Politics in the United States 1837–1860* (New York, 1976), 323–25; D. R. Tilden to Benjamin F. Wade, March 27, 1860, Benjamin F. Wade Papers, Library of Congress.

30. Francis P. Blair, Jr., to Francis P. Blair, February 18, 1857, Blair Family Papers, Library of

Congress; Joseph F. Newton, *Lincoln and Herndon* (Cedar Rapids, Ia., 1910), 114; Basler, ed., *Collected Works*, 2: 409–10.

31. Vincent Harding, *There Is a River: The Black Struggle for Freedom in America* (New York, 1981), 173–87; Miller, *Black Nationality*, 190–93; "Thoughts on Hayti" by James T. Holly, ran monthly in the *Anglo-African Magazine* from June to November 1859; African Civilization Society to Lincoln, November 5, 1863, Lincoln Papers.

32. *Anglo-African Magazine* (Sept. 1859); Philip S. Foner and George E. Walker, eds., *Proceedings of the Black State Conventions, 1840–1865*, 2 vols. (Philadelphia, 1979) 1: 335; *Weekly Anglo-African* (May 19, 26, 1860, Feb. 23, 1861); *Douglass' Monthly* (Feb. 1859): 19; (Jan. 1861): 386; (May 1861): 449; John R. McKivigan, "James Redpath and Black Reaction to the Haitian Emigration Bureau," *Mid-America*, 69 (October 1987): 139–51.

33. Mordell, ed., *Lincoln's Administration*, 234; Howard K. Beale, ed., *Diary of Gideon Welles*, 3 vols. (New York, 1960), 1: 150; Charles A. Barker, ed., *Memoirs of Elisha Oscar Crosby* (San Marino, Calif., 1945), 87–90.

34. *Private and Official Correspondence of Gen. Benjamin F. Butler During the Period of the Civil War*, 5 vols. (Norwood, Mass., 1917), 1: 130; Thomas Schoonover, "Misconstrued Mission: Expansionism and Black Colonization in Mexico and Central America During the Civil War," *Pacific Historical Review*, 49 (Nov. 1980), 611–12.

35. Ambrose W. Thompson to Lincoln, Apr. 11, 1861, Thompson to Gideon Welles, Aug. 8, 1861, Ninian W. Edwards to Lincoln, Aug. 9, 1861, Francis P. Blair, Sr., to Lincoln, Nov. 16, 1861, Francis P. Blair, Jr., to Montgomery Blair, Dec., n.d., 1861, Lincoln Papers; Basler, ed., *Collected Works*, 4: 547; Beale, ed., *Welles Diary*, 1: 151.

36. Basler, ed., *Collected Works*, 5: 48; Alfred A. Hunt, *Haiti's Influence on Antebellum America* (Baton Rouge, La., 1988), 186; *New York Times*, Dec. 4, 5, 6, 1861.

37. *New York Times*, Jan. 19, 1862; *Congressional Globe*, 37th Congress, 2nd Session, 944, 1631–34; James Mitchell, *Report on Colonization and Emigration* (Washington, 1862), 5; Basler, ed., *Collected Works*, 5: 192; *Report of Select Committee*, 13–17.

38. *Congressional Globe*, 37th Congress, 2nd Session, 1605; V. Jacque Voegeli, *Free but Not Equal: The Midwest and the Negro During the Civil War* (Chicago, 1967), 25; *Official Opinions of the Attorneys General of the United States*, 12 vols. (Washington, 1852–70), 10: 382–413.

39. Michael Vorenberg, *Final Freedom: The Civil War, the Abolition of Slavery, and the Thirteenth Amendment* (New York, 2001), 26; Joshua Speed to Lincoln, Sept. 3, 1861, Lincoln Papers.

40. Basler, ed., *Collected Works*, 5: 29–30, 144–46, 317–19; William H. Williams, *Slavery and Freedom in Delaware, 1639–1865* (Wilmington, Del., 1996), 175; Patience Essah, *A House Divided: Slavery and Emancipation in Delaware 1638–1865* (Charlottesville, Va., 1996), 162–67; Theodore C. Pease, ed., *The Diary of Orville Hickman Browning*, 2 vols. (Springfield, Ill., 1927), 1: 512; Adams S. Hill to Sydney Howard Gay, August 25, 1862, Sydney Howard Gay Papers, Columbia University.

41. Richards, *Gentlemen*, 27–29; James L. Crouthamel, *James Watson Webb* (Middletown, Conn., 1969), 173; *Papers Relating to the Foreign Relations of the United States, 1861–1862* (Washington, 1862), 704; Mitchell, *Report on Colonization*, 8–9.

42. Caleb B. Smith to Robert Murray, Apr. 25, 1862, Smith to Lincoln, May 9, 1862, Letters Sent, Sept. 8, 1858–Feb. 1, 1872, Records of the Office of the Secretary of the Interior Relating to the Suppression of the African Slave Trade and Negro Colonization, 1854–1872, RG 48, National Archives (hereafter referred to as RG 48); Beale, ed., *Welles Diary*, 1: 150–51.

43. Basler, ed., *Collected Works*, 4: 547; James Mitchell, *Letter on the Relation of the White and African Races in the United States* (Washington, 1862), 3–15; interview with Mitchell, *St. Louis Globe-Democrat*, Aug. 28, 1894; Caleb B. Smith to Lincoln, May 5, 1862, Lincoln Papers; James Mitchell to J. P. Usher, Jan. 21, 1864, Communication Relating to Rev.

James Mitchell, RG 48, National Archives; Mitchell to Lincoln, July 3, 1862, Lincoln Papers. Mitchell was a white minister, but he is sometimes erroneously identified as black. For example, Thornbrough, *Negro in Indiana*, 82; Eugene H. Berwanger, *The Frontier Against Slavery: Western Anti-Negro Prejudice and the Slavery Extension Controversy* (Urbana, Ill., 1967), 52–53.

44. James Mitchell to Lincoln, July 1, 1862, Lincoln Papers; *Pacific Appeal*, Sept. 20, 1862; Mitchell, *Report*, 5. James Oakes, *The Radical and the Republican: Frederick Douglass, Abraham Lincoln, and the Triumph of Antislavery Politics* (New York, 2007), 194, calls the meeting "a low point in his presidency." On the other hand, Richard Striner, *Father Abraham*, 173, says Lincoln held the meeting "in the hope of reducing racial tension."

45. Basler, ed., *Collected Works*, 5: 370–75; *New York Times*, Aug. 15, 1862.

46. Edward M. Thomas to Lincoln, Aug. 16, 1862, Lincoln Papers; John Bigelow, *Retrospections of an Active Life*, 5 vols. (New York, 1909–13), 1: 546; John Niven, ed., *The Salmon P. Chase Papers*, 5 vols. (Kent, Ohio, 1993–98), 1: 362; *Douglass's Monthly* (Oct. 1862): 722–23; *Christian Recorder* (Sept. 27, 1862); *New York Times*, Oct. 3, 1862.

47. *Douglass' Monthly* (Sept. 1862): 705–07; Foner, ed., *Douglass*, 4: 313.

48. *London Daily News*, in *Christian Recorder* (Nov. 1, 1862); *National Anti-Slavery Standard*, Aug. 20, 1862; Voegeli, *Free but Not Equal*, 34; *Chicago Tribune*, Aug. 22, 1862.

49. Caleb B. Smith to Samuel Pomeroy, Sept. 12, 1862, Letters Sent, Sept. 8, 1858–Feb. 1, 1872, RG 48, National Archives; *Boston Daily Advertiser*, Aug. 26, 27, 1862; *New York Times*, Aug. 30, Sept. 13, Oct. 9, 1862; *San Francisco Evening Bulletin*, Sept. 26, 1862; 39th Congress, 1st Session, Senate Executive Document 55: *Message from the President of the United States . . . Respecting the Transportation, Settlement, and Colonization of Persons of the African Race*, 13–16; Duane Mowry, ed., "Negro Colonization. From Doolittle Correspondence," *Publications of the Southern Historical Association*, 9 (Nov. 1905): 402; *Baltimore Sun*, Nov. 5, 1862.

50. Beale, ed., *Welles Diary*, 1: 152, 475–76; Niven, ed., *Chase Papers*, 1: 348–52, 393–402; Mordell, ed., *Lincoln's Administration*, 105–07; Willie Lee Rose, *Rehearsal for Reconstruction: The Port Royal Experiment* (Indianapolis, 1964), 183.

51. Beale, ed., *Welles Diary*, 1: 123; Beverly W. Palmer and Holly B. Ochoa, ed., *The Selected Papers of Thaddeus Stevens*, 2 vols. (Pittsburgh, 1997), 1: 319–20; Joseph Henry to Frederick W. Seward, Sept. 5, 1862, Unknown to Joseph Henry, Sept. 5, 1862, Lincoln Papers; *Papers Relating to Foreign Relations*, 883–84, 889, 893, 904.

52. Walter LaFeber, *The New Empire: An Interpretation of American Expansion 1860–1898* (Ithaca, N.Y., 1963), 25–31; Frederick W. Seward, *Seward at Washington*, 2 vols. (New York, 1891), 2: 227; Gaillard Hunt, *Israel, Elihu and Cadwallader Washburn: A Chapter in American Biography* (New York, 1925), 116.

53. *Papers Relating to Foreign Relations*, 202–04, 909–10; Mitchell, *Report on Colonization*, 16–19; Caleb B. Smith to Samuel Gridley Howe, October 24, 1862, Letters Sent, Sept. 8, 1858–Feb. 1, 1872, RG 48, National Archives; Roy F. Basler, ed., *The Collected Works of Abraham Lincoln: First Supplement 1832–1865* (New Brunswick, N.J., 1974), 112.

54. William Dusinberre, *Civil War Issues in Philadelphia 1856–1865* (Philadelphia, 1965), 137–47; *Congressional Globe*, 37th Congress, 2nd Session, 2502–04; Mary K. George, *Zachariah Chandler: A Political Biography* (East Lansing, Mich., 1969), 94–95; Joel H. Silbey, *A Respectable Minority: The Democratic Party in the Civil War Era, 1860–1868* (New York, 1977), 81–86; *The Crisis* [Columbus], Sept. 3, 1862. The numerous letters from politicians and ordinary northerners in the Lincoln Papers concerning the Preliminary Emancipation Proclamation almost never refer to colonization.

55. Basler, ed., *Collected Works*, 5: 520–21, 530–35.

56. Ibid., 6: 41; Quarles, *Lincoln and the Negro*, 112; Mitchell, *Report on Colonization*, 21–22; *To*

His Excellency. Abraham Lincoln, President of the United States, broadside, Oct. 1, 1862, Lincoln Papers; Howard K. Beale, ed., *The Diary of Edward Bates 1859–1866* (Washington, 1933), 268; Virginia J. Laas, ed., *Wartime Washington: The Civil War Letters of Elizabeth Blair Lee* (Urbana, Ill., 1991), 223.

57. Benjamin Rush Plumly to Lincoln, Jan. 1, 1863, Lincoln Papers.

58. Basler, ed., *Collected Works*, 6: 28–30.

59. Allan G. Bogue, "William Parker Cutler's Congressional Diary of 1862–63," *Civil War History*, 33 (December 1987): 328; Ambrose W. Thompson to Lincoln, March 28, 1863, Lincoln Papers.

60. Thomas S. Malcolm, Memorandum, Feb. 4, 1863; J. P. Usher to William H. Seward, Apr. 22, 1863, Usher to Edwin M. Stanton, Apr. 28, 1863, Usher to John Hodge, May 11, 1863, Letters Sent, Sept. 8, 1858–Feb. 1, 1872; John Hodge to Usher, May 6, 14, 1863, Communications Relating to Colonization in British Honduras, RG 48, National Archives; *New York Times*, May 18, 1863.

61. J. P. Usher to Lincoln, May 18, 1863, Usher to William McLain, Oct. 23, 1863, Letters Sent, Sept. 8, 1858–Feb. 1, 1872; James Mitchell to Lincoln, Nov. 25, 1863 (copy), Communication Relating to Rev. James Mitchell, RG 48, National Archives.

62. *Congressional Globe*, 37th Congress, 3rd Session, 283, 1293; Edward McPherson, *The Political History of the United States During the Great Rebellion*, 2nd ed. (Washington, 1865), 224–26; Montgomery Blair, *Comments on the Policy Inaugurated by the President, in a Letter and Two Speeches* (New York, 1863), 17–20; *Congressional Globe*, 38th Congress, 1st Session, Appendix, 46–47.

63. Joseph Medill to Lincoln, Feb. 17, 1864, C. M. Hawley to Lincoln, Feb. 27, 1864, Lincoln Papers; *Douglass' Monthly* (Feb. 1863): 786; Miller, *Black Nationality*, 261; Michael Burlingame, ed., *Dispatches from Lincoln's White House: The Anonymous Civil War Journalism of Presidential Secretary William O. Stoddard* (Lincoln, Neb., 2002), 167; Basler, ed., *Collected Works*, 6: 410.

64. Basler, ed., *Collected Works*, 8: 272; Michael Vorenberg, "Slavery Reparations in Theory and Practice," in Brian Dirck, ed., *Lincoln Emancipated*, 125–27; Heather C. Richardson, *The Greatest Nation of the Earth: Republican Economic Policies During the Civil War* (Cambridge, Mass., 1997), 229; Herman Belz, *A New Birth of Freedom: The Republican Party and Freedmen's Rights 1861–1866* (Westport, Conn., 1976), 72; Vorenberg, *Final Freedom*, 106.

65. Basler, ed., *Collected Works*, 6: 41–42, 178; 39th Congress, 1st Session, Senate Executive Document 55, *Message from the President of the United States . . . Respecting the Transportation, Settlement, and Colonization of Persons of the African Race*, 27–61; Charles K. Tuckerman to Lincoln, March 31, 1863, Lincoln Papers; J. P. Usher to Leonard Jerome, Dec. 12, 1863, Letters Sent, Sept. 8, 1858–Feb. 1, 1872, RG 48, National Archives.

66. J. P. Usher to Charles K. Tuckerman, April 17, July 8, 1863; April 5, 1864, Letters Sent, Sept. 8, 1858–Feb. 1, 1872; RG 48, National Archives; James De Long to Henry Conrad, June 25, 1863, Lincoln Papers; Basler, ed., *Collected Works*, 7: 164.

67. *Chicago Tribune*, March 23, 1864; *Message from the President*, 3–5; *The Nation* (Jan. 30, 1890); J. P. Usher to Lincoln, May 18, 1863, Letters Sent, Sept. 8, 1858–Feb. 1, 1872, RG 48, National Archives; James Mitchell to Lincoln, Oct. 20, 1864, Edward Bates to Lincoln, Nov. 30, 1864, Lincoln Papers; Michael Burlingame and John R. Ettinger, ed., *Inside Lincoln's White House: The Complete Civil War Diary of John Hay* (Carbondale, Ill., 1997), 217; Michael Burlingame, ed., *Lincoln's Journalist: John Hay's Anonymous Writings for the Press, 1860–1864* (Carbondale, Ill., 1998), 280.

68. Basler, ed., *Collected Works*, 6: 365; 7: 185, 243; Beale, ed., *Welles Diary*, 2: 237; Alexander H. Stephens, *A Constitutional View of the Late War Between the States*, 2 vols. (Philadelphia, 1868–70), 2: 613–14; *New Orleans Tribune*, Dec. 21, 1864. Benjamin Butler later claimed

that at the very end of his life, saying he feared a "race war" in the South, Lincoln instructed him to discuss with Seward a plan to colonize black soldiers in Panama, where they could dig a canal. Most scholars have accepted Mark Neely's argument that Butler's recollection is unreliable. Benjamin F. Butler, *Autobiography and Personal Reminiscences of Major-General Benjamin F. Butler: Butler's Book* (Boston, 1892), 903–04; Mark E. Neely, Jr., "Abraham Lincoln and Black Colonization: Benjamin Butler's Spurious Testimony," *Civil War History*, 25 (March 1979): 77–83.

69. Michael W. Fitzgerald, " 'We Have Found a Moses': Theodore Bilbo, Black Nationalism, and the Greater Liberia Bill of 1939," *Journal of Southern History*, 63 (May 1997): 293–320; Steven Hahn, *A Nation Under Our Feet: Black Political Struggles in the Rural South, From Slavery to the Great Migration* (Cambridge, Mass., 2003), 320–24; *Douglass' Monthly* (Oct. 1862): 724–25.

70. Striner, *Father Abraham*, 1–11; Miller, *Lincoln's Virtues*, 192, 228; *Milwaukee Daily Sentinel*, Aug. 29, 1862; *Harper's Weekly* (June 28, 1862).

71. Basler, ed., *Collected Works*, 8: 403.

ALLIES FOR EMANCIPATION?: LINCOLN AND BLACK ABOLITIONISTS by Manisha Sinha

The author wishes to thank John Bracey, Eric Foner, Kristen Stueber, Michael Thelwell, and the fellows and audience at the Charles Warren Center for Studies in American History Seminar, Harvard University, for their helpful comments.

1. On the freedmen's monument, see Kirk Savage, *Standing Soldiers, Kneeling Slaves: Race, War, and Monument in Nineteenth Century America* (Princeton, 1998); the kneeling slave represented the real-life fugitive slave Archer Alexander. See Christopher Eliot, "The Lincoln Emancipation Statue," *Journal of Negro History*, 29 (Oct. 1944): 471–75; Lincoln is quoted in Benjamin Quarles, *Lincoln and the Negro* (New York, 1962), 236; Allen C. Guelzo, *Lincoln's Emancipation Proclamation: The End of Slavery in America* (New York, 2004), 186.

2. W. E. B. Du Bois, *Black Reconstruction in America, 1860–1880* (New York, 1935), chapter 4. See the introductory essays of the Freedom Series in Ira Berlin, Barbara J. Fields, Stephen F. Miller, Joseph P. Reidy, and Leslie S. Rowland, *Slaves No More: Three Essays on Emancipation and The Civil War* (New York, 1992); James M. McPherson, *Drawn with the Sword: Reflections on the American Civil War* (New York, 1996), chapter 13.

3. James M. McPherson, *The Struggle for Equality: Abolitionists and the Negro in the Civil War and Reconstruction* (Princeton, 1964); Eric Foner, *Free Soil, Free Labor, Free Men: The Ideology of the Republican Party Before the Civil War* (orig. pub. 1970, New York, 1995), chapter 4; David W. Blight, "Abraham Lincoln and Frederick Douglass: A Relationship in Language, Politics, and Memory," in *Beyond the Battlefield: Race, Memory, and the American Civil War* (Amherst, Mass., 2002), 76–90; John Stauffer, "Across the Great Divide: The Friendship Between Lincoln and Frederick Douglass Required from Both a Change of Heart," *Time* magazine, Special Issue (July 4, 2005): 58-65; James Oakes, *The Radical and the Republican: Frederick Douglass, Abraham Lincoln and the Triumph of Antislavery Politics* (New York, 2007).

4. Benjamin Quarles, *Black Abolitionists* (New York, 1969); Donald Jacobs ed., *Courage and Conscience: Black and White Abolitionists in Boston* (Bloomington, Ind., 1993); Paul Goodman, *Of One Blood: Abolitionism and the Origins of Racial Equality* (Berkeley, 1998); Richard S. Newman, *The Transformation of American Abolitionism: Fighting Slavery in the Early Republic* (Chapel Hill, N.C., 2002) ; Timothy Patrick McCarthy and John Stauffer, eds., *Prophets of Protest: Reconsidering the History of American Abolitionism* (New York, 2006); For a recent dismissal of black abolitionism as merely self-interested and without any influence on Lincoln's emancipation policies, see Guelzo, *Lincoln's Emancipation Proclamation*, 76.

5. David Donald, *Lincoln Reconsidered: Essays on the Civil War Era* (New York, 1947): 36. Also see 19–21 and chapter 6.

6. David Herbert Donald, *Lincoln* (New York, 1995), 15, writes that his biography of Lincoln "highlights" the "essential passivity of his nature."

7. Mark E. Neely, Jr., *The Last Best Hope of Earth: Abraham Lincoln and the Promise of America* (Cambridge, Mass., 1993), 34.

8. Richard J. Carwardine, *Lincoln: Profiles in Power* (London, 2003); Roy P. Basler, ed., *The Collected Works of Abraham Lincoln*, 9 vols. (New Brunswick, N.J., 1953–55): 5: 492, 7: 281.

9. Basler, ed., *Collected Works*, 2: 255; Don E. Fehrenbacher, *Prelude to Greatness: Lincoln in the 1850s* (Stanford, Calif., 1962). On the Lincoln-Douglas debates, see David Zarefsky, *Lincoln, Douglas and Slavery: In the Crucible of Public Debate* (Chicago, 1990); Allen C. Guelzo, "Houses Divided: Lincoln, Douglas, and the Political Landscape of 1858," *Journal of American History*, 94 (September 2007): 391–417; Kenneth J. Winkle, "'Paradox Though It May Seem': Lincoln on Antislavery, Race and Union, 1837–1860," in Brian Dirck, ed., *Lincoln Emancipated: The President and the Politics of Race* (DeKalb, Ill., 2007), 8–28; John W. Blassingame, ed., *The Frederick Douglass Papers Series One: Speeches, Debates, and Interviews*, vol. 3: 1855–63 (New Haven, 1985), 237.

10. Foner, *Free Soil, Free Labor, Free Men*, chapter 8; Basler, ed, *Collected Works*, 2: 403–05, 408.

11. Basler, ed., *Collected Works*, 2: 256, 405. For an argument that sees Lincoln as more of a "racist," see James N. Leiker, "The Difficulties of Understanding Abe: Lincoln's Reconciliation of Racial Equality and Natural Rights," in Dirck, ed., *Lincoln Emancipated*, 73–98.

12. Basler, ed., *Collected Works*, 2: 408–09. On Charlotte Scott, see Quarles, *Lincoln and the Negro*, 3–5, 11, 18.

13. Basler, ed., *Collected Works*, 2: 409, 501.

14. Ibid., 3: 16, 179.

15. Lerone Bennett, Jr. *Forced into Glory: Abraham Lincoln's White Dream* (Chicago, 2000); Guelzo, *Lincoln's Emancipation Proclamation*, 4–5.

16. The *Anglo-African* is quoted in Quarles, *Lincoln and the Negro*, 65; Garrison is quoted by McPherson, *Struggle for Equality*, 9, 10; Blassingame, ed., *Frederick Douglass Papers*, 3: 381–82; David W. Blight, *Frederick Douglass' Civil War: Keeping Faith in Jubilee* (Baton Rouge, La., 1989), 54; "Speech of John S. Rock, Delivered at the Meionaon Boston, Massachusetts, 5 March 1860" in C. Peter Ripley, ed., *The Black Abolitionist Papers*, 5 vols. (Chapel Hill, N.C., 1992), 5: 61.

17. "Editorial by Thomas Hamilton 17 March 1860" and "Speech by H. Ford Douglas Delivered at the Town Hall, Salem, Ohio 23 September 1860," in Ripley, ed., *Black Abolitionist Papers*, 5: 72–73, 88–92; Blight, *Frederick Douglass' Civil War*, 47–58; McPherson, *Struggle for Equality*, H. Ford Douglas is quoted on 26 and Frederick Douglass on 26.

18. All quotes are from Quarles, *Lincoln and the Negro*, 39, 56.

19. James M. McPherson, *The Negro's Civil War: How American Negroes Felt and Acted During the War for the Union* (New York, 1965), 10–11; McPherson, *Struggle for Equality*, 27, 31; Wells Brown is quoted by Quarles, *Lincoln and the Negro*, 62; Rock is quoted in the *Christian Recorder*, (Feb. 22, 1862).

20. Blassingame, ed., *Frederick Douglass Papers*, 3: 428; McPherson, *Struggle for Equality*, 39, 50–51, 66–69; *Christian Recorder* (Feb. 22, 1862). For the argument that abolitionists compromised on their commitment to pacifism by supporting the war, see George M. Fredrickson, *The Inner Civil War: Northern Intellectuals and the Crisis of the Union* (New York, 1968).

21. *Frederick Douglass' Monthly* (Oct. 1861); "James McCune Smith to Gerrit Smith, 22 August, 1861," in Ripley, ed., *Black Abolitionist Papers*, 5: 113; Phillips is quoted by Stewart, *Wendell Phillips*, 229; Henry McNeal Turner is quoted from the *Christian Recorder* (March 22,

July 12, 1862); Blassingame, ed., *Frederick Douglass Papers*, 3: 483; Basler, ed., *Collected Works*, 5: 49.

22. *Christian Recorder* (Aug. 9, 1862); "Editorial by Philip A. Bell 14 June, 1862," in Ripley, ed., *Black Abolitionist Papers*, 5: 145; Douglass is quoted in McPherson, *Struggle for Equality*, 98.

23. *Christian Recorder* (Apr. 26, May 10, May 17, Nov. 15,1862).

24. Benjamin Quarles, *The Negro in the Civil War* (Boston, 1953),131; Phillip S. Paludan, "Greeley, Colonization, and a 'Deputation of Negroes': Three Considerations on Lincoln and Race," in Dirck, ed., *Lincoln Emancipated*, 29–46; Basler ed., *Collected Works*, 5: 388; Blassingame, ed., *Frederick Douglass Papers*, 3: 518, 519; Harriet Tubman is quoted by Quarles, *Lincoln and the Negro*, 86; Douglass is quoted in McPherson, *Negro's Civil War*, 39; McPherson, *Struggle for Equality*, 100–101, Phillips is quoted on 109.

25. McPherson, *Struggle for Equality*, 125–32; Wendy Hamand Venet, *Neither Ballots Nor Bullets: Women Abolitionists and the Civil War* (Charlottesville, Va., 1991), chapters 3 and 5.

26. *Christian Recorder* (June 28, 1862); Stewart, *Liberty's Hero*, 233–36. On Sumner and the Lincolns, see Donald, *Lincoln Reconsidered*, 114–25; McPherson, *Struggle for Equality*, 79–98, Mary Grew is quoted on 89, 90.

27. Rapier is quoted by Quarles, *Lincoln and the Negro*, 216; For some recent works on black abolitionists, see especially Patrick Rael, *Black Identity and Black Protest in the Antebellum North* (Chapel Hill, N.C., 2002); John Stauffer, *The Black Hearts of Men: Radical Abolitionists and the Transformation of Race* (Cambridge, Mass., 2002); Eddie S. Glaude, Jr., *Exodus!: Religion, Race, and Nation in Early Nineteenth-Century America* (Chicago, 2000); Blassingame, ed., *Frederick Douglass Papers*, 3: 440, 607; Basler, ed., *Collected Works*, 8: 332.

28. Blassingame, ed., *Frederick Douglass Papers*, 3: 606; Quarles, *Lincoln and the Negro*, 200–204, 205–06; Jennifer Fleischner, *Mrs. Lincoln and Mrs. Keckley: The Remarkable Story of the Friendship Between a First Lady and a Former Slave* (New York, 2003). For a critical reading of Lincoln's encounter with Truth see Nell Painter, *Sojourner Truth: A Life, A Symbol* (New York), 203–07.

29. Quarles, *Lincoln and the Negro*, 198–99, 207–08.

30. For a thorough discussion of Lincoln and colonization, see Eric Foner's essay in this volume. For a different view see Kevin R. C. Gutzman, "Abraham Lincoln, Jeffersonian: The Colonization Chimera," in Dirck, ed., *Lincoln Emancipated*, 47–72; Basler, ed., *Collected Works*, 5: 48.

31. "Address by Abraham D. Shadd, Peter Spencer, and William S. Thomas 12 July 1831," Ripley, ed., *Black Abolitionist Papers*, 3: 102–03; William Lloyd Garrison, *Thoughts on African Colonization: or An Impartial Exhibition of the Doctrines, Principles and Purposes of the American Colonization Society. Together with the Resolutions, Addresses and Remonstrances of the Free People of Color* (Boston, 1832). The *Liberator* is quoted by Quarles, *Lincoln and the Negro*, 119; *Christian Recorder* (Feb. 22, 1862).

32. Basler, ed., *Collected Works*, 5: 371–73; Paludan, "Greeley, Colonization, and a 'Deputation of Negroes,' " 38–46; Quarles, *The Negro in the Civil War*, 149.

33. Douglass is quoted in Blight, *Frederick Douglass' Civil War*, 139; Frances Ellen Watkins Harper is quoted from the *Christian Recorder* (Sept. 27, 1862).

34. *Christian Recorder* (Sept. 20, 1862); Quarles, *Negro in the Civil War*, 149–50; Quarles, *Lincoln and the Negro*, 117–18, 123; "George B. Vashon to Abraham Lincoln [Sept. 1862]," Ripley, ed., *Black Abolitionist Papers*, 5: 153.

35. "H. Ford Douglas to Frederick Douglass 8 January, 1863," Ripley, ed., *Black Abolitionist Papers*, 5: 167.

36. McPherson, *Struggle for Equality*, 118, Garrison is quoted on 121; John Hope Franklin, *The Emancipation Proclamation* (New York, 1963); Guelzo, *Lincoln's Emancipation Proclamation*; Blassingame, ed., *Frederick Douglass Papers*, 3: 549.

37. Quarles, *Lincoln and the Negro*, 142–51, Rock is quoted on 144; William C. Nell is quoted

by Quarles, *Negro in the Civil War*, 171; Guelzo, *Lincoln's Emancipation Proclamation*, 184–85; William H. Wiggins, Jr., *O Freedom! Afro-American Emancipation Celebrations* (Knoxville, Tenn., 1987), 59, 71–72; Mitch Kachun, *Festivals of Freedom: Memory and Meaning in African American Emancipation Celebrations, 1808–1915* (Amherst, Mass., 2003), chapter 3; Turner is quoted from the *Christian Recorder* (Oct. 4, 1862).

38. *Christian Recorder* (March 10, 1863); "Speech by John S. Rock Delivered at the Wesleyan Methodist Church, Syracuse, New York, 6 October, 1864," and "J. W. C. Pennington to Robert Hamilton 9 June 1864," in Ripley, ed., *Black Abolitionist Papers*, 5: 276–77, 306; Quarles, *Lincoln and the Negro*, 212–14; McPherson, *Negro's Civil War*, 304–07.

39. Michael Vorenberg, *Final Freedom: The Civil War, the Abolition of Slavery, and the Thirteenth Amendment* (New York, 2001); Lincoln is quoted in Quarles, *Lincoln and the Negro*, 221; Garnet is quoted by Martin B. Pasternak, *Rise Now and Fly to Arms: The Life of Henry Highland Garnet* (New York, 1995), 121.

40. Blight, *Frederick Douglass' Civil War*; Du Bois, *Black Reconstruction in America*; Blassingame, ed., *Frederick Douglass Papers*, 3: 444, 451; Basler, ed., *Collected Works*, 5: 537; James M. McPherson, *Abraham Lincoln and the Second American Revolution* (New York, 1991); Garry Wills, *Lincoln at Gettysburg: The Words That Remade America* (New York, 1992).

41. See, for example, Carwardine, *Lincoln*; Allen C. Guelzo, *Abraham Lincoln: Redeemer President* (Grand Rapids, Mich., 1999); Basler, ed., *Collected Works*, 8: 333; John W. Blassingame and John R. McKivigan, eds., *Frederick Douglass Papers Series One: Speeches, Debates, and Interviews*, vol. 4: *1864–80* (New Haven, 1991), 77.

42. McPherson, *Negro's Civil War*, 33; William C. Nell, *The Colored Patriots of the American Revolution, with Sketches of Several Disinguished Colored Persons: To Which Is Added a Brief Survey of the Condition and Prospects of Colored Americans* (Boston, 1855); Douglass is quoted by McPherson, *Struggle for Equality*, 192.

43. Ira Berlin et al., eds., *Freedom: A Documentary History of Emancipation 1861–1867 Series II The Black Military Experience* (New York, 1982); McPherson, *Struggle for Equality*, 204–07.

44. "John S. Rock to the Soldiers of the Fifth United States Colored Heavy Artillery Regiment 30 May 1864," Ripley, ed., *Black Abolitionist Papers*, 5: 274; *Christian Recorder* (Jan. 2, 30, 1864); McPherson, *Negro's Civil War*, chapter 14.

45. Berlin et al., eds., *Freedom Series II The Black Military Experience*, 362–68, 385–86, 401–02; Lincoln is quoted by Quarles, *Lincoln and the Negro*, 169–72; *Christian Recorder* (Aug. 20, 1864); McPherson, *Struggle for Equality*, 216–20; Thomas Wentworth Higginson, *Army Life in a Black Regiment and Other Writings,* with an Introduction and Notes by R. D. Madison (New York, 1997), Appendix D, *The Struggle for Pay*, 217–27.

46. *Christian Recorder* (Jan. 9, June 25, 1864); Berlin et al., eds., *Freedom Series II The Black Military Experience*, 302–12.

47. Blassingame, ed., *Frederick Douglass Papers*, 3: 607; *Christian Recorder* (Jan. 9, Apr. 30, 1864); McPherson, *Negro's Civil War*, chapter 5; Quarles, *Lincoln and the Negro*, 168, Lincoln is quoted on 177–78.

48. *Christian Recorder* (Aug. 20, 1864); Basler, ed., *Collected Works*, 6: 409–10; Quarles, *Lincoln and the Negro*, 182.

49. Basler ed., *Collected Works*, 1: 48; "Proceedings of the National Convention of Colored Men, Held in the City of Syracuse, N.Y., Oct. 4, 5, 6, and 7, 1864; With the Bill of Wrongs and Rights, and the Address to the American People" (Boston, 1864), in Howard Holman Bell, ed., *Minutes of the Proceedings of the National Negro Conventions 1830–1864* (New York, 1969), 58.

50. *Christian Recorder* (Aug. 27, Oct. 8, 1864, Jan. 7, 1865).

51. Blassingame and McKivigan, eds., *Frederick Douglass Papers*, 4: 60–69; Blassingame, ed., *Frederick Douglass Papers*, 3: 572, 604; McPherson, *Struggle for Equality*, Douglass is quoted

on 240, Phillips on 247, 287–307; *Christian Recorder* (May 21, 1864); Eric Foner, *Reconstruction: America's Unfinished Revolution, 1863–1877* (New York, 1989).

52. Quarles, *Lincoln and the Negro*, 226–30; Basler, ed., *Collected Works*, 7: 243; McPherson, *Struggle for Equality*, 240–46.

53. Basler, ed., *Collected Works*, 7: 53–56; 8: 403; LaWanda Cox, *Lincoln and Black Freedom: A Study in Presidential Leadership* (Columbia, Mo., 1981); Herman Belz, *A New Birth of Freedom: The Republican Party and Freedmen's Rights, 1861–1866* (New York, 2000); Donald, *Lincoln*, 588.

54. Blassingame and McKivigan, eds., *Frederick Douglass Papers*, 4: 76; *Christian Recorder* (Apr. 22, May 20, 1865); "Editorial by W. W. Rogers 22 April 1865," Ripley, ed., *Black Abolitionist Papers*, 5: 315–16; McPherson, *Negro's Civil War*, 308.

55. Blassingame and McKivigan, eds., *Frederick Douglass Papers*, 4: 431–36.

LINCOLN'S SACRAMENTAL LANGUAGE by Andrew Delbanco

1. Jacques Barzun, "Lincoln the Writer," in Barzun, *On Writing, Editing, and Publishing* (Chicago, 1971), 66, 81. Barzun's essay was first published in the *Saturday Evening Post* (Feb. 14, 1959) under the title "Lincoln the Literary Genius." Stowe, quoted in Douglas Wilson, *Lincoln's Sword: The Presidency and the Power of Words* (New York, 2006), 196. From Roy Basler, who called Lincoln "an indisputable master of language" (*Abraham Lincoln: His Speeches and Writings* [Cleveland and New York, 1946], 19, to James McPherson, who claims that he "won the war with metaphor" [Robert Cowley, ed., *Perspectives on the American Civil War: With My Face to the Enemy* (London, 2003), 87–102]), modern scholars have been as impressed with Lincoln's language as were his contemporaries.

2. Ernest Jones's three-volume *Life and Work of Sigmund Freud* (later abridged by Barzun's Columbia colleagues Lionel Trilling and Steven Marcus) had just been published.

3. Edmund Wilson, *The Wound and the Bow* (New York, 1947), 236.

4. Dickinson too was a 1950s poet in the sense that only a few of her poems had been published during her lifetime, and the first soundly edited modern edition appeared in 1955.

5. Hemingway, *The Green Hills of Africa* (New York, 1935), 22.

6. This view of the founders was developed as early as the 1840s by Salmon P. Chase. See Eric Foner, *Free Soil, Free Labor, Free Men: The Ideology of the Republican Party Before the Civil War* (New York, 1970), 75 ff.

7. Perry Miller, "An American Language" (1958), in *Nature's Nation* (Cambridge, Mass., 1967), 237.

8. Quoted in Janet Malcolm, review of David Shipley and Will Schwalbe, *Send: The Essential Guide to Email for Office and Home, New York Review of Books* (Sept. 27, 2007): 8.

9. David Hackett Fischer, *The Revolution of American Conservatism* (New York, 1965), 23.

10. Douglas Wilson, *Lincoln's Sword*, 90.

11. Ralph Waldo Emerson, *Divinity School Address* (1837), in Stephen E. Whicher, ed., *Selections from Ralph Waldo Emerson* (Boston, 1957), 115.

12. The comma for Lincoln appears to have functioned much as stress marks, which appear in the form of apostrophes (') and quotation marks ("), did for Thomas Jefferson, who used such marks on his reading text when delivering a public address. See Jay Fliegelman, *Declaring Independence: Jefferson, Natural Language & the Culture of Performance* (Stanford, Calif., 1993).

13. Melville to Dix & Edwards, March 24, 1856 (the book in question was *The Piazza Tales*), in Herman Melville, *Correspondence*, ed. Lynn Horth (Evanston, Ill., 1993), 288.

14. Lincoln's friend Noah Brooks reported that Lincoln told him that while "punctuation is a

matter of rule" for some people, "with me it is a matter of feeling." Quoted in Don E. Fehrenbacher and Virginia Fehrenbacher, eds., *Recollected Words of Abraham Lincoln* (Stanford, Calif., 1996), 54.

15. Edmund Ruffin, on Patrick Henry, quoted in Fliegelman, *Declaring Independence*, 14.

16. Miller, *Nature's Nation*, 232; Fehrenbacher, *Recollected Words*, 249.

17. Henry D. Thoreau, *Walden and other Writings*, ed. Brook Atkinson (orig. pub. 1854; New York, 1950), 92.

18. Douglas Wilson, *Lincoln's Sword*, 63. The "no nonsense" phrase is quoted from David Donald's biography of Lincoln (New York, 1995), 283.

19. In one scholar's judgment, Lincoln "cut the flab" from Seward's draft (Kenneth Cmiel, *Democratic Eloquence: The Fight over Popular Speech in Nineteenth-Century America* [New York, 1990], 116).

20. Don E. Fehrenbacher, "Words of Lincoln," in *Lincoln in Text and Context* (Stanford, Calif., 1987), 285.

21. Richard Carwardine, in *Lincoln: A Life of Purpose and Power* (New York, 2007), 32, notes that Lincoln may have derived the phrase "if slavery is not wrong, then nothing is wrong" from a formulation ("if those laws of the Southern states, by virtue of which slavery exists there, and is what it is, are not wrong—nothing is wrong") by a Connecticut minister, Leonard Bacon, whose book was circulating in Springfield, Illinois, in the late 1840s.

22. Quoted in James McPherson, *Hallowed Ground: A Walk at Gettysburg* (New York, 2003), 134.

23. Fehrenbacher and Fehrenbacher, eds., *Recollected Words*, 303.

24. Among the dubious attributions are some of Lincoln's most often quoted remarks, such as the comment with which he supposedly greeted Harriet Beecher Stowe at a White House reception: "So you are the little woman who made this great war."

25. Oliver Wendell Holmes, "Doings of the Sunbeam," *Atlantic Monthly* (July 1863), 7.

26. *Missouri Republican* (May 1879), quoted in George W. S. Trow, *Within the Context of No Context* (orig. pub. 1981; Boston, 1997), 8.

27. Fischer, *Revolution of American Conservatism*, passim; Diana Schaub—in a review of Ted Widmer, ed., *American Speeches: Political Oratory from the Revolution to the Civil War* and *American Speeches: Political Oratory from Abraham Lincoln to Bill Clinton*—*Claremont Review of Books* (Summer 2007), characterizes the political orator of the early Republic as "speaking to a body of distinguished equals."

28. Edmund Wilson, *Patriotic Gore: Studies in the Literature of the American Civil War* (New York, 1962), 122.

29. See Robert Ferguson, *Law and Letters in American Culture* (Cambridge, Mass., 1984), 306.

30. Thomas Wentworth Higginson, quoted in Albert J. von Frank, *The Trials of Anthony Burns* (Cambridge, Mass., 1998), 30.

31. Lowell, quoted in Cmiel, *Democratic Eloquence*, p. 116. There is a certain parallel here to what was happening in the American theater as the declamative style, associated with formal British acting, was challenged by American actors who preferred a more natural style.

32. Max Weber, "Politics as a Vocation" (1918), in Hans Gerth and C. Wright Mills, eds., *From Max Weber: Essays in Sociology* (New York, 1958), 120.

33. Roy P. Basler, ed., *Collected Works of Abraham Lincoln*, 9 vols. (New Brunswick, N.J., 1953–55), 2: 498.

34. Fehrenbacher and Fehrenbacher, eds., *Recollected Words*, 252.

35. Basler, ed., *Collected Works*, 8: 362.

36. C. Vann Woodward, ed., *Mary Chesnut's Civil War* (New Haven, 1981), 13, entry dated March 1, 1861.

37. Basler, ed., *Collected Works*, 3: 307. Foner, *Free Soil, Free Labor, Free Men*, 76, points out that

Ohio Senator Salmon P. Chase (later Lincoln's treasury secretary) was arguing in the early 1840s that the framers had carefully avoided the words *slave* and *slavery*.

38. Daniel Aaron, *The Unwritten War: American Writers and the Civil War* (New York, 1973), 343, and Sarah Morgan, *The Civil War Diary of a Southern Woman*, ed. Charles East (Athens, Ga., 1991), 74 (June 1862).

39. Fee's book, *The Sinfulness of Slaveholding Shown by Appeals to Reason and Scripture*, is quoted by Mark Noll, *The Civil War as a Theological Crisis* (Chapel Hill, N.C., 2006), 55: "The fact that one man, or race of men, may have more intellectual capacity than another man, or race of men, gives no just ground for enslaving the inferior; otherwise the most intellectual man that exists may have a right to enslave every other man—white and black. . . . Otherwise, he who has a fairer skin . . . than you or I, may have a right enslave us; and the fairest man in the world may enslave every other man." If the fragment on slavery had precedents, it also had prescience; it expresses essentially the same idea that we find nearly a century later in Martin Niemöller's famous articulation of why the defense of others is indistinguishable from self-defense: "First they came for the Jews and I did not speak out because I was not a Jew. Then they came for the Communists and I did not speak out because I was not a Communist. Then they came for the trade unionists and I did not speak out because I was not a trade unionist. Then they came for me and there was no one left to speak out for me."

40. Basler, ed., *Collected Works*, 1: 512.

41. Ibid., 1: 397.

42. Ibid., 2: 415.

43. Melville, *White-Jacket* (orig. pub. 1850; Evanston, Ill., 1970), ed. Harrison Hayford, Hershel Parker, and G. Thomas Tanselle, 150.

44. Basler, ed., *Collected Works*, 1: 448.

45. Ibid., 5: 388; 7: 49–53, and see David Blight, *Race and Reunion: The Civil War in American Memory* (Cambridge, Mass., 2001), 17–18.

46. William T. Sherman, *Memoirs* (New York, 1990), ed. Charles Royster, 670; Sam R. Watkins, *Co. Aytch: A Side Show of the Big Show* (orig. pub. 1882; New York, 1962), 162.

47. Hawthorne, "Chiefly About War Matters" (1862), in *The Complete Works of Nathaniel Hawthorne*, 13 vols. (Boston, 1883), 12: 319.

48. Edmund Wilson, *Patriotic Gore*, xxxi–ii; Louis Menand, *The Metaphysical Club* (New York, 2001), x.

49. Basler, ed., *Collected Works*, 4: 240; 2: 264, 499–500.

50. The phrase is quoted from Robert Lowell in Robert N. Bellah, "Civil Religion in America" (1967), in *Beyond Belief: Essays on Religion in a Post-Traditional World* (New York, 1970), 178.

51. Merrill D. Peterson, *Abraham Lincoln in American Memory* (New York, 1994), 380.

LINCOLN'S RELIGION by Richard Carwardine

1. Douglas L. Wilson and Rodney O. Davis, eds., *Herndon's Informants: Letters Interviews, and Statements about Abraham Lincoln* (Urbana, Ill., 1998), 576–77, 582–83.

2. William H. Herndon and Jesse W. Weik, *Herndon's Lincoln*, ed. Douglas L. Wilson and Rodney O. Davis (Urbana, Ill., 2006), 264–69; Ward H. Lamon, *The Life of Abraham Lincoln: From His Birth to His Inauguration as President* (Boston, 1872), 486–504.

3. Wilson and Davis, eds., *Herndon's Informants*, 588; Isaac N. Arnold, *The Life of Abraham Lincoln* (orig. pub. Chicago, 1884; with an introduction by James A. Rawley, Lincoln, Neb., 1994), 447–49.

4. J. G. Holland, *The Life of Abraham Lincoln* (Springfield, Ill., 1866), 239, 542; Benjamin P. Thomas, *Portrait for Posterity: Lincoln and His Biographers* (New Brunswick, N.J., 1947), 14–16.

5. Wilson and Davis, eds., *Herndon's Informants*, 346, 348.

6. William E. Barton, *The Soul of Abraham Lincoln* (New York, 1920), 225–43.

7. Most of the superior scholarly biographies of Lincoln compartmentalize, and ipso facto understate the significance of, his religion. See, for example, James G. Randall [and Richard N. Current], *Lincoln the President*, 4 vols. (New York, 1945–55); Benjamin P. Thomas, *Abraham Lincoln: A Biography* (New York, 1952); Stephen B. Oates, *With Malice Toward None: The Life of Abraham Lincoln* (New York, 1977); David Herbert Donald, *Lincoln* (New York, 1995), Doris Kearns Goodwin, *Team of Rivals: The Political Genius of Abraham Lincoln* (New York, 2005). The outstanding exception is Allen C. Guelzo, *Abraham Lincoln: Redeemer President* (Grand Rapids, Mich., 1999). Among the works that deal explicitly with Lincoln's ethical and religious ideas, the following merit particular mention: Barton, *The Soul of Abraham Lincoln*; William J. Wolf, *The Almost Chosen People: A Study of the Religion of Abraham Lincoln* (Garden City, N.Y., 1959); David Hein, "Lincoln's Theology and Political Ethics," in Kenneth W. Thompson, ed., *Essays on Lincoln's Faith and Politics* (Lanham, Md., c. 1983); Elton Trueblood, *Abraham Lincoln: A Spiritual Biography* (New York, 1986); William Lee Miller, *Lincoln's Virtues: An Ethical Biography* (New York, 2002); James Tackach, *Lincoln's Moral Vision: The Second Inaugural Address* (Jackson, Miss., 2002); Stewart Winger, *Lincoln, Religion, and Romantic Cultural Politics* (DeKalb, Ill., 2003); and the works cited in note 26 below. For a more extended treatment of some of the themes of this essay, see Richard Carwardine, *Lincoln: A Life of Purpose and Power* (New York, 2006).

8. Nathan O. Hatch, *The Democratization of American Christianity* (New Haven, 1989); Jon Butler, *Awash in a Sea of Faith: Christianizing the American People* (Cambridge, Mass., 1990); Roger Finke and Rodney Stark, *The Churching of America, 1776–1990: Winners and Losers in Our Religious Economy* (New Brunswick, N.J., 1992); Christine Leigh Heyrman, *Southern Cross: The Beginnings of the Bible Belt* (Chapel Hill, N.C., 1998); Nathan O. Hatch and John H. Wigger, eds., *Methodism and the Shaping of American Culture* (Nashville, Tenn., 2001).

9. Mark A. Noll, *America's God: From Jonathan Edwards to Abraham Lincoln* (New York, 2002).

10. This theme is given systematic and persuasive treatment in Nicholas Guyatt, *Providence and the Invention of the United States 1607–1876* (New York, 2007).

11. See, especially, Mitchell Snay, *Gospel of Disunion: Religion and Separatism in the Antebellum South* (New York, 1993); Richard J. Carwardine, *Evangelicals and Politics in Antebellum America* (New Haven, 1993); John R. McKivigan and Mitchell Snay, eds., *Religion and the Antebellum Debate over Slavery* (Athens, Ga., 1998); Elizabeth Fox-Genovese and Eugene D. Genovese, *The Mind of the Master Class: History and Faith in the Southern Slaveholders' Worldview* (New York, 2005).

12. Herndon and Weik, *Herndon's Lincoln*, 354.

13. Wilson and Davis, eds., *Herndon's Informants*, 76, 92, 106, 167, 169, 453.

14. Don E. Fehrenbacher and Virginia Fehrenbacher, c. eds., *Recollected Words of Abraham Lincoln* (Stanford, Calif., 1996), 273 [John Langdon Kaine].

15. Wilson and Davis, eds., *Herndon's Informants*, 573 [Rev. Andrew Goodpasture].

16. F. B. Carpenter, *The Inner Life of Abraham Lincoln: Six Months at the White House* (orig. pub. New York, 1866; Lincoln, Neb., 1995), 49–52, 116; Fehrenbacher and Fehrenbacher, eds., *Recollected Words*, 337; *Herndon's Lincoln*, 376, 446; Michael Burlingame and John R. Turner Ettlinger, eds., *Inside Lincoln's White House: The Complete Civil War Diary of John Hay* (Carbondale, Ill., 1997), 76, 128; Michael Burlingame, ed., *Lincoln Observed: Civil War Dispatches of Noah Brooks* (Baltimore, 1998), 250.

17. Wilson and Davis, eds., *Herndon's Informants*, 106; Douglas L. Wilson, *Honor's Voice: The Transformation of Abraham Lincoln* (New York, 1998), 73–80.

18. Wilson and Davis, eds., *Herndon's Informants*, 441.

19. Ibid., 547–50; Barton, *Soul of Abraham Lincoln*, 324, 348–49.

20. Wilson and Davis, eds., *Herndon's Informants*, 360, 464, 524, 576, 578–80.

21. Michael Burlingame, ed., *An Oral History of Abraham Lincoln: John G. Nicolay's Interviews and Essays* (Carbondale, Ill., 1996), 95–96; Wilson and Davis, eds., *Herndon's Informants*, 167–68, 358, 360, 453.

22. Arnold, *Life of Abraham Lincoln*, 81; Wilson and Davis, eds., *Herndon's Informants*, 185, 358, 360; Emanuel Hertz, *The Hidden Lincoln: From the Letters and Papers of William H. Herndon* (New York, 1940), 142, 167–68, 185, 265–66, 407–08; Roy P. Basler, ed., *The Collected Works of Abraham Lincoln*, 9 vols. (New Brunswick, N.J., 1953–55), 1: 382; Allen C. Guelzo, "Abraham Lincoln and the Doctrine of Necessity," *Journal of the Abraham Lincoln Association*, 18 (Winter 1997): 57–81.

23. Basler, ed., *Collected Works*, 2: 544–47.

24. Ibid., 3: 462 (Genesis 3: 19).

25. Ibid., 2: 479–80; Wilson and Davis, eds., *Herndon's Informants*, 183–84.

26. For the religious workings of Lincoln's mind during wartime, see especially Mark A. Noll, "'Both Pray to the Same God': The Singularity of Lincoln's Faith in the Era of the Civil War," *Journal of the Abraham Lincoln Association*, 18 (Winter 1997): 1–26; Nicholas Parrillo, "Lincoln's Calvinist Transformation: Emancipation and War," *Civil War History*, 46 (Sept. 2000), 227–53; Ronald C. White, Jr., *Lincoln's Greatest Speech: The Second Inaugural* (New York, 2002).

27. Basler, ed., *Collected Works*, 4: 482–83, 6, 244–45; Burlingame, ed., *Oral History of Abraham Lincoln*, 5.

28. Basler, ed., *Collected Works*, 5: 278–79, 403–04. On the question of the dating of the memorandum, commonly placed in Sept. 1862, but more probably originating in 1863 or 1864, see Douglas L. Wilson, *Lincoln's Sword: The Presidency and the Power of Words* (New York, 2006), 254–56, 329–30.

29. Noyes Miner, "Personal Recollection of Abraham Lincoln," Illinois State Historical Society, 46–48; Basler, ed., *Collected Works*, 5: 146, 279, 419–20, 478; John Niven, ed., *The Salmon P. Chase Papers*, vol. 1: *Journals, 1829–1872* (Kent, Ohio, 1993), 394.

30. *Diary of Gideon Welles: Secretary of the Navy Under Lincoln and Johnson*, 3 vols. (Boston, 1911), 1: 143.

31. Thomas Ford, *A History of Illinois from Its Commencement as a State in 1818 to 1847* (Chicago, 1854), 105; Joseph Gillespie, *Recollections of Early Illinois and Her Noted Men* (Chicago, 1880), 6; Clinton L. Conkling, "Historical Data Concerning the Second Presbyterian Church of Springfield, Illinois," typescript, 3 vols., Illinois State Historical Society, 1: 133–41, 176–79, 3: 8–22; Newton Bateman and Paul Selby, eds., *Illinois Historical* (Chicago, 1910), 215.

32. Basler, ed., *Collected Works*, 1: 319–21, 382–84; Harry C. Blair and Rebecca Tarshis, *Lincoln's Constant Ally: The Life of Colonel Edward D. Baker* (Portland, Ore., 1960), 8–9.

33. Basler, ed., *Collected Works*, 2: 276, 281–82.

34. Ibid., 2: 545–47, 3: 220–22, 249, 280, 301–04.

35. Ibid., 3: 234, 254, 310–12, 315–16.

36. Ibid., 2: 501, 546–47.

37. A. Smith to Abraham Lincoln [AL], 20 July 1858, J. H. Jordan to AL, 25 July 1858, Abraham Lincoln Papers, Library of Congress; *Reminiscences of Carl Schurz*, 3 vols. (New York, 1907–08), 2: 93–96; Wilson and Davis, eds., *Herndon's Informants*, 716; Walter B. Stevens, *A Reporter's Lincoln*, ed. Michael Burlingame (Lincoln, Neb., 1998), 89, 229.

38. *New York Tribune*, June 12, 15, 1860; *Albany Evening Journal*, Sept. 22, 1860; John Locke Scripps, *Life of Abraham Lincoln*, ed. Roy P. Basler and Lloyd A. Dunlap (Bloomington, Ind., 1961), 165; *Chicago Press and Tribune*, May 21, 23, 1860; *Rail Splitter* (Cincinnati; facs. ed., Chicago, 1950), 1, Aug. 15, 1860; *Illinois State Register*, June 4, Oct. 22, 1860; *Chicago Daily Times and Herald*, Oct. 27, 1860.

39. Barton, The Soul of Abraham Lincoln, 114–27; William E. Gienapp, "Who Voted for Lincoln?," in John L. Thomas, ed. *Abraham Lincoln and the American Political Tradition* (Amherst, Mass., 1986), 66–67, 74–76; Carwardine, *Evangelicals and Politics in Antebellum America*, 296–307.

40. *Northwestern Christian Advocate*, Aug. 13, 1862, July 8, 1863.

41. There is a relative dearth of distinguished scholarship on the religion of the Civil War. Essential are James H. Moorhead, *American Apocalypse: Yankee Protestants and the Civil War 1860–69* (New Haven, 1978); Randall M. Miller, Harry S. Stout, and Charles Reagan Wilson, eds., *Religion and the American Civil War* (New York, 1998); Harry S. Stout, *Upon the Altar of the Nation: A Moral History of the American Civil War* (New York, 2006).

42. Basler, ed., *Collected Works*, 4: 262–71.

43. Ibid., 8: 332–33.

44. Ibid., 4: 482–83; 5: 32; 6: 155–57, 332–33, 496–97; 7: 333, 431–32, 533–34; 8: 55–56, 399–400.

45. Ibid., 5: 478; 7: 281–82, 535–36.

46. Ibid., 6: 496; 7: 22–23.

47. Ibid., 8: 356.

48. *Metropolitan Record* [New York], Apr. 27, 1861 (letter of Archbishop John J. Hughes, read to a mass union meeting in Union Square); Chester Forrester Dunham, *The Attitude of the Northern Clergy Toward the South, 1860–1865* (Toledo, Ohio, 1942), 110–11, 134–35.

49. *Northwestern Christian Advocate*, Aug. 13, Sept. 25, Oct. 9, 16, 1861; George Peck, *Our Country: Its Trial and Its Triumph. A Series of Discourses Suggested by the Varying Events of the War for the Union* (New York, 1865), 11, 15, 31, 47–53.

50. *Northwestern Christian Advocate*, Oct. 2, 1861; *Chicago Tribune*, Sept. 9, 1862.

51. William G. T. Shedd *The Union and the War: A Sermon, Preached November 27, 1862* (New York, 1863), 9–15; Homer N. Dunning, *Our National Trial: A Thanksgiving Sermon, Preached at the Union Meeting of the Churches of Gloversville, on Thanksgiving Day, November 28th, 1861* (Gloversville, N.Y., 1861), 18.

52. Charles Hodge, "The General Assembly," *The Biblical Repertory and Princeton Review*, 36 (July 1864): 538–51; Moorhead, *American Apocalypse*, 96–104; John R. McKivigan, *The War Against Proslavery Religion: Abolitionism and the Northern Churches 1830–1865* (Ithaca, N.Y., 1984), 183–201.

53. *Metropolitan Record*, Aug. 17, 1861; *Boston Pilot*, Jan. 17, 1863. For exceptions to this general picture of Catholic conservatism, however, see the columns of the Cincinnati *Catholic Telegraph* and *Brownson's Quarterly Review*. See also Timothy F. Neville to Abraham Lincoln, June 16, 1864, Lincoln Papers.

54. Dunham, *The Attitude of the Northern Clergy*, 112; *Northwestern Christian Advocate*, May 6, 1863; Shedd, *The Union and the War*, 15–22; W. S. Leavitt, *God the Protector and Hope of the Nation: A Sermon, Preached on Thanksgiving Day, November 27, 1862* (Hudson, N.Y., 1862), 4–5; Peck, *Our Country*, 32.

55. Across the broad spectrum of Protestant churches that submitted petitions to the White House during Lincoln's presidency, the most frequent and persistent memorialists were Methodists, Baptists, Congregationalists, Reformed Presbyterians, and United Presbyterians. Of the 116 religious petitions held in the Abraham Lincoln Papers at the Library of

Congress, none originated from Catholic churches. I am especially grateful to Nichola Clayton for her assistance in transcribing and analyzing these documents.

56. Basler, ed., *Collected Works*, 4: 559–60, 5, 69; *Boston Pilot*, Aug. 30, 1862; Brooks D. Simpson and Jean V. Berlin, eds., *Selected Correspondence of William T. Sherman, 1860–1865* (Chapel Hill, N.C., 1999), 500–501.

57. Peck, *Our Country*, 169–86.

58. Charles P. McIlvaine to Abraham Lincoln, July 27, 1863, Lincoln Papers; Basler, ed., *Collected Works*, 6: 332–33; James Delany to Abraham Lincoln, Oct. 1863 (Resolutions from the Wisconsin Baptist State Convention), Lincoln Papers.

59. Victor B. Howard, *Religion and the Radical Republican Movement 1860–1870* (Lexington, Ky., 1990), 71; D. H. Wheeler to D. P. Kidder, Dec. 14, 1863, Kidder Papers, United Library, Garrett Evangelical Theological Seminary, Evanston, Illinois.

60. *Illinois State Register*, Aug. 4, 1864; *Chicago Times*, Aug. 4, 1864. For the staunch allegiance of the mainstream Catholic press to the Democratic Party and its candidates, see, for example, the columns of the *Boston Pilot* and the *New York Metropolitan Record*.

61. Allen Thorndike Rice, ed., *Reminiscences of Abraham Lincoln by Distinguished Men of His Time* (New York, 1886), 442.

62. Contemporary reactions to Lincoln's death are examined in Thomas Reed Turner, *Beware the People Weeping: Public Opinion and the Assassination of Abraham Lincoln* (Baton Rouge, La., 1982) and David B. Chesebrough, *"No Sorrow Like Our Sorrow": Northern Protestant Ministers and the Assassination of Lincoln* (Kent, Ohio, 1994), 76–77.

ABRAHAM LINCOLN: THE FAMILY THAT MADE HIM, THE FAMILY HE MADE by Catherine Clinton

1. See Kenneth Winkle, *The Young Eagle: The Rise of Abraham Lincoln* (Dallas, 2001) and David Herbert Donald, *We Are All Lincoln Men: Abraham Lincoln and His Friends* (New York, 2003). See also the most useful source, Douglas Wilson and Ronald White, eds., *Herndon's Informants: Letters, Interviews, and Statements About Abraham Lincoln* (Urbana, Ill., 1997)

2. One exception is David Herbert Donald's *Lincolns at Home: Two Glimpses of Abraham Lincoln's Family Life* (New York, 2003).

3. Wilson and White, eds., *Herndon's Informants*, 5

4. Sarah Lincoln was reputedly named after Nancy's cousin Sarah Mitchell, who had been captured by Indians and returned to live in the same household with Nancy when the two were adolescents. Sarah named her daughter Nancy, so the two bore namesakes to indicate their intimacy. Sarah Mitchell was almost ten years old when she was captured by Indians in 1790 near Crab Orchard, Kentucky. Her mother was killed in the attack, and her father drowned while on a rescue attempt, so she was an orphan when she was released from captivity in 1795 through the intervention of her grandmother, who kept up appeals to the governor to secure her redemption. Nancy helped her cousin relearn English and the ways of her own people when she was returned to her family. Wilson and White, eds., *Herndon's Informants*, 385.

5. Richard Lawrence Miller, *Lincoln and His World: The Early Years, Birth to Illinois Legislature* (Mechanicsburg, Pa., 2003), 1. Thomas Lincoln had been grabbing for a stake throughout his twenties but had run into legal entanglements over rights to land that thwarted his hopes for security.

6. I should like to thank Sandy Brue and Bertha Schmalfeldt of the National Park Service for their assistance with genealogical materials on Abraham Lincoln. Perhaps this well-

documented family tree at the Abraham Lincoln Birthplace is meant to counter some of the wild speculation, such as the suggestion by one researcher that Abraham Lincoln was the illegitimate child of John C. Calhoun and Nancy Hanks (a barmaid)—see www.greenvillesouth.com/abe.html—and the continuing folklore that Lincoln and Jefferson Davis shared the same father.

7. Indeed, when the genealogy first appeared on wall charts in the pavilion at the Lincoln Birthplace, there were *no* ancestors listed for Nancy Hanks, a serious miscalculation that was soon corrected. Not to list her mother or father was to draw attention to the issue of her contested parentage and emphasize Nancy Hanks's disputed origins.

8. This vagueness was at times a strategy, as Herndon explained his thinking on "how best to proceed" in writing his history of Lincoln's ancestry. See Wilson and White, eds., *Herndon's Informants*, 638–39.

9. Roy P. Basler, ed., *The Collected Works of Abraham Lincoln*, 9 vols. (New Brunswick, N.J., 1953–55), 3: 511.

10. Her father too remains a mystery. Sarah, Nancy's niece, gave birth to six children out of wedlock, including Sophia Hanks, who was born the same year as her cousin, Abraham Lincoln. Sophia spent time in the Thomas Lincoln home after 1818.

11. This marriage to Sparrow followed a 1789 Mercer County Court grand jury accusation, charging her with "fornication." The next year she and Henry Sparrow obtained a marriage license, and the year after that they wed. Wilson and White, eds., *Herndon's Informants*, 780.

12. In some southern families daughters might be settled on barren siblings with the expectation that they would reap financial benefit; a kind of "aunt adoption" was the custom in the early Republic. But this would never have included sons. See Catherine Clinton, *The Plantation Mistress: Woman's World in the Old South* (New York, 1982). The placement of Hanks children with the Sparrows did not fit this pattern but hinted at other issues.

13. The illegitimate birth of this particular Nancy's children has caused serious confusion for too many Lincoln researchers.

14. This field was pioneered in the modern era by the pathbreaking work of Philip Greven, with first his classic *The Protestant Temperament: Patterns of Child-Rearing, Religious Experience, and the Self in Early America* (New York, 1977), then *Spare the Child: The Religious Roots of Punishment and the Psychological Impact of Physical Abuse* (New York, 1990). Jacqueline Renier, *From Virtue to Character: American Childhood, 1775–1850* (New York, 1996) provides a survey, while a more recent volume, Steven Mintz, *Huck's Raft: A History of American Childhood* (Cambridge, Mass., 2004) affords a more nuanced and rich narrative of American childhood experiences. See also, for specific gendered and family shifts, Linda Kerber, *Women of the Republic: Intellect and Ideology In Revolutionary America* (Chapel Hill, N.C., 1980) and Christine Heyrman, *Southern Cross: The Beginnings of the Bible Belt* (Chapel Hill, N.C., 1997), as well as the pioneering Joseph M. Hawes and Elizabeth I. Nybakken, eds., *Family and Society in American History* (Urbana, Ill., 2001)

15. Matthew W. Backes, "The Father and the Middle Class: Paternal Authority, Filial Independence, and the Transformation of American Culture, 1800–1850" (unpub. diss., Columbia University, 2007), 321–22.

16. Lincoln did not have much charity toward those who did the abandonment, the casting off. For example, in later years when his wife's brother Levi Todd, who was a staunch unionist supporting Lincoln's government in a relatively hostile Kentucky environment, appealed to Lincoln for assistance, he was in desperate straits, both ill and destitute. The usually generous president failed to extend any help; Levi had been divorced by his wife for spousal abuse, something Lincoln could not tolerate.

17. Miller, *Lincoln and His World*, 28.

18. Lincoln's former law partner William Herndon seems to have launched the battles with his pronouncements about Lincoln's views on religion during a series of lectures in Springfield in autumn 1866. Letters to editors and other campaigns emerged to dispute and debate Herndon's claim of Lincoln's atheism. In his *Life of Lincoln* (1889), Herndon claimed: "No man had a stronger or firmer faith in Providence—God—than Mr. Lincoln, but the continued use by him late in life of the word God must not be interpreted to mean that he believed in a personal God. In 1854, he asked me to erase the word God from a speech I had written and read to him for criticism, because my language indicated a personal God, whereas he insisted that no such personality ever existed" (445–46). Herndon went on to say Lincoln never invoked Jesus or Jesus Christ in any of his writings or speeches. See, in particular, William Barton, *The Soul of Abraham Lincoln*, introduction by Michael Nelson (Urbana, Ill., 2005) and Richard Miller, *Lincoln and His World*, 251–59.

19. Miller, *Lincoln and His World*, 258.

20. Vernon Burton, *The Age of Lincoln* (New York, 2007), 115.

21. There are variations on this: "All I am or shall ever hope to be I owe to my loving angel mother. God bless her." William H. Herndon and Jesse W. Weik, *Abraham Lincoln; The True Story of a Great Life* (New York, 1930), 3.

22. Ward H. Lamon, *The Life of Abraham Lincoln* (Boston, 1872), 17.

23. David Herbert Donald, *Lincoln* (New York, 1996), 20 and notes on 603.

24. Lincoln confessed to his fondness for Richard III in a letter to James Hackett. Basler, ed., *Collected Works*, 6: 393.

25. Lincoln allegedly thought that illegitimate children were in some way more shrewd and intelligent, having to have in a sense "stolen" their intellectual talents. See Douglas Wilson, *Honor's Voice: The Transformation of Abraham Lincoln* (New York, 1998), 13.

26. See Winkle, *Young Eagle*.

27. Wilson and White, eds., *Herndon's Informants*, 37.

28. William Lee Miller, *Lincoln's Virtues: An Ethical Biography* (New York, 2002), 61.

29. Miller, *Lincoln and His World*, 12: On the mental instability of Lincoln's father and his mother's temperament, see Joshua Wolf Shenk, *Lincoln's Melancholy* (Boston, 2005), 11–13.

30. Miller, *Lincoln and His World*, 19.

31. See Ronald White, *The Eloquent President* (New York, 2005).

32. Wilson and White, eds., *Herndon's Informants*, 676.

33. Nancy Schrom Dye and Daniel Blake Smith, "Mother Love and Infant Death, 1750–1920," *Journal of American History*, 73 (September 1986): 330.

34. Wilson and White, eds., *Herndon's Informants*, 40.

35. Donald, *Lincoln*, 28.

36. Ibid., 28.

37. See Dennis Hanks, June 8, 1865, in Wilson and White, eds., *Herndon's Informants*, 27.

38. Donald, *Lincoln*, 32.

39. Ibid., 29.

40. Backes, "The Father and the Middle Class," 217.

41. Ibid., 321–22.

42. See Joseph Ellis, "The New American Trinity," *Reviews of American History*, 7 (March 1979), 58–63.

43. Donald, *Lincoln*, 33.

44. He continued to visit his stepmother periodically. When Thomas Lincoln died in 1851, Abraham retained a forty-acre plot of land in his own name "for Mother while she lives." All of Sarah's children were married, and each had at least seven children. By the 1850s Sarah was a grandmother to more than twenty children. She remained an energetic person, but she occasionally suffered from rheumatism. After Abraham was elected president

in 1860, he made one last visit to his stepmother before he left for Washington. During this visit Abraham and Sarah rode out to Shiloh Cemetery to visit the grave of Thomas Lincoln.

45. Donald, *Lincoln*, 13.

46. Ibid., 41.

47. Ibid., 46.

48. Douglas Wilson, *Honor's Voice: The Transformation of Abraham Lincoln* (New York, 1998), 110.

49. Ibid., 112.

50. Donald, *Lincoln*, 152–53.

51. Ibid.

52. See Charles Strozier, *Lincoln's Quest for Union* (New York, 1982), 53–55.

53. Basler, ed., *Collected Works*, 2: 97.

54. Wilson, *Honor's Voice*, 120.

55. Donald, *We Are Lincoln Men*, 24. Although Lincoln would not have been familiar with Baldassare Castiglione's *Book of the Courtier*, he would have been familiar with Sir Walter Scott's characters and perhaps been a fan of the chivalrous concept of courtly love exemplified within romantic poetry and fiction.

56. This is how he became entangled with Mary Owens, the sister of his New Salem neighbor and patron Elizabeth Abell.

57. See Catherine Clinton, "Wife Versus Widow: Clashing Perspectives on Mary Lincoln's Legacy," *Journal of the Abraham Lincoln Association*, 28 (Winter 2007).

58. Evidence of Abraham Lincoln's attachments and expressions toward other men were not unusual for his day but have been highlighted by a few scholars—most notably C. A. Tripp. See Tripp's *The Intimate World of Abraham Lincoln* (New York, 2005) and Martin P. Johnson, "Did Abraham Lincoln Sleep with His Bodyguard?: Another Look at the Evidence," *Journal of the Abraham Lincoln Association*, 27 (Summer 2006). See also Adam I. P. Smith, "Review Essay: Lincoln Scholarship and the Return of Intimacy," *Journal of the Abraham Lincoln Association*, 27 (Summer 2006).

59. See Catherine Clinton, *Mrs. Lincoln*, chapter 3 (forthcoming).

60. And over time Mary hoped that even his crisis might be forgotten, as she wrote to Josiah Holland, author of a biography of her husband in 1865, "My beloved husband had so entirely devoted himself to me, for two years before my marriage," clearly contrary to the facts. See Mary Lincoln to Josiah Holland, Dec. 1865, Justin Turner and Linda L. Turner, *Mary Lincoln: Her Life and Letters* (New York, 1973), 293.

61. Katherine Helm, *The True Story of Mary, Wife of Lincoln* (New York, 1928), 108.

62. See Karen Lystra, *Searching the Heart: Women, Men and Romantic Love in Nineteenth Century America* (New York, 1992).

63. Clinton, *Plantation Mistress*, 151–52.

64. See Abraham Lincoln, *The Collected Poetry of Abraham Lincoln* (Springfield, Ill., 1971).

65. Ruth Painter Randall, *Mary Lincoln: Biography of a Marriage* (Boston, 1953), 101.

66. Donald, *Lincoln*, 153.

67. William H. Townsend, *Lincoln and the Bluegrass: Slavery and Civil War in Kentucky* (Lexington, Ky., 1955), 193.

68. Jennifer Fleischner, *Mrs. Lincoln and Mrs. Keckly* (New York, 2003), 169.

69. Minutes of the Session of the First Presbyterian Church, 1828–62, 82. Illinois State Historical Library, Springfield.

70. See Doris Kearns Goodwin, *Team of Rivals: The Political Genius of Abraham Lincoln* (New York, 2005), 418–23.

71. Elizabeth Keckley, *Behind The Scenes: by Elizabeth Keckley. or, Thirty Years a Slave, and Four Years in the White House* (New York, 1868), 106–07.

72. Ruth Painter Randall, *Lincoln's Sons* (Boston, 1955), 180.

73. Ibid., 179.

74. Ibid., 114–15.

75. Randall, *Mary Lincoln*, 150–51.

76. Ibid, 160–61.

77. Donald, *Lincoln*, 571.

78. Goodwin, *Team of Rivals*, 684.

THE THEFT OF LINCOLN IN SCHOLARSHIP, POLITICS, AND PUBLIC MEMORY by David W. Blight

1. H. L. Mencken, *Prejudices: Third Series* (New York, 1922), 174.

2. Carl Sandburg, quoted in Merrill D. Peterson, *Lincoln in American Memory* (New York, 1994), 371; Ida Tarbell, quoted ibid., 155.

3. For Reagan's use of the four aphorisms, see Mario M. Cuomo, *Why Lincoln Matters: Today More Than Ever* (New York, 2004), 13–16.

4. Thomas F. Schwartz, "Lincoln Never Said That," *For the People: A Newsletter of the Abraham Lincoln Association*, no. 1 (Spring 1999): 4–6. For an example of a particularly egregious misquoting or fabrication of Lincoln on the Iraq War by Republican partisans, see Eric Foner, *The Nation* (March 12, 2007).

5. Newt Gingrich, "Bush and Lincoln," *Wall Street Journal*, Sept. 7, 2006; E. J. Dionne, "The Rise of the Lincoln Democrats," *Washington Post*, Sept. 5, 2006.

6. David Donald, "Getting Right with Lincoln," in Donald, *Lincoln Reconsidered: Essays on the Civil War Era* (New York, 1947), 16, 18; David Herbert Donald, *Lincoln* (New York, 1995), 14.

7. W. E. B. Du Bois, "Abraham Lincoln," *Crisis* (May 1922), and "Lincoln Again," *Crisis* (Sept. 1922), both in W. E. B. Du Bois, *Writings* (New York, 1986), 1196, 1198.

8. See Allen C. Guelzo, *Lincoln's Emancipation Proclamation: The End of Slavery in America* (New York, 2004). Other recent important Lincoln books, very selectively, include Harold Holzer, *Lincoln at Cooper Union: The Speech That Made Abraham Lincoln President* (New York, 2004); Douglas L. Wilson, *Honor's Voice: The Transformation of Abraham Lincoln* (New York, 1998) and *Lincoln's Sword: The President and the Power of Words* (New York, 2006); William Lee Miller, *Lincoln's Virtues: An Ethical Biography* (New York, 2002); Daniel Farber, *Lincoln's Constitution* (Chicago, 2003); and George P. Fletcher, *Our Secret Constitution: How Lincoln Redefined American Democracy* (New York, 2001).

9. Lerone Bennett, Jr., *Forced into Glory: Abraham Lincoln's White Dream* (Chicago, 2000), preface; Guelzo, *Lincoln's Emancipation Proclamation*, 9.

10. See David W. Blight, *A Slave No More: Two Men Who Escaped to Freedom, Including Their Narratives of Emancipation* (New York, 2007). Many recent books develop to varying degrees the "self-emancipation" thesis, but for a beginning, see Ira Berlin et al., *Slaves No More: Three Essays on Emancipation and the Civil War* (New York, 1992).

11. Charles Adams, *When in the Course of Human Events: Arguing the Case for Southern Secession* (Lanham, Md., 2000); Thomas J. DiLorenzo, *The Real Lincoln: A New Look at Abraham Lincoln, His Agenda, and an Unnecessary War* (New York, 2002).

12. See James M. McPherson, *Battle Cry of Freedom: The Civil War Era* (New York, 1988); Eric Foner, *Reconstruction: America's Unfinished Revolution, 1863–1877* (New York, 1987);

Thomas E. Woods, Jr., *The Politically Incorrect Guide to American History* (Washington, 2005). For a review that exposes Woods's falsehoods and right-wing political agenda, as well as simply sloppy pseudoscholarship, see David Greenberg, www.Slate.com, March 11, 2005. Greenberg points out that some conservative academics have denounced Woods's book, while right-wing television hosts Sean Hannity and Pat Buchanan offered it praise and considerable air time. The book demonstrates, Greenberg asserts, that the far right of the Republican Party increasingly exhibits a "scorn for intellectual authority altogether."

13. Daniel Feller, "Libertarians in the Attic, or a Tale of Two Narratives," *Reviews in American History*, 32 (June 2004): 184.

14. Adams, *When in the Course of Human Events*, 109–25, 151–55, 205.

15. Feller, "Libertarians in the Attic," 189. On Norquist, leader of the advocacy group, Americans for Tax Reform, see John Cassidy, "The Ringleader: How Grover Norquist Keeps the Conservative Movement Together," *New Yorker* (Aug. 1, 2005): 42–53.

16. On Charles L. C. Minor's book, *The Real Lincoln*, see Peterson, *Lincoln in American Memory*, 193. DiLorenzo, *The Real Lincoln*, 233.

17. DiLorenzo, *The Real Lincoln*, 264, 6.

18. "2005 Republican Freedom Calendar: Celebrating a Century and a Half of Civil Rights Achievement by the Party of Lincoln," Republican National Committee, Washington, www.policy.house.gov. Much of the text of the calendar was the work of Michael Zak, "Back to Basics for the Republican Party," a history of the GOP, available at www.republicanbasics.com.

19. Christopher Cox, "About the Calendar," "2005 Republican Freedom Calendar."

20. Ibid. Roosevelt, quoted in Donald, "Getting Right with Lincoln," 14.

21. Anne E. Kornblut, "Bush and Party Chief Court Black Voters at 2 Forums," *New York Times*, July 15, 2005; James Dao, "Republican Party Is Backing Black Candidates in Bid to Attract Votes," *New York Times*, July 1, 2005; *Morning Edition*, National Public Radio, July 15, 2005.

22. "President Bush Addresses NAACP Annual Convention," Washington, July 20, 2006, www.whitehouse.gov/news/releases.

23. Frank Rich, "He Got Out While the Getting Was Good," *New York Times*, Aug. 19, 2007.

24. Abraham Lincoln, "Annual Message to Congress," Dec. 1, 1862, in Roy P. Basler, ed., *The Collected Works of Abraham Lincoln*, 9 vols. (New Brunswick, N.J., 1953–55), 5: 537.

Index

Page numbers beginning with 287 refer to endnotes. Page numbers in *italics* refer to illustrations.